The Power of the Pen

THE POWER
OF THE PEN

The Politics,
Nationalism,
and Influence of
Sir John Willison

RICHARD CLIPPINGDALE

Foreword by
the Right Honourable Joe Clark

DUNDURN
TORONTO

Editor: Allister Thompson
Design: Courtney Horner
Printer: Webcom

Library and Archives Canada Cataloguing in Publication

Clippingdale, Richard, 1941-
   The power of the pen : the politics, nationalism, and influence of Sir John Willison / by Richard Clippingdale ; foreword by Joe Clark.

Includes bibliographical references and index.
Also issued in electronic format.
ISBN 978-1-4597-0372-8

   1. Willison, John, Sir, 1856-1927. 2. Canada--Politics and government--1896-1911. 3. Canada--Politics and government--1911-1921. 4. Canada--Politics and government--1921-1930. 5. Nationalism--Canada. 6. Journalists--Canada--Biography. I. Title.

PN4913.W49C55 2012   070.92   C2012-900105-8

1   2   3   4   5   16   15   14   13   12

Conseil des Arts du Canada   Canada Council for the Arts   Canada   ONTARIO ARTS COUNCIL CONSEIL DES ARTS DE L'ONTARIO

We acknowledge the support of the **Canada Council for the Arts** and the **Ontario Arts Council** for our publishing program. We also acknowledge the financial support of the **Government of Canada** through the **Canada Book Fund** and **Livres Canada Books**, and the **Government of Ontario** through the **Ontario Book Publishing Tax Credit** and the **Ontario Media Development Corporation**.

Care has been taken to trace the ownership of copyright material used in this book. The author and the publisher welcome any information enabling them to rectify any references or credits in subsequent editions.

J. Kirk Howard, President

Printed and bound in Canada.
www.dundurn.com

Dundurn
3 Church Street, Suite 500
Toronto, Ontario, Canada
M5E 1M2

Gazelle Book Services Limited
White Cross Mills
High Town, Lancaster, England
LA1 4XS

Dundurn
2250 Military Road
Tonawanda, NY
U.S.A. 14150

There is this to be said for the craft to which I belong, that it offers us neither great wealth nor great distinction, and that the root-motive which lures us into journalism is the public spirit which was born into us and which will not be denied expression. The worst of us are more than partisans, and the best of us are very human in the day of battle. Pope described the life of a writer as a "warfare upon earth," and that is particularly true of the life of the political journalist. The game of politics is a great game; it is played with men as the standing figures on the board, and it is full of joy to the journalist who loves his work, his country and his kind. Whatever may be our faults and our follies, our errors and our prejudices, still we do the state some service and forever sound the advance in the long and painful march towards human betterment. As Lord Houghton said of the Men of Old:

> 'Blending our souls' sublimest needs
> With tasks of every day
> They went about their gravest deeds
> As Noble boys at play.'

J.S. Willison (1905), speech on "Journalism and Public Life" to Ministerial Association, Hamilton, Ontario, March 7, 1905.
(Toronto *News*, March 7, 1905, page 4)

to Linda
my inspiration

Contents

Foreword

CANADA IS A POWERFULLY PHYSICAL COUNTRY, DEFINED BY HUGE spaces and immense resources which, unquestionably, helped make us a nation of opportunity, ambition, and frontiers. That has always been our raw material, but the decisive factors which shaped the nation were more human, often more emotional. Richard Clippingdale's rich biography of Sir John Willison demonstrates how much personal qualities — friendships, foresight, beliefs, courage — have determined our national decisions. And it reminds Canadians that issues of identity — our heritage as both British and French, our wariness of the United States — are enduring central elements in the Canadian story.

Willison is widely unknown today. But from 1886 to 1917, pivotal decades when Canada was taking shape, he had a profound influence on public opinion, particularly in Ontario, and on historic policy decisions taken by the governments of both Sir Wilfrid Laurier and Sir Robert Borden. He was editor of the Toronto *Globe* (1890–1902) and the Toronto *Evening News* (1903–1917), Canadian correspondent for the London *Morning Post* and the London *Times*, a prolific speaker and author, knighted for his accomplishments — but those mere titles understate his influence.

That was an age when newspapers made no pretence of political independence — they were "party newspapers," financed and edited to advance the interest of either the Liberal or Conservative parties. That was a two-way street: the best editors were powerful influences within the parties they supported, not some master's voice. In the tense and embattled months just before Laurier was first elected prime minister, in 1896, the Roman Catholic, Francophone leader constantly sought and accepted the advice of the Protestant Anglophone editor on how to make his case in Ontario. Clippingdale shows that "the leader was ... treating Willison as his real Ontario lieutenant".

Later, Willison also became a respected confidante of Sir Robert Borden — but that relation was more exclusively policy-driven. The connection with Laurier was deeper and far more personal. Partisanship had brought both men to Ottawa — Laurier the Liberal MP, Willison the young parliamentary correspondent for the Liberal *Globe* — but their real bond became a common enthusiasm for literature, ideas, the potential of this new nation which as French/English, Catholic/Protestant, Quebecer/Ontarian, they shared. Soon after meeting in Ottawa, Laurier invited Willison to his country home in Arthabaskaville, in the Eastern Townships, and their conversations there cemented a lasting friendship which overrode their many disagreements, including on such salient issues as whether Laurier should be elected or defeated. Willison was Laurier's prominent advocate in three national elections, and a vigorous opponent in two (1911 and 1917) others — and their world views differed on the critical questions of race, church, and the relation to Britain.

These were two strong and different men, who developed a remarkable mutual respect. For all his eagerness to embrace new possibilities, Willison remained Protestant, Ontarian, and imperialist with a profound loyalty to British institutions, and that was the perch from which he viewed his world. The friendship with Laurier led him to understand that he had to take account of a nationalist reality in Quebec (he called it "the disturbing element in our politics") whether he approved of it or not.

In his earliest days as editor of the *Globe*, Willison was urged privately by Laurier to "as much as possible ... keep a discreet silence" on Catholic–Protestant and French–English questions. By and large, it was advice he followed, focusing his attention on trade and railway and other issues which, while contentious, were not profoundly divisive in the still-young country. That commitment was tested when Laurier authorized denominational schools in the new provinces of Alberta and Saskatchewan, which Willison opposed vigorously as "clerical interference in State affairs" and attributed to "the natural race sentiments of French Canadians".

In 1906, upon receiving an honorary degree at Queens University, Willison noted that journalists "… have some popularity with Oppositions and (are) … generally distrusted by Governments." That was one factor in his political migration from Laurier. He came to admire Borden, preferring his positions on public ownership of the new railway and other issues, and wholeheartedly supporting his opposition to Reciprocity with the United States. In early 1911, Willison warned: "with our trade settled in American channels and with a vast new population with no reverence for British institutions we strengthen all the influences toward continentalism and risk the sacrifice both of a young nation and an ancient Empire."

A special value of this biography is the marriage of subject and author. Dr. Clippingdale is an historian, a public servant, and an engaged citizen, with whom I was privileged to work closely during the constitutional debates of the 1980s and 1990s. He became interested in Willison decades ago, first as a graduate student of Donald Creighton, then as a biographer of Laurier. That interest deepened as he himself became more involved in the determining Canadian issues of who we are and how we grow which, a century before, had engaged John Willison.

What distinguished Willison as a journalist was not his partisanship, which shifted and was instrumental, but his talent as a gifted observer, intelligent and well-read, with an instinct for issues that would become compelling. As a writer, an advisor, an advocate, he was able to reach beyond the stark facts, and convey the character of people and circumstances, and he applied that talent equally to his assessment of both adversaries and friends. From his seat in the press gallery above the House of Commons in the late 1880s, he looked down on Prime Minister Sir John A. Macdonald, whom his paper fiercely opposed, and often demonized. He would recall:

I was so placed that I could sometimes see shades of expression cross his face, the defiant jerk of his head when he was angry, the shrug of contempt for a mean jibe that was meant to wound, the quick, natural human manifestation of pleasure over a generous word from an opponent … few men have had such charm for his kind, or such power to inspire sacrifice and devotion … I have known gray-haired Liberals who had persuaded themselves that the Conservative leader was the favourite offspring of the Father of Evil, forever disarmed by a few quick, happy spontaneous sentences, spoken carelessly enough, but which, as he intended they should, penetrated the very marrow of their self-esteem.[1]

Willison considered himself both an interpreter and an architect of events, not simply a record-keeper or, worse, a commentator. He vigorously advanced the causes in which he believed, and had much more influence on events than most of the elected officials of his time. In this physical country, at a formative time, the Canadian resources he mobilized were insight, and argument, and eloquence. Dr. Clippingdale, the historian and practitioner, records both the power of that pen, and its historic consequences.

The Right Honourable Joe Clark, P.C., C.C.

Preface

S IR JOHN WILLISON WAS THE MOST INFLUENTIAL JOURNALIST IN Canada in the late nineteenth and early twentieth centuries, as the country finally began to realize its founders' dreams of economic growth, intellectual maturation, and world status. With his incisive pen and clear reasoning, he used the *Globe* and other Canadian newspapers and magazines, his *Times* of London contributions, his many books and speeches, and his unparalleled connections with key political leaders to become a major figure in national life. Uniquely, he was in turn at the heart of both the Liberal and Conservative parties, as a devoted supporter and close friend of Sir Wilfrid Laurier, a first employer, early booster and continuing admirer of William Lyon Mackenzie King, and a sometimes close ally and confidant of Sir Robert Borden. He played key roles in helping influence the epochal federal political shifts of power in 1896, 1911, and 1917. He also clearly articulated highly influential views on the nature and evolution of Canadian nationalism and public policy.

Willison lived and worked after the development of fast trains and the telegraph, mostly before the widespread use of the telephone, and almost entirely before radio mattered in news. The newspaper was *the* means of connecting citizens with their governments and broader life. Written correspondence, far more rapidly delivered than before, was *the* means of normal communication, unless people could count on direct daily interaction. Hence an extraordinary body of daily exchanges of views and intentions, far beyond formal "official" documents, could survive in archival holdings. The vast amount of the daily newspaper writings and publications of so prolific a journalist and author, as well as his voluminous correspondence with many very significant contemporaries, opens a wide, revealing window on extraordinary Canadian times, from soon after Confederation through the First World War and into the 1920s.

This book is not a history of Canadian journalism, politics, or nationalism in the years covered. Its aim is rather to recapture the impact and the influence of one particularly talented writer, author, political actor, and nationalist thinker, as Canada itself changed and matured in major ways. Throughout a remarkably long career, he delighted in pursuing a select series of political objectives and major interpretative Canadian themes to what he saw as their logical conclusions. Arguably, no other Canadian political journalist has done that so powerfully for so long.

Note on Abbreviations

BP	Sir Robert L. Borden Papers
CAR	*Canadian Annual Review*
CHAR	*Canadian Historical Association Report*
CHR	*Canadian Historical Review*
CIRA	Canadian Industrial Reconstruction Association
CRA	Canadian Reconstruction Association
Debates	House of Commons *Debates*
DLQU	Douglas Library, Queen's University
FOCC	From Our Canadian Correspondent
FOCT	From Our Correspondent, Toronto
FOOCT	From Our Own Correspondent, Toronto
FOOC	From Our Own Correspondent
FP	Sir Joseph Flavelle Papers (DLQU)
JSW	Sir John Willison
JWF	Sir Joseph W. Flavelle

LAC	Library and Archives Canada
LP	Sir Wilfrid Laurier Papers
Lady MW	Lady Marjory Willison
NPHSP-JSW	New Printing House Square Papers (London *Times*), J.S. Willison files
OA	Ontario Archives
OL-CU	John M. Olin Library, Cornell University
RLB	Sir Robert Borden
UTL	University of Toronto Library
UWOL	University of Western Ontario Library
WL	Sir Wilfrid Laurier
WM	*Willison's Monthly*
OA, WP	Sir John Willison Papers (OA)
WP	Sir John Willison Papers (LAC)

Acknowledgements

THE SOURCES FOR THIS BOOK ON SIR JOHN WILLISON ARE RICH and varied. More than forty years of newspapers, magazines, and other published files, along with thirty-seven archival correspondence collections, have provided extraordinary access to the daily life of Canadian politics and political journalism from the early 1880s to the late 1920s. Sincere thanks to: Library and Archives Canada; the Ontario Archives; Douglas Library, Queen's University; University of Toronto Library; John M. Olin Library, Cornell University; London *Times* "New Printing House Square" Archives; Bodleian Library, Oxford University; Scottish Record Office, Edinburgh; and the British Museum, London for permission to consult their rich manuscript correspondence collections.

Regrettably, virtually no family correspondence has survived in either the Library and Archives Canada or Ontario Archives Willison Papers. The latter collection does have, however, a valuable manuscript memoir by his second wife, Lady Marjory Willison. In 1973 I was able to interview Sir John's granddaughter, Mrs. A.W. Mackenzie, and the next year to correspond and meet with his secretary in his later years, Miss Dorothy Ferrier. Very recently, I was privileged to meet Peter Mackenzie, Mrs. Mackenzie's son, who shared family memories with me and kindly gave me access to a delightful photograph of Lady Rachel Willison. As well, there are valuable direct recollections of Sir John in various correspondence collections and printed sources, as noted in footnotes.

Over the years a number of institutions and individuals have given invaluable direct and indirect support for this project. The Canada Council, the Social Sciences and Humanities Research Council, and Carleton University provided much appreciated research funding. The late Donald Creighton of the University of Toronto wonderfully supervised my Ph.D. thesis on Willison's early career and strongly encouraged me to persevere towards a full biographical treatment. Through my teaching years at Carleton University, Dr. H. Blair Neatby and Dr. Naomi Griffiths gave me invaluable advice and assistance with this project and my academic career. Writing *Laurier: His Life and World* (Toronto: McGraw-Hill Ryerson, 1979) immersed me in that fascinating man's life, so intertwined in so many phases with Willison's. Later, working with the Honourable David Macdonald and the Right Honourable Joe Clark provided direct experience with national politics, and several years in senior levels of the public service and with national and international consulting added further perspectives on government policy challenges.

More recently, there have been two very enjoyable returns to the historical world. Ramsay Cook of the *Dictionary of Canadian Biography* asked me to write the entry on Willison for Volume XV in 2005. Then Senator Hugh Segal, the Institute for Research on Public Policy, and the Queen's University School of Policy Studies, invited me to write *Robert Stanfield's Canada: Perspectives of the Best Prime Minister We Never Had*. It was published by McGill–Queen's University Press in 2008. These experiences confirmed my resolution that I should take the time to write this full-scale study of a great Canadian political journalist.

No thanks can be adequate to the great team at Dundurn. I deeply appreciated the early encouragement and expert advice of Kirk Howard, president and publisher, and Michael Carroll, associate publisher and editorial director. It was a great pleasure to work with Allister Thompson as my editor and Marta Warner as publicist.

Finally, no thanks can be adequate for the wonderful encouragement, support and proofreading expertise of my dear wife Linda.

A "Hardscrabble" Beginning, 1856–1881

E VEN NOW, HILLS GREEN IS AN OBSCURE PLACE TO COME FROM. IT lies in central Huron County, Ontario, nearly forty miles west of London and eight east from the Lake Huron shore. In mid-1850s Canada West it was a tiny pioneer farming hamlet, a mere "post village," at the "Corners," where the county road south from Varna met the east-west base road dividing Stanley and Hay Townships. Three-quarters of a mile west of there, just in the northern Township of Stanley, John Stephen Willison was born on November 9, 1856.[1]

His father, Stephen, was thirty-eight and his mother, the former Jane Abram, thirty. Stephen was of Scottish blood, though born in Yorkshire; Jane was English. They had met and married in Oshawa, where he was a foundry foreman. Late in the 1840s or early in the 1850s, farming in the Huron Tract seemed to promise a better life. John was their third child, joining Anne, six, and George, three. The family lived in a rough one-storey log house of three or four rooms set on a few rented acres of mostly uncleared virgin timber and marshland they called "Hardscrabble Farm."[2] Stephen Willison never got far on the land. Whether from lack of ambition, insufficient experience, too little capital, three more mouths to feed or some misfortune, he was listed by the census taker in 1871 as a "labourer." Probably well before then he had started taking what occasional employment he could find as a blacksmith, stone mason, or woodcutter. He took to drinking too heavily too often, while Jane grew grey and haggard.[3]

The dark-haired "Jack" Willison grew to sturdy young manhood as a wild country weed. He would remember a happy early childhood. "There was something intimate and companionable in the forest," he would write. There were magnificent towering trees to hide behind, birds to watch and listen to, and special places of meadow and brook to delight a small boy. Very near to the family's clearing was a long tamarack marsh where cranberries could be gobbled. When he was an older boy, there were countless summer hours at the swimming hole or the mill race. "How the boy waited for the June sun to blister the face of the river," he would recall. Chores over, he and his pals would dive again and again into the tossing stream, even on Sundays, in defiance of parents and clergy. After all, he would write: "… the river in the woods, even the discoloured mill race with its obstructing saw logs and its sawdust bottom had a fascination on a hot day that made it terribly hard to remember that it was Sunday."[4]

Then there were the delightful late winter sugar-bush days with his father and brothers. "What true Canadian can ever forget the taste of the first drink of sap from the rough wooden trough on the edge of the woods," he would write, "the swift exhilarating flavour of the syrup fresh from the kettle, the first wad of taffy, the first mouthful of sugar served on a maple chip in the early stages of the jubilant sugaring?" He would remember accompanying his father into the bush in early March, to apply hammer, gouge, and wooden spike to the first sizeable maple to see if the sap was ready:

> Very likely it would run, and it was the boy's privilege
> to apply his mouth to the gash in the maple and take
> the first drink of the new season's sap welling out from
> the veins of the kindly tree. And how the boy would
> glue his mouth to that tree and try to spread it over all
> the dimensions of the gash, and reach out his tongue

and crowd down his lower lip and elevate his upper, and finally run his mouth away down to the edge of the gouge and catch the drippings as they fell from the handle…. It was a great day for the boy….

Towards midnight came the glorious taffy-pulling, as boiling syrup met clean white snow. "Taffy is strung all about camp," he would recall, "and faces are daubed and hair is glued to heads framed in fantastic bristles, and jackets and trousers are ruined for life."[5]

Such joys were all the sweeter for Jack Willison because of the stern reality of most of his daily experience. As soon as he could be useful, he began the older farm boy's routine, first on his father's acres and then as a hired hand. The older the boy, the more wearying the work. The memories that lingered were mostly not pleasant:

I underbrushed, I logged, I chopped, I split rails, I waxed fat in a lumber shanty on pioneer pork and Zurich sausage….

I know all the delights of life in the country. I have gone out on a peaceful Sabbath morning for a quiet walk in the meadow and been run out of the field by the ram with the crumpled horn. On wet days when all nature should rest I have laboured with the churn and the grindstone. I have mended the holes under the fence to keep the hogs out of the potatoes but the hogs got there all the same. I have shut my eyes to the beauty and poetry of the sunrise while, clad in a pair of overalls and one suspender, I have tramped through the wet grass of the pasture field and held out the halter in vain to the horse that had been deceived that way once too often. I have coaxed the young steer with salt in the palm of my hand only to have my advances contemptuously rejected and to be horned in the ribs in the final engagement. I have mowed the grass in the fence corners with a rusty scythe and cut great gashes just under my knee while the farmer sat behind the best team and drove the mower in ease and comfort. I have forked barley until the horns got down my back and I have pulled peas until as Macaulay says I ached for "the dark house and the long sleep."[6]

Jack's formal education was rudimentary and all too brief. Hills Green had a tiny public elementary school which he attended irregularly as chores and employment permitted. During one school year, he could not go until the last six weeks, yet he won the general proficiency award. His younger sister Mary would recall: "Jack was always a very studious boy. The teacher did not like him so well sometimes for he always had his lessons done and teacher liked to favor the girls in preference to Brother. The teacher of course was always a man." Jack's evident aptitude for learning was no doubt encouraged by his father Stephen's quite respectable knowledge of English literature, the presence in the home of a few classics, and the daily arrival of two Toronto Conservative newspapers, *The Leader* and *The Daily Telegraph*. The boy once spent some of his rare money on a set of exciting "dime novels," drawing his father's censure.[7]

School in Hills Green was over for him before he turned fifteen. By 1871, or 1872 at the latest, he was at work full-time. He had little more to learn from any local teacher, and Stephen could not afford to send him away to secondary school. He needed to earn income for himself and the family by "hiring out" — to neighbours at first, then on more distant farms. For a time he lived and worked with a German family near Hensall, four miles to the south and west of home. Some situations were bitterly disappointing. "One of my chopping experiences is memorable," he would recall. "In the fall I engaged with an old and very shrewd Scotchman, for whose daughter I had had a distinct liking, to cut stovewood for him during the winter. He was to pay me fifty cents a cord and I was to pay him two dollars and a half a week for board. I chopped for him all winter and in the Spring I owed him $5.00 and a hated rival captured the girl."[8]

In the summer of 1872, still fifteen, he had his first brush with politics. He walked the four miles to Varna to witness an oudoor debate between the Liberal and Conservative candidates for South Huron in the federal general election. He was able to elbow his way to the front of the noisy, boisterous crowd ringing the rough plank hustings set up in front of the village tavern. "It seems to me," he would write a half-century later, "that I had an instant birth into 'politics.' From that hour I saw the way along which I must go. Even now I can recall as many sentences spoken at that meeting as at any other that I ever attended. No other political event is so clear and vivid in my memory."[9]

Standing near a tavern door was likely as close as he got in those years to such an establishment. Perhaps in reaction to his father's excessive drinking, maybe with his mother's encouragement, but definitely in company with many of the local teenage boys and girls of his district, he was an enthusiastic participant in temperance lodge meetings. The Willisons were Anglican, but it was more convenient to attend the tiny frame Methodist Church just south of the Hills Green "Corners" than to find regular rides to the far-off Church of England. In the evangelical atmosphere, it was easy to drink deeply of the elixir of prohibitionism. Happily, moral crusading and social stimulation could go hand in hand, as he would remember affectionately in a newspaper account a few years later:

> Did you ever belong to the Temperance lodge in the little frame hall on the second concession? Have you ever got up at four o'clock in the morning and milked four cows and curried and harnessed the horses before breakfast and worked in the harvest field until eight o'clock at night, and then rolled down the sleeves of your flannel shirt, and put on a paper collar and walked two miles to the lodge, recited "The Accursed Wine Cup" and seconded two motions, and then walked home with Sister Brown three miles away in the other direction from where you live, let down two sets of bars, helped Sister Brown over a couple of fences, debated the right of way with large dogs, and then trudged home across the fields and by way of the side-line just in the neighborhood of midnight, feeling that life was a good time the whole year round, and that lodge night was a weekly picnic? If you say no, then you have never lived

on a farm and belonged to a Temperance lodge, and you have missed experiences that have made life richer to many of your fellows, and have been the foundation of many an eminent public reputation.

The lodge's attractions did not end there. In winter, sleighing parties were organized to visit neighbouring lodges. Bundled in the back of a bouncing sleigh with lots of opportunities for hand-holding, hugging, and kissing in the darkness, happy couples did not need alcohol to be warm and cozy. Willison would recall these wonderful outings as "ruthlessly destroying the notion that Temperance people are long-faced, and narrow-chested , and weak-limbed, and baby-muscled, and creaky-voiced, and watery-minded." On the more intellectual side, there were the many debating evenings:

> ... there were heroic struggles of contending forces to prove that Wellington was the greatest general the world ever saw, and that Napoleon didn't know enough about fighting to snow-ball a gate post and retreat in good order ... or that single life was a perpetual picnic and that married people kept on living simply because they hadn't courage enough to go away and commit suicide. And the man who was named for leader or got the first call for the next debate was for the time the king of all that community, and wasted more oratory about the barn than Webster would have found use for in a whole year....[10]

These happy social experiences aside, the brutal daily fact was that his working hours as an adolescent and young man held little enjoyment or fulfillment. From an early age he was obliged to shift pretty much for himself. He took work where he could find it. At sixteen, in the winter of 1872–1873, he left the Hills Green area to pay an extended visit to an uncle, Robert Elleker, who farmed at Salem's Corners, east of Greenwood in Ontario County, a few miles north of Oshawa. By the summer of 1873 he had hired out as a farm labourer to Lovell Harrison and Judson Gibson, close neighbours of his uncle.

The change of place was followed very soon by a political conversion. Willison had been raised in a Tory household where Sir John A. Macdonald was worshipped. But Lovell Harrison was a staunch Reformer-Liberal who subscribed to his party's great organ, George Brown's Toronto *Globe*. That summer and autumn of 1873 the paper recorded day by painful day the humbling of Macdonald's Tory federal government in the Pacific Scandal and then its resignation, subsequently confirmed in an overwhelming electoral defeat in January 1874 by Alexander Mackenzie's Liberals.

Young Willison could not help being impressed by the *Globe*'s fervour and its dramatic depiction of the unfolding political drama. He would write that he "wavered as I found life-long Conservatives falling away from the standard." Bit by bit it came to seem that the Tories could not be the proper party for an idealistic young man, and during the 1874 election campaign the eighteen-year-old was in the cheering crowd for Liberal Prime Minister Mackenzie's debate triumph in nearby Whitby. He soon took his own subscription to the *Globe* and picked it up with the rest of his mail at the nearby Kinsale post office, where the postmaster, Levi Mackey, would recall years later the "long lank country boy" with his dark brown hair and luminous dark brown eyes who very soon caught his attention because "it was plain that he was full of ambition and I remember distinctly on one occasion that he picked up a copy of the *Globe* from my desk and flatly told me that he would be on the staff of that paper some day."[11]

His working life in the mid-1870s was not greatly different, as he moved from farm to farm, hiring out for bed, board, and a little extra. But at least now there were opportunities in this more settled, established region for actually furthering his education and actively pursuing serious reading and political interests. Greenwood had an excellent school with a capable teacher who welcomed him to classes when his work permitted. Postmaster Mackey would remember that the youngster "absorbed learning like a sponge and was given the assistant teacher office during the winter of 1874 and was for a time Principal during the teacher's absence." Greenwood also had a wonderful Mechanics' Institute with a sizeable library. Soon Willison was wading through literature and poetry of the likes of Dickens, Thackeray, Scott, Pope, Dryden, Goldsmith,

Tennyson, Longfellow, and Whittier. He delighted in Samuel Smiles's *Self Help*, with its encouragement to believe in the possibility for career success, even for persons without means. Almost every week at the "Sons of Temperance" Greenwood Star Temple No. 244 and in the Mechanics' Institute debating club, he won notice for good-humoured lectures and debating performances.[12]

In 1875 or '76 he was published for the first time. It was a poem in the solemn style of Swinburne for the Whitby *Chronicle*. He soon had several prose articles printed in the *Chronicle* and in the Oshawa *Reformer*. Back in Hills Green in late 1876 to work on Frank Coleman's farm where his family rented, he sent the Guelph *Mercury* a stern anonymous prohibitionist letter on an impending liquor referendum in nearby Wellington County.[13]

Wherever he was, he read his *Globe* faithfully. One day in the early fall of 1877 he spotted an advertisement by a John A. Love, proprietor of a dry goods store in the village of Stanton, near Orangeville, Dufferin County. It wasn't journalism, but it wasn't farm work either. Maybe it could be some kind of upward step financially. He apparently wrote an impressive application, with words and phrases uncommon in would-be store clerks, and won the job. He arrived in Stanton in December and stayed for two years, boarding with the Loves. Their small daughter, Jessie, came to worship him and would remember he was tall and very good-looking, with fine pink-and-white skin, and well dressed — she would recall a white merino neckcloth with blue and black spots. He spent much of his spare time reading books and writing unsolicited articles for various dailies and weeklies. When he left Stanton in February 1880, John Love wrote a glowing letter of reference, describing him as "clever, honest, and intelligent."[14]

Armed with that, he tried unsuccessfully to secure employment with several Toronto commercial establishments and then boldly nerved himself to try to catch on with the *Globe*. The late George Brown's brother Gordon was the proprietor, and Willison sent him several of his clippings. Brown raised his hopes and spirits to dizzy heights with the note: "I believe you can do newspaper work. Come and see me. I think good will come of it." But a personal interview revealed that there were no vacancies just then. A few months later, Brown actually tried to hire him, but was vetoed by the city editor.[15] Another reporter, especially an inexperienced one, could not be afforded. The depressed Canadian economy of the early 1880s seemed to have no place for him beyond a farm labourer's or store clerk's jobs. He was twenty-three, without prospects, connections, or money.

At this point, he may have remained in Canada mostly because he could not afford to leave. He would later tell his wife that he once walked twenty miles from Toronto to Woodbridge to apply for a store job, because he had no money for the train fare. There were probably several short-term positions, none with anything but subsistence wages. He was in Barrie for a time, then back to Hills Green.

Finally, in 1880 or early 1881, he landed a store post in Tiverton, Bruce County. He worked long hours for low wages, but the town had its attractions. Local literati and the politically interested staged occasional debating evenings, and he went along whenever he could get time off work. It may have been at one of these that he met Rachel Wood Turner, one of five daughters of a pillar of local society, Mrs. Margaret Turner. Rachel — or Rae as he soon called her — was a tall, strikingly attractive girl with blue eyes and light brown hair. Acquaintance very soon turned into affection. In hours not taken up by the store and Rachel, he wrote articles for the Tiverton *Watchman* and the Kincardine *Reporter*. As for what his daily working life was like, he would write a few years later a charming recollection titled "Behind the Counter: Glimpses of the Country Merchant and his Customers" for the Toronto *Globe*. In it he claimed that a country store clerk was in the right place to find out just about everything concerning the families and foibles in his district. He experienced a wonderful education in human nature as he fought shrewd and insulting ladies for proper profit on their purchases while under the jesting scrutiny of lounging local youths. He would remember a type of woman he must have feared immensely:

> ... I have known her drag the grossest profanity from the lips of the mildest Christian; I have known the merchant driven out of the shop by her shadow at the doorway, and the clerk weep that he could not follow; I have known her buy a yard of factory at seven cents and

create a half-hour's disturbance because she could not have buttons and a five-cent spool of thread thrown in. I have known her to occupy an hour in buying:

A cent's worth of soda.

A cent's worth of salts.

A cent's worth of pins.

A darning needle, one cent.

And pay for the lot with a three-cent postage stamp and with two eggs when eggs were twelve cents a dozen, and demand a cent back in change. Every country storekeeper ten or twenty years ago knew and dreaded this woman as the supreme affliction of the business and I would not be surprised to learn that she still exists, a rare curiosity, in some of the not too remote sections of Ontario. She very rarely dies.

AN EX-CLERK[16]

He would not give up his dream of a career in journalism, and he kept on besieging Liberal papers, especially. In May 1881 he sent some of his clippings to John Cameron, owner and editor of the London *Advertiser*. "The extracts are very good," replied Cameron, "but hardly decisive, as it takes more than ability to write what may be called a smooth composition to make a journalist." He counselled that the sole way for a young man to prove his aptitude for newspaper work was by "plunging in" at the lower levels of the business — as a typesetter, for example — at "little pay, or none for a while. Valuable experience would come from occasional reporting assignments." Willison formally applied for a reporting job, but was offered only a typesetting position at three dollars a week, on three months' probation.[17]

"The offer," he would write, "held no immediate prospect of affluence and since I was twenty-five years of age was not alluring." With no savings, he faced the grim prospect of living for some time on the paltry wage offered. For some months he delayed his decision, hoping for better terms and probably canvassing other papers. He wrote Cameron again in October and managed to win a promise of a raise by one dollar weekly after the third month of satisfactory employment. The editor also commented, after receiving some fresh examples of Willison's writings, that "I think you have good stuff in you. The future would have to tell whether or not I have judged rightly. We are by no means empty on our staff but I am disposed to do what I can to allow you an opportunity."

The praise and encouragement made up the young man's mind. He was in London before month's end to sign a contract, determined to be away from the type and firmly established on the reporting staff by the time those three months were up. Before he left Tiverton he was tendered a farewell banquet at Mrs. Turner's house, at which one of his older friends gave him some rather sobering advice about journalism: "Remember, young man, that there are more devils [lowly assistants] than rich men in this business."[18] Still, the London opportunity and his developing love for young Rachel gave him reason to begin to look optimistically towards future prospects. Even as all his brothers and sisters joined his parents in the early 1880s in migrating south and west into the U.S. in search of better life prospects, his new job challenge and his relationship with Rachel Turner gave him reasons to try to build life success and happiness in Canada.[19]

II

Apprenticeship in Journalism and Liberalism, 1881–1890

For a few weeks in the autumn and early winter of 1881–82, John Willison struggled half-heartedly at the *Advertiser*'s printing case to learn the rudiments of a trade he despised. He also kept showering John Cameron with unsolicited articles, and a few were published. In his second week he was sent to cover a temperance lecture at Victoria Hall. After a few more such assignments, he was given the London East beat in the mornings. Two or three weeks later he graduated to the full-time reporting staff for the morning edition and served as a proofreader on the afternoon edition. By the end of 1882 he was earning a princely ten dollars weekly.[1]

He had much to learn, not just about reporting. The *Advertiser*'s partisanship ran deep, and staffers were expected to understand that there were proper Liberal limits to objectivity. It was hard for a man of character to be partisan enough for some London Liberals. Willison once defended a Conservative ward official charged with dishonesty and even dared on another occasion to give a purely factual report on a Conservative nominating convention. It did not help when the Tories voted a motion of thanks.[2] But mostly he was reliably loyal to his party and his editor.

He soon had a wonderful new opportunity in Liberal journalism. In December 1882, John Cameron moved to Toronto to take over the direction of the *Globe* as editor and general manager. In August 1883 he asked Willison to join him. The dreams of a post with the greatest Liberal paper in Canada were to be realized. When the invitation came Willison was ecstatic. Within two hours he secured his release from the *Advertiser* and headed north to Tiverton to tell Rachel Turner the good news. She had not yet succumbed to other suitors, and over the past two years he had taken the trip as often as his slender funds and few days off allowed. Now there was time for several days to celebrate his great news with her in a delightful Bruce County holiday setting of sunshine, swimming, and picnics. When he left for Toronto soon after Labour Day, he and Rachel were closer than ever, at least as far as Mrs. Turner would allow. And marriage was beginning to seem a delightful and none too distant likelihood.[3]

He arrived at the *Globe*'s busy building at 26–28 King Street East bright and early on the morning of September 10, 1883. Cameron's office was found, introductions made, and a desk assigned. For the first few weeks he served as the editor's private secretary. But before the year was out he was making fifteen dollars weekly as assistant night editor commenting on the "exchanges" — notes and quotes from other newspapers, local, national, and foreign. After hours he had a lonely time at first in a big strange city of 120,000. He boarded a dozen blocks east and north of the office, on Mutual Street. His landlady mothered him, and he was touched that she tried to make his room homelike and was so cheery. As his first Christmas approached, he bought her roses, even though shocked at the price, because he was determined to show that he appreciated her kindness.[4]

He knew well that he worked for more than a mere newspaper. The *Globe* had been founded and developed to a towering eminence by George Brown and his brother Gordon before Confederation. George had been *the* dominant political figure in pre-Confederation Canada West. After 1867, he had been a key supporter of Alexander Mackenzie as federal party leader and then prime minister after 1873. Mackenzie was defeated in 1878, with the federal leadership soon passing to Edward Blake. When George Brown died in 1880, brother Gordon, with the support of other members of the family, had attempted to carry on George's plans for the modernization of the business. In the unhealthy economic climate of the early 1880s, the Browns had been forced to sell more and more stock to outsiders. In December 1882 they had lost control to a syndicate organized by Robert Jaffray, a wealthy Toronto Liberal whose fortune had been founded on a thriving grocery business and in railways. The new president was James MacLennan, a law partner of Ontario Premier Oliver Mowat and a close associate of the new federal party leader, Edward Blake. Other members of the board included Jaffray; John F. Taylor, a prominent paper manufacturer; H.H. Cook, a Liberal MP; and J.D. Edgar, a former Liberal MP. It was this new board that had turned to John Cameron, a close friend of Blake's, to run the *Globe*.[5]

In the early 1880s the *Globe* was the only uncompromisingly Liberal daily in the bitterly competitive crowded newspaper market in Toronto and its large Ontario hinterland. It had the highest average daily circulation in 1883, with its morning and afternoon editions combined at close to 24,000. The weekly edition averaged 41,000. Its chief rival since 1872 had been the morning *Mail*, the acknowledged Conservative mouthpiece in the city. Once puny in comparison to the *Globe*, its role and reputation had soared under the brilliant T.C. Patteson, in company with the recovery of Sir John A. Macdonald's federal Tories from their humiliation in the Pacific Scandal. Macdonald returned to power in 1878 on a platform of protective tariffs — the so-called "National Policy." The victory was confirmed in 1882. Manufacturers and businessmen generally were enthusiastic supporters of the new government, and the Toronto city core was becoming far more Tory.

The upstart Tory *Mail* now averaged 22,000 sales daily and the semi-independent but Tory-leaning *World*, owned and edited since 1880 by W.F. Maclean, was at 17,000. The generally pro-Conservative *Telegram*, set up in 1876 by John Ross Robertson, was at around 15,000, and the *Evening News*, founded in 1881 as an afternoon edition of the *Mail* but in 1883 striking out on its own under E.E. Sheppard on a broad platform of radical political and social reform, averaged about 17,000.[6] While the *Mail* and the *Globe* sold for two cents a copy, the others were one-centers, answering what the *Dominion Annual Register and Review, 1883* termed "the steadily growing demand for cheap newspaper literature" for the masses.[7] In both political and journalistic terms, the *Globe* was in a bitter fight for survival amid the shifting tastes of its volatile market.

It was a young man's game. John Cameron was only forty; Martin Griffin of the *Mail*, thirty-six; Sheppard of the *News*, twenty-eight; Maclean of the *World*, twenty-nine; and Robertson of the *Telegram*, forty-two.[8] John Willison was twenty-seven, eager and intelligent, but he had to be aware as well of all the other young feet on the ladder rungs of his city's journalism above and below him. He would have to be quick or be left behind, never to reach the top. Too many years had been wasted already.

He served three successive sessions in the press gallery of the old Legislative Buildings on Front Street. He would remember his work as "petty and trivial and partisan…. It was of the atmosphere of the Legislature and in those days one worshipped his political idols, blasphemed the enemy and rejoiced."

Premier Mowat, though a Liberal, was a status-quo incumbent, and the Conservative leader of the opposition, W.R. Meredith, often took the more progressive social positions. Apparently Willison was impressed by this. He would record years later that he often was "in complete sympathy" with Meredith's legislative proposals.[9] But he kept that sympathy well hidden at the time, never allowing it to be reflected in his "By Our Own Correspondent" reports in the *Globe*, instead giving that column a reliably venomous anti-Conservative tone. In an early comment on the 1884 session he described Meredith as "overwhelmed with confusion" and blasted "the docility of the dull-witted mob of Opposition members."[10] It was all in keeping with the *Globe's* editorial shrillness, culminating later in the session with its denunciation of what it claimed was an undercover plot of provincial Conservatives and the *Mail* to bribe Mowat Liberals in the Legislature to change sides and overturn the government. The *Globe* even accused Prime Minister Macdonald of foul complicity, claiming that Macdonald had never shunned in the past "any political crime necessary to maintain his power."[11]

Not surprisingly, the *Globe* worshipped Premier Oliver Mowat. Never was this more evident than later in 1884, when the Judicial Committee of the Privy Council, the Empire's highest court, upheld Ontario's case in a boundary dispute against Manitoba, which had been supported by the Tory federal government. Mowat himself had argued the case in London and the *Globe* crowed: "Ontario as now definitely bounded possesses within herself all the necessaries and potentialities of a great nation. And that she was not deprived of a large part of her property is due to the courage, the shrewdness and the tenacity with which Oliver Mowat fought her battle."[12]

When Mowat returned in triumph to Toronto in September, the *Globe* enthused about his welcome home by a large cheering crowd, including some 1,500 self-styled representatives of "The Young Men of Ontario," organized by an *ad hoc* committee of young Toronto Liberals. W.F. Creelman, chairman of the committee, saw in the demonstration an "impetus to the young men of the Province" which would "awaken in them a more lively interest in its affairs." The next step was the organization of the Young Men's Liberal Club of Toronto on September 18. A.C. Hamilton told the inaugural meeting that the new club would "make it easy to get at the young men who are anxious to serve the Liberal party," and he enthused about the good to be accomplished by "bringing together a lot of young men for the discussion of political questions."[13]

During its initial season the club rapidly expanded its membership, with two hundred and fifty on the rolls by the end of February 1885 and sixty or more attending the Monday evening meetings. Debate subjects ranged from municipal taxation, electoral reform, and immigration, to the future status of Canada in the world. Among the club's leaders that first year were: Lyman Duff, future Chief Justice of the Supreme Court of Canada; T.C. Robinette, later a distinguished lawyer; H.H. Dewart, who became leader of the Ontario Liberal Party; and W.D. Gregory, who went on to be editor of the *Canada Farmer's Sun*. Gregory would later write, with pardonable partiality: "There has never been a political organization in Toronto which has had so many young men of first-rate ability as that organization had."[14]John Willison was not listed officially as a member that first year. His reporting duties may have conflicted, or perhaps he was a little shy about mixing with wealthier, better educated longtime Toronto men.

Or, just maybe, he had better things to do with the little spare time he could arrange. Back and forth to Tiverton on the weekend overnight coach sure could wear a fellow down, making Monday night no time for after-work debating. Also, the Tiverton travel offered more immediate and important rewards. "Jack" asked the lovely "Rae" to marry him, and the wedding was scheduled to take place June 3, 1885 in the

The House of Commons chamber and press gallery, 1897.
Library and Archives Canada, PA-12285

Turners' home, followed by a festive wedding breakfast. That morning, however, began in consternation at the Turner home. The issuer of marriage licenses, a rejected rival suitor of Rachel's, refused to approve one, on the grounds that the groom was not a local resident. However, he would lift his ban if Rachel asked him personally. Willison had no idea what should be done, but Rachel firmly ruled out any request. They would have their wedding breakfast and then take the train to Toronto to be married there! They were in the midst of their party when the chastened official showed up, license in hand. Mrs. J.S. Willison was a lady of spirit as well as beauty.[15]

They made their first home together at 386 Ontario Street, not far below Wellesley and about a mile north of the *Globe*.[16] He could easily walk to and from work, which was fortunate because quitting time for a reporter on a morning paper all too often was well after midnight and streetcars. However, it usually was possible now for him to get time off on

Monday nights to go to the Yonge Street Arcade, just around the corner from the office, for meetings of the Toronto Young Men's Liberal Club, which he joined on October 5.[17]

The YMLC now had more than three hundred members of a very vigorous organization. Some senior Liberals were beginning to worry about their "radicalism" and even some expressions at meetings about disloyalty to the Empire. The provincial Young Liberals' convention had taken place in September, and the Toronto club had presented most of the more radical resolutions and amendments — most notably for abolition of the Senate, liquor prohibition, and Canadian independence. But the more conservative non-Toronto delegates had heeded the promptings of senior party leaders to block the Torontonians' initiatives.[18]

John Willison had reported that convention for the *Globe*. Now he became one of the most active YMLC members. He may have been spurred to join because of the very radicalism the party elders decried. He would later describe his political views at this time as those of "a democrat, a free trader and a moderate social radical."[19] Certainly an article he wrote four years later on the 1885 provincial convention was highly critical of the older Liberals and of the young delegates who had been frightened into orthodoxy by them.[20] At a late November meeting he spoke in favour of party politics at the municipal level. In December he argued for Senate abolition, although warning that it should be treated as an ideal, not to be pushed until the smaller provinces agreed. That must have sounded like trimming to the majority, who voted solidly for abolition. Then, at a January 1886 meeting, true to his Good Templars' training, he argued fervently for prohibition — but the drinkers in the group had their blood up, and he lost.[21]

In late March 1886 his involvement in the club was cut short by his appointment to the *Globe* staff covering Parliament in Ottawa. This was everything his ambition could have asked for. National politics, for all the Mowat Ontario fanaticism of the *Globe*, meant the big time for political reporters. When Rachel said goodbye to him at the old Union Station on Front Street before he took the Grand Trunk to Ottawa, she had to know this was a critical career opportunity for him.[22] The parting may have been eased by the fact that he would be back soon enough when the session ended in the spring.

The Russell Hotel, corner of Elgin and Sparks Streets, 1898 (from William H. Carre, Art Work on Ottawa, Canada, 1898)
City of Ottawa Archives/2011.0102.1/CA-000162

The parliamentarians had gathered a month before, and sittings continued until the second day of June. Already, before his arrival, the chief fireworks of the session had been touched off — in a bitter debate on Edward Blake's motion condemning the execution the previous November of the Métis leader Louis Riel for his leadership of the Northwest Rebellion earlier that year. Blake had argued that Riel should have been pardoned as insane, and his French-Canadian colleague Wilfrid Laurier had pleaded eloquently for justice to the Métis people. Their position was largely in accord with that of Honoré Mercier's semi-separatist *parti national* in Quebec. The *Globe* loyally supported the Blake–Laurier stand, commenting: "The Métis cause was a just one. It is not possible to maintain that the leader of a just cause should have been sent to the gallows…."[23]

Twenty-four Ontario Liberal MPs dared to share publicly the general Ontario revulsion at the Blake position, by opposing his motion in

Top Left: *John Willison, 1888.*
William Topley Collection, Library and Archives Canada

Top Right: *The Honourable Edward Blake, 1886.*
Library and Archives Canada, PA-003833

Bottom Left: *The Honourable Sir Richard Cartwright, circa 1890.*
Library and Archives Canada, PA-025546

Bottom Right: *The Honourable Wilfrid Laurier, 1882.*
Library and Archives Canada, C-001967.

condemnation of the execution. In the Liberal party, as in the country at large, the fires of sectional and ethnic discord burned brightly. The Liberals just might be on the way to winning new acceptability in Quebec, hitherto the Conservatives' most reliable power base. However, with a general election inevitable in a few months, not a few in the party must have wondered if their voting strength in Ontario could be at severe risk.

During his brief first session in Ottawa, Willison was a subordinate member of the *Globe's* team there. He sent off only the occasional article, as he was under John Cameron's instructions to concentrate on familiarizing himself with the parliamentary scene and establishing personal rapport with the chief Liberal leaders. That list was long, chiefly Ontarians like Blake, Sir Richard Cartwright, the former finance minister, and David Mills, the former minister of the interior. Willison soon learned, however, from other reporters in Ottawa about the bright new star rising on Parliament Hill, and not from Ontario. John Dafoe, then of the Ottawa *Evening Journal,* would record that the speech on Riel in English by Quebec's Wilfrid Laurier had made "an extraordinary impression" on all who had heard it, that all the "big guns" in the House of Commons had been "thrown into complete eclipse by Laurier's performance."[24] After the speech Edward Blake spoke for many of the politicians of both parties when he said that it was "the finest parliamentary speech ever pronounced in the Parliament of Canada since Confederation."[25]

Willison had to be fascinated as he watched the tall, slim, elegant, chestnut-haired French Canadian from his seat immediately above and behind the Speaker's chair in the low-slung press gallery. He had spent all his life to date in English-speaking Ontario and had never before had a chance to meet any one remotely like Laurier. Yet here was a French-Canadian Quebec Roman Catholic who quoted Byron and regularly haunted the English-language literary and history shelves of the Parliamentary Library![26] For his part, Laurier was happy to linger in chats with the tall, obviously intelligent, dark-haired, bearded new reporter from his party's premier English-language paper. They soon understood that they were very alike in their intense love for the drama of politics and the romance of great history and literature.

Willison refused to be outraged, as many an Ontario Protestant was, by Laurier's position on Riel's execution. Instead, with a federal election looming in December that year, he helped to arrange an invitation for Laurier to speak at a mass public meeting organized by the Toronto Young Men's Liberal Club. There were many predictions of a negative, even unruly, reception. As the large crowd surged from the snowy Toronto night into the vast Horticultural Pavilion, there were understandable fears among leading senior Liberals that the evening could be a disaster.

In his speech Laurier identified himself as "an English liberal ... the principles which I profess ... did not come to me from the land of my ancestors. They came to me from England." He reached beyond the divisive Riel controversy to voice a moving image of Canada's dualistic but united future: "Below the island of Montreal the water that comes from the north, from the Ottawa, unites with the waters that come from the western lakes, but united they do not mix. There they run, parallel, separate, and distinguishable, and yet are one stream, flowing within the same banks, the mighty St. Lawrence rolling on toward the sea ... a perfect image of our nation."[27] Willison would write years later of that night that it had been "hard to resist the courtesy, the patience, the manly bearing and resolute temper of the eloquent leader of the French Liberals."[28]

Willison was mostly back in Toronto as 1886 gave way to 1887, reinforcing the *Globe*'s coverage of Oliver Mowat's triumphant provincial re-election in December 1886 and then the difficult federal campaign across Ontario in February 1887, when Sir John A. Macdonald's Conservatives held on to office with a reduced majority. Frustratingly for the Liberals, the Riel affair seemed to have gained them little in Quebec. The party now had been trounced in three successive general elections by the prime minister they thought they had destroyed fourteen years before in the Pacific Scandal. As Willison would write, "a long day of adversity" continued for the Liberals.[29] When the new Parliament opened in mid-April, Willison returned to Ottawa, this time with the status of "Special Parliamentary Correspondent." This first session after yet another heartbreaking defeat was a despondent time for federal Liberals, but it proved one of pivotal opportunity for Willison.

He would look back on his Parliamentary Press Gallery time as "the most happy and interesting of my life, as desirable and enviable through association with the Gallery itself as through any intimate relations with political leaders or any necessary identification with the strategy of parties." He had never been to high school. Yet here he was in what was in effect a graduate school of national politics and journalism, getting to know reporters from across the country with all sorts of backgrounds, ideas, and political identifications. He made, he would record, an "instant friendship" with Arthur Colquhoun, just graduated with a B.A. from McGill and starting out in Tory journalism in Montreal. He much admired another Conservative journalist, Bob White of the Montreal *Gazette*, whom he would remember as "perhaps the most authoritative and distinguished member of the Gallery in the eighties" with his "lucid and finished" writing on public financial questions.

There was at least a brief chance to get to know the twenty-one year-old John Dafoe, editor at the Ottawa *Evening Journal* before he left for the *Free Press* in Winnipeg. Other key Gallery members of the time were C.H. Cahan of the Conservative Halifax *Herald*, T.P. Gorman on the Liberal Ottawa *Free Press*, Fred Cook of the recently founded Tory Toronto *Empire*, A.F. Wallis of the newly independent Toronto *Mail*, James Maclean of the independent but Tory-leaning Toronto *World*, and Marc Sauvalle of the pro-Conservative Montreal *La Presse*. There was so much to talk about each day along the Gallery rail in the House of Commons and among the noisy throngs each night in the lobby, bar, and dining room at the Russell Hotel at Elgin and Sparks, where so many of the politicians stayed while in Ottawa. One didn't need to be a drinker to enjoy the company.[30]

His new Tory friend Arthur Colquhoun would recall about Willison in his Gallery days: "The man himself impressed one more than any writing that could be traced to his pen. He was courteous and agreeable, without being effusive, quick in grasping a subject, and a good talker, although prone to a rather irritating tendency to believe the Liberal party always right." In spite of that Liberal self-righteousness, he quickly impressed other Conservatives too. Just a few weeks into the new session, he was astonished to be invited with many of his new Conservative reporter friends to a dinner party at the Parliamentary Restaurant with Finance Minister Sir Charles Tupper! In the hyperpartisan atmosphere of Ottawa, he would write, the invitation was "so amazing that I hesitated to accept without authority from the office. I telegraphed to The Globe and was assured that acceptance would not be treated as a betrayal of the Opposition."[31]

He well knew of the bitter hatred of Prime Minister Sir John Macdonald for his purportedly corrupt and unprincipled ways, and it had been part of the *Globe* tradition since the days of its founder, George Brown. Now he had daily opportunity from his Gallery seat to watch the prime minister leading his government, his parliamentary party, and the nation. "I was so placed," Willison would record, "that I could sometimes see shades of expression cross his face, the defiant jerk of his head when he was angry, the shrug of contempt for a mean gibe that was meant to wound, the quick, natural human manifestation of pleasure over a generous word from an opponent or a tribute of affection and confidence from an associate…. Few men have had such charm for his kind, or such power to inspire sacrifice and devotion…. I have known gray-haired Liberals who had persuaded themselves that the Conservative leader was the favourite offspring of the father of evil forever disarmed by a few quick, happy spontaneous sentences, spoken carelessly enough, but which, as he intended they should, penetrated to the very marrow of their self-esteem."[32]

The main fascination of the session for Willison and all of the reporters and politicians he was coming to know was the Liberal leadership question. Edward Blake, it soon became clear, was not getting over the disappointment of losing the general election. The mantle of leadership always had been heavy for him, given his debilitating spasms of introspection and self-criticism. At the beginning of the session he had tried to resign, but had given way to pleas from his followers that he stay on for a time, at least nominally.[33] As the rumours of a leadership crisis swirled through the corridors of Parliament, John Cameron's intensely pro-Blake *Globe* thundered angrily: "The suggestion that any change in the Liberal leadership at Ottawa is contemplated by anyone in his senses is absurd upon its face." [34]

However, as the close of session approached in early June, Blake refused to go on any longer. He recommended to caucus on June 7 that Wilfrid Laurier succeed him, but the meeting broke up with no official word on the result. Willison haunted the corridors on the Hill and then at the Russell Hotel to find out what he could. "No one maintained a more resolute silence than Laurier himself," he would recall. "Finally, towards midnight, when the appeal from The Globe for a statement became imperative, I saw Mr. Laurier and told him that with or without his consent my dispatch would announce in the morning that he had been chosen to succeed Mr. Blake. He protested that I could have no knowledge that the statement would be accurate and intimated that he did not believe I would be rash enough to send out any such message. But I was rash enough to do so, and the message was substantially if not strictly accurate."[35] The next morning's paper carried his "Gallery Notes" with the sentence "It is understood that Mr. Laurier has been offered the leadership for the remainder of the session."[36] Soon enough, it became clear that his tenure would not be temporary.

It was nearly two weeks before Laurier's reservations about accepting the leadership were overcome. He had worried about his health and finances and whether the Liberals should select a French Canadian Catholic leader. Also, Sir Richard Cartwright and David Mills, strong rival potential leaders from the party's Ontario heartland, had substantial caucus support. The official announcement was made on June 23. Only then did the grieving John Cameron, who had hoped against hope throughout the crisis that Blake might be pressured to stay on, salute his successor editorially in the *Globe* in a restrained way, noting that Laurier "has not yet taken the highest places in purely business debate, nor displayed that intimate acquaintance with Parliamentary procedure for which Mr. Blake was so remarkable."[37]

Even at the outset of the 1888 session the paper still was adopting something of a wait-and-see attitude about Laurier, commenting: "It remains to be seen whether he possesses, in addition to Parliamentary eloquence of the first order and a character entirely stainless, the skill, the firmness, the grasp of procedure, the speedy decision, and the determination to lead, which are necessary to a leader."[38]

It was an illustration of what John Dafoe, then in the Gallery with Willison, would describe as the "doubt and heartburnings among the leaders of Ontario Liberalism" at Laurier's accession. Probably the new chief's French-Canadian and Catholic background and the widely held impression of him as an elegant dilettante were to blame. "If I ever had this impression," Willison would recall, "it was soon dispelled." That summer he received an invitation from Laurier to join him for a few days at his country home in Arthabaskaville in the Eastern Townships. This was heady stuff for a former farm hand and store clerk. "During those days," Willison would write, he talked much and I very little. In nothing that he said was there any suggestion of arrogance or boasting. But he revealed his knowledge of men and of books, his clarity and vigour of mind, his inflexibility of will and purpose. At least I thought I had discovered a man of very different quality from the amiable Laodicean who many Liberals believed had been installed in a position to which he was unequal.[39]

For Laurier, Willison, and Liberals generally, the great overriding issue in Canadian politics over the next several years was freer trade with the United States. By mid-1887 it was the obsession almost of both the great Toronto morning papers, the *Globe* and the *Mail*. The *Mail* had bolted its Conservative allegiance the year before to take up an extreme but very popular anti-Catholic and anti-Quebec stance, in reaction to the Riel furor among French Canadians.[40] In the bad economic circumstances of the later 1880s, especially in rural southwestern Ontario, the *Mail* struck a responsive chord as well with a sustained crusade for free trade, brilliantly directed by its mercurial editorial writer, Edward Farrer. By March 1, 1887 the *Mail* was solid for "commercial union" and maintained that only meaningless sentimental reasons — fears for the British connection — held back Canadians in general and farmers in particular from the economic bonanza which would result from continental free trade.

For some years the *Globe* had toyed with the free trade idea, as was proper for a good Liberal paper aware of the righteousness of the glorious free trade principles long enunciated by that greatest of all Liberals, William Ewart Gladstone in Britain.[41] But in the 1887 election Edward Blake had feared for the nation's revenues and had fretted about the potential ire of protected manufacturers. Dutifully, John Cameron had promised that the *Globe* "would not deviate a hair's breadth from that position."[42] However, as soon as the election was over the *Globe*, with an eye on the *Mail*'s circulation gain in the western Ontario hinterland, veered sharply towards "commercial union" itself.[43]

Laurier, understandably anxious to take up a "bold policy" on the economic front to attract rural Ontario support and divert attention from his Catholicism, moved quickly as leader to push commercial unionism, urged on by his chief Ontario lieutenant, Sir Richard Cartwright.[44] In March 1888 the party announced its policy, with the moderate title of "Unrestricted Reciprocity" avoiding the possibly annexationist hints in the word "union," in a resolution in the House of Commons. Gleefully, Sir John A. Macdonald and the Tories raised the spectre of Liberal disloyalty to the national future and the British connection. Debate in Parliament and the country would not be restricted to economics.

The Toronto Young Men's Liberal Club focused on the trade and national questions again and again during its 1887–88 season. Willison, often in the city when Parliament was not sitting, was nominated for the YMLC presidency, but withdrew his name. He and the incoming president, Hartley Dewart, were toasted enthusiastically at a large meeting. On November 28 he spoke for a motion favouring "commercial union." On January 16 of the new year he read a formal paper to the club on "The Future Policy of the Liberal Party." The *Globe* recorded his remarks:

> He expressed his opinion that a great mistake was made by the Liberal party in "hedging" on the tariff question in 1882 and 1887; that the great bulk of the Liberal party was in favor of a tariff levied purely for tariff; and that their enthusiasm was damped when they drew the conclusion that their leader (Blake) had feared to make that an issue. In this condition they had to meet a strong and aggressive party which took such precautions for its own safety as the gerrymander, the Franchise Bill, and a judicious distribution of subsidies, post offices, etc. Mr. Willison strongly recommended the policy of "tariff for revenue only." He also believed that they should advocate Continental Free Trade as the nearest practicable approach to Universal Free Trade....

Debate followed, with some dissent. Some questioners wondered how his "tariff for revenue" could produce same if "Continental Free Trade" actually were to be achieved. Others asked what would happen to Canadian trade and hence connection with Britain. Willison would not be the only Laurier follower to have such questions hurled at him over the next several years. And the answers never would be fully convincing.[45]

He was no policy maker at this stage of his career, only a loyal disciple of the new leader. Meanwhile, the *Globe*'s editorials made more of the leadership qualities of Sir Richard Cartwright than of Laurier. "That they [the Liberals] have considered their plan thoroughly," it assured its readers about the Unrestricted Reciprocity policy, "is sufficiently signified by Sir Richard's prominence in the matter. He is the last man to enter on a course without seeing his way clearly." It even quite explicitly compared the Cartwright-Laurier relationship to the dual Tory leadership of Macdonald and Cartier in pre-Confederation days.[46] Editor Cameron seemed nervously concerned to reassure the hinterland that this new economic policy the Tories were trying to blacken was in no way the work of some flighty Frenchman but of a good solid Ontario man — a knight of the realm even!

Willison took a very different course. His "FROM THE CAPITAL" column positively gushed unlimited praise for Laurier's speech in the trade debate at Ottawa:

> The reputations of George Brown, Alexander Mackenzie and Edward Blake will be dear to the Canadian people for many a long year to come, and on the same beadroll of fame the name of Wilfrid Laurier will have a bright and brilliant place. Steadily Mr. Laurier has risen to the duties and responsibilities of the Liberal leadership in Parliament in a way that has astonished his opponents and delighted his friends. Courteous, but ready and resolute in the House, genial, kindly and companionable he enjoys a respect and popularity almost unique among Canadian Parliamentary leaders. His ability is as great as his popularity. His speech of today must greatly enhance his reputation. He has had the fault of too many of the Quebec representatives; he has confined his attention too closely to matters of peculiar interest to his own Province and has spoken too seldom on subjects of wide

national concern. That he has a strong grasp of the great central truths of political economy, a deep knowledge of and a close familiarity with all the past and all the present of his own country, was abundantly proved in the speech he delivered … to a rapt Opposition and a silent and respectful array of Ministerialists.[47]

When the session ended in May, Willison was doubly delighted to return to Toronto. He had become a new father the month before and it was time to get to know his two twin boys, William and Walter. At work, a new and delightful assignment awaited him. On June 15 he began a regular column of editorial page comment on political and general subjects titled OBSERVATIONS. He signed himself mysteriously as OBSERVER, but his authorship soon was generally known.[48] He ranged widely in his choice of subjects: drunkenness, reminiscences of farm life, poetic humour, and political speculation. On July 2, the day after Canada's twenty-first birthday, he used a farmer's allegorical style to comment on Canada's relationship with Britain and the United States:

> We decline Cousin Jonathon's [the United States'] offer to run the farm [Canada]. We are able to get in our own harvest and attend to our own stock and catch our own fish and mind our own business. We will exchange work and lend things and be neighborly, but we will not tolerate stray cattle in our meadow nor trespassers in our corn patch…. We can't be frightened and we won't be bullied. We are of age today and we propose to manage our own affairs….
>
> We have got the farm pretty well cleared up. Up north there are still some stumps to be lifted and some stone to be removed, and away west there is a lot of good meadow that is not thoroughly stocked, and great tracts of unoccupied land that ought to be worked and cropped. But that is very much our own fault. We have allowed the neighbours to get the pick of the farm hands and have not been wise always in our conditions

of service. We will probably put the place under new management in a year or two, and get many of the old hands back, and make the whole place productive. We are not rich, but we have a great deal of experience that was costly but will prove of pertinent advantage....

It is not true that the old folks [Britain] have set the Dominion up in business. All they do for us is to send out a manager [Governor General] whom we manage. We keep him also, by the way, and he comes high.

It was very clear that Willison assumed a *de facto* self-sufficient status for Canada, whatever convenient trading arrangements might be made with the United States or whatever *de jure* attachments with Britain might remain.

He had an excellent opportunity that summer to communicate to Laurier a broad range of views on national issues. The Liberal leader was planning a rural Ontario tour, starting with a speech to the Young Liberals' picnic at Oakville, west of Toronto, and he wanted suggestions for speech themes. They were no longer in Ottawa together, so their written correspondence took over from conversation. He told Laurier that:

Ontario ... will stand a great deal of talk on the greatness of Canada and the necessity of all working in harmony, provinces working together, no race differences, full provincial rights.... Our young men are strongly Canada first, not quite Commercial Unionists, but loyal to Unrestricted Reciprocity, kindly disposed towards the States and while not quite against British connection still in favor of our exercising full material rights."[49]

He covered the Oakville picnic and accompanied Laurier on the rest of his Ontario tour, no doubt with many opportunities to provide more advice. He gave him uncritical acclaim in the *Globe*, reporting that the leader had "everywhere ... won completely the allegiance of Liberals and the respect and goodwill of opponents." Years later he would recall more soberly about that tour: "I cannot think that his [Laurier's] reputation was enhanced ... and I am confident that he was too gentlemanly for the hard, rough, uncompromising, aggressive warfare in which a political leader must engage....”[50]

At the time, however, Laurier must have been very grateful for Willison's uncritical "booming" of him in the *Globe.* The Roman Catholic French Canadian still was little known in Ontario, and the young reporter had ready daily access to its people. Certainly the ripening acquaintanceship linked Willison personally to national issues and causes and perhaps to some future career opportunity. His intense enthusiasm for Laurier gushed out when he acknowledged the leader's thanks for his articles on the summer tour:

> I only wish I had the ability to do for you in that way all I would like to do. I do not have to assure you that any service I can do you either as an individual or as a journalist will be <u>very</u> <u>very</u> cheerfully rendered.... If I can do anything for you at any time I hope you will ask me to do it.[51]

Willison was maturing now, as a writer on politics and as a Young Liberal. On October 11 the YMLC elected him president "by acclamation and applause."[52] He was in the chair in November when the club debated the options of Canadian independence from Britain or union with the United States. He voiced his support for independence, helping it to win a close vote over a strong annexationist sentiment.[53] Then, as OBSERVER in the *Globe,* he argued that "the great body of Canadian public sentiment is hostile to Annexation. The growing feeling is for Canadian nationality." He conceded that "nominally we are a dependency of Great Britain," but regarded the connection with indifference. He favoured a strong attempt at securing free trade with the United States, but not at the price of any political connection. He concluded:

> I believe simply that no people ever faced a grander destiny than ours may be if we have but the faith and the courage to work it out to its legitimate development. If we surrender our nationality it will be because

we are mercenary or because we are cowardly.... If a time in our history should come when we must choose between Independence and Political Union with the United States, let us run up a Canadian flag, let us declare Canada for the Canadians. Then we shall attract immigration from Germany, from the United States itself, and from the countries whose people will not come under the flag of England....[54]

He was warming to the nationalist theme. Early in January 1889, he addressed a crowded YMLC poetry evening meeting at the Reform Club, with many ladies including Rachel Willison present. He demonstrated a thorough familiarity with Canadian poets and stressed that "until we take our place as a nation among nations, devoted only to the working out of our own destiny, and with the single ambition to make the best of our opportunities and resources, the best that is in our people will not be developed in literature, in art, in government, or in any of the finer and higher pursuits that lie open to human effort and ambition."[55]

Very early in 1889, Willison, the *Globe*, and the Liberal party found themselves caught up in a dramatic new and divisive issue. Honoré Mercier's *parti national* regime in Quebec had awarded the Roman Catholic Church there $400,000 the previous year in compensation for properties confiscated from the Society of Jesus after the British Conquest in the mid-18th century. The money was to be divided among church societies and dioceses by the Pope. For some time, many English Canadians had found the ultra-Catholic flavour and French Canadian *nationaliste* rhetoric of the Quebec government anti-Canadian and un-British. Now there was outrage, and a group of MPs of both parties followed the prominent Conservative backbencher D'Alton McCarthy in demanding federal disallowance of the Quebec statute on the grounds that it contravened the principle of separation of Church and State and permitted a foreign power — the Papacy — to meddle in Canadian secular affairs. The two party leaders, Macdonald and Laurier, strenuously opposed the motion, knowing full well how Mercier and his supporters in Quebec would use it to fan further the flames of *nationaliste* emotion. All but eight Conservatives and five Liberals went along when division time came in the House of Commons. Yet in much of English Canada, and especially through the columns of the Toronto press, the fight against the Jesuit Estates Act went forward vigorously. As the Toronto *Mail*, continuing enthusiastically on its renegade anti-Catholic and anti-French Canadian path, put it, "Ontario is prepared, before considering itself beaten ….to insist on a revision of the constitution even though the demand should put an end to Confederation."[56]

At first, the *Globe* had followed Laurier in opposition to the disallowance idea, while the *Mail* happily drew away thousands of the Liberal organ's Protestant readers. On March 16, John Cameron abandoned that position and fell in with what had become a popular crusade. As E.W. Thomson, the paper's chief editorial writer, explained to Edward Blake: "The feeling here against the Jesuit Act is intense beyond anything in my experience, and of an enduring nature, in my judgement. Dislike of the Jesuits is part of the bone and blood of these people and no matter how wisely and how well the constitutionality of the Act may be argued for, that dislike will be fatal to those Liberal Ontarians who so argue." Five of the seven members of the paper's board of directors approved, including the president, Robert Jaffray, who met a disgusted Edward Blake's charges of opportunism with the comment: "I don't think you can be aware of the desperate struggle the *Globe* is having to maintain its Protestant and liberal readers…. The *Mail* is threatening and making heavy inroads in its circulation." Blake contemptuously wanted nothing to do with *Globe* policies formed, as he put it to Jaffray, "according to the present position of the weathercocks."[57]

John Willison did not return to the Parliamentary Press Gallery for the 1889 session; instead he was appointed sub-editor in charge of reorganizing the reporting staff.[58] It was a welcome promotion, especially since he had become a father the year before. His twin sons William and Walter would not have to suffer a protracted separation from their delighted and indulgent father. He and Rachel had a wide circle of interesting friends of their generation, principally from politics, journalism, and the Young Men's Liberal Club. Toronto fancied that it had an agreeable social and artistic milieu, and a refugee from Huron and Bruce Counties was not prone to disagree.[59]

During the Jesuit Estates controversy and what Willison would describe later as the *Globe's* variable and vacillating conduct over it, he kept mostly free of entangling himself.[60] As OBSERVER he only mentioned the issue once, commenting on February 11 that "it has to be confessed that the public throughout Ontario is profoundly stirred and that to the bulk of Protestants it is an exasperating reflection that under the constitution Quebec province can put upon its statute books such a piece of legislation." But he did not take an active part in debates Toronto Young Liberals held in which resolutions were approved calling for the abolition of French in Parliament and revision of the British North America Act to bar such Church-State relations as allegedly were involved in the Jesuit Estates Act.[61] After the *Globe* had dissociated itself from the Liberal leadership on the issue, he wrote Laurier to say: "I am still a Liberal.... I have opinions as to the present situation but I have never dogmatized as the course Liberals in parliament ought to have taken." He added later: "I have not been much affected by the ultra-Protestant movement although I am not at all convinced that it is without justification." He was sure that "the disturbing element in our politics is Mr. Mercier and his course I regard as a menace to the Liberal party."[62]

Nonetheless, Willison had to know that the Mercier *nationaliste* movement in Quebec, built initially on an anti-Macdonald, anti-Conservative, and anti-English wave of feeling at the time of Riel's execution, was playing no small part in the apparent improvement in the popularity there of Laurier and the federal Liberals. He had to be aware too that Laurier on the stump and behind the scenes in Quebec was at pains to get along with the Quebec premier and his organizers.

Willison meant to make sure that the deep Ontario hatred of Mercier's blend of clericalism and French-Canadian *nationalisme* did not extend to all things French Canadian or to a rejection of Wilfrid Laurier's leadership. Willison's Protestantism sat loosely on him, more an offshoot of his Anglo-Saxon secular liberalism than anything like a theology. He was a Church of England adherent who had attended a Methodist chapel as a boy, for convenience's sake. He now went more or less regularly to the "Low" anti-ritualistic St. Alban's Anglican services on Howland Avenue without any signs of undue interest in things religious.[63] He had known Wilfrid Laurier now for three years, and what he had heard from the French Canadian's lips in their wonderfully enjoyable chats in Laurier's House of Commons office, at his Russell Hotel rooms, or at his Arthabaskaville home, just did not jibe with the kind of narrow Catholicism and racism he associated with Mercier.

That August he joyfully accepted another invitation from Laurier to Arthabaskaville. Again he delighted in the cheery informality of Wilfrid and Zoe's little country world — the visiting neighbours with their rambunctious children, the charming squarish red brick home, set amidst maples and bright flowers and backed by vistas of timbered hills. Above all he loved the talk. He reported to his readers on Laurier's "solidity of … mind, the grasp and scope of his intellect, the taste and fancy of the critic and scholar." He stressed the Laurier "mastery of pure, strong melodious English," and found among the well-stocked library shelves firm foundation for it in many well-thumbed volumes of Shakespeare, the English historian Macaulay, and the speeches of Abraham Lincoln and John Bright. He assured Protestants that the leader had "barely patience with the dogmas of warring theologians." He emphasized freedom from clerical taint by noting the many portraits of such Liberal champions of the civil power as George Brown, Louis-Joseph Papineau, and Edward Blake which hung on the library walls.

On Laurier's Canadian patriotism he wrote that the leader "would not care to forget that he is French Canadian. But above all he is a Canadian, and Canada has no son more loyal to Canadian institutions, or more utterly devoted to the upbuilding of a great and prosperous and united Canada." Laurier, Willison argued, "cannot fight well except his heart be in it. His heart is not in the trivialities of parish politics. But this man would be a giant in some great national crisis…. He is not a Radical. He is a Liberal; a Liberal in every conviction of his mind; a strong, brave independent thinker, and a man whom duty rather than ambition, will compel to play a great part in the future of his country."[64]

During the Arthabaskaville visit, he eagerly pressed Laurier to come to Toronto for a major address as soon as possible. He first had broached the idea in June, arguing: "If you could but talk to Ontario the Liberalism you hold you would be the most popular politician in the country." He had promised that the Young Liberals would "very cheerfully" organize a large-scale rally.[65]

Senior Toronto and Ontario Liberals had rushed to smother the idea. J.D. Edgar had predicted to Laurier a "rough meeting" due to the city's aroused anti-Catholic mood and had added: "I don't think you shd speak this time for the Young Liberals — as they were far from sound on the Jesuit question." W.T.R. Preston, chief Liberal organizer for Ontario, had agreed, telling Laurier: "I think it is not desirable that we should make special effort to prove that Ontario Toryism hates you as much as ever. I think also that when you come it should not be under the auspices of the Young Liberals, whose debates and discussions on the separate school, French language and Jesuit questions make them, from a political standpoint, undesirable chaperons." At least, an annoyed Sir Richard Cartwright had urged, "some dependable person" should organize it.[66] But Laurier was determined to face the challenge of braving the "equal rights" storm and thought he could judge in whom dependability was to be found. He asked his young friend to return to Toronto and arrange the meeting. "Without consultation with the editor of The Globe, any member of the Mowat Government, or any Liberal member of parliament," Willison would record, "I secured the Horticultural Pavilion and announced the meeting."[67]

The meeting, a huge and boisterous one, took place on September 30. It was a big night for John Willison, but a trial too. He served as chairman and introduced the guest of honour, asking for "a courteous and kindly reception." Throughout his address Laurier faced persistent heckling from ultra-Protestant zealots, to the extent that afterwards a cowed Premier Oliver Mowat, who had prepared a glowing tribute to Laurier, limited himself instead to an embarrassingly few perfunctory remarks, then whispered to Willison that the advance copy of his intended speech which he had given the Globe would have to be destroyed.

Laurier bravely fought the hecklers, and there were even murmurs of admiration in the crowd when he asked them to rise above differences in religious tenets to a true liberalism and tolerance. Willison would write of that evening: "The man triumphed but the Jesuit Estates Act was still an alien and a fugitive in Toronto.... I have heard Laurier declare that the Pavilion meeting was the most severe ordeal of his public career, and that there were moments when he was mortally apprehensive he would have to abandon the struggle for a hearing. But he prevailed and never again in Ontario did the Liberal leader find an audience unwilling to receive his message…."[68] For Laurier's part, he did not regret that he had faced the Toronto storm, and he would not forget his young reporter-friend who had urged him to do so.

At the Pavilion meeting, the mere mention of the *Globe*'s name had drawn hissing and jeering. John Cameron, with Edward Thomson at his side as chief editorial writer, had conducted a vacillating editorial policy, with backward glances at the surging and uncompromising *Mail*. Willison would recall: "Those indeed were grievous days for *The Globe* staff, and the hissing at the Pavilion meeting was only a disconcerting manifestation of the contumely to which we were continually subjected."[69] The situation could not go on much longer. Sir Richard Cartwright had argued for some time that the *Globe* needed a "slashing writer" like the *Mail*'s brilliant Edward Farrer. Now J.D. Edgar, MP, a *Globe* director, urged Cartwright, as chairman of the directors' policy committee, to push the paper's president, Robert Jaffray, to strengthen the editorial department. Not surprisingly, given his own strong Unrestricted Reciprocity advocacy, Cartwright continued to push for hiring Edward Farrer, who had made his reputation at the *Mail* on precisely that issue.[70]

Very quickly it became clear that the *Globe* directors and leading Liberals at both the federal and provincial levels were determined to have not merely a new editorial writer, but a new editor-in-chief. Cartwright wanted Farrer, but others worried about his "pen-for-hire," pro-American and anti-Catholic reputations. Willison, back in Ottawa for the Parliamentary session over the winter and spring, was astonished to learn that he was being considered too. W.T.R. Preston, the party organizer, described him the only one of the principal writers on the paper not to be a "Grit party crank" in that he was not obsessed with anti-Catholicism and fear of French-Canadians. James Somerville, Liberal M.P. for Brant, confided to Willison that he was the clear choice of the Ontario federal Liberal caucus. Robert Jaffray also pushed for his appointment; so too did Laurier, who would tell him some months later that he had been "the first to suggest your name."[71] Cartwright, Blake, and Premier Mowat apparently discussed what should be done and were unsure Willison had sufficient experience, but were unable to agree on anyone else.

In late March or early April 1890, Willison was recalled from Ottawa and, without mention of the editorship, given full charge of the *Globe* for the duration of the Ontario election campaign, then about to commence. "Long before the election was over," he would remember, "I understood the situation better perhaps than Mr. Cameron or the directors of The Globe suspected. I knew that if The Globe made no capital blunder in the campaign and if the Government was sustained I would succeed Mr. Cameron, and if the Government was defeated I would not."[72]

The Mowat ministry had held office for eighteen years but now faced a very serious challenge from William R. Meredith's Conservatives, who hoped to benefit from the anti-French Canadian and anti-Catholic excitement stirred up in the province by the so-called Equal Rights Association, offspring of D'Alton McCarthy and the anti-Jesuits Estates Act agitation. The Equal Righters and the Conservatives attacked the Liberals for pandering to the Catholic hierarchy by permitting French as a language of instruction in some separate schools and by not insisting on the secret ballot in separate school board elections. Willison warned Laurier as the campaign began that Protestant feeling was running very high and "I will be much surprised if the govt. majority is not considerably reduced."[73]

Under Willison's direction, the *Globe* offered its standard defence of Mowat: that he had given Ontario honest, efficient, and economical government, and had zealously safeguarded the province's constitutional rights against federal encroachment. More boldly, however, Willison charged that Conservatives were trying to ride to power on the backs of sincere non-partisan Equal Rights feeling. The *Globe* featured support for the Mowat government's separate school policies from one of the Equal Righters' most respected spokesmen, Principal Caven of Knox College. It damned "Macdonald–McCarthy–Meredith candidates masquerading as Equal Righters in this contest.... Liberals must 'stand to their guns' and crush utterly and mercilessly this last desperate attempt of the Tory party to capture the surplus, the timber, the resources of Ontario." Gone was the vacillation, gone was the weak and almost apologetic tone John Cameron and Edward Thomson had been taking in political editorials for the past few years. War was carried to the Tory enemy, in a manner that stirred Protestant Grits to party fervour once more, while not disconcerting the

Catholic hierarchy or turning away the Catholic vote. As the campaign drew towards its close, Willison told Laurier that he was "now satisfied that Mr. Mowat is safe," adding: "I would not like to seem immoderate but I now believe that I should get the managing editorship. I can improve the Globe's standing and increase its political value. I was afraid of the task until I faced it and got the responsibility fairly upon me with the added difficulties of the existing situation."[74] To be at the helm of the storied Globe in the eye of a dangerous political storm was wonderfully exciting.

The Liberals were returned to office with fifty-four seats to thirty-seven for the Conservatives. For its conduct during the campaign, the Globe was showered with congratulations from Liberal journals and politicians across Ontario. The Reform Association of South Brant wired: "At no period in its [the Globe's] history within our memory has it been more forcible, pungent, fearless…." The St. Thomas Journal, noting that it had "not always been able to agree with the course of THE GLOBE in late years," hailed with special pleasure therefore "the vigorous and able character" of its work this time. The Guelph Mercury commented: "THE GLOBE was never better handled during a campaign." And the Norfolk Recorder remarked: "A master hand has evidently been at the helm."[75]

Willison's old Gallery friend, Bob White, now the editor of the Tory Montreal Gazette, reached across the political divide to write that "since the time of the Browns I have never known it [the Globe] to be so ably and respectably conducted. I say respectably because I am persuaded decency and due respect for opponents always help a cause, just as the reverse hurts it."[76] John Dryden, the Ontario minister of agriculture, gushed to Willison: "The result generally over the province is largely due to the extremely good management of The Globe during the campaign." Edward Blake reported to Laurier that, for the Globe, there should now be "a brighter future in the party." Laurier wrote Willison warmly to say that "on all hands I have the assurance that the course & tone of the Globe, since you have taken the practical management of the same, have been eminently satisfactorily to the party in Ontario…. I expected no less, my dear Willison, & from the bottom of my heart I congratulate you upon your success." Laurier added that he felt "quite sure now that your position on the paper is absolutely safe, but I will be glad to hear that you have the responsible position in name as well as in fact."[77]

Indeed, the official appointment as "Editor-in-Chief" and the announcement of John Cameron's return to the London *Advertiser* had come through the previous day. But astonishingly, Willison still would have a kind of probation to endure: the celebrated Edward Farrer was to be his "principal editorial writer." Willison knew nothing about this until a day or two before his own appointment was announced. Very likely Sir Richard Cartwright's enthusiasm for Farrer's experience with economic issues was the cause. Willison was to be permitted to read all Farrer editorials before publication and could submit any he disputed to a committee of directors. He would describe that arrangement as "impracticable and impossible," and he never did appeal to the directors.[78]

Willison assured Laurier that he would work "amicably" with Farrer, whose special expertise he conceded. Laurier agreed Farrer would be "very valuable," but "erratic." He contended that "good writing is doubly effective when it is known in the general public that good writing is the work of men of high character and firm opinions." He added: "I am anxious that henceforth your leading thought should be to give that tone to the Globe." Willison fully intended to do just that. "If The *Globe* is to retain its old place and to be influential, it must be respected," he told Laurier.[79] At the age of thirty-three, he had reached already one of the most prestigious and influential positions in Canadian journalism and politics, after a career of less than nine years. However, the Farrer appointment, the *Globe*'s weakened state, and the ongoing power and policy struggles within the Liberal party could easily bring him down.

Crises and Survival at the *Globe*, 1890–1893

W HEN JOHN CAMERON, WILLISON'S PREDECESSOR, RETIRED FROM the *Globe*, the Toronto weekly journal *Saturday Night* remarked acidly that he had "esteemed it his duty to be as nearly as possible unknown, to lose his identity and to be but a portion of the machinery. Men seldom get credit for ability when they thus obliterate themselves."[1] But how was John Willison, the new editor, to become a power and force in his own right within the Liberal party and in journalism? Somehow he would have to suffer — hopefully, outlast — the notorious Edward Farrer, forced on him by senior Liberals as chief editorial writer. He also would have to resist the inevitable efforts of politicians to make him a mere errand-boy. If he and the *Globe* were to rise above mediocrity, he would have to be tough and determined, ready to seize any opportunity to increase his prestige and be vigilant to make and keep his paper relevant and appealing to the great vital centre of Ontario public opinion. He would have to be diplomatic with his party superiors but in the end put his own professional stamp on the *Globe*'s policies and style.

Laurier was quick to direct him to turn the paper's attention to the trade question and strictly federal issues and to "as much as possible … keep clear" of "irritating" Catholic-Protestant and French-English issues,

The Globe *building,*
26–28 King Street West,
*1890 (*Saturday Globe*,*
Sept. 13, 1890, p. 1*)*

to "keep a discreet silence" on them. As he put it, times were "very hard" in Quebec for farmers. "So I understand in your province. This really is the most pressing reform, and this we must hold up before the public in preference to all others. Do you not believe that if the *Globe* at once enters into an active campaign, and day after day hammers on that one idea, that all other subjects will have to take a back place, and that public opinion will become powerfully agitated?"[2]

Willison was quite agreeable to pushing the trade issue, but not exclusively. For some months he had insisted to Laurier that the semi-separatist Premier Honoré Mercier of Quebec, Laurier's political ally, was "the disturbing element in our politics." Mercier won a landslide re-election the very month the *Globe*'s editorship changed hands. Mercier's rhetoric during his campaign was too *nationaliste* for Willison. He also worried about rumours of corrupt practices by the premier and his and Laurier's chief Quebec organizer, Ernest Pacaud. He wrote Laurier: "Do you think we can afford to endorse Mercier? I am afraid not. More, I think we ought to have the liberty at times to dissent, in a calm way, from the tone of his speeches and his methods."

Laurier was calm in reply: "You can certainly state your views as to his [Mercier's] policy whenever you deem it advantageous to do so, and you can point out that if blamable, the blame applies to his [Conservative] foes as well." He begged Willison to attack Ernest Pacaud "only under a strong sense of necessity. Ernest Pacaud has been almost a brother to me."[3]

Dutifully, Willison backed away from Quebec politics for a time, perhaps especially since Laurier also told him that he was contemplating resigning as leader. The chief cause appeared to be his deepening depression about the worsening sectarian and ethnic divisions in Canada. He mused: "If the game is to win, the leader ought to belong to the race of the great majority of the people of this country." Willison at once desperately tried to reassure his idol: "I believe that by the time the election comes on you will be as strong in Ontario as any other man we could put in the leadership ... much of the gratification I had in my promotion to the Chief Editorship was in the fact that you were the party leader.... If you will allow me to say it there is no man in the Liberal party who could command so much of my enthusiasm and devotion as yourself."[4] Laurier did not resign, but his warning that he might do so and why had to be taken very seriously.

However, events in Quebec very soon caused Willison to feel that he had no choice after all but to declare editorial war on Honoré Mercier and all his works. At a victory celebration in Montreal on July 2, Mercier called for a large extension of provincial autonomy via augmented financial resources and exclusive authority in enlarged areas of jurisdiction. The *Globe* exploded that "Quebec cannot be helped from the Federal treasury at the expense of the other Provinces...." It damned "the waste and extravagance in Quebec" and noted that Mercier was "not quite a terror to evil doers...." Willison explained to Laurier that it had been "wise and politic" to, as he put it, "remonstrate mildly with Mr. Mercier."[5] The federal Liberals' chief organizer in Ontario, W.T.R. Preston, now raged to the leader that the editor of the *Globe* had no business in even going that far. Preston had been a key figure in the takeover of the paper by the Robert Jaffray interests a few years before. He would recall the clear objective of that move:

> The idea was that the Globe was to be held in a perpetual trust for the Liberal party, to act as its mouthpiece. In no sense whatever was the paper to be the personal property of those under whose direction or nominal control it might come…. It was never intended that The Globe should pass from the Liberal party to private individuals, much less that private individuals should control its editorial columns to the disadvantage of any Liberal leader.

He told Laurier that he had seen Willison "and advised him very strongly to leave Quebec politics alone…. Mercier can go on any line he chooses down there, and unless some prominence is given to his actions through our papers, more especially the 'Globe,' I am satisfied that the people of this Province will be little concerned about him."[6]

Sir Richard Cartwright agreed completely with Willison's views on Mercier, but lamented to Laurier: "I heartily wish we could keep our people quiet." So did Ernest Pacaud's *L'Électeur* of Quebec City, which intoned: "Le Globe *ne représente le parti libérale en cette affaire.*" Willison tried to creep back into Liberal orthodoxy in mid-July with an editorial comment that it was "not Mr. Mercier's fault that Quebec was bankrupt, backward and toying with the castor idea of a restored New France," but that of "previous inept and profligate Conservative regimes."[7] There matters rested for a time, while crises on other fronts shook the *Globe* and the federal Liberals.

As 1891 began, Canadian politics — and a climactic general election — revolved around the related issues of trade with the United States and the national future. The *Globe* continued loyally to back the Laurier–Cartwright Unrestricted Reciprocity policy, with Edward Farrer playing his expected role in crafting editorials on the economics of it all.

On February 17, with the election in full swing, Prime Minister Sir John A. Macdonald addressed a boisterous Tory rally at the Toronto Academy of Music Building. He charged dramatically that there was "a deliberate conspiracy to injure Canada," in which some of the leaders of the Opposition were "more or less compromised." The crowd pressed Sir John for specifics and he gleefully brought forward the name of Edward Farrer, whom he described as "the philosopher and friend of Sir Richard Cartwright and the controlling spirit of the glorious and consistent newspaper the *Globe.*"

Macdonald then read from a pamphlet which he claimed Farrer had written, for American consumption, in which various economic and diplomatic pressures were suggested whereby the United States could force Canada into an economic association in the American interest. "In fact," thundered the Conservative chieftain, "the document points out every possible way in which Canada and its trade can be injured, and its people impoverished, with a view to eventually bringing about annexation." He himself, he thundered, was a Canadian first, last and all the time, adding that "a British subject I was born, and a British subject I will die.... the sooner the grass is growing over my grave the better rather than that I should see the degradation of the country which I have loved so much and which I have served for so long." The four thousand Tories inside the hall and the thousands more outside cheered the prime minister to the echo and lustily sang "We'll hang Ned Farrer on the Sour Apple Tree."[8]

Farrer's pamphlet had been stolen from a local printing shop. Willison first had heard of its existence earlier that day, from a Conservative friend.[9] The next morning, Farrer protested in the *Globe* that his pamphlet was a private piece of advice to "an American friend of mine, not in politics," concerning "what line I should take if I were an American.... I deny the assumption that THE GLOBE or the Liberal party is bound or affected by anything written, said or done by a mere writer for THE GLOBE in his private hours or private capacity."[10] But the Macdonald Conservatives had found powerful ammunition for the guns of their loyalty battery. Laurier's misgivings the year before about Farrer's "erratic ... opinions" had proven prophetic. Willison may well have wondered if his embarrassed colleague would be at his side for much longer.

From the beginning of the campaign, a potentially far worse political problem had loomed for the Liberal party. On January 28, Edward Blake, the former leader, had addressed a letter of resignation of his Liberal candidacy to the president of the West Durham constituency association, with a copy for publication in the *Globe*. Blake had never approved of the Unrestricted Reciprocity policy. He had not been consulted about it; he was unconvinced of its fiscal logic or that the Americans would agree to it; and he worried about its possibly subversive effects on Canadian nationality. For three years he had kept public silence until, on the eve of the general election, he had learned that Laurier was planning a major federal party convention in Toronto, Blake's home city, with U.R. to be to be trumpeted loudly and the former leader expected to be front and centre on the platform. Blake exploded. He would not be pushed around any longer.

The *Globe*'s copy of Blake's "West Durham Letter" reached Willison's desk just after midnight on January 28. His shock and dismay grew as he read through the eight pages of typescript. It was a root and branch denunciation of the Liberals' central platform plank. Although Blake had no love for the Tories' protectionist National Policy and favoured a moderate revenue tariff, he believed Canada's tax needs and American hostility made that impracticable. He warned that Americans who favoured U.R. did so for essentially annexationist reasons. As a blow to his party's election hopes, it promised to be fatal.[11]

Willison desperately sought to head off disaster. He quickly found that the letter had not been sent as yet to any other paper. In the morning he stalled Blake for a few hours by writing him that he assumed immediate publication had not been intended, as his copy of the letter had been marked "personal." That afternoon he laid the letter before the paper's directors. He would remember "the depth of gloom" which pervaded that meeting. No one doubted that the statement would be fatal to Liberal prospects in the election, but the unanimous judgment was that Mr. Blake would insist on publication and that it must appear. That evening he and David Mills, a Liberal MP and legal expert, drafted what Willison would recall as a "feeble, inconsequential editorial" to accompany the letter's text in the *Globe*. However, late that night Willison resolved to make a last personal effort to dissuade Blake from his course.

The next morning he called on Blake. The ex-leader was furious: he knew Willison had been given full authorization to publish. He wanted this done at once or threatened to take his letter to the *Mail*. When Willison begged him to consult Laurier first, Blake snapped that Laurier had not had the courtesy to consult him before calling the Liberal convention. Blake's brother Sam and Premier Oliver Mowat likewise failed to budge him. Once again, the *Globe's* directors authorized publication. Willison, to their amazement, disobeyed. He asked if Blake would delay publication until he, Willison, could meet Laurier and explore possibilities for accommodations on the trade and convention issues. To his relief, Blake agreed.[12] Willison then wired Laurier, who came to Toronto the next day to meet Blake. Agreement was reached that Blake would postpone publication until after the general election in return for Laurier's pledge to cancel the Toronto convention.[13]

John Willison's achievement was, as his contemporary John Dafoe would describe it, "a political not a journalistic feat." He kept after Blake as the campaign wore on to close ranks completely with his fellow Liberals and even to forget his post-election publication plans:

> If you must think that he [Laurier] has been ill advised in committing so much to U.R. can you not suppress your frank criticism of U.R. which would be fatal at this time, put forward a policy of free trade with the U.S. on the best terms that can be obtained, stand for West Durham, make a 'Midlothian' campaign in these last weeks of the contest, and go into parliament in a position to control the policy of the future. Apologizing for all this mass of words and all this presumption, I am your devoted admirer.[14]

Willison's reference to "Midlothian" recalled the aged W.E. Gladstone's speaking tours in that Scottish constituency in 1879 and 1880. Gladstone, a former prime minister, had emerged from retirement to fight a furious battle against Disraelian foreign and imperial policy. The old man had won the seat, sparking a national overthrow of the Tories. Public opinion then forced aside the official Liberal leaders to bring Gladstone's return to power.[15] It was a famous hour in the history of Liberalism, and neither Willison nor Blake could have been ignorant of the implications of recalling it. Whether Laurier approved or was consulted is unclear, but the ploy failed. Blake remained silent and aloof until election day, his determination to air his grievances immediately afterwards unshaken.

On March 5 the Liberals were defeated nationally, but the Tory majority sank to thirty-one. In Ontario the Laurier forces slimly won the popular vote and took forty-four of the ninety-two seats. The U.R cry seemed to have helped the party in the *Globe*'s hinterland north and west of Toronto, where it swept almost every seat. "Well we are defeated," Willison wrote Laurier philosophically, "but we did not do badly."[16]

The real humiliation came the next day, when Blake's "West Durham Letter" finally was published. The *Globe* confined its accompanying editorial to two main points. First, it welcomed Blake's indictment of the "no growth" Tory protective tariff National Policy. Second, it attacked what it chose to describe as Blake's "political unionism" policy from a nationalistic and pro-British position. Blake had been vague and obscure in any positive advice he offered, and the *Globe* seized cleverly on one particular sentence: "Assuming that free trade with the States, best described as commercial union, may and ought to come," the ex-leader had written, "I believe it can and ought to come only as an incident or at any rate as a well-understood precursor of political union." The *Globe* pronounced coldly and cruelly: "These words may be taken to convey his [Blake's] mind upon the subject of our fiscal and political future." It utterly ignored the totally contradictory thrust of his main clearly nationalist argument against U.R.:

> I do not add to the many matters with which you [the West Durham Liberals] have been necessarily troubled any speculations of my own as to our future.
>
> It is not needful that I should. Whatever you or I may think on that head, whether we like or dislike, believe or disbelieve in political union, must we not agree that the subject is one of great moment, towards the practical settlement of which we should take no serious step without reflection, or in ignorance of what we are doing? ...

> Yet let us never despair of our country.... [If Canadians] do but wake from our delusive dreams, face the stern facts in time, repair our errors, and mend our ways, there may still remain for us, despite our troubled past, a future, if not so clear and bright as we might have hoped, yet fair and honourable, dignified and secure.[17]

Considered in its entirety, Blake's letter was not that of an annexationist, but rather of a sorrowing nationalist, albeit a somewhat pessimistic one. Blake confirmed that in a note to the *Globe* a few days later, citing "contradictory inferences to which a sentence in my Durham letter, detached from its context, has in several quarters unexpectedly given rise." He went on to state that "I think political union with the States, though becoming our probable, is by no means as yet our inevitable future." Ironically, his words provided a partial reinforcement for the *Globe*'s claim. He later told Laurier that the *Globe*'s attitude and that of several of his former parliamentary colleagues had caused him to conclude that he was "in fact dead to them & had lost their private friendship & personal sympathy as well as their political confidence."[18] Whether Farrer, Willison, or both of them were responsible for the *Globe*'s cunning characterization of his views is unknown. Willison certainly never tried to blame Farrer.[19] Politics is a dirty game and so too is party journalism.

There was a brief pause in politics and Liberal infighting in June, as Canadians everywhere reacted to the death of Prime Minister Sir John A. Macdonald in Ottawa. The *Globe* headlined that "Canada's Affection for Sir John Macdonald Universally Manifested" but, perhaps mindful of its decades of criticism of him, limited itself editorially to remarking that "this is not the proper occasion for attempting a judicial review of the man's character and achievements. On the part of those of us who have been his antagonists a respectful silence is becoming...."[20]

Wilfrid Laurier, however, abandoned past partisanship to lead his party in mourning the old adversary with what Willison later would characterize as a "remarkable eulogy" of his great rival in the House of Commons. "It may be said, without any exaggeration whatever," Laurier judged, "that the life of Sir John Macdonald from the date he entered Parliament is the history of Canada" and, while recalling that Sir John "of late has imputed to his opponents' motives which I must say in my heart he has misconceived, yet I am only too glad here to sink these differences and to remember only the great services he has performed for our country — to remember that his actions always displayed great originality of view, unbounded fertility of resource, a high level of intellectual conception, and above all a far reaching vision beyond the events of the day, and still higher, permeating the whole, a broad patriotism — a devotion to Canada's welfare, Canada's advancement, and Canada's glory."[21]

The normal petty and partisan tenor of politics returned soon enough, and the *Globe* was fully caught up in it. That summer, Sir Hector Langevin, the federal minister of public works, became embroiled in a scandal concerning the peddling of government contracts in exchange for election funds. The *Globe* commented on August 1 that the revelations were "still more startling evidence of the corruption that is eating at the vitals of the body politic.... The reputation of the country is at stake...."[22] And of course for the *Globe*, that of the post-Macdonald Conservative party.

But five days later a new scandal began to emerge — involving Liberals. The accused was Willison's least favourite Liberal, or near-Liberal, Premier Honoré Mercier of Quebec. It seemed that Mercier's party had received $100,000 from the contractors of the Baie des Chaleurs railway, to whom his government had given substantial subsidies. Ernest Pacaud, Laurier's close friend and organizer, was one of the men directly implicated. The *Globe* warned at once that if the charges, laid by a respected Ontario lawyer with knowledge of the railway's affairs, were true, it would treat Mercier, Pacaud, and company "precisely as it expects decent Conservatives to treat the federal boodlers, that is to say, it will ask for the condign punishment of the wrongdoers without regard to rank or station."

Less than two weeks later, after only the opening days of testimony before a Senate committee, the *Globe* concluded that "the *prima face* case against Mr. Mercier is complete.... Mr. Mercier was tempted to follow in Sir John's footsteps ... has even bettered the lessons of that master of corruption — and between the two Quebec is left rotten to the core." *L'Électeur* of Quebec City, Pacaud's paper, raged: "Le Globe *abandonne ses amis au premier feu.*" But in late October, before a judicial commission, Pacaud confessed his personal guilt and the *Globe* concluded that "the responsibility for his acts must rest upon those who wrongfully armed him with power."[23]

DISCORD IN THE PAIRTY.

LAURIER—"STOP! STOP! THIS TUNE WILL GET US INTO NO END OF TROUBLE WITH THE FRENCH VOTE!"
WILLISON—"VERY PROBABLY. BUT, MOST RESPECTED SIR, DON'T FORGET TO REMEMBER THAT THIS IS NOT YOUR ORGAN!"

DISCORD IN THE PAIRTY. J.W. Bengough cartoon, Grip, *April 9, 1892. Willison is the organ grinder, with Edward Farrer as his "monkey." Toronto Reference* Library

It was crystal clear from the outset of the controversy that Willison, not Edward Farrer, was in charge of the *Globe* on these issues. Willison would record that "powerful influences" in the Liberal party were "outraged by my candour and treason." At one point he was warned by a *Globe* colleague that he was to be fired. John Cameron even hurried back from London to advise him to resign first. Robert Jaffray, the paper's president, told him two years later that several political leaders, including Farrer's patron Sir Richard Cartwright, had demanded his dismissal, but that the board of directors had refused.

While the situation was still uncertain, Rachel Willison told her husband: "Jack, you must either stop worrying or resign!"[24] But Willison insisted to Laurier that he had taken a position that "suits the temper of ninety-nine per cent of Ontario and that no other would be tolerated. To take any other course would be fatal to *The Globe* and fatal to you as leader of the Liberal party as far as this province is concerned…. Your position is difficult — so is mine." W.D. Gregory affirmed to the leader that the *Globe*'s stance on Pacaud and Mercier "has rendered that scandal less effective than it might have been."[25]

The whole affair gradually faded into the background of Canadian politics. In December, the provincial judicial commission in Quebec found against Mercier, who then was dismissed by the lieutenant governor. In March 1892, the Conservatives won a landslide provincial election victory. The *Globe* followed Laurier in endorsing selected "reform" *parti national* candidates but hailed the "wave of popular indignation" that swept over Quebec. For machine Liberals in that province, however, as J. Israel Tarte, MP, advised Laurier: "*Le sentiment est fort prononcé contre le Globe.*"[26] Tarte had special personal reasons for his enmity. Although he was now on his way to becoming one of Laurier's Quebec lieutenants, he had been elected in 1891 as a Conservative and the *Globe* recently had identified him as having taken "tainted" campaign donations. Tarte's *Le Canadien* listed several bitter *Globe* editorials as just following on "*une longue série d'injures à l'adresse des gouvernements précédents et, en fait, de notre race et de nos institutions.*"[27] Willison would have regarded such a charge as preposterous, but there was no question that the *nationalisme* and ultra-Catholicism which had been so much a part of Mercier's appeal in Quebec had done as much as the corruption which had been uncovered to turn the Torontonian into an open foe.

The trade and national question continued to be a festering sore for the federal Liberals. Edward Blake still believed that they had adopted in

U.R. a too-radical position. Some party members and sympathizers, such as Professor Goldwin Smith of Toronto, believed it not radical enough. The *Globe* had noted in September 1891 that a group existed, "becoming more numerous every day," who saw "political union with the States as the only practicable solution" to the nation's economic stagnation and population loss. Edward Farrer, with his continentalist reputation, was still at the *Globe*. In December, Premier Mowat, a staunch loyalist for the British connection and Canadian separateness from the U.S., wrote an open public letter to former Prime Minister Mackenzie in which he worried about several recent articles or sentences in the *Globe* "tending in an annexationist and anti-British direction." He hoped that his fears were groundless.[28]

They were not. The *Globe* had begun to "tilt" towards political union earlier that fall. On October 5 it commented that "in a country that can be kept together only by the use of lubricants in the form of bribes and boodle" there was now a widespread feeling of uneasiness and despair." Two days later it remarked: "It is not pessimism but the simple unadorned truth to say that the future of Canada is now far from secure.... This much is certain, that Sir John A. Macdonald and Toryism have destroyed the fair prospect that lay before the country, and rendered the task of rehabilitating it vastly difficult." On November 21 it lamented "a policy of commercial isolation which dooms our resources to idleness and expatriates the flower of our youth at the rate of 100,000 a year."[29]

Premier Mowat could see all too well that in the *Globe*'s expressed pessimism about the national future there was something definitely bordering on political unionism. His letter to Mackenzie was a dramatic warning to the paper to turn back before being confronted with the open enmity of the head of Ontario's provincial Liberals. The *Globe* denied that "casual expressions" in its columns constituted approval of political union but declined to join Mowat in optimistic estimates of the national future or in words of praise for the British connection. "The panorama of our future greatness," it observed, "has been unfolded on every stage ... but every ten years we receive a shock through being brought in contact with the stern prose of the census." It wondered "when the beatific vision is to be realized, and whether we can borrow enough money to keep us going until the prophets have been justified by the event."[30]

As the year drew to a close Premier Mowat complained bitterly to Laurier:

> The Globe is now creating an annexation party out of members of the Reform [Liberal] party, and has accomplished more in that direction than I was aware of when I wrote my open letter addressed to Mr. Mackenzie. I find that at meetings in the rural parts, in even my own constituency, the Globe is being cited to old Reformers as going for annexation, and that this is bearing fruit amongst them. I presume you disapprove of this and might do something to prevent further harm in that direction.... If nothing can be done, an open division of the party is inevitable, and its consequent destruction.

The premier wanted Laurier to make "a very distinct declaration ... against political union as a price too great to pay for unrestricted reciprocity." He had a clear idea who was leading the *Globe* astray: "Farrer seems to have made lively annexationists of the whole Globe staff and directorate...." He also assumed that Sir Richard Cartwright "is contemplating and desiring political union. If that is to be the policy of the Dominion Liberal party, I cease to be a member of it."[31]

Mowat may well have been correct in his estimation of the extent of the *Globe's* political unionist drift at this time. W.D. Gregory, an important Toronto Liberal and a leader of the Continental Union Association, would remember:

> Robert Jaffray, then head of the Globe, was in full sympathy with the movement and Willison used to say that four out of six or seven Liberals were supporters of political union. Jaffray once gave an interview when in the United States expressing his views. He perhaps did not know that he was giving an interview. When he returned to Toronto and the interview was published, he repudiated it, but Willison later told me that there was no doubt whatever that it was absolutely correct.... Willison

and I used to discuss the matter of political union a good deal and I remember telling him that I felt "in my bones" that it was right and must some day prevail. Willison, I think, thought much the same as I did.[32]

Whatever impression Willison may have given Gregory, Jaffray, Farrer, or anyone else involved with the *Globe*, he never openly declared himself a political unionist. It clearly was prudent for him not to offend colleagues and Liberals who were. Whether over the "national" question, Mowat's criticisms of the paper, the Quebec scandals or the health of the federal party, he was at this juncture deeply worried about the future. Despite all the earlier tensions with Edward Blake over recent months, he urged the former leader in December 1891 to "soon re-appear in federal politics because I do not know whether the country or the Liberal party is in the worse position and you are the only man who can extricate either."[33]

The Liberals' situation soon became bleak indeed. Between December 1891 and mid-March 1892, they had to fight by-elections in twenty-one federal constituencies in Ontario, opened in most cases by court action. In the recent general election they had won thirteen of them; they retained only two. Willison would judge that Blake's letter and related controversies about it had been "infinitely damaging to the candidates of the Liberal party."[34] In late March, the satirical Toronto weekly *Grip* jested that "a bad tooth, in the Grit jaw bone" was to blame, and recommended "some pulling" — of "the Cartwright molar, the Unrestricted Reciprocity incisor and any others that are shaky."[35] In fact, earlier that month the *Globe* had begun something like that kind of operation. On March 18 it had stressed that "a vote of the people of Canada would show a very large majority in favour of the continuance of the present relations of Canada with Great Britain...." It urged Canadians to cease squabbling over political union and turn their attention to building up a strong economy. In late April it even published an editorial hailing "Ontario's Grand Old Man" — Oliver Mowat.[36]

Then on July 27 Edward Farrer's departure from the *Globe* was announced. Goldwin Smith, the expatriate Oxford intellectual who had moved to Toronto via the U.S. and was the most prominent political unionist Liberal in Ontario, advised Laurier that "the Mowat presence has gradually rendered Farrer's position untenable." Mowat's prestige had been crowned that year with a knighthood, on the advice of the federal Conservative government.[37] Neither Farrer nor Willison, in letters to Laurier about the departure, claimed any direct Mowat role. But Farrer did remark that the *Globe's* position in the Liberal party had become "a difficult, almost a perilous one on several issues — rendered all the more so of late because of Sir Oliver's strong stand and reactionary associations."[38]

The month before Farrer's role at the *Globe* ceased, Edward Blake's brooding presence on the fringe of the federal Liberals and their policies also came to an end. The former leader left Canada in June to accept an Irish nationalist nomination to the House of Commons in London. Once Blake was gone, the Liberals might be much freer to jettison or modify their U.R. policy without being so open to taunts from their Conservative enemies that they were surrendering to him. Furthermore, Farrer's absence potentially enabled the *Globe* to play a new and creative role on this and related "nationalist" issues, with Willison at last free to direct editorial expression on them.

Willison was one of the first Liberals to propose a practical and politically acceptable means of drafting a new platform so that the general voting public, especially in Ontario, could be favourably impressed. On July 16, the *Globe* called for the "holding of a great council of the Liberals of Canada." In early August he sent Laurier a long letter about where he thought the party should go on the trade issue:

> I feel that the general line of the party ought to be much the same as during the last four or five years but in view of the best information I can get I am convinced that little can be said about [trade] discrimination against Great Britain and that we must not admit the idea of a common tariff [with the U.S.]. There are many Liberals who would go further than this — much further, but there are many Liberals who will not go further and the loyalty cry and hatred of Sir Richard keep the Conservatives a solid body. I feel, too, that incidentally we should assail the N.P. [National Policy] on every

occasion and urge a general reduction of duties. We want Reciprocity if we can get an arrangement on terms that will not infringe on our national integrity. If we cannot make an arrangement with the States we must radically reduce and reform the tariff.

Then too, we should attack the Senate, the cost of govt., the failure of the Immigration policy, the franchise [election] laws, the extravagance and dishonesty in administration. This may not be a very radical programme, but is there any other to hand? Then we should thoroughly organize the party and get it well united behind the platform. That I hold can only be thoroughly done by means of a convention.... I do not see why a Reciprocity policy and low tariff policy cannot be run together.[39]

Along such moderate lines the *Globe* proceeded in the following months, stressing that "every effort" should be made by Canada to negotiate a trade treaty with the U.S. "for the widest possible measure of reciprocity upon terms not inconsistent with the maintenance of our independence." As for the continuing discouraging emigration and trade statistics, the paper now described these "as an incentive to action, not as an argument for despair."[40]

Just as Willison was settling in as uncontested editor-in-chief of his paper, he became aware of lingering criticism of him, even some real hostility, within the Liberal party. "I have been told," he wrote Laurier on September 2, "that you have been led to suspect the loyalty of Mr. Jaffray and myself to you as leader. May I simply say, once for all (I know you will believe me) that there is no man in or out of Canadian politics so completely acceptable to both of us." Perhaps Laurier had caught wind of Willison's at least seemingly pro-Blake mood of a few months before. Possibly he felt that the *Globe* had swung too far, too fast towards Sir Oliver Mowat's views on trade, national, and pro-British questions, or that Jaffray and Willison had been equally to blame with Farrer for the "disloyal" image the paper had helped to give the party in the recent past.

Willison created even more Liberal enemies for himself and the *Globe* later in 1892 — this time on a transportation issue. In the 1880s, the *Globe* and the party had attacked the Canadian Pacific Railway as the pampered monopolistic pet of the Tories. During the 1891 campaign, the *Globe* had bitterly assaulted the CPR, charging: "At Ottawa its will is law. All other interests big or little are thrust aside to suit its everlasting cry for more." But in October 1892, the CPR was interested in providing a "fast Atlantic steamship service" and the *Globe* recommended that the Liberals put aside their traditional hostility to a company which it said had become "a part of the national life" and had "performed with admirable thoroughness the vital parts of their contract with the people of Canada." The paper suggested a package deal in which the CPR would develop the steamship line as a feeder for its railway and vice versa. The federal government would lease its Intercolonial Railway in the Maritimes to the CPR in return for a low rate structure and running privileges on it for the Grand Trunk Railway. The government would save its annual $500,000 loss on the Intercolonial, which sum it could use to subsidize the steamship operation.

It was a thoughtful, serious proposal. Willison was making it his business to study the whole complex question of transportation, so vital to Canadian development, and offer some fresh analysis. The *Globe* stressed that it favoured a system of state control of all the great transportation facilities as the "the ideal one for a democracy." But, as long as the Tories were in government, it added, state control of transportation really meant "political management ... government for a party instead of for a people." The *Globe* pointed out that in the U.S. the trend was to accept private ownership in return for strict regulation and the enforcement of reasonable non-discriminatory rates, and urged: "We should avail ourselves of the enterprise of the Canadian railway corporations, but we should compel them to deal fairly with the people."

It was the kind of approach prescribed in the American Interstate Commerce Act of 1887, but it prompted blazing indignation among Maritime Liberals. There had been rumours the federal Tory government had been contemplating sale of the Intercolonial to the CPR. L.G. Power of Halifax raged to Laurier: "The proposed transfer of the I.C.R. to the CPR is most unpopular throughout the Lower provinces, and were it not for the *Globe*'s stupid conduct, the mere suspicion that the Government favoured it would have done them much harm." Professor Goldwin Smith in Toronto sadly reported to a friend: "The Globe … appears, I am sorry to say, to have fallen under the influence of the Canadian Pacific Railway."[41]

When pointed attacks on the *Globe* on the issue, rumoured to be inspired by Sir Richard Cartwright, appeared in the *Mail* and the Ottawa *Free Press* and Willison heard Laurier was in agreement with them, he fought back in an angry letter to the leader: "I am told that you are not at all satisfied with the course of the *Globe* and that Sir Richard Cartwright is waging a campaign against me.... I propose to fight for my own hand and … he will hardly find me as weak a victim as he may anticipate." He assured Laurier that the paper "is as anxious to serve the Liberal party as it ever was, as loyal to you and the Liberal policy, but we must have some freedom of utterance...." More calmly, he apologized for lack of prior consultation.[42] The storm soon passed, as other issues became paramount.

In the midst of the brief furor over transportation, he reminded Laurier of his proposal for a national policy convention to draft a "tariff reform and reciprocity platform" for the next election. "Now things are drifting," he remarked pointedly in December 1892, "and it seems to me the chaos becomes more complete every day."[43] Three months later, Laurier formally announced that the convention would be held in Ottawa in late June 1893. A delighted *Globe* commented that the policy emphasis at the rally should be on "the best means of lightening the taxation of the country and of removing burdens from trade, agriculture and manufacturing...." With a view towards emphasizing a non-continentalist emphasis, it hailed the proposal from Louis Davies, Liberal MP from P.E.I., that several types of goods exported almost exclusively to Canada from Britain be allowed a preferential duty. The *Globe* urged giving Britain "the better treatment which so large a number of our people are willing to extend." The developing strength of lower tariff sentiment in the U.S., it argued, could be stimulated by measured Canadian tariff reductions on selected American products. Revenue needs, it stressed, not the whims of manufacturers, should dictate tariff levels, and marked reductions in government expenditures could make possible significant tariff reductions.[44]

These were very much the lines on which the June Liberal convention proceeded. The unanimous election of Sir Oliver Mowat as chairman symbolized the party's intense desire to divest itself of any "disloyal" image. The delegates decided the tariff under a Liberal government would be reduced to "the needs of honest, economical and efficient government" and was to be "so adjusted as to make free, or to bear as lightly as possible upon, the necessaries of life, and should be so arranged as to promote freer trade with the whole world, more particularly Great Britain and the United States." Specifically on trade with the U.S., there should be a treaty to "include a well considered list of manufactured articles" in a "broad and liberal intercourse."[45]

There was much reason for Willison to be delighted at the trade stance. The convention had charted a defensibly nationalist course, only mildly continentalist in trade matters and not implying a lessening of British connection in either economic or constitutional aspects. It would antagonize few electors and rally just about all Liberals. The heydays of Cartwright and Farrer, with their zealous theorizing about radical continental free trade, and of Edward Blake with his relentless intellectual hair-splitting, were over. Wilfrid Laurier's apprenticeship as leader, when he had learned that the "bold policy" of U.R. was too inflexible, too precise, too radical to be safe as a national rallying cry, had passed too. John Willison was now firmly settled in as editor of the *Globe*. He was scarred somewhat from the internecine party and *Globe* struggles of his first three years in the chair of George Brown, but he clearly now was a figure of critical importance in the national Liberal party. His views had not always been met with general approval, but he had shown intelligence and flexibility in articulating his positions. In his manoeuvrings to survive in his job and come out on the winning side in party squabbles, he had proved adroit. He was fast becoming the most influential federal Liberal in Ontario, Laurier's real lieutenant in the province.

There were continuing major challenges. In the sluggish economics of the early 1890s, none of Toronto's six dailies had been able to stop their circulation figures from declining. The *Globe*'s daily average had dropped from 27,616 in June 1890 to 21,166 three years later. But if more people could afford to buy newspapers and Liberals could have reason again to feel more confident in their political prospects, all that could be turned around. Since September 1890, thanks to the Jaffray syndicate, the *Globe* had impressive new modern six-storey headquarters on the south of Melinda Street running an entire block west of Yonge to Jordan. The latest in modern presses, elevators, sky-lights, and inter-office communications made for a fitting home for a great newspaper.[46]

Now there were important new staff additions. With the troublesome, idiosyncratic Farrer gone, the steadier yet highly experienced John Ewan, two years Willison's senior, was appointed as chief editorial writer. He had graduated from the *Globe*'s reporting staff to be Ottawa correspondent of the *Mail* and then news editor of the *World*. Working with him were the fiery pro-labour radical, John Lewis, and the gifted municipal affairs specialist, Stewart Lyon. In 1895, Samuel Wood, on staff since 1891, took on editorial responsibilities for economic and fiscal questions.[47] John Lewis would describe the quartet of which he was a member as "Willison's happy group of editorial lieutenants," working in the atmosphere of "a very pleasant social club, characterized by a feeling of freedom, confidence and security…."[48]

John Willison, his party, and his newspaper were emerging from painfully difficult years of trial. No doubt major challenges would lie ahead, but from his spacious fourth-floor office overlooking the teeming Yonge Street traffic, he must have believed that he had good reason to face the future with renewed enthusiasm.

IV

Triumph, 1893–1896

T HE EXECUTION OF LOUIS RIEL AND THE GERMINATION OF THE Jesuit Estates controversy had helped to restore in the 1880s some of the ethnic and sectarian bitterness which in pre-Confederation days had bedeviled the relations of Protestants and Catholics and of English-speaking and French-speaking Canadians. In the early 1890s, in spite of the primacy of the trade and loyalty issues, the unfortunate divisions deepened; by the middle of the decade they were necessarily the central concern of Canadian politics and political journalism. John Willison had an extraordinarily difficult task as editor of the chief Liberal journal in Ontario. He had to steer through the treacherous waters of bitter linguistic and religious squabbles to the satisfaction of his predominantly Anglo-Saxon and Protestant community, while at the same time providing powerful support for the elevation to the prime ministership of the French-speaking and Roman Catholic Wilfrid Laurier. All the while, he was developing — and, as far as prudence permitted, articulating — some controversial views of his own on the constitutional, religious, ethnic, and cultural shape of Canada.

Some of the hostility to Catholic and French-Canadian distinctive-ness and to Mercierite *nationalisme* which had blazed so strongly in Ontario in 1889 and 1890 flared up in western Canada as well. Also, the now overwhelmingly English-speaking and Protestant majority there was not inclined to tolerate the continuity of dualistic educational provisions of earlier times. Sentiment for educational standardization, efficiency, and economy pointed towards the end of separate schools; and concern about the growing influx of immigration from continental Europe spurred support for "national schools" and one "national language" to help shape disparate elements into a single community.

Standing in the way of these emotions, principles, prejudices, and goals lay the educational and linguistic provisions which had been enacted for both the North-West Territories and Manitoba in the 1870s. The North-West Territories Act of 1875 had authorized minority denominational schools, and an amendment in 1877 had made both English and French official languages in the courts and government institutions. The federal Manitoba Act of 1870 likewise had authorized bilingualism as well as the protection of "any right or privilege with respect to denominational schools which any class of persons have by law or practice in the Province at the union." In addition, if any subsequently granted school right or privilege were adversely affected by the Province, an aggrieved denominational minority might appeal to the federal Cabinet and, ultimately Parliament, for remedial action.[1]

A western tour in the summer of 1889 by the fiery Ontarian foe of Jesuits and dualism, D'Alton McCarthy, a Conservative MP, helped precipitate the bitter Canadian ethnic-sectarian divisions of the 1890s. McCarthy urged a Calgary audience to press Territorial authorities to request Ottawa, still in ultimate control over the region, to end official sanction for the French language. This was done, and on the strength of that petitioning McCarthy moved an appropriate resolution of the House of Commons the following winter. He did not get all he wanted, but the English-speaking majority in the House did authorize the Territorial Assembly to regulate its own language provisions. In addition, 1892 Assembly ordinances brought the two separate school systems under effective Territorial control.[2]

McCarthy also spoke at Portage La Prairie, Manitoba, in August 1889. He called on Manitobans to help "make this a British country in fact as it is in name." There were rumours before the visit that Thomas

Greenway's Liberal provincial government was determined to abolish dual languages and provincial support for separate schools. Now Attorney General Joseph Martin, sharing the platform with McCarthy, pledged just such action.[3] Within a year Manitoba ended any official status for the French language and, in the Public Schools Act of 1890, stopped tax support for separate schools.[4]

French-speaking Canadians were angry at the curbing of language rights in the Territories and Manitoba, although there seemed little that could be done constitutionally or politically to reverse the actions taken. Just about all Catholics, of whatever language, were agreed on the need to protect denominational education. The Manitoba Act provided the mechanism for fighting back.

The federal Conservatives, facing a difficult general election in 1891, declined to risk disallowing the Public Schools Act, but sought judicial clarification of the constitutionality of the Manitoba legislation. The Judicial Committee of the Privy Council (JCPC) in London upheld that law in 1892, sending the federal government back to the courts to decide whether the ensuing appeal to it from the Manitoba Catholic minority was constitutional. The JCPC then ruled in January 1895 that the Manitoba minority *did* have the right to appeal to the federal government and Parliament and *did* have a clear grievance; but the government and Parliament were free to grant redress or not.[5] After five years of manoeuvring and evasion, politicians and their newspaper supporters would have to deal with the issue in the arena of party warfare as a federal general election loomed.

From the beginning of the squabble, federal Liberals were as uneasy as their Conservative counterparts. Sir Richard Cartwright warned Laurier as early as the summer of 1889 that he did not see how the party could be held together if the question became a federal one.[6] Laurier too was apprehensive at this point and resolved, as he told a Quebec friend, to "*laisser les événements se dessiner avant de faire des commentaires, qui pour le moment, n'auraient d'autre effet que produire de l'irritation en certains lieux.*" [leave events to sort themselves out before making comments, which, at this time, would have no other effect except to produce irritation in certain quarters.][7] His most specific public statement during the four long years of litigation came in 1893 to the House of Commons, when he remarked that if Archbishop Taché of Manitoba was correct that the Manitoba public schools were actually Protestant, this would be "a most infamous tyranny." He said that he wanted the Conservative federal government to fully investigate the facts before he would offer any definite advice.[8] His private views, expressed to Oscar McDonnell, a French-speaking journalist, were that only if such an investigation showed the public schools to be, in effect, Protestant, would he "*risquerais tout pour empecher une pareille tyrannie.*" [risk everything to prevent such a tyranny.]

If the schools really were non-denominational, he would favour a settlement on the New Brunswick and Nova Scotia models.[9] There all schools were "public" and non-sectarian, but administrative edicts and local practice had permitted the grouping of Catholic teachers and the provision of after-hours non-compulsory denominational religious education. However, there could be no open articulation of so precise and moderate a view until the political circumstances permitted. A Liberal party which could remain uncommitted to specifics on Manitoba schools might remain, at least for public consumption, reasonably united.

It was immensely difficult for Laurier to keep French-speaking and Catholic Liberals on one hand and English-speaking and Protestant Liberals on the other from taking up dogmatic positions from which later retreat to reasonable compromise would be impossible. Even the party's major newspapers were bitterly divergent in their views. *Le Canadien* in January 1892 described the Manitoba issue as not so much a religious squabble as "*une question nationale,*" which had to be resolved with justice for the Catholics there, or the English-speaking Protestant majority across Canada might view it as a good example of how to "*faire de nous des anglais à coups de bâtons.*" [make us English by force][10] For its part, Willison's *Globe* quickly took a very definite pro-Manitoba government line. In early 1891 it predicted that the Liberal party "will no doubt follow the straight path and stand up for provincial rights as it has so often done before." In March 1892, while the JCPC was considering the Manitoba case, the *Globe* remarked, in language with which Dalton McCarthy would not have quarrelled:

One language and a system of national schools are the true conditions for the development of a national sentiment, and while it is not proposed to violate the compromise which is at the very basis of the Confederation, and thereby endanger the whole fabric, it is the common hope that outside the two old Provinces, one language and national schools shall prevail.

When the JCPC upheld the Manitoba Schools Act in 1892, the *Globe* rejoiced, terming the issue of a public school system there "settled." Still, possibly on instructions from Laurier, it mused about a "friendly arrangement on the Maritimes model after the passions aroused by the struggle have abated." Willison wrote to Laurier, suspecting, as he put it, that "you may differ with us" over Manitoba but argued that "in view of our position in favour of provincial rights and the decision of the Privy Council [JCPC]" upholding the constitutionality of the schools legislation, "to argue for remedial legislation for Manitoba is quite out of the question."

In response to the Catholic and French-Canadian pressure for remedial action, the *Globe* remarked in 1893 that "hardly a member of Parliament for Ontario could vote for interference except upon peril of his seat."[11] Perhaps because of the uncompromising character of Willison's and the *Globe*'s positions, Laurier may have been less than frank with the editor about his own views. After the right of the Catholic minority in Manitoba to appeal its case to the federal government and Parliament was upheld by the JCPC early in 1895, Willison claimed to him: "Your own statement made to me more than once was that when you had to decide you would decide for Manitoba."

Laurier replied: "I do not remember that I spoke of my intentions ... in so strong and positive terms as you mention."[12]

The *Globe*'s absolute refusal to countenance federal remedial action to any degree in any circumstance infuriated leading Quebec Liberals like J. Israel Tarte, preparing to organize Laurier's home province in the next federal election. He spluttered to Laurier that the *Globe* was as bad as D'Alton McCarthy and that its policy makers "*n'ont d'autres horizons que celui de Toronto,*" that they were but "*diminuitifs de George Brown,*" *dont ils ont — grâce à Dieu — ni la force, ni le talent.*" [have no other horizons than those of Toronto … pygmy copies of George Brown with, thank God, neither the strength nor the talent.][13] For its part, the *Globe* classed Tarte in the "extremist camp on sectarian and language matters." Willison told Laurier that Tarte "seems to hold the view that because he is a French Canadian he has a divine right to direct the universe."[14]

There was some justice to Willison's indignation, but also some accuracy in Tarte's description of the "*horizon de* Toronto" which bounded Willison's attitudes. But he and the *Globe* were justly proud of their stern hostility to the extremist Protestant Protective Association, a secret ritualistic society whose members swore not to employ or vote for Catholics, whom they regarded as aliens unfit for citizenship. The *Globe* commented that "no man who is anxious for the continued existence and growth of the Canadian Confederation can conscientiously give his adhesion to the exclusion of Roman Catholics from political trust and honour." The paper was uncompromising in its hostility to the PPA, especially when it campaigned against the Mowat Liberals in a provincial general election in 1894.

When Mowat triumphed once again, and as the *Globe* turned to other issues, that limited "*horizon de* Toronto" could be glimpsed on occasion. Over the summer of 1894, the paper carried a series of articles by John Ewan, its leading editorial writer, on the attitudes of French Canadians to such things as the spread of English in Quebec. "Real national unity," Ewan wrote, "cannot be had until some one language is everywhere understood and spoken, and the prevalence of English speech all over this country, as well as the fact that this is a British Country, indicates that this one language should be English."

The *Globe* had commented editorially some months before on Quebec's attachment to separate schools and the French language, asking its readers to be "tolerant of the eccentricities and patient with the prejudices of the minority." It counted on the "ripening conviction of Quebecers" to end denominational schools as educationally inferior; and it was confident that "the ultimate result" of their thinking and experience was that "English must come."[15] Whether that sort of comment was due to Willison or other members of his editorial team is unclear. But the general tone and thrust was consistent.

The crucial political stage of the Manitoba schools issue commenced with the JCPC's pronouncement of January 29, 1895, throwing the decision for or against remedial action on the "well founded" grievance of the Catholic minority to the federal government and Parliament. As the Conservatives pondered what to do next, the Liberals knew that the time soon would come to break their own silence. George Ross, an Ontario provincial cabinet minister, counselled Laurier to come out for a "judicial" approach, restoring separate schools by federal remedial legislation, in simple obedience to the highest court. Laurier allowed as to how such an approach would be "the only justifiable one" and certainly would make him "extremely popular" in Quebec. However, he worried about the "tactical aspect" in Ontario — there was no point in moving in advance of public opinion. He asked Ross to "see Willison and express to him the views which you express in your letter. He must be made ready to take up that question, for at any moment, it may be forced upon him."[16]

Even before the JCPC decision, Willison had been sent advance warning of it from Edward Blake in London. He had passed this on to Laurier, who had urged him to be "very cautious" in his treatment of the schools question in the *Globe* and "not to venture any opinion until the Government have shown their hand and told what they are going to do."[17] Willison did not rush to editorial comment, especially since the *Globe's* building had been destroyed by fire on January 5, and it had been forced to re-locate as temporary guests of the rival Tory *Empire* over at its Adelaide Street headquarters.[18] In early February, the *Mail* had absorbed the *Empire* and a pro-Conservative *Mail and Empire* had emerged as a potentially very dangerous rival to its Liberal tenant. In one of its first numbers the new paper had accused Laurier and the Liberals of keeping silent on the Manitoba issue in order later to be in a position to censure the federal government whatever its course of action.[19]

On March 5, Willison wrote Laurier: "It is impossible for a newspaper to go on and on and not have an opinion. From the first we have opposed interference in Manitoba. We cannot now turn heels over head...." This was in explanation of a three-column editorial the previous day, which he had prepared with Robert Jaffray and George Ross and which he described to Laurier as being "as judicious as possible." In the editorial the *Globe* acknowledged the JCPC's "weighty and deliberate pronouncement upon a question of right and wrong...." But it argued that the same court's earlier upholding of the constitutionality of the school legislation in Manitoba had somewhat blunted the force of the new ruling. It reasoned that any federal interference would only stir up further sectarian bitterness and strife. It hoped that "the people of Manitoba will be just … will be generous" and cited with approval the Nova Scotia and New Brunswick practical school compromises. Similar generosity by Manitoba Protestants would be forthcoming, the *Globe* argued, if only outsiders would just leave the province alone. Willison urged Laurier to "consider carefully the position before condemning our attitude."[20]

Laurier was diplomatic in his reply, sensing that on the Manitoba issue Willison and the public he sought to reach were very volatile and sensitive. He assured the editor that "your article is so broad, so generous and so admirable that we can find in it much to help us." But he added:

> Let us now look a little ahead. You say that from the first the Globe has opposed interference with Manitoba. Before you further emphasize that position, would you not reconsider it? To condemn interference absolutely and in all cases would simply revolutionize our constitution. Why should an appeal be given to the minority if in no case was interference ever to take place? Think of this before you take any further step, and further steps do not take, I pray, until unavoidable, and then only with such caution as in this instance.[21]

The thrust of the advice gave Willison strong reason to suspect that Laurier was preparing to support remedial action.

There was immense party pressure on Willison to change his position. David Mills, the Liberal constitutional expert, warned the leader that the *Globe* was "dead against us … and all our misfortunes will come from its course…. We must have an official organ and if the Globe people feel that this is too humble a position we must look about and find newspapers that will…. If nothing is done to check the daily issue of drivel by putting the other side you must count on a protestant feeling as great as on the Jesuit question."

Mills was fearful that the *Globe* would drive all Catholics into the Conservative camp. Willison even was provided by certain party luminaries, according to his later testimony, with an editorial in which the *Globe* would reverse its position. He refused, with the full backing of the paper's president, Robert Jaffray, and the respected Principal Grant of Queen's University, who seconded his reading of Ontario opinion. His resolve may have been stiffened by a marked rise at last in the *Globe*'s circulation, from 20,966 at the end of February to 23,911 less than two weeks later.[22]

He soon had even stronger backing for his stand's soundness. On March 21, the federal Conservative government sent a sharply worded remedial order to Manitoba, demanding the restoration of full provincial and local tax support for Roman Catholic separate schools.[23] Even Tarte of Quebec realized that the tone and substance of the order threatened to make the Tories immensely unpopular in English Canada. "The government is in the den of lions," he exulted to J.W. Dafoe, his Liberal emotions overpowering his French Canadian and Catholic ones. "If only [Manitoba Premier] Greenway will now shut the door."[24]

The *Globe* argued that Manitobans "deserve better treatment at our hands than to have the laws which they have passed deliberately and with full knowledge of their own conditions, destroyed by a body to whom these conditions are unknown, acting without inquiry and without adequate consideration."[25] Willison explained to Laurier that the "very absolute remedial order" had altered the political situation "very materially." He thought that a straight "Provincial Rights" opposition by the federal Liberals to the order would "very nearly if not certainly carry the country." He anticipated sixty seats in Ontario and most of those in the rest of English Canada. "What could we do in Quebec? Could we carry ten or fifteen seats there?"[26]

Laurier was not quick to reply. He was mired for a time in deep depression, fearing for his Quebec base, burdened by health and financial problems, and musing to a friend that on a sectarian and ethnic problem like Manitoba schools, "an English leader would be much stronger than I can ever be and everything confirms me in that opinion." He would, however, do "nothing rash."[27] At last he wrote Willison to say that he was as yet unready to make up his mind on the merits of the appeal of the Manitoba Catholics, although "what information I have on the matter strongly inclines me to the side of the minority." He begged Willison to "bring back public opinion to the tariff."[28]

Willison answered his leader that "I very much doubt if in any conceivable case federal interference in a province could be effective." He thought this especially so where the courts had already ruled the law in question constitutional. Besides, he would not have the *Globe* change ground out of apparent fear for the Catholic vote. "I do not object at all to separate schools for Manitoba," he stressed. "I would be quite willing that they should be re-established tomorrow.... But Manitoba has taken a course, and as long as she chooses to adhere to that course interference from Ottawa, in my humble judgment, will be futile and mischievous, possibly disastrous."[29]

Laurier responded that the Judicial Committee's January judgment "has placed a new complexion upon the whole matter." He argued that the principle of interference had been "formally admitted" in that opinion. "This is fact," he asserted, "to which we cannot close our eyes, and in view of that decision the attitude of the *Globe* seems to me altogether too positive, too absolute."[30] However, he also told Frank Anglin, an Ontario Catholic, that the *Globe*'s stand and the evident effort of the Conservative press in Ontario to depict the remedial order as a mere piece of friendly advice to Manitoba provided clear proof that "there is a deep rooted feeling" in the province against interference in Manitoba. He reminded Anglin that the *Globe* "has within the recent past done some good work in favour of religious tolerance. The fact that it is now so uncompromising in its attitude is certainly evidence that such a feeling not only exists but might be liable to break out at any moment." He had decided, he told Anglin, "not to open my mouth until Parliament meets, and am enabled by personal intercourse with the members of my party, to ascertain how far the protestant community can be carried." He suspected that the Conservatives would feel obliged now to back away from remedial legislation, and that "the only recourse left, to have the claims of the minority admitted, would be by negotiations."

Willison too remarked to his leader that "the best thing if it could be at all accomplished would be some sort of agreement between Manitoba and the Dominion Government."[31] Through April and May, Willison and Laurier allowed their debate to cool down, Laurier even inviting him to

Ottawa for a friendly chat.[32] When Laurier told the House of Commons on April 19 that he had no intention of helping the government decide its policy by suggesting his own plan, the *Globe* approved, terming the attitude "moderate and judicious."[33]

In June, the Manitoba government passed through the legislature a "memorial" resolution utterly rejecting restoration of Catholic separate schools, which it described as having been inefficient educationally. It complained that the federal government had no idea of the *real* conditions in those schools and offered to assist in making possible a thorough study of the situation. For the *Globe*, Manitoba's "willingness to have the case thoroughly investigated strengthens their case materially, and leaves no possible excuse for following up the remedial order with any further hasty and ill-advised action."[34] There matters would rest until it became clear whether the Conservative federal government would respond to this rebuff from Manitoba with remedial legislation.

The Conservatives were no longer led by men of the calibre of Sir John A. Macdonald or his brilliant successor, Sir John Thompson, who died suddenly in December 1894. The new prime minister, Senator Sir Mackenzie Bowell, reacted to the Manitoba memorial with characteristic irresolution. On July 6 he put off the possibility of introducing remedial legislation until a new session of Parliament the following January, in hopes of being able to arrange some compromise beforehand. Three French-Canadian ministers resigned in protest three days later. Two eventually came back, but the government party's disunity was all too apparent.[35] In Ontario, many Protestant Tories were absolutely opposed to any remedial action ever. Their leader was N. Clarke Wallace, MP for West York and controller of customs, who also was grand master of the Orange Association of British North America. Wallace told the Toronto Orange celebration on the "Glorious Twelfth" of July that he was in full support of Manitoba's public schools policy and was only staying in the government in the hope that, somehow, remedial legislation would never be forthcoming. In addition to Wallace's subdued rebellion within the party, there was a movement outside its ranks of former members such as D'Alton McCarthy. "McCarthyism" threatened to attract restless Conservatives in several approaching federal by-elections in Ontario.[36]

Willison could sense all too well how strongly the anti-remedial feeling was developing in Ontario. "I do not want to preach to you," he wrote his leader on July 7, "but I cannot refrain from telling you that if you can avoid any declaration in favour of remedial legislation it will be an enormous advantage in Ontario. Be sure that this province will destroy any party that attempts arbitrary interference with Manitoba. The feeling has grown enormously strong. Be sure also that the Liberals are gaining in Ontario steadily and that nothing can save the Tories if you can maintain your present ground."[37] He wanted Laurier to stay away from declarations, but did not follow that advice himself. Ten days later the *Globe* published a strongly worded editorial entitled NO COERCION. The Conservative government was taunted to dissolve Parliament and take the issue of Manitoba schools to the electorate:

> … and we can promise that the result will be an eye-opener for those who imagine that public opinion can be trifled with….
>
> As to what is going on in Quebec, we believe that, left to himself, the French-Canadian citizen cares very little about the question of Separate Schools in the North-west; but it is quite possible that he may be worked into a state of excitement by the appeals of politicians who will tell him that the French-Canadians of Manitoba are being oppressed by the majority….[38]

Laurier exploded, sending Willison a blistering letter in which he charged that the *Globe*'s indictment of Quebec politicians "is as much an attack on the Liberal party as on the Conservative party." Quebec Liberals too believed that there was oppression in Manitoba. "The Globe seems to be of the opinion that the whole of Canada is composed of one Province," he charged. He was shocked that his Toronto friend could not see that there could be no reconciling the conflicting opinions of the various sections of the party "except by an honourable acknowledgement of those differences with the view of effecting a compromise of the same." He regarded the editorial as "a very serious reflection on me personally and it has been a most painful surprise to me."[39]

Willison was appalled. Differences he might have with his leader, but he had never meant to touch off such fury. Alone in his office in the rebuilt *Globe* building on the morning of July 20, he wrote out an emotional apology to the man he had worshipped for almost a decade:

Dear Mr. Laurier,

Your letter pains me more than any letter I ever received. I know in my conscience that if there is one thing I have had in my view ever since I visited at your home in Arthabaskaville it has been to build up your reputation and influence. No one here thought we were attacking you. No visitor to the office seems to have thought we had attacked you. I have heard no one say so, except from <u>Ottawa</u>. All this session three or four men at Ottawa (from Ontario) seem to have made it their business to find grievances against the Globe and myself. I found that to be the case when I was in Ottawa. I am not infallible but I do as well probably as they would if they were in my place. However you certainly were not among that number. Looking over the article I am bound to say that I think there are some rash sentences and that in this case there may be ground for complaint. It does seem to attack the Liberals. An unfortunate thing too is that it appeared the day the vote was to be taken on the McCarthy resolution [condemning the government for promising remedial legislation, on which the Liberal party was declining to take a position]. Of course our expectation was that the debate was to close the night the article was written, and it was only the next morning that I found the debate was carried over for a day. As to the general question I will not attempt to discuss it. I have been worried very much this week. My boy has diphtheria and it may be that I was not as attentive to the editorial page as usual. This is for yourself only. I do not want anyone to think that I would hide behind my home trouble. All this I have said because I am not satisfied with the article on reading it over and because I am sure that in view of all the difficulties of your position a personal attack upon you by the Globe would be very ungenerous. As for myself I would just about attack my own father.

Yours very truly,

J.S. Willison

P.S. At the same time I must repeat that no one in Ontario and no Ontario paper in Toronto or elsewhere, seems to have thought the article an attack on you. I see however as I have said that it could be turned into an attack.[40]

Laurier was touched by the letter and apologized in turn for having been so uncharacteristically blunt. He conceded that the *Globe*'s views were quite possibly "a reflex expression" of opinion in Ontario generally. He quite understood, he claimed, that the paper had to avoid going counter to public sentiment. He felt, however, that the criticism "was carried rather farther than a friend might expect from a friend. It may be that I was unduly sensitive, but as I am responsible for the attitude of the party in the House I took the point as effectively though perhaps unconsciously directed at me."

He understood that many English-speaking Liberals were impatient for the taking of a definite stand, yet he could see nothing but loss in causing division among Liberals while the Tories seemed about to destroy themselves. He assured Willison that he did not wish to see the *Globe* "boxing the compass — as it did in previous years" but he hoped that Willison could "make due allowance for the difficulties of my own position."[41] It seemed still true what Laurier's close Arthabaskaville friend, Emilie Lavergne, had assured Willison three weeks previously, that he "thinks everything of you, you know — in this good opinion he is never shaken by his entourage."[42]

The willingness on Laurier's part to forgive and forget may have had something to do with the fact that on July 19, he, Israel Tarte and John Charlton, a strongly Protestant Ontario Liberal MP, had decided privately, as Charlton would later write, that the Liberal party "would oppose the Remedial Bill and remedial legislation, and that our party should approach the position they took in opposition from such a standpoint and with an array of such reasons as they thought proper." The Winnipeg *Free Press*'s John Dafoe would recall: "All through the winter and spring of 1895 Tarte was sinking test wells in Quebec public opinion with one uniform result. The issue was Laurier. So the policy was formulated of marking time until the government was irretrievably committed; then the Liberals as a solid body were to throw themselves against it."[43]

The *Globe*'s continuing message now was that the federal government ought to agree to Manitoba's offer of an investigation of the school situation. The prestigious Principal George M. Grant of Queen's University lent his reputation to that idea in a series of articles for the paper in September. In October, Laurier travelled through Ontario with the message of conciliation. At Morrisburg he explained that he would approach Premier Greenway of Manitoba "with the sunny way of patriotism, asking him to be just and fair, asking him to be generous to the minority, in order that we have peace amongst all creeds and races which it has pleased God to bring upon this corner of our common country."

Tarte's *Le Cultivateur* promised French Canadians that Laurier would settle the whole question within three months of achieving power, and that he would receive "*une grande majorité*" in Ontario.[44] The prospect of such a result promised to strengthen Laurier immensely in Quebec.

Late in the year, however, the Liberals' situation darkened ominously. Two federal by-elections were held — in North Ontario on December 12 and in Cardwell on December 24. The Liberals fared badly in both contests. In Northern Ontario the Conservatives swept to a convincing win over Liberal and Patron (farmers' party) candidates after their candidate championed the extreme anti-remedialist views of N. Clarke Wallace, who resigned from the Bowell government on the eve of the contest. In Cardwell the Liberals finished a distant third, with less than one-sixth of the vote. The winner was an anti-remedialist McCarthyite, just ahead of the official Conservative. "One thing staggers me," wrote Laurier in alarm to Willison. "There seems to have been a stampede from our ranks to McCarthy! ... I rather believe that the radical policies of McCarthy of no separate schools, no commission, no listening to the complaints of the minority, has captured our people."

Willison responded that bad organization also had been a factor in both seats but argued that the McCarthyite votes reflected the public's readiness to support whatever candidate could most likely defeat the now hated Tories. "To my mind," he contended, "it is quite possible to make an arrangement with the Patrons and for that matter Mr. Wallace to go in a body against the Government.... Of course we could not accept Mr. Wallace's anti-Catholicism nor his protectionism but you will find that he will rapidly moderate his views if we show him any prospect of recognition." Willison added that he had been in touch with Wallace already. He also reassured Laurier that once the Liberals in Parliament had taken a clear and united stand for investigation and conciliation but against remedial action, the "sober second thought" of Ontario would be with them, rather than with splinter groups.

Notwithstanding the recent tensions with Laurier, it was abundantly clear that the leader now was treating Willison as his real Ontario lieutenant. Cartwright and Mills were figures of the past. Other parliamentary Liberals were not yet of the stature required. Willison told Laurier plainly as the year ended that "we have not a leader with a following" in Ontario. "If we could get Principal Grant into the field," he suggested, "he would at once take the position of a leader for Ontario and with you in Quebec ... would make a combination that could not be resisted."[45] It was an interesting idea, but Grant was on the academic sidelines while Willison was operating very much on the political field, in the very midst of the action. Laurier hoped the next by-election in Ontario, in West Huron in mid-January 1896, would see a Liberal victory on a straightforward "conciliation" platform. On Clarke Wallace, he warned that it would be "rather difficult to find a common ground of action for us and for him" but agreed "it would be well to know exactly what he wants and what concessions he would be ready to make. Let me know at your earliest convenience."[46]

Happily for the Liberals, the West Huron battle took place just as the Conservatives were experiencing their worst internal crisis in decades. On January 4, seven ministers resigned in protest against Sir Mackenzie Bowell's failure to supply resolute leadership. Nine days later, Bowell was obliged to pledge that he would resign after the coming session in favour of Sir Charles Tupper of Nova Scotia, a father of Confederation and the

High Commissioner to Britain, who would return home to lead the government in the House of Commons. The very next day, the electors of West Huron gave the Liberals victory by two hundred votes. The *Globe*, perhaps for Laurier's eyes especially, hailed the win as showing that "the great broadminded Protestant population of this country are not at all disposed to oppress or harass a small minority of their fellow countrymen in Manitoba."[47]

The reconstituted Conservative government brought down its remedial bill in the House of Commons on February 11. Under its provisions separate schools were to be restored in Manitoba under a special Catholic board of education and with full access to local taxation. But less than a month before, Manitobans had signalled their endorsement of their government's public schools policy with a landslide re-election of Premier Greenway and his colleagues. Parliament's five-year term would expire in April.[48] The stage was set for the final act in the schools crisis and for potentially a pivotal federal political change.

Laurier at last unveiled his policy to Parliament and the public. He declined to offer amendments, but moved that the remedial bill not be given second reading for six months, by which time the existing Parliament would have ceased to exist. To his Catholic supporters he pointed out that the Tory bill did not and could not ensure that provincial grants would go to the Catholic schools. He damned the proposed legislation as but "a half-hearted and faint measure … to be administered by a hostile government." He would not support federal interference until "after full and ample inquiry into the facts of the case, after all means of conciliation have been exhausted, and only as a last resort." His motion won the votes of all Ontario Liberals, sixteen Ontario Conservatives led by Clarke Wallace, D'Alton McCarthy, and his follower William Stubbs, all but six of the Quebec Liberal contingent, and all the Liberals from the other provinces. The bill passed second reading on March 20 by only eighteen votes, a considerably smaller margin than the government usually enjoyed.[49] A Liberal–McCarthy–Wallace filibuster effectively blocked passage, last-minute negotiations with Manitoba produced no compromise, and the issue was thrown at last to the electorate, with polling day scheduled for June 23 and the new Tupper government facing Laurier's eager Liberal forces.

All the main Liberal arguments had been laid down in the *Globe* for months — that Manitoba not be coerced, that the facts be explored, and that conciliation under the proper auspices could succeed. The paper now added two new themes. It expressed repugnance at the intervention of the Roman Catholic hierarchy, especially from Quebec, in the election; as well, ironically, it launched a major effort to convince Catholic voters in Ontario that they need not fear a Laurier government. It was true that a few powerful prelates, led by Bishop Laflèche of Trois Rivières, explicitly equated Liberal votes with fearful sin. However, the collective *mandement* of the French-Canadian bishops, issued on May 17, was so vague and mild that all but eight of the Liberal candidates in Quebec supported it.[50]

Israel Tarte, now amazingly friendly to Willison, advised him: "We will be able to face the *mandement* without much loss, I think. Do not be afraid to discuss it freely although with your usual calmness and moderation in tones." Laurier concurred, advising that the anti-*mandement* line "ought to be worked to some advantage" and that "an appeal ought to be made to the Catholics … to assert their determination to act in harmony with their fellow citizens of O[ntario]."[51] Obediently, the *Globe* delighted, for the sake of its Protestant readers, in denouncing the bishops' efforts as "an anachronism that must be relegated to the ages in which it belongs." For Catholics, it rejoiced when Premier Sir Oliver Mowat, long the defender of constitutional school rights in Ontario against extremist Protestant assaults, announced that he would join a Laurier cabinet. LAURIER, MOWAT AND VICTORY was the *Globe*'s banner headline during the closing weeks of the election battle. An editorial proclaimed that the paper's "one desire is that the Catholics of Manitoba should be well and generously treated."[52]

No small contribution to a very colourful *Globe* effort were the brilliant cartoons of the celebrated J.W. Bengough, the man whose countless contributions to the satirical weekly *Grip* had convulsed Canadians for more than two decades. Bengough particularly enjoyed poking grand fun at the legendary vanity of old Sir Charles Tupper and the desperate effort he was making to keep both pro-remedial and anti-remedial Tories together until the votes were in.[53]

Ever since January, when the worst of the Bowell cabinet crises had unfolded, the *Globe* had been making impressive circulation gains. On

January 1, the daily average for the previous week stood at 26,150; on February 1, 27,650; and on April 1, 29,400. By the week of the election itself, the figure had soared to 33,100, far ahead of the chief morning rival, the Conservative *Mail and Empire*, standing virtually still at 23,109. Without a doubt, the *Globe* had won thousands of new readers during a period when the Manitoba schools question was far and away the chief political issue before the newspaper public in Toronto and its hinterland.

Willison was hailed on the campaign trail by Liberals delighted with his and the *Globe's* special contributions to the cause. Young Jesse Middleton, later one of his reporters, would remember that he "got a thrill" at a Laurier rally in Chatham when the chairman introduced Willison — "a tall man with a well-clipped brown beard; and with a pair of luminous eyes" —as one of the most famous party leaders. The climactic night of the election victory came in Toronto when the city's new Massey Hall was overrun by excited Laurier worshippers at an exuberant rally. A hastily arranged overflow meeting in a nearby auditorium absorbed only a small portion of the extra thousands. The mere mention of the *Globe* brought thunderous cheers. How different it all was from the tense evening at the Horticultural Pavillion seven long years before, when Laurier had struggled to be heard and the *Globe* had been hissed.[54]

It was victory all the way. Confounding traditional patterns and Conservative expectations, Laurier took a 49–16 "favourite son" majority out of Quebec. In Ontario he gained 43 of the 92 seats, an increase of eleven over the number held at dissolution. Three Patrons, two McCarthyites, N. Clarke Wallace, and forty-three Conservatives — including at least seven pronounced anti-remedialists — rounded off the Ontario totals. In the six Toronto and York ridings, where the Tories had enjoyed huge success in almost all the seats for years, the Liberals took three. Sir Charles Tupper's strong personal campaign, a pro-Tory Catholic vote tendency in Ontario, and the fact that the Liberals had stayed out of half a dozen races where other anti-government candidates were likely to run stronger, held down Laurier's harvest in Ontario. However, as Willison put it to Laurier, "… upon the whole … we have done very well and without the school question to break up the machine and destroy the enemy in their strong places, I doubt if we could have succeeded." Mostly, he savoured the national triumph, exclaiming to his leader: "For years my desire has been to see you Prime Minister and more than half of my rejoicing over the victory of Tuesday is over your own advancement to the first position of the country."

Laurier, clearly moved, replied: "I know that I never had a more sincere friend than you."[55]

With Laurier victorious and the *Globe's* circulation soaring, Willison happily basked in the warmth of winning. The celebrating Liberals packed around the paper's offices on election night cheered him repeatedly. The next day, he was mobbed at a party celebration at Cobourg, east of the city, and lauded for having made the *Globe* "the grandest newspaper ... on the continent." Cameron Brown of the Belleville *Sun* praised the paper's "independent moderate tone" during the campaign which had won, he was sure, a great many new readers as well as votes. Arthur Hardy, Premier Mowat's senior lieutenant in the Ontario government, gushed: "The opinion is universal that the Globe never did such work in a campaign. It is almost equally universal that the Mail never did worse."

The consensus was that the *Globe's* consistency and its blend of anti-remedialism with a moderate conciliatory tone had contrasted sharply with the *Mail and Empire's* flip-flopping. Tory activist William David McPherson, a defeated candidate and later a provincial cabinet minister, congratulated him unreservedly as "one of the leading victors.... As one viewing the contest from the Opposition camp I can testify to the great party service of The Globe. I think it can fairly be said that without the great services of The Globe the Liberal party would have been defeated." In spite of the clear powerful pro-Tory impact of the Catholic hierarchy in Ontario, even Frank Anglin, the Catholic Liberal Ontario MP, testified to Laurier that "the strong anti-coercion appeals of the Globe helped us..." Mrs. Elizabeth O'Brien, wife of the defeated Conservative William O'Brien, sent Willison an especially interesting letter:

> I don't suppose you are old enough to know where "The Globe" was once. As a girl in Conservative circles I heard it was almost a synonym for lying and defamation, personal attack wholly unscrupulous & I fancy the attack was largely merited.... For some time I

have heard Conservatives say it was the <u>best</u> newspaper
in Canada, as a newspaper....

...I admire your conduct of your paper during the
campaign, the fairness, discretion, talent and honesty.[56]

Meanwhile, Laurier was putting together a new administration, one
of the strongest ever seen in Canada. Three provincial premiers — Mowat
of Ontario, Fielding of Nova Scotia, and Blair of New Brunswick — took
Justice, Finance, and Railways and Canals. Clifford Sifton, the best and
the brightest of Greenway's cabinet in Manitoba, soon came to take over
Interior and the responsibility for settling the West. Prime Minister Laurier moved quickly to put his own stamp on the Manitoba schools im-
broglio, to the satisfaction of most Canadians. By early November he
had reached a compromise with Manitoba. Public funding for separate
schools would not be restored; instead there would be a number of accommodations within the single public schools system. At the end of the
school day, students could be separated for such religious education as
either the local school board chose to provide or set numbers of parents
of particular denominations wished. There would be no compulsion of
attendance at such exercises. Where the proportion of Catholic students
warranted, Catholic teachers would be appointed. Where ten pupils in
any school spoke the French language or any other language than English
as their mother tongue, teaching would be on a bilingual basis. Manitoba
then passed appropriate amendments to its education laws.[57]

Not surprisingly, the *Globe* pronounced the settlement entirely acceptable, fully in keeping with its provincial rights principles, yet justly conciliatory. What was more, the "national character of the schools has been
maintained...." On the question of bilingual provisions, clearly an effort to
compensate French-Canadians for the failure to win on the separate school
front, the *Globe* did have to swallow some past pronouncements about the
need for a single language in the West. After all, it suggested, "the education
of all children must be given in the simple words that they understand."[58]
Then too there was the question of loyalty to one's own government.

It may be that Willison's role in the shaping of Liberal policy on
Manitoba schools, though highly important, was not quite as decisive as
he believed. He would tell John Dafoe a quarter-century later:

> If the <u>Globe</u> had followed Laurier's advice the whole party would have been committed to remedial legislation, Laurier himself would have been openly committed, and it would have been impossible to make such an effective fight as was made in 1896.... Nine days or so before the general election … he [Laurier] said to me, "I do not want to be too confident, but I think we will win. Whether we win or lose I want to say to you that if you had not driven us to the course we have taken I would not have a party left except in the Province of Quebec. I should have seen at once that the position of a Catholic leader with a Catholic policy tailing in behind Tupper would have been impossible. If we are beaten you will never find me complaining that you forced us into a wrong position."

There is no reason to doubt Willison's recollections of Laurier's words to him. Their correspondence through the painful confrontation in 1895 was quite consistent with such an interpretation. Yet a knowledge of other Laurier correspondence, as early as 1893, would seem to indicate that the Liberal leader very early in the Manitoba squabble strongly suspected what his ultimate policy would be.

If Willison's uncompromising provincial rights case in the *Globe* helped to confirm Laurier's views, so too did Israel Tarte's perceptive soundings in Quebec and the disastrous effects on the Tories of their pro-remedial policy. Also, Laurier's arrival at a policy Willison could accept and support owed more to the leader's political pragmatism than to any acceptance of the editor's uncompromising "no coercion" attitude. This Laurier, understandably, had found "altogether too positive, too absolute."[59]

In the context of the times, Willison was not an ultra-Protestant or anti-French bigot. His support for Laurier over a difficult decade in Ontario and his stern opposition to the PPA had shown that. Yet he clearly saw nothing of merit for Canada in giving any effective protection for either separate schools or the French language beyond what the constitution absolutely directed. He had stood on those principles and on his conviction that most Ontarians, thousands of them actual and potential *Globe* readers, shared them. It was very clearly his strategy on Manitoba schools which had been adopted.

Nevertheless, his French-Canadian and Catholic leader now had a mighty principal power base outside Ontario, among his own people. Perhaps the debate the two of them had shared in 1895 merely had been adjourned. However, the sweet summer of 1896, with political victory and newspaper success in magnificent combination, was a time of unalloyed triumph.

V

New Horizons in the Mid-1890s

"YOU ARE ON THE WAY OF BEING SOME DAY THE DELANE OF Canadian Politics," observed Laurier to Willison in January 1895, recalling the legendary mid-nineteenth century editor of the London *Times*.[1] The federal Liberals' victory of June 1896 and the *Globe's* circulation advances in the intervening eighteen months further convinced Willison's friends of the splendour of his future.[2] In July 1896, E.S. Caswell of the Methodist Book Publishing House told him: "You are making a name in Canadian journalism — & I hope ere long in public life — that will stand as high as that of George Brown. But should I thus limit your upward climb?" Willison's newspaper constituency was growing and not composed merely of Liberals. T.C. Patteson, a thorough Tory who had edited the Toronto *Mail* in the 1870s, wrote him in December 1895:

> The Globe is certainly now the best paper — a long way - ever published in Canada. Temperate in its comment and vigorous in all departments — you have a good man at the bellows.... And tho' I don't agree with the politics of the Globe, there can be nobody

who objects to the tone in which the difference of opinion is expressed, while the converts or waverers made by the Globe's style of comment are ten times as numerous (I am sure) as those made by the old style of polemical writing.

John Cameron, Willison's predecessor at the *Globe*, gleefully reported to him late in 1896 on the paper's growing popularity even in downtown "Tory" Toronto: "When I was at the Rossin House [a city hotel] the news vendor there informed me that sometime ago it was their custom to take fifteen Globes and thirty Mails, but that now the situation is exactly reversed, and they take thirty Globes and fifteen Mails."[3]

The early years of Willison's editorship were marked not merely by his journalistic achievements and his rise to prominence in the Liberal party but also by the broadening and deepening of his intellectual awareness and the significant development of his social associations. Largely self-educated, having risen from pure poverty, he had to win entry into the world of the social and intellectual elite of his day practically on merit alone. Acceptance came only gradually. It was helped along by his occasional special articles, which some of his friends hoped were signs of a literary rather than merely a journalistic talent. His "Observer" article on Laurier in 1889 was described by Mrs. J. Wilson of St. Thomas, wife of a Liberal MP, as "the most perfect of the kind ever written." A young Toronto friend, D.E. Cameron, termed it "the best thing of its kind you have yet done. Your friends are proud of the way you are developing."

A special article in June 1895 on the political scene in Canada prompted J.D. Edgar, a Liberal MP but also a poet (*This Canada of Ours*, 1893) and soon, in 1897, to be elected to the Royal Society of Canada, to write: "Your sketch ... is so able & picturesque that I say to all my friends that there is no other man in Canada who could have written it but yourself."

Mme. Emilie Lavergne, Laurier's devoted soulmate, also admired the article Edgar had found so attractive, writing him that it was "absolutely just in every sense of the word & written by that clear pen which can be so incisive." She beseeched him to come back to

Arthabaskaville to sit again with Laurier and herself: "Oh, if you were here what a lot of things we would discuss!" When later that summer *The Printer and Publisher* lauded Willison as a newspaperman, she found the treatment "not satisfactory to me. It does not give you the credit you deserve as a writer." This was praise indeed from a *grande dame* with several years of residence in Paris and London and an excellent knowledge of politics, literature, and history. For his part, Laurier considered the article "good" but "scarcely doing you justice both as a writer and a journalist."[4]

His many friends had to assume it was Willison's writing they were reading when they picked up their Monday morning *Globe* on January 7, 1895. The chief editorial — composed in the *Empire*'s office, set in its type and printed on its press was, as always, anonymous. The terrible fire which had destroyed the *Globe* building late Saturday night had left its staff exhausted tenants in their Tory enemy's premises, As the Dutton *Advance* would put it of the *Globe* at this juncture, "Everything is lost, save its name." But still the writer of the editorial could summon up the spirit and humour for a memorable note:

GRIT SOLILOQUY IN A TORY OFFICE

A man who Moulds Public Opinion and Guides the Destinies of a Nation ought to be superior to his surroundings. An overindulgence on mince pie should not betray him into pessimism, nor the finest Canadian sunlight shed its light over a sky darkened by reflections on the evil consequences of the policy of the Enemies of the Public Weal, his political opponents to wit. As to being affected by the trifling circumstances of writing in a Tory office, that would be a lamentable exhibition of a lack of gall that makes oppression bitter. Sound doctrine is sound, and heresy is heresy — and yet there are the heretics offering you the run of the house, and is the temperature about right, and which desk would we prefer, and wouldn't we be more comfortable on a chair with a leather seat, and while our intellectual assurance of the rankness of

the heresy is unimpaired the heart assenteth thereto
with something less than its usual vigor.[5]

But far more than good humour was on display from John Willison
in this crisis. A nineteen-year-old University of Toronto student, Bob
Coats, was at the *Globe* during the terrible post-fire hours and would
testify to Willison's "day of captaincy and achievement" in rallying the
staff and overcoming the almost impossible odds of publishing somehow
an amazingly respectable paper only a little more than twenty-four hours
after the disaster.[6] He was becoming an inspiration, even a legend, to
his staff. Young Marjory MacMurchy, a new assistant to the editor of
the *Women's Globe*, recalled her first impression: "He came in quickly,
but with an air, tall, dressed delightfully, quietly but perfectly…. He was
dark, good looking, well turned out, distinguished," with "altogether an
impressive, effective, stimulating appearance. He was 39 years old."[7]

By the mid-1890s, Willison had developed a wide circle of
interesting friends in Toronto in business, academic life, the law and
among literati. Among them was John King. Q.C. King had moved
to Toronto in 1892 from Berlin, Ontario, and came to serve as the
Globe's lawyer in the libel and slander cases inevitable for newspapers.
His wife Isabel was the daughter of the 1837 Upper Canada rebellion
leader, William Lyon Mackenzie. Willison came to know and like the
Kings. He happily paid John to write some special legal articles and
in November 1895 took on his engaging son William ("Willie") King,
twenty and just graduated with a B.A. from the University of Toronto, as
a reporter to cover police court proceedings. Willie King's young friend
Bert Harper visited him there a few weeks later and enthused to him
that that he undoubtedly was working for a paper that "represents the
triumph of Canadian journalism." The job helped Willie assemble the
funds for post-graduate studies at the University of Chicago the next
year. Willison met him often to discuss public issues and promised to
pay him for future special articles on Willie's labour relations and social
reform interests. "I think a great deal of Mr. J.S. Willison," recorded
Willie in his diary in July 1896. His "In Chicago Slums" piece in 1897
was followed by one in 1898 by "The Sweating System in Canada,"
about unfair labour practices.[8]

"Willie" (William Lyon Mackenzie) King, 1891.
Library and Archives Canada,
C-007336

Another good friend was Professor James Mavor, a political economist at the University of Toronto. He and Willison became members of a non-partisan social and political discussion group called the Fifteen Club. Another member was the leading lawyer Samuel Blake, Edward's brother. In May 1894, Willison invited Professor Goldwin Smith to attend the group's "closing social meeting for the season." Smith, the former regius professor of modern history at Oxford University, had moved to Toronto in 1871 and was a noted author and essayist. For some time he had been dubbed popularly as the "sage of the Grange" [his Toronto house], the unquestioned intellectual giant of Toronto. He had been the founding president in 1874 of the National Club, the social and intellectual sanctuary for so-called "Canada First" Liberals, and he and Willison had come to meet there increasingly, as the young journalist's income and reputation had grown. In 1896, Willison became a full member and stayed on the club roster for the rest of his life.

Smith had been discussing national and international questions with Willison for some time, so the invitation was logical, as was Smith's to him in 1895 to be a member of his own evening discussion group, the "Round Table Club." In addition to Smith, Willison, and Professor Mavor, charter members were: W.J. Alexander, Professor of English at University College; Edmund Walker of the Bank of Commerce; James Bain, head of the Toronto Public Library; O.A. Howland, a Conservative MLA and author of *The Irish Problem* (1887) and *The New Empire* (1891); W.L. Clark, Professor of Philosophy at Trinity College; T.A. Haultain, private secretary to Goldwin Smith and eventually his literary executor and biographer, who had already written *The War in the Soudan* (1885) and *Versiculi* (1893); Provost Welch of Trinity; Maurice Hutton, Professor of Classics at University College; and Ramsay Wright, the noted biologist. No papers were read, but the members in rotation were each responsible for the introduction of a subject for conversation. The association with the club must have been intellectually rewarding for Willison, especially because of its habit of entertaining distinguished visitors to the city.[9]

As editor of the *Globe*, Willison was in a position to promote Canadian writers. He had met the poets Wilfrid Campbell, Archibald Lampman, and Duncan Campbell Scott in Ottawa in the late 1880s, and in 1892 agreed to let them write for the *Globe* a weekly literary column called "At the Mermaid Inn." The *Globe* told its readers that Campbell's "Mother" was "the greatest poem that has come from the pen of a Canadian, and one of the greatest poems of this time" and that Lampman was "as true a poet as rings today." It argued that "while there is much in our literature that is mere trash there is much that has heart and life in it, some that shows humanity in its very nakedness, that goes to the heart of human hope and passion...."[10]

Willison continued *Globe* support for Canadian literature, as he put it in a letter to Wilfrid Campbell in 1897, that went "to the heart of human hope and passion." He sent Campbell in June that year "$10 for the Jubilee Poem. I think a great deal of it." Pauline Johnson thanked him for his 1895 review of her first volume of poetry, *The White Wampum*, gushing: "One thing I feel always assured of, and that is the most excellent treatment from the good old 'Globe.' It always has the kindliest things to say of me." The poet and novelist Charles G.D. Roberts expressed delight in 1897 for "the most kind and gratifying notice" the *Globe* gave his volume of poetry *Around the Campfire*.[11]

Willison seems to have been closest personally to Gilbert Parker among the Canadian writers of that day. The expatriate Canadian was making a great name in London as a prolific producer of fiction, much of it set in a romantic Canadian setting of early colonial days. Parker was rarely in Toronto, but from London and New York he kept Willison posted on his career, subscribed to the *Globe* and inquired about the Toronto scene. In December 1896 he thanked Willison for "your good words about the Seats [*Seats of the Mighty*].... You must tell me all about Canadian affairs when we meet, and while the ladies gossip, we will set the world right!" In February 1897 he wrote from London that he was sending the editor "the uniform edition of my books.... It is born of a weak moment of gratitude...." Parker wrote later that year that he would be in Toronto soon and "above all else, & beyond everything, I shall have the great advantage & joy of meeting good men like yourself, who are one with me in trying to combine best of life & love of country in the daily round...." He came in April 1896, and during a testimonial banquet at the National Club, Willison toasted him and Canadian literature generally, rejoicing that the press could display "a special pride" in writers such as Parker, Roberts, Campbell, and Lampman "because they have won honorable places in the commonwealth of letters."

He especially lauded Parker for his great writing from London — "proving that in literature as in business, in politics, in science, we breed on this stretch of northern territory men that are the equal of any race on the Father's footstool...." He concluded:

> They tell us sometimes that we have no history. Why, on this strip of soil empires have waxed and waned. A wonderful native race has ruled, declined and vanished.... At old Quebec the modern spirit seems to walk reverently, as though in the very presence chamber of time. Then away in the west we have an unpeopled empire, where, if we will, we may build up a newer and better civilization than any the world has seen.... Then we have a right to remember that the Canadian

is a British citizen; that he is a neighbour to a great free nation who speak the Imperial language; that his hand touches imperial problems, and that if he will he may be a citizen of the world, and deliver his message to all the nations who speak the Queen's tongue.

Perhaps sensing a personal yearning on Willison's part, George Ross, the Ontario minister of education, remarked in his speech that "with greater development of our national strength Canada would be no longer provincial, and its editors, like those of the Thunderer [London *Times*], would shape policies for the empire...."[12]

As the mid-1890s unfolded, both Willison's broadening associations and the changing circumstances of the times were acting to convince him and many of his friends that the future greatness of Canada and loyalty to a vital British connection were perfectly complementary.

In the early 1890s he still had articulated a nationalist, non-imperialist, even somewhat moderately continentalist point of view. His childhood and youth in rural western Ontario in the 1850s and 1860s had been lived in the very shadow and heavy influence of America's democratic idealism and its powerful popular culture. All his life his writing style strayed easily into the American "or" rather than the Canadian "our" usage. His parents and siblings all had migrated to the U.S. In so many ways he felt, as he would tell an American audience years later, that "we are bretheren."[13] When George Parkin, a leading member of the Imperial Federation League in Canada, gave a lecture on his cause in Toronto in December 1892, the *Globe* was harshly critical, asking: "Why remain blind to all but the mistakes and failings of the United States? Mr. Parkin was full of passionate eulogy for the mother English nation, but has not a kind word for the great sister English nation...."[14]

The paper's viewpoint was very consistent with views Willison had often expressed personally since his first days in the Young Men's Liberal Club. Earlier that year he had attended Grover Cleveland's re-nomination for the American presidency by the Democratic National Convention in Chicago, preceding his re-election, and had written Cleveland to say that "I simply admire your political principles and regard you as the best type of statesman this generation has produced."[15]

By the mid-1890s a very definite shift had occurred in his views. Britain and the United States had become embroiled in an acrimonious dispute in 1895 over the boundary between Venezuela and British Guiana. President Cleveland had threatened, if Britain would not agree to arbitration with Venezuela, that he would "arbitrate" the question himself, by force if necessary. Secretary of State Olney had added that "any permanent political union between a European and an American state" was "unnatural and inexpedient."[16] The *Globe* angrily retorted that, for Canada, it was "of her own free choice that she remains a member of a world-wide empire, with world-wide responsibilities." As Willison put it to the National Club in Toronto in December 1896, he and many other Liberals had been shocked by the American behaviour out of their "illusions" about Canada's prospects for peaceful progress towards separate Anglo-Saxon nationhood. "With the issue of President Cleveland's menacing message," he emphasized, "we felt the solid ground beneath our feet, and knew that we too were born into the splendid privileges of British citizenship."[17]

That change in sympathy for the British connection was foreshadowed and made easier by the Liberal party's shift on trade policy after 1892. Previously, the Conservatives had contrived to associate defence of the National Policy Tariff with loyalty to Britain in a manner infuriating to Liberals. As Willison remembered in his National Club speech, "… we could not know whether we were required to be loyal to a tariff, a party leader or a great free-trading empire…. In a British country loyalty had become a party cry, and the flag a party emblem."

With the Liberals' convention resolution in 1893 in favour of "freer trade with the whole world, more particularly with Great Britain and the United States" and evident American hostility to trade compromises with Canada as the decade wore on, that problem disappeared.[18] Canadian Conservatives even opened themselves up to Willison charges in the *Globe* in 1895 of "England-cursing protectionism" by hostility to better Canadian tariff treatment of Britain.[19] No longer need a good Liberal and his newspaper be defensive about their "Britishness."

Some of Willison's new personal associations in the mid-1890s were likely quite influential in the introduction of a consciously imperialist element into his nationalism. In particular, he came into the orbit of that eminent cleric and educator, Principal George Monro Grant of Queen's University. Grant was twenty years Willison's senior, a graduate with distinction from Glasgow University and a confirmed believer in imperial unity. In his book *Ocean to Ocean* (1872), he argued that a nation "cannot be pulled up by the roots ... cannot be dissociated from its past, without danger to its higher interests. Loyalty is essential to its fulfillment of a distinctive mission — essential to its true glory." He lauded the "subtle, indirect influences that flow from unbroken connection with the old land, those living and life-giving forces that determine the tone and mould the character of a people."[20] He was an early and active member of the Imperial Federation League in Canada and of its successor organization, the British Empire League. He supported Sir John A. Macdonald in the "loyalty" election of 1891.

Otherwise, since the Pacific Scandal of 1873, he had not voted for the Conservatives, because of the corruption he saw in their regime. Once the Liberals had abandoned Unrestricted Reciprocity, he no longer worried about dangers to the Imperial tie but looked primarily for a moral upgrade in federal politics and the cultivation of mutual tolerance among Canada's various ethnic and religious groups. He believed university men should help influence society's advance in these areas. This was one of the reasons for his foundation in 1893 of the *Queen's Quarterly* and his delight at accepting Willison's offer of space in the *Globe* for a series of articles on "A Policy for Canada."

Willison's earlier attacks on partisan excess and corruption in politics by both parties made the *Globe* a natural vehicle for Grant's reforming campaign, especially since there was no truly "independent" paper of wide circulation to turn to. To a fellow "independent," Goldwin Smith, Grant remarked in 1896: "As to an organ, we are indeed badly off, but since Willison has had a free hand the Globe is fair and reports its opponents with remarkable fairness."[21]

In his 1893 *Globe* articles, Grant wrote that the "terrible revelations" of 1891 — the McGreevy–Langevin and Mercier–Pacaud scandals — had "made me for the first time in my life ashamed of being a Canadian." He called on his countrymen to "go forward to make our land one worth living for...."[22] Reaction to the scandals and graft in public life brought Grant and Willison together, Grant's biographers record, "and acquaintance deepened into friendship." In an interview published in the *Globe* the next year Grant asked: "Can we get administrators who are determined that the commandment 'Thou shalt not steal' must be observed? Till that is settled, it is useless to talk of anything else."[23] Since Honoré Mercier's 1892 exit from office in Quebec, anti-corruptionists like Grant were left with the Conservative regime at Ottawa as their chief target. Thus the opening of the *Globe*'s columns to Grant could serve Willison's partisan purposes very nicely.

There were other grounds for co-operation. In 1893 and 1894, the Protestant Protective Association sought support from Ontarians for its doctrine of exclusion of Roman Catholics from public office, the franchise, and Protestant employ. Grant proclaimed to a *Globe* reporter: "We need a union of all good men in Canada, and we dare not say to any man that he must abandon the religion of his mother before he can expect to be treated as a citizen." This was useful ammunition for the Liberal government of Ontario in its electoral battle of 1894 against the Conservatives and the PPA. In addition, as Grant explained to a fellow imperialist, the Conservative Castell Hopkins, defeat of Premier Sir Oliver Mowat would be gratifying for his old political unionist foes and therefore "we could not afford to have such a man defeated at such a time."[24]

Grant continued to style himself as an "independent," but he was by 1895 something of a "fellow-traveller" with the Liberals. Willison asked him that year to visit Manitoba and report on the educational situation there.[25] Although Grant's contention in his articles after the visit that the Manitoba Catholics did have a legitimate grievance about their separate school rights was not quite to the *Globe*'s liking, his opposition to federal "coercion" of the province in redress of that grievance was. Grant called for investigation and conciliation rather than remedial action, perfectly in harmony with Laurier's "sunny ways" approach.[26]

Willison later wrote that in his first years as editor of the *Globe*, "no one gave me wiser counsel than Principal Grant...." It was not merely that he shared attitudes with Grant on a wide range of issues. He also was deeply impressed by the man himself, by his integrity, intelligence, and patriotism. Just before the federal election of 1896, he advised Laurier to "get Principal Grant into the field" as his Ontario lieutenant and thus "make a combination that could not be resisted.... Why could we not get such a man with us?"[27] Grant preferred, however, as he once put it, "to be one of the guides of the people, to stimulate them to independent judgment, honour and righteousness...." That he guided and stimulated Willison towards imperialist sympathies seems clear from the editor's obituary of his friend in 1902:

> His part in our public life was more subtle than that of the publicist of the usual type, and the harder to appraise....
>
> .... The Canadian point of view has changed with the years, and our national outlook to-day is, on the whole, that which was Dr. Grant's principle through life. With the full force of a most effective personality, a personality which was persuasive as well as compelling, he strove to promote the habit of thought which would conceive of the individual as part of the whole, of the Province as member of the Dominion, of Canada as a factor in the British race, and of the British race as related to humanity. Born in what was then an isolated eddy of the current of the world's life his political message to his country seems to have been to get into the main stream.[28]

Willison had less to do personally in this period with the colourful Lieutenant-Colonel George Taylor Denison III, cavalry enthusiast and president of the British Empire League in Canada. Denison had been one of the leaders of the Canada First nationalist Liberals in the 1870s, then had swung to support Sir John A. Macdonald in response to the continentalist tendencies in Liberal ranks in the later 1880s and early 1890s. Denison's drift towards amicable relations with the federal Liberals by 1896 illustrated the degree to which Liberals in Ontario were more and more giving the impression of being pro-British. Seventeen years Willison's senior and with his military experience and writings, he was for a considerable time worlds away socially from the editor. Politically, the gap to close was even wider.

Colonel George T. Denison, 1909. (facing title page of his *The Struggle for Imperial Unity: Recollections and Experiences*. Toronto: Macmillan, 1909)

In 1888, he helped organize a Toronto branch of the Imperial Federation League with the call for members to "rally around the old flag and frustrate the designs of traitors." He denounced the *Globe*'s printing of some annexationist letters to the editor that year as "rank treason." Later he damned Edward Farrer as "one of the conspirators who are working for annexation."[29] He even wrote his friend Lord Salisbury, then prime minister of Britain, that the *Globe* was "more anxious to stir up a spirit of annexation in Canada than to see Reciprocity carried out or even the Liberal party immediately in power if pledged to British connection." He was prepared to support Premier Mowat's Liberal candidate in a provincial by-election in 1892 because, as he explained to Salisbury, it would be a "pat ... on the back for his loyal anti-annexation letters.... I urged my friends to draw a clear-cut distinction between an honest loyal leader and the disloyal traitors and conspirators who have wrecked the Reform party."

Then Farrer left the *Globe* and the 1893 Liberal convention sanctioned a new non-continentalist trade policy, which Denison described to Lord Salisbury as "most significant," making the annexation danger "flatter than ever." By the end of 1894 he happily wrote Salisbury about the utterly changed federal political situation: "Even if there were a change ... there will not be the danger there would have been in 1891 for the annexation party is practically dead."[30]

By early 1895, according to a Conservative friend of his and Willison's, Arthur Colquhoun, Denison was dropping in at the *Globe* office "in a friendly way." In early 1896, he wrote Laurier in commendation of his support for increased militia expenditures following the Venezuela crisis, and in May assured Lord Salisbury that the federal Liberals were "now very careful not to squint towards the United States. In fact, they remind one of the Indian's tree that was so upright that it leaned a little the other way."[31] He also involved himself in efforts to get Premier Mowat to move to the federal sphere at Laurier's side; and when Mowat agreed to enter a Liberal cabinet in the event of election victory, he in turn, supported by the *Globe's* president, Robert Jaffray, pressed Denison to carry the party's colours in West Toronto.[32] Denison preferred not to enter directly into political life, but his forgiveness of Liberals for past sins was now complete.

Willison understood the political significance of the alliance with Denison. Soon after the 1896 election victory, he confidentially showed him some of the new Laurier government's draft proposals for settlement of the Manitoba schools question. He explained to Clifford Sifton that "I have thought it of importance to keep him [Denison] in sympathy with the new government, and because he represents an element that has been hostile to us in the past."[33] A very close personal friendship very quickly now began to develop between the two men. It was part of the complex of influences making Willison's Canadian nationalism more British and imperialistic.

Arthur Colquhoun also contributed to that escalating process. A Conservative journalist, he was five years Willison's junior. Born in

Montreal of a wealthy Scottish father and a mother descended from the old Upper Canada "Family Compact" aristocracy, he won academic honours at McGill University in literature and history. He entered the newspaper world with the Ottawa *Journal* and met Willison in the Press Gallery on Parliament Hill in 1886, where they began, as Willison described it, "an instant friendship...." Later he moved to Toronto as assistant editor and then managing editor of the Conservative *Empire*. Likely it was he who offered the burned-out *Globe* people refuge in the *Empire*'s premises in 1895. He was named later that year to the editorial staff of the merged *Mail and Empire*. From the mid-1890s he also was editor of the trade journal *The Printer and Publisher*, in which he gave his good Liberal friend full credit for restoring the *Globe* to a position of prestige and influence. He commended Willison's practice of reporting Conservatives' speeches accurately and avoiding virulence in editorial comment. With its exhaustive reporting and analysis of key issues, he judged that "The *Globe*, under its present control, is a great source of strength to the [Liberal] party. It goes into many Conservative homes, and must be doing a missionary work which the next election may show."[34]

Colquhoun was doing his own missionary work. He was a staunch champion of imperial unity whom Hector Charlesworth described as "a type of the complete Tory gentleman of the old school." His positions with Conservative newspapers and his educational credentials won him access to teas and dinners at Heydon Villa, Colonel Denison's Toronto home, from early in the 1890s. He did his best to keep the Colonel fully informed on the progress of the imperialist cause among journalists. In June 1896, he explained to Denison that, while the "country press" was apt to be lukewarm, "some of its best friends are Liberals who control newspapers. They should be enlisted on our side." The enlistment was for the sake of imperialism, not Conservatism.

For Willison, personal associations with leading imperialists, indications in the Venezeula dispute of a possible threat to Canadian separateness in North America from a revived American unfriendliness, and his party's liberation from its old embarrassing continentalist and anti-Empire image, combined to induce in him a new receptiveness to imperialist arguments. In December 1896, with the high protectionist Dingley Tariff in the works in Washington and stringent American "anti-alien" legislation annoying and affecting many Canadians, he demonstrated to the National Club in Toronto just how far the process had gone:

> Some of us who have an aversion to jingoism in all its motives and phases feel humiliated when we see fellow-Canadians flung back across the border like criminals, and we are told that we must surrender our national integrity for human trade relationships.... There seems nothing for us but to emulate British forbearance, to be patient and not peevish, neighbourly but not servile, to take care that it is not by us that the offence cometh, to lean upon our imperial relationships and to remember that
>
> 'This is the law of the jungle,
>> as old and as true as the sky,
> And the wolf that shall keep it may prosper,
>> but the wolf that shall break it must die,
> As the creeper that girdles the tree trunk,
>> the law runneth forward and back
> For the pack is the strength of the wolf and
>> the wolf is the strength of the pack.'

It was fitting that Willison, who had long been very emotional in his championing of Canadian nationalism, who admired and was close to several romantic poets and novelists, should close his remarks with a quote from Kipling, then the chief poet of British imperialism. Colonel Denison gleefully wrote Prime Minister Lord Salisbury in Britain about the "striking speech" of Willison, whom he described as "a man in the utmost confidence of the Liberal party." It was, he claimed, an illustration of the "vast change" in Liberal opinion on the Empire tie.[35]

As his imperialism solidified, his confidence in Canadian development to maturity did not falter. Indeed, his nationalist faith was confirmed and strengthened as the country slowly began to free itself in the mid-1890s from the grip of economic depression. As he later would put it to Sir William Van Horne, president of the CPR, his views on the West were "revolutionized" by his trip through the region in 1895.[36]

After that journey he wrote a series of lengthy articles for the *Globe* on transportation and settlement. The major one, accompanied by seventeen large photographs, filled four full pages of the Saturday *Globe* on October 19, 1895 on "The Harvest in the Canadian Northwest." At first, it was only to be termed "Special Correspondence of The Globe," as was the case with other letters in the series, but Van Horne of the CPR managed to see an advance copy and informed a subordinate, who contacted Willison, that the essay was "very much the best that has been written on our N.W. The value would be enormously increased if it could appear distinctly as from the Editor-in-chief of the Globe. As from a special correspondent it would be open to the suspicion of having been written up for advertising purposes.... If Mr. W. has no objection to its appearing as suggested I think you would be justified in taking say 120,000 copies and perhaps more could be used to advantage."

Van Horne doubtless was thinking of the article's usefulness as immigration propaganda for the West, including CPR-owned land, in Eastern Canada, Britain, and the United States. That this propaganda had been written by the leading publicist of the federal Opposition must have made it potentially very persuasive indeed. Along the same lines, the deputy minister of the interior in Ottawa wrote Willison just before publication that his minister wanted to know how much per thousand copies the paper would charge the government for immigration promotion purposes. The official added that it would be particularly valuable as "from your own pen."[37]

Willison began his article by recalling the patriotic enthusiasm of the western reports of Charles Mair and G.M. Grant of a quarter-century before. "The Canadian who has not seen western Canada," he remarked, "has not reached his full stature and can have but a poor appreciation of the magnificent estate of his countrymen." He referred briefly but enthusiastically to the agricultural and mineral wealth awaiting exploitation in the North-West Territories and British Columbia, but his chief focus was on Manitoba itself. He was conscious of the widespread impression in the East that the West was "a country of small patches of splendid fertility separated by wide stretches of barren, drouth-stricken, unfruitful land." In fact, he stressed, "in Manitoba alone barely 25,000 farmers, of a population of less than 200,000, were producing 60,000,000 bushels of grain and shipping 23,000 head of cattle eastward. He saw room in the province for at least 100,000 farmers and a proportionate increase in productivity, and had little sympathy for the pessimists who worried about monopolistic grain elevator companies and the rigours of the climate. In the "spirit, purpose and intelligence" of Manitobans he found "a fair guarantee that elevator charges will not go unregulated, and that the farmer will not be left for long at the mercy of any corporation." He was sure that through irrigation, the careful choice of strains of crop and wise attention to the experience of older residents there was no reason why the province — indeed, by implication, much of the northwest generally — could not be fantastically productive.

It was the wheat boom that impressed, even awed him most:

> There are in this western country as wonderful pictures … as one can find on the face of this old earth, but the scene that will live longest in the memory is … the first full sight of the prairie wheat fields. We who have thought of Manitoba as a pioneer country, scarcely redeemed from the virgin condition, who know only of the square fields and scant meadows and narrow orchards of the older provinces – mere patches they would be on the face of the prairies – are struck with an utter surprise by the extent, the beauty and the wonder of a Manitoba harvest….
>
> As we ran into the Lasalle settlement we got our first sight of the prairie wheat-fields. Then on for hours and hours we pass over an enchanted land, through mile upon mile of yellow swinging grain, clean-stemmed, stalwart, triumphant, rare in its splendor and spendthrift in its promise.

Men failed in western agriculture, he admitted, but he believed there were thousands of individual success stories, cases of men who had journeyed west with little but energy and intelligence and had built towards prosperity and pride. "There may be a touch of enthusiasm in this writing," he conceded, "but where is there a Canadian but feels a thrill in the possession of this western country?" He foresaw that with the spread of accurate information about the region, there would flow into it Americans, English, and Scottish tenant-farmers, northern Europeans, Ontarians, and "thousands of young Canadians in the United States of the second and third generation who probably could not do better than to come to the land of their fathers and restore to us some of the strength that has been taken away." In closing he wrote: "Here are virgin lands and an advanced civilization; the opportunities of a new settlement, the comforts, conveniences and advantages of an old community. The country stands open to all the world, and man cannot long neglect a land that God has filled so full of plenty."[38] A worship of the West and a fascination with its potential for a rich contribution to national growth and prosperity were now significant elements of Willison's nationalism.

One of his greatest satisfactions, however, was that he had a wonderfully happy home environment to offset the frenetic atmosphere of politics and the press. Since early in the decade and his editorship, the family had rented a large house on the north side of St. Joseph Street, west of Bay and near Queen's Park. Rachel reigned there, as beautiful as ever, with a marvelous skill at domestic management. She was an essential, imperturbable counter to his frettings about the tensions of the work day. The twins, Walt and Bill, were healthy, boisterous, affectionate eight-year-olds with more energy than could safely be contained. Walt was fair-haired and easy-going, Bill darker, more turbulent. Dad was rarely home to tuck them in — not getting back from putting the *Globe* to bed until 1 or 2 a.m. In the mornings Rachel guarded his sleep until a set time, when the twins were unleashed to bash, yelling, through the bedroom door and leap on him for a furious wrestling session, with Bill likely ending up atop his head. The family was completed in the early 1890s with the arrival, already teenaged, of the attractive Hazel Wright, Rachel's niece, who would stay a dozen years as a help with the boys and a special companion to her aunt. In every way, she was a daughter.

When he was able to be home and had writing to do, he liked to work with the family around him, which did not seem to bother his concentration at all. His family was very obviously the principal joy of his life, and he hoarded his limited time in their midst. He was so marvellous at reading aloud to the children that one day, when a well-meaning visitor substituted for him, one of the twins bluntly told the man: "I would rather listen to Dad for half an hour than to you all day." He was no stern Victorian father, instead being much too indulgent. Rachel's affectionate comment was: "Jack, as a father, you are a joke!" His own family had broken up long ago, and in 1888 his mother had died far away in the United States. There was a special sweetness for him in the domestic happiness he felt privileged to enjoy. He even took the boys along with him to his office when he could. In August 1896, cub-reporter Willie King recorded in his diary that he "played three games of checkers" after work at the *Globe* with eight-year-old Willie Willison, "in each of which I was beaten."[39]

Thus John Willison entered on his years as the chief English-Canadian newspaper spokesman and leading strategist for the new Laurier regime at the height of his powers and personal happiness. He was forty in 1896, in love with life itself, glorying in all the challenges of mind and pen that his career was bringing. He had travelled far and fast on strong ambition and intense energy. He was full of confidence in himself and in the growth to greatness of Canada. His contacts outside politics and journalism, in many cases with men of other than just Canadian sensibilities, were helping him to be newly interested in the wider world, especially Britain and the Empire. Fresh opportunities and challenges lay ahead.

A Nationalist and Imperialist, 1896–1902

THE FIRST SIX YEARS OF THE LAURIER GOVERNMENT WAS A TIME WHEN rapid boisterous national growth, recurrent storms of anti-American feeling, and a marked increase in enthusiasm for the Empire were central features of Canadian life. The *Globe*, chief newspaper organ of the governing Liberals, had much to say on them all, as did its editor personally.

Through this time, John Willison's confidence in Canadian material success was strengthened immensely, and he became properly Torontonian in associating the new growth with tariff protection. He continued to view the United States as both a good and bad model for Canadians, while American hostility and indifference to Canada helped push him toward an increased interest in the Anglo-Canadian relationship in political, military, and economic spheres. His rising protectionism did somewhat blunt his imperialism, causing him to shy away from Empire free trade. And in political and military matters he did his best to be a loyal follower of Laurier's go-slow approach. Still, unlike Laurier, his emotions truly were engaged on the side of the imperial idea. More and more he thought of himself as both a Canadian and a Briton. All the while, the *Globe* went from strength to strength in its circulation battles with its Toronto contemporaries. It did seem that Willison's trends of thinking on nationalism and imperialism were highly acceptable to many in his Toronto and Ontario community.

During the 1896 election campaign and through the early months of the Laurier government, the old enmity between the federal Liberals and business interests was largely put aside. Willison had advised his leader as early as November 1894 that victory "will be won by the party that can best command the confidence of the best elements of the country." Three weeks before polling day, the *Globe* published a Laurier statement that "the intention of the Liberal party is not and never was to establish absolute free trade in this country" and that manufacturing required "stability and permanency." The *Globe* echoed the pledge, vowing that the tariff "will be reformed by business men upon business principles."[1] After electoral victory, Willison was quick to apprise Laurier of the sharp antagonism on Bay Street to Sir Richard Cartwright, the old arch-free trader, even advising that he should be excluded from cabinet. Laurier did not go that far, but did deny Finance to Cartwright. The *Globe* stressed editorially that Liberal tariff moves would be "of a constructive not of a destructive character."

J.B. MacLean of the MacLean Publishing Company congratulated Willison on the "cautious, I might say conservative … course you have taken." He advised that the *Globe* was being "watched very closely by manufacturers and businessmen, and was "growing in favour among them."[2] This process was furthered as Laurier appointed a business-inclined tariff commission, with orders to travel the country and undertake exhaustive study before recommending changes. "I am sure that your government grows steadily stronger with all the best people in Ontario," Willison exulted to Laurier in November.[3]

Early in the new administration's term it became clear to Willison that American political leaders, with their high protectionism, stringent anti-alien laws with anti-Canadian implications, and hard-line views on the Alaska boundary issue, were in no mood for cultivating good relations with Canada. The *Globe* observed in December 1896 that it was now "impossible to doubt that American policy has been guided by the notion that Canada can be induced to enter the Union by making political union a condition of improved trade relations." If this view continued to dominate, and no reasonable trade concessions were to be forthcoming from the Americans, the *Globe* affirmed, "we shall have nothing to expect in that quarter and we shall be free to direct our attention elsewhere."[4] When Willison learned that the Laurier government was considering preferential treatment of British manufactures, he gave, as he later described it, "instant support to the proposal as politically advantageous, as agreeable to Canadian and British feeling, and as a method of escape from the position in which advocacy of free trade with the United States has involved the Liberal party."[5]

In the first budget of the Laurier government, brought down by W.S. Fielding in April 1897, a Canadian minimum tariff was promised any country that would offer Canada similar or lower rates. The minimum rate was to be 12.5 percent lower than the general tariff until July 1898 and then 25 percent lower. Britain, with her policy of free trade, obviously would be *the* beneficiary. Duties against the high protectionist Americans would remain unchanged — something which pleased Canadian manufacturers no end! As Sir Joseph Pope, formerly Sir John A. Macdonald's secretary, recorded in his diary, the moves "have made a big hit, and completely taken the wind out of the Conservative sails." For old Liberal free traders, the *Globe* offered the consolation that "if we cannot enlarge the free trade area on this continent, then we may enlarge the free trade area within the British Empire and build up there a new and prosperous British commonwealth."[6]

The year of the Fielding tariff was also the sixtieth anniversary of Queen Victoria's accession to the throne. In June political leaders from all over the Empire gathered in London to take part in the magnificent Diamond Jubilee celebrations and to meet with the aggressively imperialist Colonial Secretary, Joseph Chamberlain. The poet Rudyard Kipling published "Our Lady of the Snows" in the London *Times* to celebrate the Canadian tariff initiative favouring Britain, with the final stanza reading:

> A nation spoke to a nation,
> *A Queen sent word to a throne,*
> *Daughter I am in my mother's house,*
> *But mistress in my own,*
> *The gates are mine to open,*

As the gates are mine to close,
And I abide by my mother's house,
Said our Lady of the Snows.

In the same spirit, Lord Salisbury, the British prime minister, exulted to his Canadian friend George Denison about the "rallying of the [Canadian] Liberals to the Imperial idea." The spectacle of this new British enthusiasm for Canada caused the *Globe* to observe that the Empire "seems to be approaching the hour of some great evolutionary step in her progress."[7]

At the Jubilee in London, Laurier was now Sir Wilfrid, his knighthood symbolic of British lionization. In his speeches he moved powerfully but cautiously to put himself in touch with the spirit of imperialist emotions. A scant four years before, he had reflected privately that the British tie was gradually eroding and that the time for Canadian independence was "not I think very far away." Now he seemed of another opinion. His speech in Liverpool reflected this. He noted that "never before" had the words "colony" and "nation" been linked, and added:

> All thoughts of separation disappear, thoughts of union, of a closer union, take their place. Today the sentiment exists in Canada in favour of a closer union with the motherland. The sentiment exists in Canada — nay it exists across the ocean — from continent to continent, and today it encircles the earth. What is its future? It is a subject upon which I would hardly venture an opinion.

But his key words likely were in the cautious resolution he pushed successfully through the Colonial Conference of the various governments of the Empire, that "the present political relations between the United Kingdom and the self-governing colonies are generally satisfactory under the existing condition of things."[8]

Willison was delighted as a Liberal by the immense political boost Sir Wilfrid Laurier received by his spectacular role at the Jubilee. In November the Liberals won a decisive by-election victory in the traditionally solid Tory seat of Centre Toronto. An ecstatic Willison

"Home Sweet Home." *J. W. Bengough cartoon*, Globe, *September 1, 1897, p.1).*

told cheering party faithful that night "we are going on until this whole city belongs to the Liberal Party."[9] He was delighted too by what the Jubilee seemed to signify about the quickening of imperial spirit. The *Globe* stressed: "It matters not whether one is friendly or hostile or indifferent to Imperial unity, he cannot close his eyes to the fact that events are steadily marching in that direction. We cannot say what vistas will be opened to the view as the march proceeds; but what has already happened indicates that a page of history more wonderful than any romance is unfolding itself."[10]

Even Canadian anti-imperialists recognized change was in the air. The year before, Willison's continentalist Toronto friend, Goldwin Smith, had told Laurier: "The British connection is merely a dying dolphin." Now Smith lamented to an American friend that Laurier was "going deeper and deeper into imperialism."[11]

Willison was fascinated by the surge of imperial feeling in Canada and excited by the quickened interest in Canada that Laurier had experienced in Britain. He determined now to go himself as soon as possible to explore everything he could at the Empire's centre. He bought passages as well for Rachel and young Hazel. They sailed in late July, after the Jubilee's crowds, confusion, and inflated prices had subsided. They were "somebodies" with a handy batch of introductions from Governor General Lord Aberdeen and from Laurier. Throughout August and September, they toured and observed with tireless energy, thrilled by their first overseas experience.[12]

He sent ten special articles back to the *Globe* and would remark later that one could not "realize to the full the pride and glory of British citizenship until he had visited the Isles over the seas, touched hands with England's life, and felt the presence of those infinite forces which beat and throb in the marvelous life of old London." One of his former staffers, Joe Atkinson of the *Star*, told him that when seeing the dispatches from Britain "I felt I was reading the impressions which the old world makes upon a thorough going Canadian."[13] Willison certainly was thrilled by the cultural and historical heritage of Britain. He visited St. Paul's, Westminster Abbey, Hampton Court, the Tower, Westminster, and many other storied sites, remarking:

> A Canadian cannot be robbed of his full part in the great inheritance of British tradition and British valor and British literature and British freedom.... The grey hairs of a nation are honourable if the life has been deep and true, and all down through wonderful centuries these islands have been the pillar of fire by night and the pillar of cloud by day in the sacred cause of human

freedom. It is this rich past that gives a touch of arrogance to the Englishman and the scepter of leadership to the British peoples.[14]

His articles were primarily a report on trends in British thought and action concerning the Empire and on the role Canada might play in its future. He explained that Britain's diplomatic isolation and the economic challenge to her from powerful, populous protectionist countries, especially Germany and the U.S., were pushing the British to look anew at the self-governing colonies as "integral parts of Britain."[15] Canada's unconditional grant of a trade preference had made Laurier "the hero" of the Jubilee, who had "put Canada before the British people, not as a sucking infant clinging to the mother country, but as a free self-governing kingdom...."[16]

"At last," he rejoiced, "there is prospect of a real revival in Great Britain of interest in Canada and Canadian affairs." In this climate, he urged, no time must be lost by Canada in a vigorous search for British investment and immigrants.[17] This aggressive approach was of a piece with the policies of Canada's new minister of the interior, Clifford Sifton, with whom the editor had become very friendly. Sifton had invited him to Ottawa for a long chat en route to his ship in Montreal.[18] If Canada was to be intimately involved in the "new imperialism," they could agree, it should be on a thoroughly profitable basis.

Willison loved his trip through England, describing with affection "the enduring peace and beauty" of the countryside.[19] However, he was shocked and appalled by the social misery of so much of industrial England, describing "the grey and pallid faces" of workers and their sickly-looking families and that "... no otherwise than in the presence of this misery and infamy does one so rejoice that his lot is cast in a new country, with its wide leagues of virgin fields and all its royal opportunities and privileges, or feel so resolute to oppose the further reproduction of old world conditions overseas." He was heartened that British social reform and democracy were rising to meet the challenge of urban poverty, but he wanted no settlement of the sufferers in Canada's open lands, as "the taint cannot be eradicated in one generation."[20]

There was more, much more, goodly portions of it filled with references to poetry and literature, as well as detailed political reporting. The ten articles won wide praise in Canada for Willison, whose "JSW" initials headed each. A Toronto lawyer friend, Frank Denton, told him that "many, many people are speaking of and praising your articles." Mrs. J. Wilson of St. Thomas remarked that she "felt as if a new 'Autocrat of the Breakfast Table' had risen in the literary firmament." The novelist Gilbert Parker thought them "quite the most comprehensive and thorough things of the kind that I have read...." Arthur Colquhoun would remember them for "their insight and their emancipation from the narrow outlook derived exclusively from the atmospheres of North America."[21]

For all his enthusiasm about Britain and the Empire, Willison still hoped for progress towards wider Anglo-Saxon co-operation. In his final article from Britain he wrote of the American: "If he learns to know England thoroughly his voice can never again be raised in any jingo chorus against the British people, and in proportion as these two communities come together civilization advances and Christianity gains." To reinforce that point, the *Globe* pointed out, by way of a J.W. Bengough cartoon in November, that there were "two great Anglo-Saxon models" for Canada, each with its virtues and defects. Bengough entitled the sketch JACK CANUCK AT SCHOOL and portrayed him observing Uncle Sam and John Bull standing on tablets listing the strong and weak points of each:

UNITED STATES

PRO	CON
Social Equality	*Slickness*
Free Schools	*Trickery*
No Sectarianism	*Boss Rule*
No State Church	*Brag*
Unity	*Bad Faith*
Loyalty	*Weak Administration*
National Spirit	*Gov't by Injunction*
A Solid Middle Class	*Protectionism*
Shrewd Sense	

BRITAIN

PRO	CON
Freedom of Trade	*Ireland*
Liberty	*Privilege*
Pure Judges	*Rule of Rank*
Fair Play	*State Church*
Equal Laws	*Landlordism*
Good Administration	*Church Schools*
National Honor	*Vested Wrongs*
Solidity	*Slowness*[22]

Not surprisingly, Willison and the *Globe* voiced support for America when she went to war with Spain in April 1898. The *Globe* credited the Americans' "disinterested pity" for the oppressed Cubans as "the real impulse" for the conflict and wished them well. It also was pleased at Britain's evident sympathy for the American cause and hoped that knowledge of this in America would further Anglo-Saxon harmony. To the Toronto Canadian Club in June 1898, Willison remarked: "Nothing promises more for humanity at large and for the race than the rapprochement which now promises between Great Britain and the United States." He jokingly "expected before long" to see his friend, Colonel Denison, "burning fire crackers on the fourth of July — (Laughter)." However, he added, if an alliance there was to be, he wanted the United States to do "one half the wooing."[23]

The Anglo-Saxon harmony theme which underlay both imperialism and dreams of Anglo-American alliance had clear racist overtones, all too normal in the writing and thought of Willison's time throughout the western world. Sometimes the *Globe* mused about the dangerous side of Anglo-Saxonism, as the term Anglo-Saxon "may carry with it an impression of narrowness, intolerance or self-sufficiency. We may admire the sterling English qualities, the energy and sobriety, the love of order and freedom, without desiring to Anglicize the whole world, and without ignoring the virtues and talents of others. Every race has something to teach and something to learn."

Yet the *Globe* could slip all too easily into that very intolerance it decried. In July 1898 it condemned the "cowardice and the lack of chivalry shown by the aristocratic gentlemen of Paris, in the terrible bazaar fire which occurred there last year, and the same characteristics exhibited by the sailors of the Bourgogne in the recent disaster." It asked why "in high and low alike when the supreme test came these men failed to exhibit that self-control and manly heroism which to the English-speaking man is as the very breath of life." It concluded that modern France's lack of religious feeling was at fault.[24]

Willison was amazed that highly religious French Canadians seemed more infuriated by the racist aspect of the editorial than its anti-atheistic overtones. Laurier complained to him that Quebec Conservatives were using the editorial to "fan the wounded pride of the French Canadians" and that he too found it "offensive." Willison responded that he was "scarcely able to regard" it "as a very terrible affair," and merely regretted that it "could be turned against us."[25]

In January 1899, Willison went south to meet Laurier in Washington, where Canadian–American negotiations on trade, boundaries, fisheries, and other subjects were in progress. It was a chance to report for the *Globe* on the talks and on American attitudes to Canada and Britain. He also badly needed a holiday after an alarming illness the month before. As he explained to the prime minister, he had suffered "a general physical collapse from over-work ... the machine had run out while it seemed to be running all right." One morning he had been seized by great pain just after reaching his office. He was carried home to St. Joseph Street in a cab, recalling later that he was "perfectly indifferent" to whether he lived or not. His doctor diagnosed persistent indigestion and warned him to find more exercise and relaxation. One result would be that he would take up lawn bowling, once weather in Toronto permitted. A more immediate relief could be found in Washington and a couple of weeks of convalescence in North Carolina.[26]

He reported back to *Globe* readers that "many of the undersized politicians ... unquestionably supported by a great body of public opinion" in the States were as Anglophobe and anti-Canadian as ever, notwithstanding the friendly feeling in both Britain and Canada towards the States. He was especially struck by the tough, uncompromising positions taken by American negotiators during the negotiations then foundering in Washington. Trade, Bering Sea sealing, coastal fisheries, alien labour laws, and the Alaska boundary were all at issue, and when the talks were broken off by an exasperated Laurier, Willison wrote in the *Globe*: "… in proportion as we grow in strength, in national dignity and in old-fashioned British confidence in ourselves we shall grow in the respect of our neighbours to the South, in influence in the empire to which we belong."[27]

His American visit was also a time for some biting *Globe* editorial comment, very likely written by him, on the post-Spanish-American War mood and problems in the U.S. The paper noted that Americans were "still in the height of the war fever. Their poets regard the life of peace as cowardly. They … think they are in the 'van of the race' only when conquering with arms. The sooner they turn from such hallucinations and take a rational view of national life and national destiny the better for the American people. Their danger is at home and not abroad, and during this period of national eclipse the hold of the aggressive forces from which they have suffered much and will suffer more has been tightened."

The *Globe* explained that these "aggressive forces" were capitalist trusts, monopolies, and worker exploitation. "It is in affecting domestic reforms that the highest heroism is displayed," it argued, "and we must recognize our real heroes. We have the experience of other nations before our eyes and it clearly points the path of honour and marks the quicksands and quagmires along the path of real national development."[28]

Gone were the days when many Canadians believed their futures depended on some favourable treaty with the United States. As the *Globe* put it in January 1899, it was CANADA'S TURN NOW to grow to quick maturity in the coming century, after the style of the Americans in the one before. Immigration was beginning to pour in, from Britain, the States, and continental Europe; industrial expansion was accelerating enormously; agricultural settlement, productivity, and profitability were expanding by leaps and bounds. In short, Canada was on the way to "be classed among the great communities of the world, albeit allied with the mother country."[29] Willison typified this spirit in a triumphant address to the Toronto Young Men's Liberal Club in December 1898, exulting:

> It would be idle to gainsay the fact that Canadians to-
> day are in a firmly self-reliant mood, that the spirit of
> nationalism is stirring all across the Confederation,
> that we are going into the work of nation-building
> with head high and courage strong, and faith that is
> not easily to be daunted.... And so it would seem to me
> that we would be pessimists and weaklings beyond all
> men if we did not meet these imperative demands and
> take at the tide the fortune for which we have looked so
> wearily and so long.[30]

On through the winter, spring, and summer of 1899, the *Globe* now devoted far less space to imperial vistas for Canada. Far more went to celebrate, publicize, and help to promote the dramatic, exciting, amazing national economic boom.

Suddenly, dramatically, everything changed. Willison and his newspaper were swept up that fall in the popular enthusiasm which developed in English Canada for the sending of volunteers to fight for Queen and Empire in South Africa. A crisis had simmered in that distant land through the summer and into the fall between Britain and the two Boer republics, after negotiations over the political rights of their English-speaking "Uitlander" populations had broken down. Laurier had moved, and the House of Commons had passed, a resolution of sympathy and support for the Uitlanders' cause, but few Canadians had dreamed that more than words might be called for. Until mid-September, the *Globe* made only passing references, strictly in the news columns, to the South African situation. On September 14 it called mildly for a compromise reconciliation of the interests of Boer farmers with those of British miners and mine-owners; and it could not imagine that the Boers would be so foolish as to appeal to force in the dispute. Within two weeks the unthinkable began to look very probable, as the cable despatches from South Africa pointed to an outbreak of hostilities at any hour.

"There appears to be a general belief," the *Globe* announced on September 29, "that in case of war ... a Canadian regiment will be sent...." This was a bold statement. Weeks earlier Laurier had told Frederick Borden, the minister of militia: "I do not favour at all the scheme of sending an armed force to Africa…. We have too much to do in this country to go into military expenditure."[31] But pressure mounted when the colonial secretary cabled the governor general, Lord Minto, to express his appreciation of private offers to serve. On October 4, in an interview with the *Globe*, the prime minister dismissed as "pure invention" the *Canadian Military Gazette's* story of the previous day concerning details of a planned contingent and declared that the government had no authority from parliament to send men overseas. The next day he wrote Willison to warn that an effort "systematically planned and carried by some military men" was being launched before public opinion in order to force the sending of a contingent and that he did not think it a "wise policy … to take a share in all the secondary wars in which England is always engaged."[32]

Already he knew that Willison's attitude was very different. The super-heated Empire feeling of Toronto was all around the editor, and his past few years of imperialist associations and rhetoric combined with the excitement of an overseas crisis to make him absolutely certain that Canada *must* go to Britain's aid. The day before Laurier wrote, the *Globe* had dealt at length with how a contingent should be organized — "Canadians from Colonel to drummerboy" — and had asserted that sending it would be "a national declaration of Canada's stake in the British Empire."

Willison was at first unsure of the government's intentions and wrote Clifford Sifton to complain bitterly of the "intolerable" situation, whereby news of preparation for a contingent had gone to the *Military Gazette* instead of the *Globe*. Sifton wired back that the cabinet's policy was "wholly undetermined," and Laurier's letter made his opposition all too clear. Willison would write years later: "As editor of The Globe I was in a difficult position. I told Laurier that he would either send troops or go out of office, but gave a rash pledge that The Globe would not suggest the despatch of contingents in advance of the decision of the Cabinet."[33]

Laurier was scheduled to attend international celebrations in Chicago from October 7 through 10. John and Rachel Willison were invited guests on the trip, with Lady Laurier, the Siftons, L.O. David, a close Laurier friend, and Raymond Préfontaine, the Mayor of Montreal. Back and forth to Chicago on the Grand Trunk the group worriedly discussed the South African situation and the government's dilemma. As Willison would remember:

For three days we discussed the Imperial obligation of Canada and the possible political consequences of a decision against sending contingents in all its phases, if not with unanimity, at least with good temper and complete candour.... It is fair to explain that Sir Wilfrid contended the war in South Africa, if war there should be, would be a petty tribal conflict in which the aid of the Dominions would not be required, and that over and over again he declared he would put all the resources of Canada at the service of the Mother Country in any great war for the security and integrity of the Empire. When we reached London on the homeward journey we learned that the South African Republics had precipitated the conflict. Laurier had not believed that war was inevitable and he was greatly comforted by assurances received at Chicago, through British sources, that the Republics would submit to the demands of Great Britain or the conditions would be so modified as to avert hostilities and ensure a settlement by negotiation. During the journey between London and Toronto he was very sober and silent. He recognized that the Canadian Government must reach an immediate decision, but he would not admit that the fact of war necessarily involved Canada in the conflict.

When we parted at Toronto, I urged that as soon as he reached Ottawa he should announce that the Government would send troops to South Africa. But he was still reluctant, unconvinced and rebellious.

Willison also would remember that he "never doubted that Laurier's ultimate decision would be in favour of contingents. For that among other reasons *The Globe* said nothing to embarrass the Government or to excite public opinion."[34]

Opinion among public and politicians was excited enough already. The Conservative mass-circulation Montreal *Star* denounced the government for "humiliating and disgracing" Canada. On October

11, with Laurier still hesitating, it had banner headlines reading: OUR COUNTRY MUST BE KEPT BRITISH: ALL CANADA RISES IN ITS MIGHT AND FORCES THE HANDS OF THE GOVERNMENT. The shrill tone was matched in the Ottawa *Citizen*, the Toronto *Mail and Empire*, and practically the entire English-language Tory press. Former *Globe* editor John Cameron warned Laurier to "not let this patriotic feeling be headed by the Tories. You must guide it and head it yourself." In cabinet, Laurier was pressed strongly by Ontario ministers, led by William Mulock, to send troops. Just as adamantly, the French Canadians sided with Israel Tarte, who argued that there should be "not a man, not a cent for South Africa."[35]

On October 13, Laurier caved in, conceding later to Willison that "public feeling in the English provinces was too strong to be opposed." The cabinet authorized the recruitment, equipping, and transportation of a thousand volunteers, to be paid and kept in service by the British. English-Canadian pro-contingent opinion was to be appealed to through this decisive executive action, avoiding legislative delay. The moderate expenditure, voluntary aspect, and a "no precedent" pledge were designed to mollify anti-militarists, principally among French Canadians.[36]

In spite of the government's actions, there remained, as Willison explained to Laurier, "a very great uproar in Toronto" because of the small size of the contingent, the fact that the men would be paid and sustained in the field by Britain, and the general impression that the government had been held back from stronger moves by Quebeckers like Israel Tarte. The *Globe* tried to calm feeling with the contention that the sending of troops overseas was "an entirely new departure for Canada," not to be lightly undertaken. It stressed that there was "no crisis in sight" and that "Britain needed at once not masses of colonial troops but an indication of ... good-will, and ... to the world a practical example of the growing strength and unity of the empire."[37]

Very soon, expectations of easy British victory and no continuing pressure on Canadian Liberals were exploded. Throughout October, Boer forces advanced into the British colony of Natal and laid siege to Kimberley, Mafeking, and Ladysmith. On October 30, Sir George White and the cream of the British regular army were defeated at Nicholson's Nek. The possibility of a rising of Boer Afrikaners in Cape Colony was very real.[38] That same day, 1150 Canadian volunteers sailed from Montreal, accompanied by a number of correspondents, including Charles Frederick Hamilton of the *Globe*. As war fever mounted sharply, so too did the *Globe*'s circulation. By the week ending October 14, the daily average was 36,975; for that ending October 21, 39,291; the October 28, 41,583; and November 4, 43,416.[39] The Empire was in danger and Canadian boys were rushing to the rescue. "Strong feeling here that Government should proceed at once to organize another Regiment," Willison telegraphed Clifford Sifton on November 1, "and in case situation in South Africa becomes graver or European complications develop there we should call Parliament and vote supply." Early in December, General Methuen was defeated with heavy losses in his attempt to relieve Kimberley.[40]

Willison's emotions now were thoroughly engaged. He was utterly fascinated by the drama and devoted to the Empire's cause. In a speech on December 8 to the Employing Printers Association of Toronto, he remarked, in response to a toast to OUR COUNTRY AND EMPIRE:

> One rises to this toast tonight under very unusual conditions. We are all absorbed in the struggle in South Africa. Those of my social creed and of my political faith have no love for war.... But we are, too, loyal Britons, and our patriotism is at its best when our country needs us most. This is the day of her need and the day of her trial, and all that we have of blood and treasure is at her service.... We today with the inner vision see a thousand of our fellow-Canadians marching along the red line of danger, across the wide bare plains of Cape Colony to the relief of a beleaguered British garrison. We may not hope that any of these will escape the peril of battle, but we at least feel proud confidence that they will hold the honour of their country as a sacred trust and that not through them shall Britain come to shame (cheers).

He was thrilled that "soldiers of the Queen" had answered her call for aid from throughout the British world in order to

maintain her imperilled sovereignty in the Transvaal, to

establish the solidity and integrity of her empire, to keep undimmed the splendour of British traditions, and to extend the sway of British institutions so that still

'The triumph may be won
For common rights and equal laws,
The glorious dream of Harrington
And Sidney's good old cause.' (cheers).[41]

Then came the "Black Week" for the British Empire, December 11 through 16. General Gatacre blundered into defeat at Stormberg; General Methuen's army was thrown back from Magersfontein Ridge with a thousand casualties; and then the British main force attempting to relieve Ladysmith was outmanoeuvered at Colenso, losing 1,000 men and most of its artillery. The British commander-in-chief even counselled the surrender of Ladysmith.[42] The *Globe* now saw the stakes in South Africa to be the very integrity and survival of the Empire:

> If the Boers can succeed South Africa is lost, and if South Africa can be wrenched from her [Britain's] grasp by a few embattled farmers, what is to hold together her widely scattered dominions and dependencies in this stern world where the strong hand is the only title-deed to material possessions?

On December 18, a second contingent was authorized by the Laurier government, with the *Globe* noting "an almost universal feeling that every unit of the empire should do its share, or even more than its share, in making the result [of the war] as certain as anything can be." But when he pressed Laurier to ensure that Canadian soldiers in South Africa be paid full Canadian rates, the prime minister demurred, citing lack of national unity on the war, given widespread dissent in Quebec. Willison warned him that he was making "a tremendous political mistake" which could cost him the voting support of the main cities and towns in Ontario through the rebellion of their "men of character and influence…. It will be said that you have done the least possible when you should have done the most possible…."[43]

Laurier did announce later that year that Canada would give her volunteers in South Africa the difference between British and Canadian pay, and the Canadian contribution in men ultimately reached more than seven thousand. There were no more complaints from Willison, who even admitted the "absolute reasonableness" of Laurier's concern for Quebec opinion, although he himself had to be more concerned with feeling in Ontario. Two years later, he told the prime minister that "my own feeling is that under all the circumstances Canada has done exceedingly well."[44]

For all his enthusiasm for Canadian participation in the Boer War, Willison became quite disturbed early in the crisis at the intense bitterness between French and English in Canada. In November 1899, he asked his poet friend Wilfred Campbell: "Are we quite sure where we are going? Is it Canada First or Second?"

When Henri Bourassa, the Liberal MP for Labelle, resigned his seat in protest against the sending of Canadian troops without Parliamentary approval, the Globe described his action as "mistaken" but as having sprung from "the best of motives." It was not that the paper was uninterested in seeing French Canadians develop an Empire loyalty; it was a question of choosing the right means to this end. "If after 140 years the French Canadian is not as enthusiastic a Britisher as those of us who derive our origin from the British Isles we need neither be surprised nor discouraged at it," it commented. "Let us cease worrying him, let us frankly recognize his peculiar position, and let us treat him with unvarying friendship and generosity, and there need be no anxiety about his ultimate attitude towards the empire and its highest and grandest aims."[45]

In January 1900, the Globe's Charles Frederick Hamilton reported the first engagement of the Canadians, and the next month "scooped" the world on their Paardeberg victory, where they distinguished themselves with a brave charge at a critical stage in the battle. Readership soared. Willison's friend C.R.W. Biggar remarked to him: "Was it not Murat Halstead who, commenting on [U.S. Civil War General] Butler's remark about war being Hell, said it was a Hell of a time for the newspapers?" For 1900, the Globe's circulation climbed steeply to an average of 47,120, up from 36,729 in 1899. The Mail and Empire shot up too for this period, from 31,167 to 41,181.[46] In the week of Paardeberg, the Globe averaged

56,233 copies, and on the day following the capture of the Boer capital of Pretoria in June 1900, it reached the then-phenomenal total of 63,000.[47]

Goldwin Smith, almost alone in Toronto in his denunciation of the war, admitted to W.D. Gregory that the "engrossing excitement of the war" was making people "take papers for war news and nothing else."[48] The doldrums during the early phases of Willison's editorship were long gone. The *Globe* had become immensely popular in Toronto and the Ontario communities in its circulation hinterland.

Such, however, was not the case for the federal Liberals in the province as a general election approached in the fall of 1900. Conservative propagandists attacked Laurier as "not British enough." It was charged that his government's policy on South Africa had been dictated by Israel Tarte, the minister of public works. Reports of recent purportedly anti-British statements by Tarte in France were further grist for the Tory mill. In a Paris speech in June 1900, Tarte had proclaimed the continuing "Frenchness" of French Canadians, even that they were becoming "more French" and that by their natural increase they would be one day a majority in Canada.[49] The *Mail and Empire* asked: "Is this country to remain British, is it to grow stronger and stronger under the flag; or is Mr. Tarte's hope for separation to be endorsed in this period of Imperial progress elsewhere?" The Toronto *World*'s banner for election day was ARE WE TO BE BRITISH OR ARE WE TO BE FRENCH?[50] The result in Ontario was 55 seats to 37 for the Conservatives.

This was in stark contrast to the rest of the country, where the Liberals enjoyed a victory of landslide proportions, especially in Quebec. Laurier's power base now lay firmly on his solid block of support in his home province, to a lesser extent on his "good times" appeal in the Maritimes and the West.

Before the Boer War, prosperity, and Laurier's Jubilee prestige had seemed about to guarantee a smashing Liberal triumph in Ontario, too. There even had been in November 1897 that amazing by-election win in Centre Toronto as a possible harbinger. Willison's reactions now, as a Laurier man and an imperialist, were bitter. "The vote in this province was to me painful and distressing, although I generally take defeat with a good deal of philosophy," he wrote Laurier. "I thought that Ontario had voted in blind ignorance of your work and character and I resented the verdict accordingly."

SIR JOHN'S RIGHTFUL SUCCESSOR.

SPIRIT OF SIR JOHN—My old party may have my effigy with them in this campaign, but the record and influence of my life as a statesman is with you, Sir Wilfrid.

"Sir John's Rightful Successor." (*J. W. Bengough cartoon,* Globe, *October 26, 1900, p.1*)

His resentment was directed especially at imperialist leaders such as Principal George Parkin of Upper Canada College, to whom he exploded: "I think I have done something to lead the Government in the direction of the Imperial ideal. My only reward was to fight in Ontario the most disastrous battle that the Liberal party ever fought." He argued that Laurier had done "great things" for imperial unity — the British preference and the sending of the contingents in particular — which had threatened to endanger his position in Quebec. Yet, he complained to Parkin, most Ontario imperialists had in 1900 "climbed on Conservative platforms and denounced Sir Wilfrid Laurier for not having moved fast enough." He was "more than willing to work with the Imperialists," he affirmed. "I am not willing to be dragged at the wheels of their chariot as a spectacle for my political opponents. If we are to do the work of the Imperialists they must show some gratitude and take some risks...."[51]

The events of 1899–1900 demonstrated powerfully to Willison that his long crusade for Laurier in Ontario was farther away from success than it had been since the early 1890s. And he now could see just how complicated and difficult a task it would be to bring a Liberal government no longer dependent on Ontario to an imperialist position peculiarly popular there. For the sake of both his party and imperialism, it was to be hoped that the next few years would be quiet as far as any fresh imperialist crises were concerned.

However, Willison was by now too sincere and committed an imperialist to avoid altogether participating in the inevitable ongoing debate about the future of the Empire and Canada's role in it which the events and emotional currents of recent years had engendered. When the contingents went off to South Africa, the *Globe* had commented that "Canada has made a new departure, and has taken a new position in the councils of the British nation...." That meant that "we share the responsibility, and we cannot shift that responsibility upon any British statesman...."[52]

But how could this sharing be brought about? If there were to be some federal parliament of the Empire, of what importance would a small Canadian minority be? In the foreign policy and defence establishments, how could Canada effectively participate in the making of policy?

"For the present," the *Globe* remarked in March 1901, "we see nothing that can be done except to await events, and act upon the circumstances as they arise; in fact, do just as we have been doing."[53] Yet it also advanced on occasion vague ideas about the Empire's future — such as that it was "a league in which, when common action is called for, the Parliaments of the various communities will deal with the matter." As for increasing military expenditures and moving into naval activities, it was reluctant to see much done for the time being, beyond putting Canada "in a thoroughly self-respecting position" concerning "the defence of Canadian and British interests in this part of the world." Mainly, Canada should concentrate on domestic growth which "will give us the strength for war if war should be forced upon us." Commenting on statements by Reverend Armstrong Black that Canada would never take its true position as a nation without a "baptism of blood," the *Globe* stressed that it was "entirely opposed to the idea of setting up military glory as an ideal for the nation."[54]

On economic aspects of the Anglo-Canadian relationship, the *Globe* was much more specific. When Joseph Chamberlain, the

British Colonial Secretary, called in April 1900 for progress towards "an Imperial Zollverein in which there would be free trade between the portions of the Empire and duties as against strangers," the paper asked: "Is Great Britain ready for protection? Are we ready for free trade? ... Such a scheme would involve 'fiscal revolution' in Britain and could hardly be agreed to by maturing industrial societies like Canada and Australia, until their populations had enormously increased." It praised the Laurier government for having done "what could be done without waiting for revolutions" — by giving British imports a "substantial preference."

Canadians were advised to concentrate on improving their export products, transportation, waterways, and harbours in order to be well positioned to "take advantage of our position in the empire, and of any measure for the advancement of Imperial trade that the British Government may adopt. But our duty and our business lie close at hand."[55]

Late in June 1902, a Colonial Conference met in London, in conjunction with the coronation of King Edward VII. Leading imperialists throughout the British world looked to the meeting to provide, in the words of George Parkin, the "turning point" for the Empire.[56] Joseph Chamberlain convened the delegates with the message that the "weary Titan staggers under the too vast orb of its fate," and invited the self-governing colonies, now that they were "rich and powerful," to take a "proportionate share of the burdens of the Empire." He favoured a Council of the Empire and evolution towards Empire free trade. The Admiralty and the War Office called for colonial contributions to the Royal Navy and an imperial army.[57] These positions were hardly surprising to Laurier or Willison, and they pretty much matched Canadian imperialists' objectives, as set forth in the speeches and writings of men like Principal Parkin and Colonel Denison.

Willison had shared a Hamilton platform with Parkin on St. George's Day that April. Parkin had urged more or less the Chamberlain program, and had maintained that Laurier, even though he had "led this country a long way on the lines of Imperialism," had become "frightened and afraid as to the Quebec vote." He had argued that the prime minister "could bring the French Canadians into a proper way of thinking on the matter if he would boldly determine to do so."

Willison, for his part, had cautioned his audience that "we should proceed slowly and cautiously in any project for the imposition of new duties on the colonies or new obligations on the mother country.... Imperial consolidation went hand in hand with colonial self-government."[58] He then went on to write Colonel Denison privately to say he thought Parkin was acting "unwisely" in contending that Laurier was failing to move Canada towards imperial unity because he was prisoner of the Quebec vote. Editorially the *Globe* observed: "It is only a united Canada that can contribute effectively to the maintenance of a united empire."

Parkin commented to Denison on Willison's view: "As a matter of historical experience we must expect this. Some men are naturally built to drive the wheel forward; nature intended others to act as a drag." Arthur Colquhoun remarked to Denison: "The root of the trouble is Laurier and his absurd dread of 'militaryism' and the *Globe* is trying its best, as a loyal friend and supporter, to cover his retreat and confuse the issue."[59]

There was no question that Laurier shrank from major Canadian activity in military or naval defence. That would be, he told Willison shortly before the Colonial Conference convened, "absolutely repugnant to the convictions of all my life...." Willison, as the events of 1899–1900 had shown, was not so appalled. In February 1902 he had conceded to Denison, after the colonel had detailed to him the vulnerable military and economic positions of the British nations: "The facts presented certainly call for a very serious consideration." Shortly afterwards the *Globe* set forth editorially a frank statement on the defence aspect of imperial relations:

> Canada is growing wealthier, and it is becoming clearer that it ought not to depend on any other set of taxpayers for protection. That is not jingoism, but self-respect and fair play. At the same time, it is unreasonable to expect the Canadian people at once to solve the problems which confront them. The country is in a state of transition. It is passing from the state of sonship to that of brotherhood, and it is natural to expect some delay and hesitation in readjusting the conditions.[60]

In one area of imperial policy, the prime minister and his chief journalistic supporter in English Canada were fully together: Chamberlain, Parkin, and Denison were utterly on the wrong track with their talk of imperial free trade. Laurier told Premier Ross of Ontario that he doubted Chamberlain could shift the great mass of British voters toward duties, and therefore higher prices, for non-Empire imports. And he was certain that Canadians remained determined to keep British manufacturers from thwarting Canadian ambitions toward industrial maturity. Willison backed this view, telling the prime minister that "we could not accept any material reduction of the present duties against the Old Country." He confronted Parkin with the charge that Canadian imperialists were not frank with the public in recognizing Canadian national interests — "yet all these men who know the facts conceal and evade, and allow Sir Wilfrid Laurier to be denounced for rejecting something that Canada could not accept...."[61]

Willison's chief fear about the Conference was, he explained to Laurier, that "you will reject preferential trade if offered on the basis of a contribution to defence, in order to conciliate Quebec." This "would enable the Conservative politicians to appeal to English and Protestant feeling against Quebec, and I only write this note in order to emphasize the importance of doing everything possible to avert such an issue."[62] He remembered the 1900 election all too painfully.

The fears proved groundless. Chamberlain could not deliver serious alterations in the British tariff. Also, with the Boer War over and Canadian, Australian, Cape Colony, and other colonial leaders anxious to concentrate on economic rather than military objectives, the projects from the Admiralty and the War Office did not seem urgent priorities. Laurier easily side-stepped Chamberlain's imperial council proposal with his preference for continued — but more frequent — prime ministers' conferences. He also promised local militia improvement and the establishment in due course of local naval forces.[63]

The *Globe* was delighted and relieved. It noted that it had been Britain, not Canada, which had stymied progress on the trade front, proving that a comprehensive deal "is not the easy thing that the Conservatives imagined." On defence it observed that there was a "general desire that Canada shall do its fair share of the duty of defence, and that desire was voiced by the Ministers at the Conference. There is an equally general desire that not one iota of the right of self-government shall be relinquished or even placed in the slightest peril."

The Canadian imperialists did not criticize Laurier at this point, even Colonel Denison conceding that he had made every effort he could on the economic front, and agreeing that it would in current circumstances be "inadvisable for Canada to be asked to spend money on defence in any other way than under the direction of our Government, and by the hands of our own officers." But he warned that if Laurier's promises in London about strengthening the militia and beginning to move into naval defence proved "merely talk, and no direct improvement and advance is made in our defence, then naturally one would feel dissatisfied."[64] For the time being, as he explained to Joseph Chamberlain early the next year, while he felt like "starting a regular campaign" to force progress in defence, "the difficulty is it would hurt Laurier in whom we base our greatest hopes of getting the French to join us in a proper scheme of Imperial defence. They have to be educated and a French Canadian alone can do it."[65]

Denison very soon would come to feel that Laurier could not be brought to champion significant defence improvements. Eventually, Willison would too. The key to the editor's arriving at that point would be what the *Globe* described as "days of stress and storm" threatening both Britain and Canada, when inevitably there would be a new sense of urgency in both countries about responding to defence and foreign policy concerns.[66] But in 1902, a Liberal who was a nationalist and an imperialist comfortably could remain all three. Meanwhile, Canada's extraordinary economic growth as well as his own and the *Globe*'s amazing success continued to build.

VII

Toward Independent Journalism, 1896–1902

"WHEN THE LIBERAL PARTY CAME INTO OFFICE IN 1896 I WAS trusting, hopeful and enthusiastic," Willison would remember. Into his rejoicing and satisfaction, however, came the sobering reminder from Premier Hardy of Ontario that he was now the foremost publicist for *two* Liberal governments. "Your position is a very delicate one and its importance cannot be overrated."[1] The next six years underlined his exceptional importance within his party and as Canada's leading editor. They also witnessed his steadily increasing alienation from the personal frustrations of party journalism and of political partisanship itself.

An early jolt to his pride came with his failure to convince Laurier to appoint Robert Jaffray, the *Globe*'s president, to the Senate. Willison complained to Laurier that this was "humiliating" for the *Globe*, but even worse was the "utterly distasteful" fact that "under the circumstances of my relationship to the applicant I must continue to appear as a lobbyist."[2] As it happened, George Cox, another member of the *Globe* directorate, got the senatorship. Very soon it became clear that he and Jaffray were managing to get a great deal more from the new Liberal government, much to Willison's even greater distaste and personal embarrassment.

The beginnings were innocent enough. Since the early 1890s, Willison had been fascinated by transportation issues. He had proposed dealing with the CPR over its interest in winning fast Atlantic steamship rights in exchange for removal of its exemption from rate regulation in the West. These stands had not endeared him to inveterate anti-CPR Liberals, but they had showed a consistent pragmatism in his transportation development ideas. One of his specific proposals in 1895 had been that the federal government take advantage of the CPR's interest in building a railway spur from its main line into the Kootenay coal region of southeastern B.C. He had argued that any such line, vital to the development of the region, inevitably would have to link up with either the CPR or the American Great Northern. On nationalist grounds he had preferred the CPR, if a deal could be made whereby it surrendered some of its charter freedom from rate control on its main transcontinental line. Even before the change in government in Ottawa, Laurier and President Van Horne of the CPR had expressed interest in the Willison proposals.[3]

On the very day the Liberals took office, the *Globe* renewed its campaign for a Crow's Nest Pass deal. A few weeks later, a special correspondent, T.C. Irving, was sent to the Kootenays after President Jaffray worked out, as he explained to Willison, "a fair division of the expenses" with the CPR.[4] Irving reported back in glowing terms of potentially $40 million in mining output from the area and that in twenty-five years there could be a million miners and their families there. He also warned of American ambitions to control the region and its profits.[5] Negotiations proceeded in Ottawa between the government and the CPR, and the *Globe* called in November for federal aid to the CPR for a Crow's Nest Pass line in return for "real and effective control of operations on that line and on the Corporation's main transcontinental line through the west."[6]

Unhappily for Willison and the *Globe*, the Crow's Nest Pass question did not involve merely a railway — fabulously lucrative concessions in coal lands and construction contracts were also at stake. In 1888, British Columbia had chartered the B.C. Southern Railway to build a line into the area; and two years later the province had added an inducement of 65 million acres of land. In late 1896, a Toronto syndicate led by S.H. Janes purchased an option on the B.C. Southern and proposed to sell this to the CPR for $100,000 and a contract for construction of the Crow's Nest Pass project, begging Laurier for "immediate" action on federal aid.[7] As Ottawa negotiations lagged, the Janes syndicate lost its B.C. Southern option to another Toronto-based group, and in mid-January the Conservative Manitoba *Free Press* revealed some interesting news about the new group:

> Mr. Robert Jaffray, Managing Director of The Globe and Senator Cox, pecuniarily interested in The Globe, are at the head of a syndicate that have taken over the charter of the British Columbia Southern Railway, which controls several million acres of land, including the coal deposits in the Crow's Nest Pass, and are now negotiating with the Government for construction of the road. Hereafter when the Toronto organ takes a pronounced attitude on any public matter involving Government favors, it would be well to regard it with an amount of skepticism appropriate to their value.[8]

The *Globe* sputtered that Jaffray and Cox had not taken over the B.C. Southern charter, but merely "a small portion of the coal lands."[9]

There was immediate and intense concern in Liberal circles. The Victoria *Times* reported "virtually unanimous" opinion in the West for a government-owned line into the Kootenays. John Shields of Toronto warned the prime minister that "sinister and dangerous influences in your Cabinet and out of it" were intriguing with the CPR. Richard Armstrong of Confederation Life told Laurier that it had become "common street gossip that the CPR had bought up a large number of the leaders of your party for cash, interests in mines, lands etc.... and the betting is that it is only a matter of days when you will succumb."

Liberal stalwart Peter Ryan complained bitterly to his leader that Robert Jaffray's enrichment would be "at the expense of my party's life and honour." Laurier responded that "we have no engagement of any kind. The articles of 'The Globe' reflect the opinions of the 'Globe' people alone." The Conservative press intensified its attacks, with the Toronto *World* charging on February 27 that Jaffray and Cox had sold their option on the B.C. Southern to the CPR and were using their *Globe* and

Liberal connections to force both the railway and the government to grant them "extravagant and criminal concessions."[10]

Willison was heartsick. He assured Clifford Sifton, the minister of the interior, that he had been "wholly ignorant" of the Jaffray coal mine interests when he had launched his Crow's Nest campaign. When he had found out the truth, he added, he had felt barred from proposing a government road to carry Jaffray's coal to market. "As you know," he continued, "from the first my opinion was that the C.P.R. should build this extension on condition of surrender of monopoly privileges and reduction of rates on certain through staples...." Not until the *World*'s attack, he avowed, had he known anything of the sale of the B.C. Southern charter to the CPR by Jaffray and Cox. A reversal of editorial policy at that point, he had decided, would have been too humiliating. "I had then to go on and make the very best fight I could in order that public opinion in Ontario might not be turned overwhelmingly against the *Globe*," he explained. "I do not like the position, but what would you have done under the circumstances?" Sifton agreed that "our friends ... have put you in a very difficult position, and it will be a great triumph for your skill and capacity if you succeed in getting through all right."[11]

Willison's humiliation was far from over. Early in April, William McInnes, a young Liberal MP from Nanaimo, B.C., charged in the House of Commons that the *Globe*'s Crow's Nest policy had been "characterized by cant and deception" aimed at the gift of the route to "their masters," the CPR. When the *Globe* exploded editorially that McInnes was "a liar and a slanderer," Laurier expressed his "shock" to Willison; and McInnes retorted that it was impossible not to believe that the paper had engaged in "deception and fraud." He was amused that Willison "would have us believe that he is immaculate in his sanctum.... No business is transacted in that way. There is not a newspaper in the country that would be worked that way. We all know that the man who pays the piper can select the tune."[12]

Hector Charlesworth was the editor's close friend and would recall of this time: "Willison found himself in the position of a man regarded by intimates as one who had been a stool pigeon, and by those less friendly as a crafty manipulator of graft." Charlesworth believed that it was at this time his friend first began to conceive the idea to "rid himself forever of the yoke of party journalism."[13]

The immediate need was to shore up his reputation. Laurier helped, inviting him to Ottawa to brief Liberal caucus members on the full sweep of his transportation views. Then in May he summed them up in a lengthy published pamphlet, *The Railway Question in Canada*. It offered a clear and detailed argument for hard, pragmatic bargaining between governments and railways to help to win rate regulation and establish effective railway commission oversight in return for selective concessions. The special case of the CPR, with the challenge of its existing chartered freedom from rate control, was stressed.[14] Stewart Lyon of the *Globe*'s Ottawa bureau soon reported back: "Your position is becoming more generally understood all the time." Joe Atkinson of the Montreal *Herald* wrote Willison that the pamphlet was "the first attempt ... to deal comprehensively and upon basic principles with the problem in Canada." Premier Hardy congratulated him on "a very timely production," and Edmund Walker of the Bank of Commerce hailed "a remarkably fair and most admirable statement of a very complicated and difficult question."[15]

On June 11, the government unveiled its Crow's Nest Railway plan, after agreement with the CPR. The corporation would get a subsidy of $11,000 per mile, but the completed line would be subject to federal rate and service regulation. On the CPR main line, eastbound rates on the shipment of wheat and flour to Fort William on Lake Superior were reduced substantially, as were westbound commodities of crucial importance to beginning settlers. Finally, the CPR would hand over to the federal government 50,000 acres of such coal lands as it received from B.C. under the B.C. Southern Charter. The package was remarkably similar to what Willison had been calling for, except for the failure to establish a railway commission or re-negotiate an end to the CPR's general freedom from rate regulation. As well, the special provisions about the coal lands undercut some of the charges of the *Globe*'s critics. A.G. Blair, the minister of railways and canals, stressed that it was the "somewhat inconsiderate legislation" on the B.C. Southern franchise that had raised questions about a coal lands monopoly and that federal possession of the lands would prevent that and control prices.[16]

Willison had cause to be delighted with the broad thrust of the agreement but knew that he very much needed not to be seen as automatically "pro-CPR." In April 1898, the *Globe* warned that the government should not give in to CPR pressure against application by the Corbin interests in the U.S. to build the Kettle River Valley Railway into the Kootenays. When the House of Commons, in a free vote, turned down the Corbin proposal, with some Liberal ministers and MPs siding with the majority, the *Globe* acidly observed that "the politicians in Ottawa" were "dominated" by the CPR. Laurier bluntly warned him to back off, and Clifford Sifton joined him in expressing annoyance. Willison stuck to his position, explaining to Sifton that "from time to time causes of friction must arise between Governments and friendly papers except the friendly paper is to be a mere echo and therefore without either character or influence."[17]

But the *Globe* angered no Liberals when it persistently attacked the CPR's historic and continuing closeness to the Conservative party. It noted that the Tories had supported even more favourable terms for the CPR on the Crow's Nest Pass line and had been a solid chief voting block against the Corbin application. "All along the line a determined effort is being made to drag the CPR back into politics," the paper charged in November 1898, "to make it the ally of the Conservative party, and to have its influence thrown against the Liberal candidates in the constituencies."[18] When President Van Horne of the CPR indignantly denied the charges, Willison responded to him that "a contingent" of Tory politicians and newspapers "hound the Liberal Press and the Liberal Government as the bond-slaves of the Canadian Pacific" while the rest "stand by the Canadian Pacific as their special friends and champions."[19] When Van Horne explained to him that some "smaller-minded" Conservatives were upset with the railway for its necessary dealings with the Liberal government, Willison responded candidly:

> I fear the position in politics of the CPR at this moment is very like the position of the Globe; we are under fire from both sides and are perhaps unlikely to get justice when we thoroughly deserve it…. I have a very strong opinion that a paper which is believed to be a mere organ of a corporation is useless to itself, useless to the country, and trebly useless to the corporation for whose defence it is supposed to exist. On great questions of national policy on which the country and the CPR must

stand together, I have little fear that you will have occasion to find fault with the Globe's policy; and I hope it is now so manifest that the Globe is not a mere creature of the CPR that it will be able to face the corporation cry to some purpose when the road really needs defence at the hands of the Canadian press.[20]

Far more important for Willison than mere CPR questions, however, were what he saw as the great pending national issues of this period of extraordinary railway development. He wanted that development properly regulated, through a federal commission. He had been stressing that objective for some time, but the prime minister now openly disagreed, describing the idea as "premature." Andrew Blair, the minister of railways, warned that it would incur the political hostility of both the CPR and the Grand Trunk.[21] Another of Willison's key proposals was that the government drop the old Tory policy of direct cash subsidies for railway construction and replace them with offering to guarantee bond interest. Clifford Sifton at once warned him that an end to subsidies would be politically suicidal.[22] It seemed that no new railway ideas were wanted by his Liberal friends in Ottawa. Four years later, bond interest guarantee would be a key component in their new national transcontinental project. By then, of course, it was their idea. Liberal editors, like Conservative ones, were expected to popularize ideas, not propose them.

They also were expected to be slavish propagandists during election campaigns. In the March 1898 provincial contest, the governing Liberals, their hold on power at last beginning to slip away, needed all the help they could get. A colourless Premier Arthur Hardy was opposed by the vigorous Conservative leader, James Whitney, who charged the Liberals with waste, graft, favouritism in the civil service, allowing the school system to decay, and electoral corruption. The Globe, now a modern big-city newspaper with a mass circulation, much of it among non-Liberals, gave Whitney's impressive campaign pretty much factual coverage. Even before the election fight began, Premier Hardy remarked to a federal minister that Willison was "drifting as steadily as a man can to a position of perfect independence" and that he cared "a good deal more for what he calls the management of the Globe than he does for the party." Now, at the height of the battle, he snapped to Willison: "Bite someone or something occasionally just to show that you want to hurt somebody now and then. While we are all personally abused you scarcely even criticize the enemy." Willison would record: "I was concerned only for The Globe's reputation as a newspaper and could not be convinced that the speeches of the Conservative leader should be ignored." The provincial Liberals survived in government for the time being, but were severely weakened.[23]

There would not be a federal election for some time, but opportunities and occasions for Willison's collisions with his political "masters" in Ottawa abounded. In March 1898, Postmaster-General William Mulock imposed a new higher rate on the mailing of newspapers outside a ten-mile limit. Willison exploded to the prime minister that this was "absolutely outrageous" treatment of the *Globe* and the few other papers "as have enterprise enough to get a general circulation...." Laurier curtly commanded him to back off: "Beware of a quarrel with Mulock, because then you quarrel with us." Willison lashed back at what he told Laurier was his "ungenerous" tone, and asked: "Why should we be especially punished because a Liberal government obtained power in Canada?" The prime minister apologized and courteously invited him to Ottawa for a calming chat. The new postal rates were not changed, however.[24]

In January 1899 a fresh quarrel developed — over federal Liberal policy on the Senate. Willison had favoured abolition of the upper house ever since his days in the Toronto Young Men's Liberal Club. Now Prime Minister Laurier's approach to "reforming" the Senate was to Liberalize it. The *Globe* denounced the Senate's "uselessness," its "obstructive power" and the "essentially vicious character of ... the selection by the dominant party of the day." Laurier's only Senate reform proposal was for resolution of conflicts between the House of Commons and the Senate by a joint vote. He argued that in "a country of different elements and interests," an upper house was a "necessary safeguard." He saw no need to seek change in either the method of Senators' appointments or their veto. He conceded to Willison that this was "too mild for your radical views, but we have done enough for the time being...." The *Globe* then printed an editorial a day against the Senate over the next two weeks. There was faint praise for Laurier's idea as an improvement, but, as Willison explained to his leader, the *Globe*'s traditional abolitionist policy could not be abandoned without damage to its reputation and self-respect. He concluded:

> I still think, although I know you do not agree with me, that for the *Globe* to be a mere echo of the Government on every question makes the paper of little use to the government and gives it little influence with the people when the government really needs effective newspaper support.

As the *Globe* continued its anti-Senate campaign, the Tory *Mail and Empire* amusedly commented that its Liberal rival was putting on "an ungenerous exhibition ... when you bear in mind the value of coal lands."[25]

Election scandals — many involving Liberals — were plentiful in 1899 at both the federal and provincial levels. Early that year the provincial Liberals had won a by-election, but in the summer court hearings confirmed voting malpractices, and the seat was vacated. The *Globe* did not hesitate to condemn the "intolerable nuisance" of such evils and called for "the most severe and effective" laws to prevent them. Then in July came charges of Liberal illegalities in two Ontario federal constituencies. The *Globe* approved when Laurier referred the charges to the Commons Committee on Privileges and Elections. But when the testimony before the Committee's hearings turned out to be very embarrassing for the Liberals, the paper abandoned any kind of pro-Liberal fight. Bogus ballots, the stuffing of ballot boxes, and the forging of election officials' signatures had come to light, and, even before the final report was issued, the *Globe* coldly observed that such perpetrators "will not infest the Liberal camp if it is plainly shown they are not wanted." It stressed that "the duty of finding a remedy rests mainly with the Liberal party which now holds power both in Ottawa and in Toronto."[26]

Partisan Liberals were furious. Judge B. Russell stormed to Willison: "If you did have to anticipate the verdict the very least you might have done is help your friends instead of playing into the hands of the enemy." Laurier expressed his fury that Willison had not consulted him about the editorial. Roden Kingsmill, the *Globe*'s Ottawa bureau chief in Ottawa, reported that the Liberal caucus "have varying degrees of indignation. The smaller the man the madder he is…. Sifton wants to know how the party is going to get along without the help of the newspapers." However, a fellow Liberal editor, R.L. Richardson of the Winnipeg *Tribune*, assured him that "the reputation of the Globe and your own reputation are of much more value to yourself and the country than the triumph of any political party by methods which we all cursed so vigorously in days gone bye…."[27]

Another of Willison's problems in these years involved the *Globe's* reporters in the press gallery in Ottawa. Under the former Conservative regime, they had scrambled unrestrainedly after stories. Now such behaviour could be politically embarrassing. When Willison sent George Simpson to Ottawa, he asked Clifford Sifton to "spend a little time with him so that he may start right not only as the *Globe's* news correspondent, but as the practical exponent of the Government's policy…." Such harmony proved difficult to maintain. In the spring of 1899 Willison learned some Liberal MPs were claiming that Roden Kingsmill, Simpson's successor, was a Tory. Sifton explained that Kingsmill was displaying "a particularly loving disposition toward the Tory reporters." Willison may have remembered his own cross-party friendships in his press gallery days when he kept Kingsmill in Ottawa another year, dismissing the criticism contemptuously as being from disappointed applicants for his post.[28]

Clearly all was not now well with the news relationship between the Laurier government and the *Globe*. In September 1899, Willison was furious to learn of a new cabinet appointment from Ontario only through leaks to other Toronto papers. He complained to Sifton: "Speaking as a journalist I cannot tell you how much I long for the old days of opposition." Days later, he was stunned to discover details of a Canadian military contingent for South Africa in the *Canadian Military Gazette*. The *Globe* had been told nothing. Willison asked Sifton: "Would it not be far better that the pretence of close relations between the Globe and the Government should cease and that in all those matters we should become a free lance like our contemporaries…? The present situation is intolerable."[29]

He was increasingly of the view that disharmony between government and the press was normal, even healthy. In November 1899, he spoke to the U of T Political Science Club about journalism and where it should be going. Journalists, he contended, should be "trained thinkers," preferably with university degrees, able to produce "a creditable literary product" and be "a sane well-balanced progressive force in public affairs." He hailed the growing influence of the American social sciences on journalism in that country and looked eagerly for a similar development in Canada. He stressed the need for the press to be in "very responsible hands." A sensational press could cause "grave national and international mischiefs." Too many Canadian newspapermen still were "more ready to misrepresent an opponent than to meet his argument, more ready to appeal to the meaner prejudices than to the higher sentiment of the community, more ready to run at the heels of popular clamor than to stand steadfast for the principles and policies which one's inner conviction and sober judgment approve." He did not think that party affiliation for the press needed to be more than "a minor evil. There is an independence within the party organization which largely influences party policy." He claimed that the party system gave to "the radical and progressive elements of the community" a disproportionate influence because often it was "easier to move the politician ... than the great inert masses of the people."

A "more ominous and more dangerous" influence on newspapers was "the growing power of corporations and ... great aggregations of capital in few hands." This could get in the way of the press's "mission" to serve "the plain unorganized and unsubsidized people." However, he claimed, there was "as yet no reason to conclude" that the corporations dominated press or public life. He added an allusion to his and the *Globe*'s recent bitter experiences:

> At least this is true, that no public journal can be influential as the mere mouthpiece of a corporation, and perhaps we could have no better evidence of this than the efforts of party papers ... to convict public men and public journals of compromising relations with corporations which do not exist in fact.

At its best, he concluded, the press should be "necessarily and legitimately an agitator, very often a voice crying in the wilderness; always, if it performs its true functions, seeking to better social and material conditions." It should run in advance of governments to "develop public opinion, to liberalize and energize the social and industrial forces, to utter the voice of the people ... always in the serene confidence that good will come out of free discussion."[30]

Willison's closest friends would have had reason to be puzzled by the optimistic thrust of his speech. The party system restrained freedom of expression — *but* it had positive values which were overriding. The influence of corporations on politics and the press was dangerous — *but* little of it existed in Canada. Given Willison's recent frustrating experiences with pressures from both politicians and plutocrats, he must have seemed to confidantes to be less than candid.

At just this time, in November 1899, he was seeing more clearly than ever how negatively his approach to political journalism was viewed by powerful elements in the Liberal party. A group of Liberals were undertaking to purchase the Toronto *Star* as an evening party journal. Laurier appears to have launched the operation; and Senator George Cox, Postmaster-General William Mulock and several other prominent Toronto Liberals provided the backing. Cox and Mulock were both shareholders in the *Globe*. A leading candidate for the editorship of a Liberal *Star* was Joseph Atkinson, late of the *Globe*, then the Montreal *Herald*. Willison enthusiastically supported his protégé. Atkinson eventually secured the position but only after assuring himself broad editorial freedom — something opposed by Mulock among others. At one point in the negotiations Atkinson wrote Laurier:

> I understand the motive of Mr. Mulock is to have not only an evening Liberal paper, but one that will be more 'ardent' and reliable than the Globe in the support it gives the party.... A newspaper is a good ally but soon becomes useless as the subservient organ of a party.[31]

Willison decided that early in the new year of 1900 he would make it clearer than ever that his *Globe* most definitely was no "subservient organ." On January 9, the paper carried a detailed and elaborate "Programme for Parliament." In addition to a call for full payment by Canada of the contingents of troops sent to South Africa, and "some more definite determination of our responsibility for the defence of the empire," there were eight other points, almost all reiterations of earlier editorial opinions. The different policies now were linked together, however, in what amounted to a manifesto for *Globe* liberalism. Number (2) was a call for a federal railway commission. Number (3) referred to "such dealing with the Senate as will re-establish government by the people," with perhaps a national plebiscite on any constitutional amendment. Number (4) was a call for "resumption" by the federal government, "or for a more satisfactory allotment," of the CPR's granted lands in the West that had not yet been taken up, "and the initiation of measures to make the lands granted to the railways subject to taxation…." Number (5) touched on the need to re-organize the Canadian High Commission in Britain on a more effective commercial basis. Number (6) called for a federal insolvency and bankruptcy law. Number (7) called for provisions in future railway subsidies for eventual repayment, with outright grants of money or land for colonization lines only. Number (8) called for a "thoroughly non-partisan civil service." And Number (9) was a plea for redistribution of federal constituencies by Superior Court judges.

Numbers (2) and (4) had been pushed by the *Globe* since the early days of the Laurier government. Number (3) represented, even with the mention of the referendum, a far more moderate stand on the Senate than the abolitionism of the previous year. Numbers (5) and (6) had been proposed in Willison's published letters from England in 1897. Number (9) was essentially what he had suggested to Laurier in May 1899 — in response to which the prime minister had remarked that he appreciated "the full force of your remarks." Only number (8) was a new departure; even here, however, the *Globe*'s antipathy to partisanship and patronage in the public service was clearly on record. In sum, the *Globe*'s "Programme" was merely a composite of its major editorial proposals of recent years.

Laurier was not amused. He at once wrote Willison to say that the "Programme" was "of such advanced radicalism that I am at a loss to realise why such a powerful paper as the Globe should further it & still less do I realise that you should have brought such an amount of timber to us as a government. Many articles there are in that programme which cannot be touched for 25 years." Also, he "would have expected that as a personal friend you would have talked this whole matter with me before putting it so prominently before us." Probably Laurier's attitude was all too familiar to Willison. "As far back as 1897," he would recall, "he said to me 'I wish the Globe would stop urging reforms. Reforms are for Oppositions. It is the business of Governments to stay in office.'"[32]

"I think you take our little programme ... too seriously," Willison replied. There was "nothing in it that we have not advocated over and over again, in a score of articles, for the last ten years." He did not expect immediate implementation, "but it does seem to me to be a programme that ought to be carried out." On the matter of personal friendship:

> ....I fancy there has never been a time when the Globe's friendship or my own was seriously needed that they were not very much at and in your service. That is a point which I refuse to admit is in issue at all. So far as I am concerned I stand where I have always stood your devoted personal friend and the devoted friend of the government. Of course I have never admitted that this should mean that the Globe should never seem to go a step in advance, and should never offer a criticism of any government measure. Such a paper I conceive would be useless to the government and a curse to the community. There is no point at which I fear danger to the government except that of railway subsidies. Believe me, however, that the subsidies of last session are extremely distasteful to our people, and even your own great personal popularity, backed by a score of Globes, could not save the government in this province if another vote of similar dimension were made. This is not due to any exaggerated alarm on my part but to expressions of opinion which I get from all over the country.

Laurier conceded that he really had "no serious objection" to the programme, except on the issue of payment for the Canadians in South Africa, but he still regretted that the *Globe* had given such strong publicity to "a series of reforms which it is impossible to take up and on which it would be impossible to unite the party."[33]

It was increasingly evident that Willison's position in Canadian affairs was one of enormous prestige, beyond that of a mere servant or publicist for his party or any of its leaders. In March 1900, he was elected president of the Canadian Press Association. Professor G.C. Workman of Toronto congratulated him for "promoting independent and elevated journalism throughout our country." Professor F.H. Wallace of Victoria College praised the "fair, decent gentlemanly tone" he saw in the *Globe*. "It is refreshing to read a paper which does not blackguard its opponents nor lie on behalf of its friends. The judicial tone, the absence of sensationalism, the broad sympathies of your management are most agreeable to me. Long may 'The Globe' prosper in its effort to elevate Canadian journalism."

Then in May, on the motion of the poets Wilfred Campbell and Duncan Campbell Scott, the philosopher William Clark, and the historian John George Bourinot, Willison was elected a Fellow of the Royal Society of Canada. Bourinot explained to him that the choice was "in recognition of your contributions to economic science, your efforts to elevate journalism and your sympathetic encouragement in your journal to science and letters in the Dominion."

"Your election was a special one," wrote Wilfred Campbell, "and you owe it to no one, but to your own ability as a writer, and to your distinguished services to journalism." Bourinot completed his explanation of the Society's action with the observation that "I & others have felt that Journalism should be represented in the Society & your claim to be that representative was so superior to that of all others in this country that you were enthusiastically elected…. You will find it very pleasant to meet so many interesting people — not politicians."[34]

For much of the rest of that year Willison can have had little time for anyone but politicians. A federal general election was held in November, and through many months previous to it, the war for votes got hotter and hotter. As the year wore on, the "Programme for Parliament" was replaced by attacks on the Tories. Nevertheless, the *Globe's* degree of partisanship often proved not shrill enough for many Liberal partisans. Willison's explicit instructions to his parliamentary reporters were not in line with the expectations of many party MPs. Robert Dunbar, a *Globe* Ottawa staffer, acknowledged in March 1900 in a letter back to Willison that "we are as far as possible to give as much space per day to the Conservatives as to the Liberals and to be absolutely impartial in our manner of expressing what the members say...." He added that Liberal MPs were complaining bitterly that they "did not get a fair shake in the Globe." MPs also denounced Roden Kingsmill for being far too generous in his reporting on the tribute Sir Charles Tupper, the Conservative leader, paid to Canadian troops in South Africa. By the summer, Kingsmill was gone, sacrificed to the party's zealots.[35]

Shortly before the federal election, Premier George Ross of Ontario, Arthur Hardy's successor, warned Laurier that "only the most strenuous efforts" in the province could hold the Liberals' strength there. As the campaign began, he excitedly wrote Willison: "What has become of your rapier? ... You are letting the enemy off far too lightly." Willison tried to oblige with searing editorial attacks on Tupper and the Tories as weak and reactionary.[36] But the Globe's campaign news reporting remained Willison-style. Many Liberals were furious. J. Hunter of Toronto wrote Willison in disgust at the "flaming headlines, flash light photos" and columns of detail "heralding the triumphant tour of Sir Charles Tupper." W.C. Black, Liberal MP for Paisley, bitterly denounced the "glaring headlines" about Tupper. "Liberals should not be saturated with this stuff," he raged to Willison. "Lots of people go with the hurrah and we want the hurrah on our side, now. Will you be good?"[37]

That very morning the Globe had carried a remarkably fair and exhaustive report of Sir Charles Tupper's Toronto rally of the night before. It had been, the paper commented, "a splendid demonstration" and a "great success in every way." Perhaps mindful of complaints such as had come from Hunter and Black, the Globe made sure when Laurier's own Toronto visit took place that it pulled out all the stops on superlatives about the success of the three "gigantic meetings," the "royal honours to Laurier" and the "prodigious demonstration" of Torontonians "in their thousands" along his route. The prime minister's main address was described as "magnificent," those of his lieutenants merely "splendid."[38]

That surely was pro-Liberal enough for any party enthusiast. But Willison refused to go beyond positive boosting of his own party to vicious attacks on their opponents. He must have been sorely tempted when the Tories printed a facsimile of the Globe with the normal Junius masthead quotation ("The Subject who is truly loyal to the Chief Magistrate will neither advise nor consent to arbitrary measures") altered to read: "The Subject who is truly loyal to the Grit Party will get his coal lands at remarkably reasonable rates." As for the openly biased anti-Liberal news coverage and inflammatory editorials of the Tory *Mail and Empire*, the *Globe* denounced "journalism that has lost its conscience." In contrast, its own final editorial appeal of the campaign was devoted to outline an appropriate agenda for a progressive re-elected Liberal government and a clear testament for Willison Liberalism:

> ... We desire to escape here those industrial conditions which breed labour wars and agrarian riots in other lands. We want to perpetuate here government by the people and for the people, and not government by plutocrats for plutocrats. We want government by a responsible House of Commons elected by a free people, and not government by an autocratic Executive or an irresponsible Senate. We want laws to protect labour, and not laws to facilitate industrial combinations. We must insist that the Government shall be a model employer, and shall lead in the movement to shorten hours of work and to maintain standard wages. We must improve and develop our channels of water communication and subject the great railway system of the country to adequate public control. We must prevent railway discrimination in favour of particular individuals or particular communities, and provide that the interests of Canadian producers and manufacturers shall not be prejudiced by preferential treatment of foreign shippers. We must sacredly respect existing contracts, but we must not consent to any extension of engagements which exempt great blocks of territory from public taxation. It is over these great issues that the battles of the future must be fought; and it is our privilege and our obligation to maintain the Liberal party as the party of the people, to keep step with the advancing tide of social reform, and to make this the model State among all the British commonwealths.[39]

As with the "Programme for Parliament" of a few months earlier, this was years in advance, in most particulars, of the policies and rhetoric of the Liberal government in Ottawa.

And, it seemed, not especially impressive to the voters in Ontario: they gave the Conservatives fifty-five seats to thirty-seven for the Liberals. Elsewhere, the government did very well and retained power by a comfortable margin. Liberal victors twitted Liberal losers. J.S. MacLean reported to Willison from Montreal that Liberals there were "sore on Ontario and think leaders and organizers no good." J. Israel Tarte complained to Willison that "your policy of constantly apologizing for the Ontario Liberal Party being associated with Quebec will never, in my humble opinion, give us any foothold in your province."[40]

Willison chafed under these attacks for a few weeks, and then exploded, telling Clifford Sifton: "Since the recent election … the Globe has been subjected to a line of criticism to which I call your attention. I write you because I think you pretty sane on most subjects." The complaint, he noted, was that the paper was "not bitter enough," that it did not "deal as savagely as it should" with Conservatives, and that it gave "too much space" to their speeches. He estimated the paper probably devoted "five columns to Liberal speakers for every column it gives to Conservative speakers," and added:

> … I think this is hardly what a newspaper ought to do. There is not another civilized country in the world where newspapers venture to discriminate in favour of one party or the other…. The idea of a great newspaper suppressing the speeches of its political opponents is to me so absurd and stupid that it is simply not worth discussion.

He praised Sifton for having risen to political prominence without personal abuse of opponents. "Is it fair," he remarked, "that I should be asked to do what the self-respecting public man will not do? Have I not the same right to respect myself and my profession as have my critics? He concluded, with bitterness and exasperation:

> Personally I resent the assumption of every Liberal politician that I am his hired man, and that he has the right

to dictate or shape my course as a journalist. I claim as much freedom as any other Liberal…. You must not think that I am a "kicker" or that I am dissatisfied with the Government. But some of our so-called friends are demanding too much. I say very frankly that I do not think they can teach me how to run a newspaper…. When I go down to Ottawa or into a private Liberal meeting these men with incredible insolence and presumption undertake to discipline me as though I were their servant. I do not want to be driven out of Liberal associations nor do I want open quarrels with Liberal politicians. I have always been willing to take kindly advice from any quarter. But I am not willing to be the football of every querulous and disgruntled Liberal in the country, many of whom feel they may attack the Globe when they cannot afford to attack the Government and one of these days I shall exhaust my vocabulary, which is not always as pacific as they may suppose, on some of these people, and shall make an occasion to fight the quarrel out in the open.[41]

Sifton delayed his reply ten days in order to "let my ideas settle a little." He did not think "the party generally" wanted savageness or bitterness from the *Globe*. "I think the general opinion is that it lacks aggressiveness, stands too much on the defensive, and in politics seems to regard everything the party does as having to be defended instead of carrying the war into Africa. I share that opinion myself…." He was quite ready to admit, nevertheless, that Willison was "the best judge" on how to conduct his paper as a business enterprise but added that "if The Globe will not be aggressive politically we must have a paper that will — hence I thought it a good move to establish The Star." He thought that in a campaign "the object of the party is to get the public mind saturated with its own views and ideas." The *Globe's* painstaking fairness, he argued, made "not the best kind of literature" for the Liberals. He thought a "great party newspaper" could "alter its tactics during an election fight, put more ginger into its fighting, rake the other side and devote its space to its own friends and when the campaign is over go back to its former style." He concluded:

> As to your personal feelings — I don't think anything could be more unfortunate for yourself or The Globe than to allow the least feeling of irritation to be apparent. You must allow for the natural feeling of irritation in the minds of a party which, so far as Ontario is concerned, suffered a reverse. You are big enough to see that we have gloriously routed our traditional enemies who are reduced to a leaderless and discomfited mob. Let us make use of our strength to build up ... our party and show a united front....[42]

Willison replied that he had "not the least fault to find with the way you put your case," but his own view had been only "very slightly modified" as a result and further argument seemed pointless. "So far as my experience has gone," he remarked, "there never was a political party that did not put the responsibility for its reverses on its newspapers."[43]

He had other problems to worry about. The *Globe*'s declared editorial enmity against "government by plutocrats for plutocrats" once more came to appear to be compromised by the private interests of Robert Jaffray and George Cox. In January 1901, the paper repeatedly expressed concern for the mining entrepreneurs in B.C. who were at the mercy of monopoly railways, principally the CPR. The paper once again stressed the need for a federal railway commission with power to control rates and prevent discrimination. President Shaughnessy of the CPR then charged publicly that behind the *Globe*'s words were arrangements with the Jaffray-Cox Crow's Nest Pass Coal Company and the American J.J. Hill's Great Northern Railway for the supplying of great quantities of coal. Shaughnessy wrote Laurier to charge that "some of the gentlemen connected with the Crow's Nest Coal Company have schemes that are inimical to this Company and through the 'Globe' they opened an attack on the Company with a view to arousing an unfriendly public sentiment so that it might strengthen their hands with your government." In mid-March, the New York *Commercial Advertiser* reported that Hill had purchased 30 percent of Crow's Nest Coal Company stock. Fears were expressed in Parliament about American takeover of B.C. coal fields, smelters, and railways. As a result, when Crow's Nest sought a federal charter for a B.C. Southern Railway, it was turned down. It did get a provincial charter, however.[44]

Once again, as in 1897, the propriety of the *Globe's* special pleading was suspect. "It does not so much matter whether things are true or not," observed *Saturday Night* about the paper's role, "but it does matter what people believe is true." The tray for incoming letters on Willison's desk bulged with protests, signed and unsigned. One especially colourful one was addressed to "Mr. J.S. Willison, Proprietor of Cox and Jaffray's morals, and Editor (daylight editor) of the Globe." The refusal of the federal charter helped calm the uproar, as did the *Globe's* argument that it made no sense to prohibit export of B.C. coal to the States.[45] But Willison's problem remained: how could he fight off the super-partisans of his party who wanted the *Globe* to be their cheap political rag, when his own and his paper's integrity was being questioned?

One way was to continue to press for a federal railway commission with powers over rates and such issues as rights of way, company organization, and expropriation regulation. In April 1902, the paper rejoiced at the announcement by the Minister of Railways, Andrew Blair, that a bill for creating such a commission soon would be presented to Parliament. However, the proposal was not pressed forward in 1902, although Laurier assured Willison that it would be one of "several go ahead measures" in 1903.[46]

Railway issues more generally were now overshadowing every other national concern. The pressure throughout Canada for a second transcontinental railway grew tremendously throughout 1902. On November 3, Charles M. Hays, an aggressive American railroad man who was general manager of the Grand Trunk Railway of Canada, William Wainwright, the line's vice-president, and the *Globe's* Senator George Cox, now president of the Bank of Commerce, petitioned Laurier for federal assistance in building an extension of the Grand Trunk to the Pacific. They sought a cash subsidy of $6,400 per mile and a land grant of five thousand acres per mile on a route from their existing terminus at North Bay, Ontario, to Port Simpson, B.C. Laurier wrote Willison about the scheme that very day, stating that it was "of very great importance, with which we shall have to deal at an early day, but before we take it up, it requires some very careful consideration."[47]

Willison responded quickly. He could see the "great importance" of a new transcontinental. "My own view leans a good deal to Government railways," he informed the prime minister, but he knew that "no government is likely as yet to make government construction and operation of railways its general policy." Therefore, everything would hang on whether "terms and conditions … satisfactory from the public standpoint" could be negotiated with the Grand Trunk. He added firmly: "… I do not wish to be understood as lobbying for Mr. Cox or the Grand Trunk nor have I the least intention of agitating the project in the Globe until I know what the Government intends to do." Senator Cox had wanted him to go to Ottawa immediately to "discuss the Grand Trunk project with ministers," he told Laurier, but he had not seen "any excuse" for so doing.[48] John Willison now was going to be very wary about his own and the Globe's implication in any railway scheme.

Meanwhile, his relations with the provincial Liberals were going from bad to worse. Increasingly, he came to see the government at Queen's Park as unacceptably illiberal and unprogressive. In 1901 and 1902, on major issues involving education, hydro-electric power, and electoral corruption, he came as close to an open breach as was feasible for an editor of the Toronto Globe.

A major debate of the 1901 session of the provincial legislature concerned the financial situation of the provincially-supported University of Toronto. The opposition Conservatives demanded sharply increased subsidies, as recommended by a commission of experts. The Conservatives also sought diminished government control in favour of increased power to the board of governors, and they wanted the "sons and daughters of the relatively poor" to have an "open door" at the university. The Liberals increased grants only slightly and refused to make any significant alterations in the governing structure or fee schedule. Premier George Ross explained to Willison that this was as far as his rural-dominated caucus would go. Universities served only three per cent of the population and were the responsibility of individuals, a leading Liberal MLA told the Assembly.[49]

Editorially, the *Globe* stood with the government, but with no evident enthusiasm. One evening that summer Willison gave the University College Alumni Association at the U of T his own opinion, in response to a toast to "The Legislature." According to the *Globe's* report, he said that he "would have had rather more pleasure in answering to the toast ... if the Legislature had dealt just a little more generously by the University of Toronto than it had seen fit to do. No greater responsibility rested on the Legislature than to provide, even munificently, for the cause of education." He wanted to see "the educational system from the bottom to the top made absolutely free to the poorest child of the poorest family in Ontario." He would look in vain to the Ross Liberals for agreement with such a philosophy.

The hydro issue involved Toronto's demand that the province permit it to transfer power from Niagara Falls at rates lower than the Toronto Electric Light Company was prepared to grant. Since 1899, the Liberal government had refused. Premier Ross was president of Manufacturer's Life, whose first vice-president, Henry M. Pellatt, was president of the Toronto Electric Light Company. The staunchest defenders at Queen's Park of the private utilities were in the Liberal cabinet and caucus. In 1899 they had amended the Ontario Municipal Act to prevent any municipality from competing with a private utility. Instead, the company would have to be bought out at a sum fixed by arbitration. In February 1902, a Conservative motion for direct provincial generation of hydro power at Niagara Falls for cheap sale to municipalities was defeated by the Liberals. The *Globe* regretted that, commenting that "only by the action of the city itself ... can Toronto be put in touch with the marvelous development of electrical energy at Niagara." The government's claims that "further study" was needed on the whole question were damned with the faint praise of being "plausible," but it insisted that the city's request should be "heard and granted next year." This was tantamount to a disassociation of the *Globe* from the Ross Liberals on the power question.[50]

Nevertheless, during the provincial general election campaign in March and April, 1902 the *Globe* did its best to be the government's loyal ally. Willison knew well, as he advised Laurier, that there would be "a hard contest with the results in doubt." Ross stressed the government's commitment to the development of the agriculture and minerals of northern "New Ontario," and the *Globe* dutifully followed that lead. But, Willison warned Sifton in Ottawa, the Liberals were "absurdly confident." Thanks to their go-slow policies on such urban-related issues as university education and hydro, they were slaughtered in major cities, winning none except Kingston. Overall, they kept a slim majority of seats, fifty-one to forty-seven, but the Conservatives took a slight majority of the popular vote. By the end of July, court decisions had reduced the government majority to one.[51]

Premier Ross, in consultation with Laurier and other key Liberal leaders, decided to explore possibilities for a "grand coalition" with the Conservatives and discussions were initiated in late summer. Willison, he would later recall, was convinced the Liberals should simply resign, but as he put it, "there would have been a suspicion of betrayal if, as editor of *The Globe*, I had attempted to exercise the freedom which I believed the circumstances demanded." So the paper openly called for coalition "against all self seekers, dishonest trimmers and corruptionists.... There is not a single issue between the two parties which is worth an hour of intrigue or the expenditure of one dollar in a manner that will not bear the light of day." The editorial, as the *Canadian Annual Review* commented, "created a political sensation."[52]

The Conservatives then contemptuously denounced the Liberals' coalition proposal as "simply absurd." Premier Ross turned tail, denied authorship, and assured bewildered Liberal partisans: "We are just going to fight; that is all we are going to do."[53] The *Globe* was left to suffer as a defeatist sinner. Willison summed up his response to these events and the situation in which he found himself in a carefully crafted editorial on November 19 that was a clear warning to provincial Liberals not to try to cling to office through corrupt manipulative politics:

> Common sense tells us that Grits and Tories are much the same kind of people. The baser sort in both parties are equally capable of buying votes, and they are equally capable of buying the evidence that votes have been bought. The better element in both parties hate both practices. The only policy for this better element is to realize that the real enemy is not the Grit or the Tory, but

the corruptionist. Between the two parties, the heavier obligation lies on the Reformer. He has made himself the champion of free institutions, of government by the people. When a man calling himself a Liberal is guilty of any of the practices to which we have referred he is not an enemy of Toryism, but a traitor to Liberalism and free institutions.

The years of compromise and pretence as a partisan Liberal journalist were over for Willison. Nine days later, he resigned as editor-in-chief of the *Globe*. Premier Ross was not surprised, writing him to say: "I have observed for some time that the bent of your mind was in the direction of less Partyism and a higher standard of political ethics as well as of political discussion."[54] The Liberal government of Ontario now entered its last stages, dying a pathetic death amid new scandal and shame. Willison had a new editorial responsibility outside the Liberal party, and he joined unreservedly in the kill. In 1905, when that was accomplished, he responded to a Liberal militant who had charged him with "treason" to Liberal principles: "If your leaders had been faithful to Liberal principles it is very unlikely that I should ever have been in this office, or should ever have ceased to be editor of The Globe." There was the federal side too. As his friend John W. Dafoe of the Manitoba *Free Press* would write of Willison's last years at the *Globe*:

> Probably disillusionment and dissatisfaction followed hard on the triumph of 1896, and these moods were strengthened by the gradual revelation to himself that if he were making policies they would be different in their spirit and objectives from those put out by the Laurier government. Between 1896 and 1902 Willison began to find the political climate in which he lived inhospitable.[55]

It was more than a question of divergence from two governments. Party journalism hobbled him, kept him from being fully free to promote his own ideas and his own reputation. He told the students at Queen's University in 1901: "… after all, the citizen who speaks his own mind, rests on his own judgement even in the face of press or caucus or pulpit, is the only man worthy of representative institutions."[56] What was more, he probably had taken about all he could take of being shoved about for petty partisan purposes or the potential enrichment of other men. Yet party journalism, his own skills in partisan manoeuvre and personal connection, as well as the party-arranged backing of wealthy men with compromising private interests, had allowed him to rise in twenty-one years from the store-clerk's counter in Tiverton to the pinnacle of his profession in all of Canada. He was not a rich man. The days of a journalist like George Brown founding or buying his own daily were long gone. A suitable vehicle for Willison's prominence and ambitions required massive financial support. Where was that to come from, without undermining, even fatally compromising, the very independence he had come to yearn for?

VIII

A Study of Laurier — and Willison

O N JUNE 5, 1900, THE TORONTO PUBLISHING FIRM OF GEORGE
Morang and Company formally invited Willison to undertake a biography of George Brown in their ambitious "Makers of Canada" series.
Willison demurred, but then Morang came back with the idea of a Laurier study instead. This time, after many months of indecision, he agreed.[1]

He had been moving for years towards attempting a major historical
work. Probably his literary ambition had been stimulated by the generally favourable reactions to his "Observer" sketch on Laurier in 1889,
his special reports from the West in 1895, his articles on Imperialism
and the railroad question in 1897, and his essay that same year in the
Canadian Magazine on "The Premiers of Ontario Since Confederation."
After that last effort Arthur Colquhoun had told him: "… if you allow the
coming years to slip away without venturing more & more into purely
literary work you will throw away a gift. It may mean some sacrifice of
time, health, energy, but positively you <u>ought</u> to deal with some period
of our modern political history."[2] To Laurier, after work on the biography
was well under way, Willison confessed: "… as you know, I have always
been particularly fond of the study of men and events and if I had been
a less busy man such a work would have had a great fascination for me."

Now he made the time, and with some very partisan motives too. "The thing that determined me finally was the result of the last [federal] election in Ontario.... I thought that Ontario had voted in blind ignorance of your work and character and I resented the verdict accordingly." He had "long thought," he added, that "a proper presentation of your life work with a running history of the Liberal party since Confederation would be of great value" and concluded:

> I am vain enough to think that if I can make the time I can write a book that will do good, and notwithstanding our occasional very small differences of opinion it is not necessary for me to say that my personal devotion to yourself and, for that matter, my positive affection for yourself have never undergone any change.[3]

Thus a journalist turned to history — or, at least, to a kind of history, "a book that will do good" for his leader and party.

The preparation of Willison's two-volume *Sir Wilfrid Laurier: A Political History* occupied about a year, from July 1901 into the summer of 1902.[4] The time had to be snatched in bits and pieces out of the swirling daily chaos that was an editor-in-chief's unavoidable routine. Much of the mining of source materials was handled by others. John S. Maclean, the *Globe's* correspondent in Montreal, searched the Fraser Institute there for books, pamphlets, and documents on both the Roman Catholic church and Liberal politics in Quebec. W.H. Dickson, the paper's Ottawa bureau chief, rummaged through the Library of Parliament, and officials of both the Legislative Library of Ontario and the Toronto Public Library supplied newspaper files and government documents. Willison organized the material and corresponded with Laurier on hundreds of details.

The prime minister's first reaction to Willison on hearing of the project was that he doubted the "advisability" of publishing a biography in his lifetime because "the judgment of his friends might have afterwards to be revised by those who will come when his whole career can be reviewed." He was "quite sure," however, that "if my biography has to be written, the work could not be placed in more sympathetic and friendly hands than yours." By mid-1902 he confessed: "I am now awaiting your book with some impatience."[5]

After four months of work, Willison reported to Laurier that the project had "quite outgrown the original plan. It will now amount to something like a history of Canada since Confederation. Perhaps it would be more accurate to say a history of the Liberal party since Confederation. While I make you the central figure, it will deal with many of the chief questions that have arisen during the last thirty years."[6]

Toward the end of the completed work Willison summed up his attitude to Laurier's public career — that it was "remarkable for consistent and unchanging devotion to three great objects: the assertion and maintenance of the principle of federalism, ardent and unflinching championship of civil and religious freedom, patient and courageous resistance to the denationalizing tendencies of racialism, sectarianism and provincialism."[7]

The first theme to be developed was Laurier's "ardent and unyielding championship of civil and religious freedom." As Willison sifted through his material, particularly that sent from Montreal, his excitement mounted and his admiration for Laurier, which had remained strong in spite of all their policy differences over the years, intensified. It was the spectacle of the struggle in Quebec in the 1850s, '60s, and '70s between Liberalism and *ultramontanist* Catholicism that astonished, fascinated, and thrilled him. Admiringly, he portrayed Laurier's emergence by the end of this period as the prime champion of enlightened secular British liberalism against the dark forces of clerical pretension and political reaction. Surely this would stir English-Canadian Protestants to admiration! He wrote Laurier:

> I have thought for fifteen years that I knew something about you. As a matter of fact until I began this work I knew nothing. I have now studied your career from the beginning and am amazed at its continuity, its purpose and its consistency. I am ashamed of some of the rash and foolish things I have written ever since you became leader of the Liberal party. But if I knew so little about you how must it be with the English-speaking people

generally? In fact the history of the Liberal party of Quebec is a sealed book in the English provinces, and it is time it was opened.[8]

Open it he did: seven of the sixteen chapters in Volume I were on little else.

He recounted the "formidable ascendancy" which *ultramontanism* had acquired among Quebec's Roman Catholics by the 1870s, the decade of Laurier's emergence as an important Liberal leader in the province. *Ultramontanism* was a set of aggressive clericalist doctrines about the domination of church over state and the supremacy of papal authority. It had a strongly *nationaliste* slant in a French Canada surrounded by the vastly greater numbers of English-speaking Protestants in North America. One striking feature had been the unremitting war which several bishops, especially Bourget of Montreal, had waged in the '50s and '60s against the *Institut Canadien*, a cultural and literary society of mainly "young, progressive and independent thinkers." For prelates such as Bourget intellectual enquiry outside clerical discipline and supervision was anathema, and by 1858 they had achieved control or forced the closing of all the *Institut*'s branches outside Montreal. The organization there had been continuing its "prudent but determined resistance" when the young law student Wilfrid Laurier had joined it in 1863 and thereby, in Willison's view, "struck his first blow for civil liberty, and registered his first protest against ecclesiastical domination in the realm of the human intellect and in the field of public affairs." In 1865–66, as a vice-president of the *Institut*, he had participated in its struggle against Bourget's dictation in reading matter and program. By 1869, when the Vatican condemned the group and threatened Catholics who remained in it with excommunication, Laurier had left Montreal to hang out his lawyer's shingle in Arthabaskaville. Nevertheless, as Willison put it, the young man continued to "bear the consequences of his identification with the society."[9]

For Laurier and many other members and ex-members of the *Institut* were Liberals, and any electoral ambitions they might have were bound to conflict with the Church's explicit hostility in constituency after constituency. Bishops and *curés* warned the faithful of certain damnation if they voted for the accursed "heretics." The courts overturned some of these electoral decisions on the grounds of the "*influence undue*" of the clergy, but the force of the clerical hostility remained awesome.[10] Laurier was obliged to meet it election after election in the 1870s. In 1877, already a junior minister in Alexander Mackenzie's federal Liberal government, he defined his personal political faith before the *Club Canadien* at Quebec City in what Willison described as his "noteworthy speech" on "Political Liberalism."

The biographer explained that it was to allow his readers to "grasp the full significance" of this speech that he had devoted so much space and attention to the Quebec political scene over the previous thirty years. Now he gave the address a place of special importance, analyzed it exhaustively, and appended a full text, in the original French. He portrayed the young Laurier as by this time the brightest shining light in the glorious struggle of Quebec Liberalism against the evil darkness of clerical pretension. Here was a French-speaking Roman Catholic who was properly imbued with all the wonderful principles of British Liberalism! Laurier had claimed that Quebec Liberals were not of the radical anti-clerical and revolutionary school of continental Europe. They were, rather, inheritors of the traditions of Fox, Grey, Brougham, Russell, and Gladstone: "... there are our models, there are our principles, there is our party!" He had quoted with approval Tennyson's verses about Britain as a land where "freedom slowly broadens down from precedent to precedent." He had admitted that "some young enthusiasts" among the '*rouges*' in the 1840s had been carried away by radical continental liberalism and, in their extreme anti-clericalism, had truly given defenders of the Church cause for alarm. As a result, clerical reactionaries and Conservative politicians had been able to keep political liberalism in Quebec on the defensive as "a heresy carrying with it its own condemnation."[11]

Yet Laurier, as Willison put it, had declared "uncompromising resistance to the arrogant assumptions" of the *ultramontanes*, and had "boldly affirmed the right of the Catholic elector to control his own franchise, rest in his own judgment, and exercise all the freedom and authority of independent citizenship." He had warned French Canadians that if they sought to make Catholicism the basis of one party, then English Canadians, a far larger group, would respond by making Protestantism, anti-Catholicism, and hostility to French Canadians the foundations of another.

Willison took pains to show that Laurier's bows to British Liberalism were part of a general deep admiration for, and participation in, the cultural and political traditions of Britain and of English-speaking civilization generally. Attendance as a twelve-year-old at a Protestant school had had "a distinct and lasting effect upon his character and opinions" — making him tolerant of the language and beliefs of English Canadians. As a young law student and then lawyer, he had been "quick to recognize the fact that on this continent English must be the language of commerce, of politics, and of literature, and that a command of English speech was essential to full and effective participation in the life of the community." Accordingly, Willison explained, Laurier had read deeply in the great writers, poets, historians, and essayists of the English language, raising him, in the poet Louis Fréchette's opinion, to "the distinction of being almost without a peer among the English-speaking debaters of the Dominion."[12]

Willison relied upon this early "Englishness" he had established for Laurier to keep his hero untainted, uncompromised by the anti-Confederation and often separatist character of the *rouge* party of the 1860s. As Willison put it:

> He came upon the scene at the birth of Confederation, surrounded by eager agitators touched by the revolutionary zeal of continental Liberalism and still verging upon the excesses of the old Rouge programme. The spirit of his political surroundings was hostile to the Confederation settlement ... and profoundly apprehensive of the effects of Confederation upon the social and political fortunes of the French population. In face of all these adverse circumstances he perfected his English speech, read his English books, developed the Constitutional temper of British statesmanship, and found in the principle of federalism ample guarantees for all the legitimate rights and interests of the race and the province to which he belonged, and the wider basis of a common nationality and a united British commonwealth.

Yet Willison had to admit that his hero had opposed Confederation. For a few months in the winter of 1866–67, he had edited *Le Défricheur*, and in the only known surviving issues from that period were two spirited anti-Confederation editorials. In the principal one "we politicians of the Papineau school" argued that the proposed union would be "the tomb of the French race and the ruin of Lower Canada." But Willison added that the "spirit of the writing is that of *Le Défricheur* rather than that of Laurier." He commented that it would have been "difficult" for the young editor to have abandoned the paper's traditional policy and tone. Still, he had to concede that Laurier was in this period "in sympathy" with the general *rouge* anti-Confederation line. At any rate, he stressed, Laurier "heartily accepted the union when it became an accomplished fact; and no man in Quebec was more influential in reconciling the dissentient elements in the French Province to acceptance of the settlement and in infusing into his French compatriots the broader spirit of Canadian nationality."[13]

The second of the "three great objects" of Laurier's career, according to Willison, was "the assertion and maintenance of the idea of federalism." Willison never explained just what this "idea" — he also called it a "principle" — was. It certainly was not federalism as envisaged by the Fathers of Confederation, with a dominant federal authority armed with "peace, order and good government" responsibilities as well as full taxing and disallowance powers. It seems rather to have been federalism as viewed by Sir John A. Macdonald's anti-centralist opponents, before and after 1867. This was good Liberal orthodoxy, and Laurier could be shown to have voiced it at practically every appropriate opportunity since the commencement of his legislative career as an MLA at Quebec City in 1871. He opposed "dual representation," arguing that if a man sat in both Parliament and a provincial legislature, he could be forced by his federal party to subordinate his province's interests. As an MP, he had defended the provinces' rights to lucrative liquor licensing revenues and he had attacked savagely the Macdonald government's use of the disallowance or veto power against provincial legislation as counter to the proper spirit of federalism. This attitude, it was claimed, had been carried into the Jesuit Estates Act disallowance issue in 1889 and on into the Manitoba Schools crisis later.[14]

Willison observed that Laurier had maintained a "discreet and judicial attitude" on the Manitoba question while it was before the courts. His difficult position and eventual policy were summed up this way:

> He did not believe that a policy of coercion could succeed. He was thoroughly persuaded that sympathetic treatment of minorities was conducive to national stability and national solidarity. He shrank from a quarrel with the Church to which he belonged. He could not think that the forces which the Remedial Order would range behind the Government could be successfully resisted. He had fought many a battle against presumptuous federal interference with provincial legislation; and while bound to admit that Manitoba's control over education was limited by constitutional restrictions, he was yet convinced that only by the free action of the legislature could the Catholic people receive effective and enduring redress of any grievances arising out of the abolition of the Separate School system. He could not argue the question as one of abstract provincial rights, nor could he contend for absolute restoration of Separate Schools, if it could be established that under the Public Schools system the conscientious convictions of Roman Catholics were fairly respected. Thus he favoured investigation, condemned the policy of the Remedial Order, and pleaded for a settlement by a compromise and conciliation.

Sir Charles Tupper's Remedial Bill had been, Willison believed, "a full satisfaction of the demands of the Catholic bishops." Their battle in support of it and then against the Laurier-Greenway "settlement" of the issue he regarded as "the most desperate attempt at clerical coercion which even Canada has ever witnessed." He recalled the "ultimatum" which Father Lacombe had addressed to Laurier on behalf of the bishops that he support the Remedial Bill or suffer their wrath in the constituencies.[15]

Interestingly, Willison brushed over the far more moderate *mande-ment* which the bishops had issued before the 1896 election to which most of the Liberal candidates in Quebec had pledged their allegiance. The important thing Willison wanted to emphasize was that Laurier was an anti-*ultramontane* who "could not now sacrifice the professions and the convictions of a lifetime at the dictation of the heads of the Church to which he belonged and whose pretensions to supremacy in the civil sphere he had always opposed." He praised the Liberal leader for his "raw courage" in opposing the Remedial Bill in Parliament and then on the hustings in 1896. As prime minister, he had led the way to a reasonable compromise settlement of the schools issue, in spite of bitter opposition from the Catholic hierarchy. "The struggle for a free voice and a free vote was won in 1896," Willison rejoiced, "and the name of Wilfrid Laurier must be forever associated with the long contest and the final victory." Laurier's devotion to "the principle of federalism" and his "ardent and unflinching championship of civil and religious free-dom" were tied together and given special emphasis in this comment on the election result of 1896:

> To the Liberals of Quebec, maligned, misrepresented, and misunderstood from the very birth of Confederation, faithful through long years of adversity to the essential principles of civil and religious liberty, we owe the deliv-erance of Manitoba from the policy of federal coercion and the pacific settlement of a quarrel which threatened the self-governing rights of all the western communities.[16]

This was an agreeable portrait for Willison to paint, but it was not altogether an accurate one — important details were lacking. Willison must have recalled that the Liberal leader had tried time and again dur-ing the controversy to impress on him that Manitoba's "provincial rights" were, in fact, severely restricted in education, describing Willison's con-trary view, now repeated in the biography, as "altogether too positive, too absolute." Willison admitted this many years later, writing to John Dafoe: "If *The Globe* had followed Laurier's advice, the whole party would have been committed to remedial legislation."[17] But a half-dozen years on, the biographer shunned any qualifications of his hero's pursuit of "great objects;" and, perhaps, the "counselor" who believed he had convinced his chief of the soundness of a position did not wish now to detail the process of enlightenment. After all, this was a study that was to "do good" for Laurier and the Liberal party; the Manitoba problem was finished, solved. Why give readers an excuse for thinking of it in terms of shades of grey rather than of black and white? Besides, Laurier's public stance in the later stages of the crisis could be connected so neatly — and, for English-Canadian Protestants, so appealingly — with his earlier provincial rights and anti-*ultramontane* pronouncements that, for Willison, the temptation hardly could have been resisted.

The third of the "great objects" of Laurier's public career which Willison emphasized was the "patient and courageous resistance to the denationalizing tendencies of racialism, sectarianism and provincialism." He celebrated Laurier's early experiences with Scottish Presbyterian schooling, his McGill Law School days, his maiden speech in the Quebec Assembly when he had spoken of French and English "united under the same flag," a Toronto address in 1886 in praise of British institutions and "one nation," and numerous other examples of the same broad, generous, tolerant Canadianism. Such a Laurier, the biographer wanted his readers to believe, could be counted on to see the future of the nation and of its Empire connection in terms not at all redolent of parochial French Canadianism. He recalled the generosity of the prime minister's British preference tariff of 1897 and his leading role at the Queen's Jubilee that same year.[18]

Willison bitterly condemned the Conservatives' "race cry" in 1899 and 1900. He remembered their "rash and intemperate utterances" against Laurier in particular and French Canadians in general for hesitating at all in favouring dispatch of troops to South Africa. Laurier, he stressed, had very soon recognized the "overwhelming demand" of Canadians for a contingent. What had counted, he argued, had been the prime minister's thorough commitment to the British cause in the war and his praise for the volunteer soldiers' brave efforts for "Canada's glory, the glory of the Empire, and above all, to the cause of justice, humanity and liberty." This then was Willison's contemptuous answer to the Tory charge in Ontario in the 1900 federal election that Laurier was "not British enough."[19]

Development of the main themes about the heroic Laurier, champion of civil freedom, federalism, and national unity, did not always hide from view Willison the enthusiast for public ownership of railways, the budding protectionist, and the advocate of closer Imperial co-operation.

On transportation, he judged the abandonment by the Macdonald Conservatives of the public ownership approach to major railway construction "the gravest national mistake in all our history." He conceded that Laurier and other Liberals in opposition had not stood for public ownership, and he deplored what he saw as their often excessively negative reaction against the sometimes "heroic" private CPR. With the Liberals in office, he remarked, there was "an excellent prospect that the right of public regulation of charges over the whole Canadian Pacific system will soon be regained" through mutually beneficial arrangements between the government and the CPR. There was no direct mention of those bitter Liberal party squabbles over railway policy which had so discomfited Willison since the early 1890s. If he could not praise, he would not blame. It would not have been seemly in a propagandist biography.

As for the tariff issue, he could not avoid at least implicit criticism of Laurier and the Liberals. The indifferent success of the high protectionist National Policy during the Tory ascendancy was emphasized. Laurier, he stressed, had been a moderate protectionist before 1887, and had been drawn into the radical Unrestricted Reciprocity policy primarily because of terribly bad economic conditions. After all, Willison recalled, the late 1880s had been "a time of gloom and doubt, of suspicion and unrest, of rash opinion and premature judgment, of failing faith in our institutions, of hostile examination of the central props and pillars of our national edifice." He condemned the Tories' "Loyalty campaign" of 1891 as one of "shrieking, of denunciation, and of violence" which, however, had "no doubt appealed with peculiar force to the sentiments, the prejudices, and the interests of powerful elements of the Canadian people." He conceded that in the Liberals' campaign "the note of continentalism had distinct utterance," and that "in too much of the Opposition literature" there had been "that deep note of pessimism and tone of contempt for sentimental considerations which are always offensive to the national pride and the sturdy self-reliance of Anglo-Saxon peoples." He detailed his party's more positive and more moderate approach to the trade question at the

1893 convention, in the 1896 campaign and in the Liberal government's budget of 1897. As prime minister, he claimed, Laurier

> … understands that it is not easy for a small community to adhere to free trade, in the teeth of powerful protectionist neighbours with a vast equipment of developed industries. Whatever weakness there may be in the position from the standpoint of sound economics, it is the fact that no modern community is willing to limit its activities to the single industry of agriculture…. It is necessary also to face the fact that protectionism is a vital part of modern nationalism.[20]

Willison even reflected that "important Canadian industries now profess to be suffering from the competition which the British preference directly sanctions and promotes." He called on his readers to realize "what small option" this left Laurier in the area of Empire preferential trade. Clearly, for Willison, Canadian industrial protectionism could not be sacrificed for imperial preferences.

Nevertheless, he believed that the "signs of the hour point to growth in Imperial unity, if not so directly to an Imperial trade alliance." He argued that the moderate Canadian tariff preference for British products, the imperial penny postage, contributions to the Pacific Cable and Atlantic steamship links, and the sending of contingents to South Africa had made Canadians "feel that they are discharging, in full measure, all their legitimate obligations to the Mother Country." However, he wanted his readers to see that there was "yet a further word to be said" on the defence side of Empire co-operation. He noted the British efforts at the Colonial Conference of 1897 and subsequently to encourage the self-governing colonies such as Canada to assume a major role in Imperial defence, and the general colonial response that internal development in new countries was so costly as to effectively preclude such a move for some time. This was precisely Laurier's position that very summer of 1902 at the Imperial Conference, as Willison's biography of him was receiving its final touches. Willison allowed for the "force and validity" of the development-first view, but added:

The sea power of Britain is the fortress of British trade, and the main guarantee of peace in the world; and whether in peace or in war, the maintenance of these world-circling fleets bears heavily upon British taxpayers. We enjoy the protection and security which this armament maintains, and while we may be reluctant to vote direct contributions to be expended by the British authorities, it is not at all clear that we should not make an indirect contribution of men and ships to the navy, and relieve Britain of all responsibility for the defences of Canada. These responsibilities we should have to meet if we were an independent country, and we have no right to accept a less obligation as a part of the British Empire…. There is, therefore, a further word to be said on the question, and Canada will hardly shirk any obligation which falls upon her as an integral part of the British dominions.

He mentioned the "active and increasing interest" in Colonel Denison's plan for a special duty of 5 percent on all goods imported into Britain and the colonies to provide a common fund for Imperial defence. Thus, far more clearly than in the editorial columns of the *Globe*, Willison was setting forth his personal preferences concerning Canada's imperial policy. It was his one major explicit intrusion over a point on which he had a substantive difference with his hero-subject. Laurier made noises in London in 1902 about naval defence, but the next several years were to show that he put no premium on action, that he did not feel the urgency of the matter in anything like the way his biographer did.

Willison's *Laurier* was not a work of objective historical scholarship. It was half a partisan document and half a personal tribute in a nineteenth century one-dimensional style. To the extent that it was history, it was of the Whig approach, with "grand themes" traced to their inexorable triumph. The partisanship was never complete: Conservative as well as Liberal leaders came in for their share of praise. Indeed, his treatment of the careers of Sir John A. Macdonald and Edward Blake can only have left Tories believing their old chief had been handsomely treated and his rival's failings as a leader of men accurately described. But for all that, the book was about Laurier and the Liberal party, with other men only bit players in the drama.

The biography was completed in the summer of 1902 and publication was in February and March 1903.[21] Immediate newspaper comment was quick and varied, though largely positive. Most enthusiastic, predictably, were the Liberal organs. The *Globe*, which Willison had left two months previously, heartily approved the depiction of Laurier's "strength, moderation, justness and nationalism." The London *Advertiser* liked the "fresh light" on Laurier's "valiant struggle" against *ultramontanism* in Quebec. The paper noted approvingly: "Under the placid surface there has been a force, a persistence, a resolute adherence to definite ideals. The Liberals of Canada will draw new faith in their leader, new affection and admiration for him, from Mr. Willison's pages." The Manitoba *Free Press* agreed: "We must look in his youth for the sources of his mature strength, and in this volume much is revealed that must make Liberals more then ever satisfied to have him as their leader." *Le Soleil* of Quebec City reprinted without dissent a translation of the *Globe's* approving comment, complete with the anti-*ultramontane* emphasis.[22]

Leading Conservative papers mixed criticisms and praise. The *Mail and Empire* considered the work "ably written" and "the result of earnest and laborious research" but it attacked what it claimed were sins of omission by the author — for example, the failure to condemn Laurier for using the "race cry" in Quebec in 1885–87. The Montreal *Gazette* wished the book has been "less redolent of the caucus, but inasmuch as such a book was to be written, one is glad that it was entrusted to a gentleman at once able and honest." *La Presse* of Montreal hailed "*la plume vigoureuse et élégante de* M.J.S. Willison" which, it confessed, made even good Quebec Conservatives willing to state about Laurier: "*Nous le combattons, mais nous sommes fiers de lui.*" [We fight him, but we are proud of him.][23]

The magazine and independent newspaper press was generally very laudatory. Norman Patterson in the *Canadian Magazine* praised "the greatest biography yet produced in this country" for "its method, its breadth of view, its wideness of research, its clearness and fairness, and last, but not by any means least, the excellence of its style." But he chided Willison for "occasionally passing by weak spots with a journalist's adroitness." The "Book Worm" in *Saturday Night* hailed "a genuinely important political history" but added: "It is rather to be doubted if the effort is as valuable on its biographical as on its historical side.... Truth is the daughter of time, and only as great figures recede into the distance can we accurately seize their shape and proportion." Yet overall, the reviewer judged that the work "seizes upon the imagination and holds it under a potent spell." P.D. Ross of the independent Ottawa *Journal* wrote the review that pleased Willison most, spending much time on Laurier's "trial by fire" against the *ultramontanes*, and concluding:

> The book must, we think, tend greatly to remove what has undoubtedly been an impression among even well-informed people that Laurier's political life and character have lacked force and virile continuity....
>
> ... it cannot be denied that the ascendancy of Laurier in the Dominion has tended to a remarkable amelioration of theological and racial jealousy and suspicion. Mr. Willison has endeavoured to present a development of this kind as the greatest aid or effect of Sir Wilfrid's political life, and we think he has made out a strong case.

Willison wrote Ross to say that he had "penetrated to the very spirit of my work. It would be mere pretence to deny that I am very glad that the book has been well received generally."[24]

Major attention was given to Willison's books in Britain, no doubt largely because of Laurier's importance on imperial issues of trade and defence. For the *Times Literary Supplement* the "main interest" was the tracing of "the gradual rise and formation, under the influence of a distinguished intellect and a naturally well balanced mind, of a new force in Imperial politics which is represented by the Liberal party in Canada." The *Spectator* hailed the "very full and valuable" treatment of trade and tariff questions. The *Morning Post*, while praising the coverage of imperial issues, described the books as "somewhat longwinded," and thought they suffered from "the fault of treating all the Canadian geese as swans." The *Monthly Review* remarked cleverly: "We get the case for Canadian Liberalism as fairly as counsel for the defence could be expected to state it." The Yorkshire *Daily Post* thought the political history was written in an "even" manner, but the biographical treatment suffered from "excessive hero worship." Further on that line, the *Daily Chronicle* complained of the author's "unescapable panegyrics" about Laurier, and remarked that "the most heroic of heroes ought not to be so searchingly tested" as to be praised in such fashion.[25]

Probably the most scathing criticism Willison ever received about his book was contained in a private letter in April 1903 from Joseph Flavelle, a leading Toronto industrialist and financier, who bluntly stated that he was "at wide variance" with Willison on most of his handling of the trade, transportation, and commercial aspects of Laurier's career. He found many of the sections on these subjects "as singular for what they do not say as for what they do say…." Liberal policy on them, he thought, had been too often "dangerous, unprogressive and lacking in business acumen and grasp." He damned what he saw as the long Laurier and Liberal records of negative and "destructive" attitudes on both the National Policy tariff and the CPR, and observed: "I find not only no trace of this in your book — which perhaps is natural — but actual approval." He thought "this must have done some violence to your real convictions." He added that the accomplishment of the extraordinary prosperity in place by 1903 without a reciprocity treaty with the Americans "pointed to the utter discreditment of the utterances of the Liberal Party…." In business, financial and transportation affairs, Laurier had shown, by Flavelle's reckoning, "impotence and weakness, an over-emphasis of local troubles and a failure to see the large results." He added: "… the story of his creative work in the line of business development cannot be written; there is nothing to write…." He was "inclined to think that a 'History of the Liberal Party' ought to tell some of its failures — ought to speak plainly of some of its defeats — ought to tell some of the errors of its leaders, as well as magnify their virtues and successes. Else what real merit will there be in its study?"[26]

Willison's response to this blast is not known. Some discounting of the critique on account of Flavelle's business perspectives and traditional Conservative associations would be fair. It was all too true, however, that in Willison's almost nine hundred pages on Laurier that there was almost no detail on any constructive policy achievements in economic development or social reform. Willison generalized that Laurier's administration was "distinguished for progressive social legislation, for sympathetic recognition of the changing relationship between labour and capital, and for intelligent comprehension of the new responsibilities imposed upon governments by the capitalistic organization of modern industry."[27] However, there was scarcely any backing for that sort of statement, and little reflection on the government's failure to respond positively or significantly to the kinds of proposals Willison himself had pushed on them — for a railway commission, a new railway subsidies policy, an increased public ownership in the railway field, Senate abolition, and civil service reform.

Of course, the biography was to "do good," not recite problems and failures. Thus Laurier was depicted as a resolute upholder of civil freedom against clerical dictation, a thorough "provincial rights" federalist, and an uncompromising champion of national unity and the imperial connection. These were the three "great objects" of Laurier's career, and concentration on them was almost total. In 1902 and 1903, in spite of his abandonment of "Liberal" journalism, there was no personal estrangement from Laurier. In particular, learning the details of the dramatic anti-*ultramontane* roots of Laurier's career particularly had "amazed" him. His own denominational Christian experience once had been country Methodist and was now calm "low-Anglican" moderation at St. Alban's Church on Howland Avenue and latterly St. Paul's Bloor Street. Now his personal enthusiasm for his hero-subject on grounds of religious liberalism was stronger than ever. On all the main themes of the book, he still could be comfortably a Laurier man, though no longer a Liberal journalist.

Meanwhile, the largely favourable reaction to the biography was clearly a significant boost to his already substantial prestige. The dividends from it would come initially in royalty cheques; what other form they might take only the future could tell. He now was very publicly not just a leading journalist but a noted author. His new status came even as he moved his family from temporary rented accommodation on Spadina Road into a lovely three-storey residence, 10 Elmsley Place, just east of Queen's Park. It became the family's new centre of operations and rallying point in 1902, on a rental basis. By August 1904 he had scraped together enough capital to purchase a lease from the Elmsley Estate. It was a pleasant walk to downtown, and the Ontario Legislature and the University of Toronto were just easy strolls away.[28]

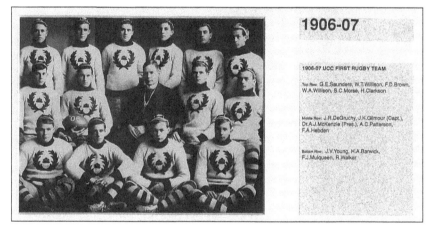

Above Left: Ten Elmsley Place, Toronto. Uncatalogued photo, St. Michael's College Library, Toronto
Above Right: The Library of 10 Elmsley Place. Ph. 5, 1931, St. Michael's College Library, Toronto
Bottom: The 1906–07 Upper Canada College First Rugby Team. Upper Canada College Library

For the rest of his career he did most of his major writing there. The "gallery room" upstairs housed his letters, papers, and files, but he habitually wrote elsewhere — in the winter downstairs in the living room inglenook by the huge fireplace, in summer out on the screened verandah and often, in any season, in the midst of his two-storey library on the ground floor. It was huge but soon enough overflowing with books to the ceiling. A winding staircase ladder led to the upper reaches. In one corner was a curved window nook. At one end was a raised dais for writing. Across the hall was Rachel's sitting room, which came to be graced with Louis XIV-style furniture and oriental rugs. She loved to entertain and was happily active in the Imperial Order Daughters of the Empire and the Toronto Ladies Club. Sons Walter and Bill were teenagers now and enthusiastic, athletic students at Upper Canada College. For all the family their lovely home was a congenial base and refuge.[29] For John Willison it was a fitting setting for the exciting new career opportunities which lay ahead.

Independent Journalism and Independence, 1903–1905

Tʜᴇ ᴡᴇᴀʟᴛʜʏ ᴘᴀᴛʀᴏɴ Wɪʟʟɪsᴏɴ ɴᴇᴇᴅᴇᴅ ʙᴇғᴏʀᴇ ʜᴇ ᴄᴏᴜʟᴅ ᴅᴀʀᴇ to leave the security of the *Globe* and launch himself into the uncertainties of independent journalism turned out to be Joseph Wesley Flavelle. Two years Willison's junior, he was a tall, bearded, balding Peterborough native who came to Toronto in 1887 with Gunn's, wholesale provision merchants. In the early 1890s he bought into the William Davies Company, pork packers, and became its general manager. By 1902, in his early forties, he was a millionaire, Toronto was being called Hogtown, and the William Davies Company was the largest pork-packing firm in the British Empire. He was also a director of the Bank of Commerce, a director and vice-president of the Imperial Life, president of the National Trust, vice-president of Robert Simpson's and a director of Canada Life. There were other businesses, many investments and several major involvements in Methodist church work, education, and philanthropy. He was nominally a Conservative, primarily on National Policy grounds, but without bitter partisanship or particular enthusiasm for contemporary Conservative leadership.[1]

"EQV" in the *Canadian Magazine*, likely after conversation with Flavelle, wrote in January 1903 that the entrepreneur had been "set

J. W. FLAVELLE,
PRESIDENT NATIONAL TRUST COMPANY; MANAGING
DIRECTOR THE WM. DAVIES COMPANY,
TORONTO.

Joseph Flavelle, 1902.
Library and Archives
Canada, C-023692

thinking" the previous year by the editor's speeches on the educational and moral value of newspapers. "We met as strangers who previously had but the most casual acquaintance," Flavelle explained to Goldwin Smith. It was Flavelle who made the initial approach:

> If I furnish the capital, will you join me in the production of a paper in which you can give expression to your views upon public affairs without being interfered with in the interests of party, church, corporation, or any interests which will seek to influence your judgment to cause you to be partisan.
>
> I shall appreciate discussing with you any question affecting public interests upon which we may differ, but

when we have so discussed the subject, the view as finally determined by you to be truest to the public interest is the one which will find expression in the paper.

I will at no time ask you to write a line, or to make reference in any way favourable to any interests with which I am identified, whether of a business, corporate or church character.

I do not desire to be known as newspaper proprietor, or to secure advantage of any sort for myself. I only desire to be of some service to the community in which I live, and shall be grateful if you give me the opportunity, by permitting me to join with you in such an enterprise.

From you, Mr. Willison, I want no pledge other than that you will say you will seek to express your honest opinions upon public matters, undeterred by personal, party or any other influences which will keep you from saying what you think ought to be said in the public interest.[2]

The exact timing of Flavelle's unexpected offer is unclear, but by August 1902 the two men were exploring eagerly the prospects for purchasing an existing paper or starting a new one.[3]

Intermediaries, including Willison's friend Arthur Colquhoun, who was anxious to join in the new venture, approached William F. (Billie) Maclean, MP, the owner and editor of the *World*, an "independent Conservative" morning paper, and William J. Douglas, manager of the official Tory morning journal, the *Mail and Empire*. Flavelle had what he termed "a natural shrinking from taking on any low grade evening paper."

Willison must have been tense indeed as the discussions dragged on for weeks that fall. Rachel, visiting relatives in Tiverton, wired him on October 1: "Whatever you do I shall be satisfied." In November Flavelle told Willison that they had been "jockeyed" by Maclean, who really hoped they would buy the *Mail and Empire* so that he could pick up its partisan Tory readers. However, the *Mail and Empire*'s owners asked for $1,000,000, and Flavelle advised Willison that reasonable terms for it "will probably be impossible." Interestingly, the same interests also owned the *Evening News* and were prepared to let it go for

$150,000 and the satisfaction that the new Flavelle operation would not be competing with them in the morning field. Willison would not be required to purchase stock and his starting salary would be the then princely sum of $7,500.[4]

On November 28, the Toronto press carried the announcement of Willison's resignation from the *Globe* and of the new project. Two days before, Flavelle had received Willison's agreement to the step with deep emotion:

> I will not attempt to deny how much I am moved. I remember when my wife consented to be my wife.... This decision you have made means so much to you, may mean so much to the country, that I feel I must not intrude with my rude hand, but you will let me say how deeply I prize your confidence, and how much I am indebted to you for giving me the opportunity of working with you.[5]

As his new business associate welcomed Willison to what clearly would be an extraordinary partnership, his oldest and dearest political friend generously blessed the new role. Two weeks before the resignation and the venture into independent journalism were made public, he and Rachel were guests of Sir Wilfrid and Lady Laurier in Ottawa. Amid the warmth of their closeness, he told Laurier of his plans. As Arthur Colquhoun recorded, "the judgment of Laurier was that he did not see how Willison could turn away from such an opportunity.[6]

Willison's friends and associates all agreed that his move was an event of major significance for Canadian politics and journalism, but they divided sharply on whether they regretted or welcomed it. Partisan Liberals put the accent on regret and on doubt the new enterprise would succeed. Premier George Ross warned him that he could become "a voice crying in the wilderness." James Young, veteran politician and editor, sorrowed that an independent paper "wd. lead you into antagonism with your formerly expressed opinions. Public men seldom achieve distinction and success under those circumstances." John Cooper reported on Liberal caucus reactions in Ottawa that "already they are trying to make themselves believe that you were never of much importance."

Most non-Liberal or non-partisan friends were more positive and encouraging. Professor William Clark of Trinity College wished him "better fulfillment" and many years of happiness and usefulness." Dr. George Parkin of the Rhodes Scholarship Trust blessed the "new venture" and told him it was "one of the healthiest signs of the times for us here in Canada. You have always seemed to me the nearest approach to a <u>fair</u> man that our party press has produced here in Canada ... and that you should have so good a field now open to you to exercise this quality of fairness is a matter of the greatest public moment." To the best wishes of that leading Canadian imperialist was added the strong approval of the respected continentalist Goldwin Smith, remarking to W.D. Gregory: "Willison is a very good man, and, from what I can learn, Flavelle's object is patriotic."[7]

Purchase of the *News* at 106 Yonge Street was completed on December 10. On January 19, 1903 it appeared for the first time under Willison's editorship. A special editorial, THE NEWS AND ITS AIMS charted its future course. There would be "an independent course in politics," but without contempt for political parties or partisans. There would be "frank and free discussion" of issues in the fashion of the New York *Post*, the Springfield *Republican*, and the London *Times*. The *News* aimed to be "a good soldier in the 'irrepressible conflict' between public and private interests, and to have an honourable part in the enduring struggle between the unorganized people and the organized corporations." It declared its "freedom from all entangling alliances and its detachment from all selfish interests."

Willison was scarcely settled in at his new desk before his first great political battle began, over the so-called "Gamey Affair." In May 1902, Robert Roswell Gamey had been elected the Conservative M.L.A. for Manitoulin. Then, in late January 1903, he announced a switch to the Liberals for the sake, he claimed, of the better development of northern Ontario. But on March 11, when the Legislature convened, he rose in his place to announce that his switch had been arranged by the Provincial Secretary, J.R. Stratton, in exchange for the control of local patronage and two thousand dollars. Gamey claimed that he had only pretended to switch parties, in order to obtain evidence of Liberal corruption. A shaken Premier Ross appointed a judicial royal commission to investigate Gamey's charges.[8]

The lead editorial in the *News* on March 12 was titled A SHAMEFUL STO-RY. It suspected Gamey had taken "grave risks with his own reputation," perhaps at one point fully intending to be bribed, but it saw the guilt of the government as "damning and conclusive to the last degree," and called for the "exclusion" of Stratton from public life and "the overthrow of the administration in whose behalf he operated." Even the staunch Liberal W.D. Gregory warned Laurier that the Ontario government "cannot continue in office without injuring the party."[9]

The royal commission reported in June, clearing Stratton and condemning Gamey, who apparently had pocketed some of his bribe and, at one point in the proceedings, fearing perjury charges, had fled to Buffalo, N.Y. The *News* agreed Gamey was a scoundrel but added that "the judges cannot mean to contend that it is proper for Governments to bargain for the support of Opposition members in return for the patronage of their constituencies … it was a bribe, and a bribe even though it were solicited." It commented that there was "a disposition to embalm the Commission's report among the curiosities of judicial literature and to consider the Gamey charges in the light of political experience and from the standpoint of human probability."

Predictably, however, many Liberal partisans were outraged. P.S. Armstrong of St. Mary's condemned the "lynch law attitude," and a correspondent to the *News* styling himself "Real Old Liberal" raged that Willison had "forfeited the respect of honest men forever."

To Laurier, Willison explained that "the methods revealed in the Gamey inquiry seriously discredit the whole Government. That may be a rash view but it is my honest view and I must give it expression." He understood partisan Liberal annoyance, but as he put it to Laurier, "the theory that I have turned Tory is absurd and I have no fear that the notion can become a permanent impression." In any event, his "independent" admirers, especially in academe, warmly praised his stance. The poet Wilfred Campbell rejoiced to him that "there is one paper with a true independent spirit…. I feel like you that we are tyrannized over by party."[10]

Of course, for many Liberals the words "Tory" and "protectionist" were inseparable. Toronto industrial business and its financial backers were virtually unanimously for effective protective tariffs, and Willison already had travelled a long way towards that position at the *Globe*. Now in the *News* he called in February 1903 for a "New National Policy" through which "the East will consider transportation as a national question, and the West the tariff as a national question."[11] Clearly, the imminence of major national decisions on new transcontinental railway development suggested that kind of trade-off, in the face of traditional Western anti-tariff sentiment.

A further reason for renewed tariff debate sprang from the bombshell announcement in May 1903 of Joseph Chamberlain, the British Colonial Secretary, that he favoured reciprocal preferential tariffs within the Empire, to foster common economic progress and imperial unity. Willison was naturally sympathetic to these objectives, but his nationalism and protectionism were far more powerful motivations. The *News* admitted, following Chamberlain's statement, that there would be undoubted trade benefits for Canadian resource exports in Britain, but was unwilling to see Canada gain this "at the expense of certain Eastern industries." Earlier American and British indifference to Canadian industrial development had forced Canadians, the *News* recalled, to "build for ourselves.... In that spirit we must continue to rear our national structure." It expressed the hope that something moderate and partial could be worked out among the Empire countries, and contended that "a system of preferences on the basis of moderate protection for colonial industries, and higher duties against foreign countries is both possible and practicable." Willison stressed to Governor General Lord Minto: "... we shall not readily forego the ambition to make this a great industrial community, somewhat on the lines of the Republic."[12]

In September 1903, Chamberlain resigned from the British government to carry his "Fair Trade" crusade to the people. By February 1904, the *News* was able to make a very accurate prediction of his failure to reverse Britain's commitment to free trade and state a very definite prediction as to the implications for Canada:

> We in Canada may as well face the situation. Free trade is still the chosen fiscal faith of Great Britain. The sentiment against the taxation of food is formidable. The [British] Liberals ... seem certain to come into office with the next general election. Years may elapse before the policy of imperial preference can succeed in the

mother Country. In the meantime, Canada will have grown in strength and population, and we shall probably be much less concerned for tariff consideration from Great Britain or any other community.[13]

All this did not mean at all that Willison had renounced the imperialist faith he earlier had come to hold with a convert's fervour. Not trade but defence was his proposed area of concentration. He advised the governor general that this was "a new question for Canada."[14] As the *News* put it in May 1903, "In Canada no apprehension of foreign war prevails. The idea of national expansion has seized upon our minds, and we are intent upon making a great nation…. The Canadian idea is sound, so far as it goes, but every great Empire needs some defensive organization just as every city needs a police force, and Canada is forgetting that fact."

In September of that year it proposed "a reasonable annual contribution to the Royal Navy and the creation of a naval militia." It argued that "for shame's sake and for need's sake, we must do something to help the Navy on which our national scheme of existence depends…. A contribution to the Navy is Canada's next step towards Empire building."[15] But as Willison would write years later about these times of unprecedented prosperity and growth, there were only "isolated voices" on the need for a Canadian naval effort, and "those who pleaded and admonished were unheard or treated merely as fretful or garrulous imperialists."[16] Until something dramatic occurred, the *News* and its editor could get nowhere on the naval or any other defence issue.

On both the tariff and naval defence, enough had been said already, of course, to give anti-protectionist and anti-imperialist federal Liberals some handy evidence for their suspicions that John Willison was turning Tory. But as yet no fundamental clash with Laurier had developed. Indeed, at the April 1904 Press Gallery dinner in Ottawa the prime minister went out of his way to praise Willison. John Ewan, still with the *Globe* and serving as an Ottawa correspondent, witnessed that off-the-record tribute and at once wrote his old boss to report: "He mentioned your name, saying that you were one of the influential men of the day & so on. He did it so well, too. It really required some courage for the leader of the Liberal party to do what he did at this juncture."[17]

By early 1904 a new phase in Canadian railway development may have helped the prime minister find his kind words for Willison. Through much of 1903 and on into 1904, the paramount national political issue in Canada was the Laurier government's mammoth National Transcontinental–Grand Trunk Pacific railway project. Through much of the evolution and publicization of its essentials, Willison and the *News* were strongly supportive. The initial version of the project was unveiled by the prime minister in the House of Commons on July 30, 1903. The terms owed at least as much to the Liberal party's political concerns in the various provinces and regions as to pragmatic transportation planning or cost estimating. The thriving agricultural and mining west yearned for an alternative non-CPR link with eastern markets; Ontario and Quebec dreamed of important new northern settlements; and the Maritimes wanted the winter eastern terminus for the new route. Laurier and his ministers believed that these powerful pressures and dreams, coupled with escalating immigration and building export markets for natural products in Britain and Europe, meant that a bold new national railway project begged to be launched.

There was division in the cabinet and understandable hesitation over the best approach. Andrew Blair from New Brunswick, minister of railways and canals, wanted a government-owned line, at least from Quebec to Winnipeg, to serve as a common carrier. Sir Richard Cartwright of Ontario headed a group that opposed so expensive an approach, preferring federal construction bonds for an expanding Grand Trunk. Clifford Sifton from Manitoba urged that the government should force the western-based Canadian Northern and the eastern Grand Trunk to cooperate in constructing necessary links for their two systems. However, the Canadian Northern owners, Mackenzie and Mann, and the Grand Trunk's controlling manager, Charles M. Hays, blocked any co-operative arrangement, and Laurier did not believe in public ownership of so large an entrepreneurial enterprise.[18] The prime minister strove instead to entice the Grand Trunk into a deal that would minimize the cost of the project to the government and yet satisfy the various regional ambitions.

A substantially correct outline of the resulting agreement appeared in the *Globe* on July 3. The government would construct a line from Moncton, N.B. to Winnipeg and lease it to the "Grand Trunk Pacific" for fifty years; and the GTP would build from Winnipeg to the Pacific with government aid, mainly in bond guarantees.

Willison, delighted, wrote Laurier: "My impression is that your solution will satisfy the country and give strength to the Government." He no doubt was delighted also by the government's introduction of a railway commission bill, something he long had called for.[19] His enthusiasm soared after the prime minister formally launched the plan with a brilliant speech in the House of Commons on July 30. Laurier spoke of the "national as well as … commercial necessity" of fully opening the West to the hundreds of thousands of settlers who were starting to flood into the country. He was certain that Canadian industrial development would advance phenomenally as the new line distributed Canadian products to this vast new population. "The flood of tide is upon us that leads on to fortune," he cried. "If we let it pass, the voyage of our national life, bright as it is today, will be bound in shallows."

The *News* at once pronounced Laurier "a giant when a great political task has to be performed." It praised him for resisting the "powerful influences of the CPR and the Canadian Northern," and it rejoiced that he had steered almost entirely clear of subsidies, in favour of the bond guarantee approach, which Willison long had championed. The paper regretted that public opinion seemed not yet prepared for the more "radical" step of public ownership, but pronounced the new Grand Trunk Pacific agreement the most favourable deal for the public interest ever concluded in the railway field in Canada. It warned the Conservative federal opposition, now led by Robert Borden of Halifax, that they "can hardly meet the situation with any less radical or less comprehensive proposal. The time demands a constructive policy, and in that way only lies credit for the Opposition"[20]

It was a suitably "independent" line for the kind of paper the *News* claimed to be. Probably to Willison's astonishment, Robert Borden began to offer precisely the public ownership policy he wanted. Initially, Borden told the Commons that Laurier's plan would "set back" the cause of public ownership for fifty years and that the government's dreams of never having to carry through on its bond guarantees to the Grand Trunk were delusive. He was not yet ready to put forward a detailed alternative, but that was promised in the near future. For the first time in twenty-two years of political journalism, Willison was drawn into ad-miring comment on a Conservative federal leader. The *News* speculated that the Tories at last, for the first time since Macdonald, might just have a properly "national" leader. If he could indeed put forward a compre-hensive alternative, he would "grow in stature and in public confidence" and his party could be seen once more as "a governing organization."[21]

The full shaping of that alternative took nearly a year. Borden start-ed with piecemeal proposals. In August he played deftly to Maritime opinion by proposing that the government-owned Intercolonial, with perhaps some additions, be the Maritimes section of the new system. He wanted the private Canada Atlantic, in central Ontario, to be pur-chased by the government to extend the Intercolonial to Georgian Bay, and that waterways and a government-purchased North Bay–Fort Wil-liam CPR section be the links to the West. There should be realistic careful study of the economics of the proposed Quebec–Winnipeg line through the northern regions of Ontario and Quebec before any final decision was made about it. The *News* hailed the "large measure" of public ownership and urged serious non-partisan consideration of both the Laurier and Borden options. Willison did not have a personal close-ness to Borden, but very likely a contributing factor in the paper's open-ness towards the Conservative leader's position was that Joseph Flavelle had advised Borden on several financial aspects, while adding that "on the last analysis the News will express Mr. Willison's views." Borden had thanked Flavelle profusely for his "great assistance," remarking that he had been "an inspiration."[22]

The government's plan, substantially intact, passed Parliament in late October. But trouble soon developed. The Grand Trunk's directors began to doubt the financial soundness of the deal and squeezed new conces-sions from the government. On April 5, 1904, Laurier presented them to the Commons. Most dramatically, the government's guarantee of interest on the construction costs of the mountain line would now be 75 percent of the *total* cost, without the ceiling that had previously been prescribed; and the railway would now be permitted five years' grace on default of interest payments before the government would be allowed to act against it. The prime minister claimed that the new terms were "no violent de-parture" from the original provisions.[23]

In the interval since the previous August, Willison and the *News* had pressed vigorously for the extension of the publicly-owned Intercolonial, and he had stressed privately to Laurier in January 2004 that his adoption of that position would be "an admirable political stroke, would make the Intercolonial very like a national system and give it influential control over through freight rates." He assured the prime minister that, whatever their difference on that or any other policy, "my personal feeling towards you was never stronger." Laurier graciously replied: "In the position which you occupy it is essential that you should speak your mind freely, and in the very nature of things you must differ with me on many points." He went on to reiterate his continuing opposition to extensive government ownership of railways:

> Government ownership is quite feasible in Australia, where there are no rival lines to compete with, and in some other countries similarly situated.... But on this continent, I am afraid that we must come to the conclusion that a Government railway having to compete with lines in the hands of private companies administered by keen and sharp business men, is bound to be a heavy loser.[24]

That was just too absolute a rejection of public ownership for Willison. And as the details of the revised Grand Trunk Pacific project became known, the *News* was frank in its disappointment, commenting that the government, "while bearing all the risks, is giving the prospective benefits to the private interests which would not jeopardize their own money." Echoing an earlier Borden comment, it mourned: "Private operation of a public railway is assured for fifty years. Public ownership is put back for a half a century — perhaps permanently."[25]

Then came Robert Borden's House of Commons speech of May 26, just before third reading on the revised Laurier position. Borden claimed that the "growing sentiment of the people" was moving inexorably towards "the conclusion that that road, constructed by the people of this country should not only be owned but operated by them." He added:

We do not propose that the voice of the people should be stifled, and we declare that if the Conservative party is returned to power at the next general election, it will enact such legislation as will enable the will of the people to prevail over the will of the corporation....

... By expropriation, or by any other fair and just policy, we shall carry out the will of the people. Let the people determine whether Canada shall have a government-owned railway or a railway-owned government.[26]

The *News* rejoiced. "The contrast is dangerous to the Government," it concluded. "Mr. Borden's speech and resolutions change the whole face of Canadian politics. The issue which he presents must affect the party relationships of a great body of the electorate, and will unquestionably determine the result of the next general election." At last Willison found himself supporting a major Conservative policy and opposing a major Liberal one. He explained to Laurier: "You cannot know how hard it is for me to go against your Government. I do not imagine that it is of much consequence to you; it is a constant distress to me. I was intensely anxious to go with the Government on the Grand Trunk Pacific, but what can an advocate of state railways do under the circumstances? I have not made the situation. It was made for me." Laurier was quick to reassure him generously: "Disagree you and I will, on many questions, but so far as I am concerned, that will not in any way deter from my old friendship for you...."[27]

As it turned out, Borden's bold move did not turn out to "change the whole face of Canadian politics," nor turn the *News* into an enthusiastic newspaper ally of the federal Conservatives. Even in its first flush of enthusiasm for Borden's position, the paper noted that "many senior members of the Conservative party, many men in influential positions, will deeply resent this radical departure."

In June, a number of Montreal financial leaders, many of them Conservatives, published a statement against public ownership both as a general principle and as applied to the transcontinental. The Conservative press was openly divided. The result, when the general election campaign began in the fall, was at best a fitful and querulous Conservative campaign on the railway issue. As Willison later would write, "there was so much of incoherence and uncertainty … that the country was not impressed." Accordingly, the *News* did not formally support the Conservatives in the election, although it did continue to push the public ownership position which it described repeatedly as a public necessity. Laurier's landslide election win in November practically "settled" the railway question, the *News* admitted on the morrow of the vote, and it conceded that the public ownership principle had received a "decided check."

As 1904 closed, Willison congratulated Laurier and wished him "from my heart a very happy Christmas season, good and improving health, and many more years of public usefulness…."

The prime minister thanked his "sincere friend" and remarked generously: "You have done a great work during the year. Your paper is becoming stronger every day. In your increased success I take a very deep interest…."[28]

That kind of generosity was possible for a victorious prime minister at the height of his power. It was also typical of the lofty Laurier. It was not possible from the embattled provincial Liberals in their last death throes as a governing force. Once more, as in 1903 over the Gamey affair, revelations about Liberal electoral corruption and Willison's unambiguous response to them were at the heart of what had become a complete estrangement. In the autumn of 1904, election trials in North Norfolk, North Perth, and Sault Ste. Marie resulted in the unseating of their MLAs — all Liberals. Revelations about the Sault were particularly damaging for the Ross regime: with the collusion of the Attorney General, James Gibson, twenty impersonators had been steamed to vote across Lake Superior from Michigan aboard the *Minnie M*.[29]

In the wake of the unseatings, the *News* acidly remarked that the determination of the provincial Liberals to cling to power at any cost had "compromised the party for a generation." James McMullen, an old Liberal friend, wrote to Willison to protest his "bitterness" against Ross and his ministers. Had they not handled the affairs of the province well? To another critic Willison conceded that, but argued the electoral fraud sin was mortal. In November 1904, as the opening of a provincial general election campaign neared, the *News* reminded voters: "… there is but one issue. The electoral corruption that has spread over the Province."[30]

The campaign on which Willison was launched was distasteful to him, notwithstanding his deep convictions about its necessity. "The citizen who dares to step out of his party alliances," he had told the Canadian Club of Toronto earlier that year, "is likely to be regarded by one-half of his former associates as a fool and by the other half as a knave, and he is indeed fortunate if ten per cent of the community can be persuaded that he is not settling a private grudge with politicians who had rejected his counsel, refused him office, or denied him some other recognition which he coveted." He confided to E.S. Caswell that "there was no man in the Ontario Government who has not been my friend, and the hardest thing I have had to do in my life is to take the course which I have taken."[31]

The provincial general election was called for January 25, 1905. The *News* called on "the independent electors of Ontario" to "vote for a change ... give the new Government a working majority, and hold it to a strict responsibility for its actions." To Laurier Willison explained: "All I want to say ... is that I cannot take any course other than the one I am taking, that I am sure I am walking in what Goldwin Smith calls the path of 'honor' and 'duty,' that I have confidence that you will understand me even if you regret my action and that at any rate you will not think that I am actuated by unworthy motives." As the campaign ended, the *News* summed up Willison's core objective: "If we punish corruption in this Government and judge its successors by as severe a standard, the whole tone and character of public life will be elevated, and Government, if only from sheer self-interest, will drive the corruptionist out of business, and make their appeal to the judgment and conscience of the community."[32]

At last the Ontario Liberals were humbled, after thirty-four years in office. James Whitney's Conservatives took sixty-nine seats to twenty-nine for the Liberals. A large share of the credit for the overturn had to go to "independents" like Willison, Goldwin Smith and Samuel Hume Blake who had denounced the party they once had championed. The *Canadian Annual Review* was certain that the *News* had been "the leading external influence" in pushing Liberals and independents into the Tory column. Newspaper circulation figures illustrated that impact. In January 1904 the daily average sales of the *News* numbered 25,413. By June 1, the figure rose to 33,439; by January 1, 1905 it reached 37,467; and for the final week of the election it was at 39,830. Daily averages for 1904 and 1905 were 33,173 and 38,282. During the same period the *Mail and Empire*, the official Conservative organ, declined from 45,463 to 41,135, even as its provincial party was winning office. The Liberal *Globe* rose a mere seven hundred, to 51,915.[33] Clearly, the Toronto daily that gained a substantial new readership as the provincial Liberals were hounded from office was the *News*.

Its editor barely had time to catch his breath before he found himself in a new struggle with the Liberal party, this time at the federal level. The issue involved the separate school laws of the new provinces of Alberta and Saskatchewan, which were created by Parliament during the 1905 session. Willison's past attitudes on federalism and provincial rights, his concern that the new provinces in the west be free to enjoy the same degree of autonomy as the older provinces, and his aversion to the national heterogeneity which he believed separate schools encouraged, brought him into sharp and bitter conflict with Sir Wilfrid Laurier. For Willison, it was a final and immensely painful separation from his best friend and idol and from the political party in whose service he had invested two decades of his talent, enthusiasm, and idealism.

In the North-West Territories Act of 1875, provision had been made for the establishment of minority Protestant or Roman Catholic tax-supported separate schools. Territorial Ordinances of 1892 and 1901, however, had severely modified the truly "separate" character of such schools, subjecting them to control by a single educational authority regulating teachers, curriculum, and textbooks, and limiting religious instruction to a mere half-hour at the end of the school day.[34]

By 1904, the North-West Territories contained over 450,000 people and pressure was mounting on the federal government to grant provincial status. Laurier publicly pledged to work out terms following his re-election, and privately assured Archbishop Sbaretti, the Vatican's Apostolic Delegate in Canada, that he would deal with the schools issue according to, as he put it, the "letter and spirit of the constitution." He promised him that "the system of separate schools now in existence shall be secured and beyond the power of the provincial legislature as provided by Section 93 of the constitution, either to abolish or even prejudicially affect such schools."[35]

From Willison's first days at the *News* he had stressed his support for untrammelled autonomy for any provinces to be created in the West. "The Western communities will not be denied the right to determine the character of their local institutions," the paper pronounced in January 1903. In May that year it indicated its fear that the Roman Catholic hierarchy and its political allies might try to make separate schools "the price of autonomy." It repeated that line in mid-1904, warning both the Church and the Laurier government against "disregard of the wishes of the people of the Northwest." That comment was sufficiently pointed to draw the attention and ire of the prime minister, who wrote him to say:

> Why, in the name of patriotism, attempt to resurrect the now dormant school question? Why, when we have profound peace, attempt to prejudge public opinion? The school question will come up again all too soon. It will come in a very different form from what it was in 1896, but with the same bitter passions on both sides, and again it will be my lot to fight extremists and to place and maintain the question where it has been placed by the British North America Act.... Let me ask you also to remember that the work of effecting the union is far from complete. The work must be continued in the same spirit in which it was conceived, and I certainly indulge the hope that you and I will always find it easy to stand on that ground.

Willison replied that he would be dismayed to see the whole matter "quietly settled" in Ottawa. He stressed that his non-coercion policy on separate schools in the west "was my position upon the Manitoba question and I do not see how it is possible to take any other position with respect to the Territories." He promised, nevertheless, to give his "very earnest and sympathetic attention" to Laurier's arguments, but added: "I do not think I shall reach any different conclusion from the one I have stated." For his part, Laurier made clear that he would "ask no quarter from you or anyone if when the time has come to face and solve that new question, I do not solve it according to your conception of right."[36]

Laurier's smashing triumph in the November 1904 general election was followed by the announcement as the new Parliament convened on January 12, 1905 that the government would bring in autonomy legislation for the Territories. Through the remainder of January and early February, Premier Haultain of the Territories negotiated in Ottawa with a team of federal ministers led by Laurier. Little time was spent on the schools issue, to the annoyance of Haultain, apparently because Laurier saw no point in reiterating irreconcilable differences. The actual drafting of the education clauses was the responsibility of Charles Fitzpatrick, the minister of justice and a Roman Catholic. The minister of the interior, Clifford Sifton, who normally would have been prominent in finalizing any policy concerning the West, was in the southern United States for his health. Sifton was opposed in principle to separate schools, but he was prepared to agree to the entrenching in the new provincial constitutions of the very limited system which had evolved in the Territories. He had made this clear to Laurier before going south.[37]

On February 21, Laurier introduced into the House of Commons the Autonomy Bills creating the new provinces of Alberta and Saskatchewan. He left the schools issue to the very end of his speech, but then tackled it head on. He warned: "… the old passions which such a subject has always aroused are not, unfortunately, buried." He would approach the problem with "the Canadian spirit of tolerance and charity of which Confederation is the essence." He chose to base his policy on the historical guarantee of denominational school rights, Section 93 (1) of the British North America Act, which read: "Nothing in any such [provincial education] law shall prejudicially affect any right or privilege with respect to denominational schools which any class of persons have by law in the province." He reminded the House of the educational clauses of the North-West Territories Act of 1875 through which Parliament, as he put it, "unanimously, deliberately and with their eyes open, introduced into the North-West Territories the system of separate schools." Accordingly, he stated: "We have to decide this problem upon the very terms of the legislation which was introduced in 1875." Clause 16 of the bills creating the new provinces declared that each should be considered in law already to have been a province at the time of union (1905) and hence subject to the provisions of Section 93 of the British North America Act, "in continuance of the principles sanctioned under the North-West Territories Act."

Not content with a merely constitutional justification for separate schools in the new provinces, Laurier chose to identify himself with a theoretical case for denominational education itself. He "never could understand what objection there could be to a system of schools wherein, after secular matters have been attended to, the tenets of the religion of Christ, even with the divisions which exist among his followers, are allowed to be taught." He cited the U.S. experience with lynchings, divorces, and murders, and contrasted this with the "almost total absence" of them in Canada, stressing: "... for my part I thank heaven that we are living in a country where the young children are taught Christian morals and Christian dogmas."[38]

Willison was appalled at the Laurier position. As he would later explain to a close Liberal friend, Frank Beer:

> If you have ever read my history of the Liberal party you know that my estimate of Sir Wilfrid Laurier is based chiefly on his devotion to the federal principle and his resolute resistance to clerical interference in education. Probably half of the book deals with questions of this character and Sir Wilfrid knew well that it was largely to present this view of his public career that my book was written. With the Western Autonomy Acts he turned squarely in the other direction and with my book in existence I had nothing to do but break political connections which on personal grounds as well as on political grounds I greatly cherished. If I had defended the Western Autonomy Acts in face of what I had written in the book I would have been a joke from one end of the country to the other.[39]

The *News* was quick to respond to the Laurier speech, with the sarcastic comment: "The theory that our national morality is due to the separation of our children will not bear a moment's consideration." It was certain that the "federal principle" required freedom for new provinces to determine their own practices in education. It argued that "the best chapters" of Laurier's career had been his "long struggle against *ultramontane* ascendancy in Quebec," recalled that the Ontario Liberal party "had its birth in resistance to sectarian institutions," and emphasized that "provincial rights has been the bedrock of Liberal policy." Accordingly, the new Laurier policy "suggests a great betrayal of Liberal principles, and a flagrant denial of the faith of the founders of Canadian Liberalism." On March 8 the *News* carried for the first time a banner on its front page which was to be a feature for the next two months: A FREE WEST, A COMMON SCHOOL, PROVINCIAL RIGHTS AND RELIGIOUS EQUALITY.[40]

Laurier and Willison corresponded briefly, only to reiterate their absolutely conflicting views. Laurier pleaded that "this is a difficult country to govern ... there are conflicting elements to reconcile and to harmonize." He argued that Section 93 of the British North America Act had been drawn up "to lay down once and for all the rules by which the unfortunate subject of separate schools was to be regulated." Willison responded that he could give "no respect at all" to "the contention that we are constitutionally obliged to create an educational system for the Western Territories," and added:

> ... while I have all this respect for the natural race sentiment of French Canadians no man could be more strenuously opposed to clerical interference in State affairs. And from Confederation down the plain meaning of the constitution has been deliberately perverted to serve the ends of the Roman Catholic Hierarchy. Further, the Hierarchy have never touched education except to check, embarrass and prevent the free play of human intelligence. With these views I am bound to oppose, and oppose with all the powers I possess, the North-West Bills. I am sure you could not have expected me to do otherwise, and you know how much rather I would fight with you rather than against you. I know, of course, that the measure cannot be defeated in Parliament, but I cannot think that is a reason for silence or slackness.
>
> With profound regret that we should be separated on this issue.

The Honourable Clifford Sifton, 1900. Library and Archives Canada, PA-027943

Laurier asked him to put aside the merits or faults of separate schools and argued that "the whole point is one of good faith under the constitution." But he recognized their impasse and observed philosophically: "So let us agree to disagree."[41]

Willison was by no means alone in his stand. Even within Liberal ranks the reaction among prominent English-speaking Protestant leaders in Ontario was markedly unfavourable. Former premier George Ross told Laurier he wished he had left the schools issue alone. Senator Mc-Mullen attacked the prime minister for "a direct subversion" of Liberal principles. Senator L.M. Jones reminded him of his reputation from 1896 as a champion of provincial rights and lamented he had "changed his mind and reversed his position." Newton Wesley Rowell, a prominent Toronto lawyer and rising provincial Liberal, challenged the attempt to apply Section 93 to any province beyond Ontario and Quebec. Only they, he argued, had entered Confederation with freely adopted systems of separate schools. There were, he warned Laurier, "hosts of Liberals" who agreed with his opposition. Perhaps most seriously of all, the *Globe*, under Willison's successor, Rev. J.A. Macdonald, broke openly with the prime minister. Macdonald explained to him that the *Globe* was "shut up by its own past as well as by present convictions and conditions" to support of full provincial freedom in education.[42]

There was trouble in the Cabinet, too. The worst blow of all came on February 27 when Clifford Sifton, the minister of the interior and leading minister from the West, resigned. Sifton had rushed back to Ottawa from his vacation when Laurier's schools policy was announced. He had been prepared to accept constitutional entrenchment of the existing semi-public schools in the Territories, as set forth in the Territorial ordinances of 1892 and 1901, but not the old 1875 absolutely separate ones. The minister of finance, W.S. Fielding from Nova Scotia, also had been out of town when Laurier's proposed clause had been drafted. He too was alarmed by it, but Sifton advised him: "… one resignation will probably accomplish the desired result." Other ministers too may have been disaffected. By March 1, Laurier admitted to a Quebec colleague: "… *nous allons avoir une crise ministérielle*." But he was quick to add that he had not lost all hope of a compromise.[43]

A compromise there was. The new education clause in the two bills for the new provinces of Alberta and Saskatchewan was made public on March 20 and introduced in the Commons two days later by the prime minister. Its terms were in accord with Sifton's position, that the guarantees of Section 93 of the BNA Act would apply specifically only to the severely modified separate school privileges under the Territorial Ordinance of 1901. Laurier later claimed that he "never had any intention to give anything else to the minority.…" But as his later very admiring biographer, O.D. Skelton, would remark: "No explanation could fully explain. Critics contended that if he had intended to re-establish denominational schools of the earlier type, then for the first time he had been forced to retire from a position which he had deliberately taken; and if he had merely meant to continue the existing schools, this should have been made clear beyond question."

The new terms reunited the Liberals in Parliament, except for a handful of Quebec MPs led by Henri Bourassa, who denounced what he saw as a betrayal of Catholic rights. Even the *Globe* pronounced itself satisfied, commenting that the new provisions were "widely and essentially different" from the original ones.[44]

Willison was not mollified at all. The *News* declared that the amended clauses "differ from the old in setting forth in detail the kind of Separate Schools to be perpetuated in the west," but "they are identical precisely in their constitutional aspect, and in their infringement of Provincial Rights." It condemned Liberals in Ottawa for bowing to "sectarian control," and was certain that their surrender would "sow the seeds of certain strife and struggle in the future." The *News* claimed to see further clerical interference in discussions said to have taken place between Mgr. Sbaretti, the papal delegate, and the Manitoba government, over the extension of that province's boundary. Sbaretti was said to have suggested that the extension could be expedited in exchange for concessions to Catholics under the Manitoba school laws. "Whether we look at the proposal to fasten Separate Schools on the West, or at the conduct of Mgr. Sbaratti, the *News* thundered, "we find the same course of evil — clerical interference — and we must seek the same remedy — the entire separation of Church and State.[45]

Even some of Willison's friends, a number of them allies thus far in the fight on the education clauses in the Autonomy Bills, urged him to be more moderate. W.D. LeSuer, the historian and essayist, warned that "all this talk about the hierarchy" was "actually throwing into the shade the main question of the constitutionality and justice of the pending legislation." E.S. Caswell, former head of the Methodist Book Publishing House, denounced the "bitterness and ever growing spirit of <u>violence</u>" of Willison's campaign. "I cannot see that enough is involved to justify a great hubbub being raised." John Lewis, one of Willison's own editorial writers, cited "the danger of getting into an old-fashioned no-popery attitude." Willison himself admitted to the federal Conservative leader,

Betrayed and Thrown. N. McConnell cartoon, News, March 23, 1905, p. 1

Robert Borden, his "daily regret ... that such a question must be discussed. But I have seldom felt so strongly upon any subject and so must stay in the fight." The *News* remarked: "We are solemnly warned against saying the measure has a sectarian basis. What other legal basis can be found for a measure that on legal and constitutional grounds is too weak to stand a moment's consideration. We are warned against religious and racial strife. Let the blame rest on those who are, by this unwarranted measure, wantonly breaking the peace that has existed ever since the settlement of the Manitoba School question nine years ago."[46]

Willison stood side by side now, on the Autonomy Bills issue, with Robert Borden and the federal Conservatives. He and Borden were beginning to correspond confidentially now, as the journalist had done so frequently and so closely and for so long with his long-time idol and friend, Laurier. Borden had matched Willison's thorough provincial rights stand and Willison, delighted, told him that the Conservatives "have commended themselves to the English-speaking majority, and as a result will probably gain some strength in all the English provinces."[47]

Two federal by-elections in Ontario, in the London and North Oxford ridings, called for June 13, provided an early opportunity to test that theory. The *News* sought to sway traditional Liberal supporters in the ridings with the claim that a Liberal vote now would be "a vote to dishonour Liberal traditions, to set aside the principles of George Brown, and to declare that a generation of devotion to Provincial Rights was a sham and a mistake...." But, it argued, "if you vote against the Government candidate you will vote to give freedom to the West, to save the constitution, to respect Provincial rights and it may be that even at this eleventh hour the Government will heed your remonstrance and so amend the bills now before the House of Commons so as to give full Provincial autonomy to Alberta and Saskatchewan."

The Liberals won both seats, in London by a higher majority than in 1904, and in North Oxford by their smallest margin in years. In the city seat, the increase seemed to come from Catholic voters; in the rural one the decrease was among predominantly Scottish Presbyterian electors, the traditional "backbone" of Ontario Liberalism.[48] It was possible that in future contests for less reliably Liberal seats, that kind of trend in overwhelmingly Protestant Ontario might be fatal for the Liberals.

That prospect can have been little comfort for Willison amid the discouragements of 1905. Not only did Laurier win the Ontario by-elections, but Liberal governments were elected handily in the new provinces of Alberta and Saskatchewan. Willison later would write that "outside of Ontario the autonomist agitation left the deeps of public opinion in the English provinces undisturbed." He even came to judge that the actual practice of the Laurier educational clauses "have been so interpreted as to maintain the integrity of the public school system as developed under the old ordinances of the territorial government."[49] In 1905, however, still feeling hurt and betrayed by what he clearly sincerely believed had been a complete turning away by Laurier from his 1896 provincial rights schools policy for Manitoba to anti-constitutional imposition of separate schools in Alberta and Saskatchewan, he was not ready to believe any such thing.

By the time he had come to his later conclusion, Willison's bitterness against Laurier had disappeared, in spite of a host of political differences that supplemented those of 1905. As early as 1908, there was a small measure of rapprochement, when Laurier thanked him for a message which "has removed a load from off my heart." At Laurier's death, Willison would recall: "I feel still the fragrance of all his consideration for myself, and notwithstanding that I separated from him politically he was kind to the end." Willison's second wife, in an unpublished memoir she wrote following his death, recalled a conversation they had had a decade after the Autonomy Bills split with Laurier:

> It was plain to see that it had made a great difference to him and had been possibly the most difficult decision of his life.... He believed that common schools were essential to national unity. As far as I know he never changed his mind on that question, and he believed that he had taken the only course he could take.... Laurier had changed his mind on that question, not he. But after telling the story without heat or emotion merely as a story, he added that to leave one's party was one of the hardest things that a man had to do. A man lost his friends, his associates. There was much ill-feeling.... He concluded that he did not know whether he would do it now or not, he did not see what else he could do. But he added, 'I would advise my boys never to leave their party; it is too difficult, too painful.'[50]

For John Willison in the spring of 1905, the Liberal and Laurier years were over. He was on his own.

X

Challenges of Independence, 1905–1908

IN APRIL 1905, EDWARD CASWELL, AN OLD LIBERAL FRIEND OF Willison, accused him of heading "to all intents and purposes a Tory paper." Charlie Hamilton, Willison's Ottawa correspondent, urged "going slow at times to convince people we are still fair." Willison himself assured another Liberal friend that he was "not the bond-slave of any party, and I venture to think that my future course will make that plain."[1] It would not be easy.

In provincial politics, with the Ross Liberals defeated, there was an early pro-Whitney tone, aided perhaps by the premier appointing Joseph Flavelle to the Toronto liquor licensing commission and as a member of a royal commission on the University of Toronto. Relations soured for a time in November as Flavelle and his fellow commissioners quit over the firing of their expert inspectors on partisan grounds. Flavelle angrily told Whitney that the firings were "so at variance with Mr. Willison's and my own views as to what is in the public interest, that the News will be outspoken and insistent in its condemnation of this or similar acts of your government." The *News* did then denounce the "spoilsmen" of the Tory administration. Whitney remarked to a Tory colleague that "Willison has been waiting for an opportunity to pitch into us in order to show the Grits who have been throwing mud at him that his paper is not the Whitney organ." When Queen's University awarded the editor an honourary doctorate of laws in April 1906 "in recognition more especially of your eminent services to Canadian journalism," he joked that it was "my own peculiar fortune to have some popularity with Oppositions, and to be generally distrusted by Governments."[2]

He tried his best to rebuild and keep in place some bridges to old Liberal friends. He had a long "heart to heart" with the lawyer George Lindsey, whom he had known since the Young Men's Liberal Club days of the 1880s, assuring him; "Neither towards Sir Wilfrid nor Mr. Ross have I any personal ill-will...." He told his Ottawa correspondent Charlie Hamilton in April 1906 that he wanted to be "really independent," to "give the News a character for the most rigid independence of men and parties." That July he even published a lead editorial analyzing Laurier's strengths as a leader, with evident generosity:

> He has ridden through heavy seas and kept his head and his temper. He has faced gusts of hostile opinion, steady, calculating and resourceful, and has known just when to stand still and when to advance. With it all there has been an air of magnanimity, a touch of magnificence, and much restraint and dignity.

Looking to the Liberal future, he no doubt was delighted in June 1907 when Charlie Hamilton followed the spirit of his instructions in reporting in his Ottawa column on speculation in the capital that "Willie" King (now styled William Lyon Mackenzie King), who had served as deputy minister of labour since 1902, would be "a most suitable recruit for Ontario Federal Liberalism." King was very gratified, writing in his diary that the commendation was "most generous ... I am ... most pleased that an independent rather than a party paper should have been the first to announce a probable venture into public life."[3] He can have been in no doubt that Willison, his former employer and his family's longtime friend, remained a notable admirer of his talents.

Beyond politics, Willison was receiving more than a little praise. Montreal's *Le Nationaliste*, in a feature article, described him at this phase of his career as "*un brilliant journaliste et ses écrits sont de ceux qui commandent l'attention et qui font penser même ses plus irréductibles adversaires.*" [a brilliant journalist and his writings are such as to command the attention of even his bitterest opponents][4] In December 1905, he was invited to speak to the Canadian Club of Boston on "The Spirit of Canada." While warmly friendly to America, he wanted his audience to know that "the day of our strength is at hand, and long before this century has run its course, Canada will be a power among the nations…."[5]

The poet Wilfred Campbell saw a newspaper account and "not only agreed with the sentiments but appreciated the fine style in which it was written." A group of Toronto's business and academic elite, led by Edmund Walker of the Bank of Commerce and Sir Sandford Fleming, the famous CPR engineer and now the chancellor of Queen's, put together funds for the publication of 2,500 copies of the speech as a pamphlet entitled *Anglo-Saxon Amity*, which they distributed to British and Canadian MPs, members of the U.S. Congress, governors of American states, and newspaper editors throughout Canada, Britain and the U.S.[6]

Probably unknown to his Toronto sponsors, he had found already, and on a regular basis, a useful avenue of approach to a non-Canadian readership. During his 1897 trip to England, he had made some useful contacts in London. Since then, important and well-placed Canadian friends there, such as George Parkin of the Rhodes Scholarship Trust, steadily helped him widen his circle of correspondents and acquaintances in top imperialist and press circles. On Parkin's urging, L.S. Amery, the Colonial Editor of the *Times*, lunched with Willison in Toronto in July 1905. Then Fabian Ware, the editor of the London *Morning Post*, second only to the *Times* as an imperialist paper, sought Parkin's advice later that summer on a Canadian correspondent. By early October, Ware's associate, Richard Jebb, had come to Toronto, likely with the encouragement of Governor General Lord Grey, to invite Willison to take up the position. Ware explained to Willison that it was "of the greatest importance that the British people obtain accurate information regarding Canada…."

Willison's contributions to the *Post*, in keeping with the paper's tradition, were to be anonymous, as "From Our Own Correspondent — Toronto." Informally, his authorship gradually became known on both sides of the Atlantic, though it was never openly acknowledged. The involvement was worth far more to him than his average annual pay of seventy British pounds. Unbound by Canadian party constraints and freed for greater candour by the anonymity principle, he was able to press forcefully a strongly Canadian nationalist imperialism in one of the best available vehicles for reaching the breakfast tables of the British governing elite.[7]

In January 1906, the general election victory in Britain by the free trade Liberals dealt a severe blow to the imperial preference cause. Willison knew as well that imperial military or political centralization would be opposed resolutely by Laurier. He had believed for some time that Canadians generally, in the midst of great boom years, were prepared to give only cursory attention to defence issues. His imperialist faith remained strong, but he was determined to mix it with realism, especially for British readers. Joseph Flavelle urged him to "inform Englishmen that we are not supplicants for favours; we are not weaklings looking to the motherland for strength, but a vigorous rapidly enlarging community...."[8]

Consistent with this, Willison warned the British in his first major article for the *Post* in November 1905 that it was "doubtful if there is any general opinion in this country in favour of a contribution to Imperial naval defence," but he speculated that there was developing a "vagrant, unorganized sentiment of Canadian nationalism, not hostile to British connection," prepared to support beginning a Canadian navy to "make Canada the independent ally of Great Britain." On the idea of some imperialists for a permanent Imperial council, he warned of "that formidable body of Canadian opinion which is jealous for Canadian autonomy." In a December 1906 article he wrote: "Nothing is more certain than that we become more and more an independent nation within the British Empire.... It is certain that during the last few years there has been a remarkable growth in Canadian national feeling."

Richard Jebb and Fabian Ware expressed delight at Willison's candour and the thrust of his "autonomist" views. Jebb wrote that "serious Imperialists like myself will come to rely more and more on your judgment of Canadian events and tendencies than upon any other accessible individual opinion." Ware found Willison's articles "admirable" and reported that "everybody I have told that you are writing for us have told me that I am extremely lucky."[9]

Willison's main challenge remained to make the *News* a success as a newspaper and a force in public life. The dramatic controversies of 1905 had been painful for him, but they had helped to swell the newspaper's circulation average from 33,173 the year before to 38,282 in 1905. However, Joseph Atkinson's Toronto *Star* was moving up even faster, from 31,221 in 1904 to 38,489 in 1905. Alarmingly, the 1906 figures showed the *Star* at 42,313, while the *News* had dropped slightly, to 37,581. Atkinson was building his circulation success on an aggressive news policy, with political crusades distinctly secondary. The *Star* was prepared to send its reporters almost anywhere in the world for a good story and had more of them than any other two Toronto papers. Its editorials were simple, punchy, and populist. It was frightening competition, pulling farther and farther ahead in both sales and advertising in the main Toronto market. The greater appeal of the *News* outside the city helped sales but did little to pull in a competitive share of downtown retail advertising. By 1907 Flavelle was putting an extra $50,000 a year into the paper.[10]

Flavelle's support continued to be far more than just financial. The two men had agreed in 1903 on Willison's independence, and the bargain was kept. In 1906 the *News* lashed out against the "cynical carelessness" of the Toronto Railway Company holding the city's streetcar franchise, for their "refusal to observe solemn agreements" for satisfactory service and due regard for municipal concerns. This prompted Sir William Mackenzie, the company's president, and his friends to appeal to Flavelle. The *News* even denounced Mackenzie as "an arrogant, tyrannical man." When Z.A. Lash, Edmund Walker, and E.R. Wood, colleagues of Flavelle's on the boards of the Bank of Commerce and National Trust and heavy investors in Mackenzie's various enterprises, pressured him to muzzle Willison, Flavelle flatly refused. If that displeased his corporate colleagues, he was prepared to resign his directorships.[11]

Willison and Flavelle were not always on the popular or populist side of public disputes. Instead of being mere followers of opinion, they often preferred to champion ideals. That could mean a clash with some popular view.

In 1907, the *News* wandered into a disastrous fight with the Whitney provincial government and the powerful electric power movement. The paper's viewpoint outraged many Ontarians, especially when it came to be all too plausibly associated with certain of Flavelle's financial connections. At issue were the established interests of the private Toronto Electrical Development Company and its sister concern, the Toronto Electric Company, controlled by Sir William Mackenzie, Frederic Nicholls, and Sir Henry Pellatt. Electrical Development's stranglehold on Niagara production and its sale to municipalities throughout southern and southwest Ontario had been loosened by the Whitney government's creation of the public Hydro-Electric Power Commission under Adam Beck. Now the City of Toronto sought to take over its own power distribution, but Toronto Electric Light refused to negotiate a purchase deal, so the city chose to build its own plant and take its supply from the public HEPC rather than Electrical Development. Toronto voters were asked to approve in a special vote on January 1, 1908. It became evident that the provincial government, though regretting that a negotiated solution had not been found, was sympathetic with the city's stand, which fitted well with its own public power objectives.[12]

Willison long had been favourable to those objectives. In May 1907, the *News* damned the companies for exorbitant rates and urged them to be reasonable in the purchase negotiations with the city. When these failed, the paper commented acidly: "The Pellatt–Nicholls syndicate has itself to blame for the hostility of the Government, the city and the general public." The *News* firmly asserted that provincial and civic competition with the private interests would be a "violation" of existing contracts and would "frighten off" the kind of foreign — especially British — investment needed for Canadian development. Accordingly, it called in editorial after editorial throughout the rest of 1907 for public "expropriation" at fair cost of the companies' properties and franchises as the only honourable course if Ontario, through "confiscation," was not to sink "to the level of outlaw states." This line was anathema to the more extreme public power newspaper champions such as the *World* and the *Telegram*, which damned any compromises with the "grasping capitalists" of the "Electric Ring." The electors of Toronto agreed, voting three to one for the city's policy of competition. Six months later, Premier Whitney was elected in a landslide.[13]

In intensity and duration, the editorial campaign of the *News* on the power issue rivaled its crusade over the Autonomy Bills. Willison explained to Frank Cochrane, the minister of mines, that he "simply had to cry 'Halt' in deference to my long settled convictions of what is just and proper for a Government to do." He added: "You know that I have no private interest in the matter."

There were many suspicions that the same was not true for Joseph Flavelle. National Trust, of which he was president, served as trustee for the Electric Development Company's bondholders. Premier Whitney speculated to his brother that the rage of the *News* was "in order that the pockets of Mr. Flavelle may not be injured," that "what Willison has been saying in the 'News' against Power Policy has really been the views of Flavelle and against Willison's inclination." Later, according to Whitney, Willison approached him "to see if there is no way to come to an arrangement." Willison indignantly denied to his friend W.R. Riddell that he was "the slave of Mr. Flavelle's purse." However, as one of many critics, W.E. Saunders, put it to him: "I think the real reason why I am so sorry over your stand is that it makes me feel that your independence cannot be relied on."[14]

Even worse difficulties for Willison now became evident. Through the winter of 1907–08, the financial markets were in disarray, and Joseph Flavelle decided that he had reached the end of his willingness to bear the drain of the *News* on his finances. The year before, he had revealed to a close business friend that the paper had become "a financial burden almost too heavy to bear." The hard fact was that the cost of running a successful big-city daily newspaper was increasing by leaps and bounds as the need to appeal effectively with news and features to a mass readership became paramount. More than ever before, journalism had to operate as a big business.[15]

Flavelle later would estimate that in all he had lost $350,000 to $400,000 on the *News*.[16] When Willison learned of Flavelle's intentions, he sought advice from his closest friends on what he should do next. He had to be aware that he was at one of the great cross-roads of his career. Could he hope, at all realistically, to find as understanding and wealthy a patron for independent journalism as Flavelle had been over the past five years? Could the sponsorship of Conservative partisans be possible or palatable after the fight over the power question? Had bridges to Liberal associations been burned forever? Should he turn from being an editor to concentrating on more of the kind of special correspondence he was doing for the *Morning Post*? The questions must have piled on top of one another for many months throughout 1908. Only gradually were there any clear answers. While Flavelle looked to sell the *News*, Willison sought solid ground for his career. He was fifty-one years old.

Could a renewed Liberal association be possible? He still had many longtime Liberal friends. J.M. Clark, whom he had known since the 1880s in the Young Men's Liberal Club, had written feelingly in 1907 with condolences on news of Willison's father's death in the western U.S. Willison's close friendship with George Lindsey survived intensely. When Lindsey's father, a noted Liberal historian, died in April 1908, Willison wrote a eulogistic editorial in the *News*. Lindsey was immensely grateful: "You are very kind, considerate and good, you always are, you have touched me very deeply and I very sincerely thank you." Even a key figure in the Ross provincial administration, the former attorney general J.M. Gibson, sought to mend fences, telling Willison during the power controversy "how much I have admired your articles" because of their focus on "how much has been done and is being done ... to affect the financial credit of this country."

Willison remained close to Clifford Sifton, the former federal minister of the interior who had resigned his portfolio during the Autonomy Bills furor but remained a Liberal MP. In 1907, Sifton had been courted by Laurier to re-enter the government, and he had kept Willison fully informed, even to the extent of wiring him to come to Ottawa for an urgent consultation and of detailing to him in the end his reasons for declining the prime minister's offer. In turn, in February 1908 Willison sought Sifton's counsel as soon as Flavelle's intention to drop the *News* was evident.[17]

He did not stop with Sifton, also approaching the top Liberal of them all, Sir Wilfrid Laurier. After three years of no contact between them, he decided to try to break the ice. His letter and Laurier's reply beautifully illustrated what they once had been for each other, and how beyond any other motives for what they wrote, there was a mutual desire to restore at least something of their old intimacy:

Toronto
Feb. 3, 1908
Dear Sir Wilfrid,
Often I wonder if the relations between the Prime Minister and his former organist are ever to be restored. You may say that it is my fault that they were interrupted. That is true perhaps and yet on the subject of division there seemed to be only one course for me to take. I recognize, however, that that question is settled and that no good object could be served by its revival. As I grow older earlier associations seem to increase in value and I confess that my personal affection for yourself has not been overcome. For some time I have wanted to say this even if there should never be any further communication between us.
Yours very truly,
J.S. Willison

Ottawa
Feb. 5, 1908
My dear Willison,
Your letter has removed a load from off my heart. I cannot find fault with a friend if he differs from me, but loss of friendship is painful; in your case it was particularly painful. You thought I was wrong and I thought I was right. But no more of this; let it rest in oblivion until such time as meeting again as of old, at the fireside, talking of this, that, and the other thing, that one also may turn up.

I am happy to think that we may be friends again, and I will look forward eagerly and with a good deal of impatience for the pleasure of seeing you.

In the meantime believe me ever, my dear Willison.
Yours very sincerely,
Wilfrid Laurier[18]

There was no mention by either of them of the new circumstances for Willison at the *News*. Laurier may not have known about them. On Willison's side at least, however, the re-establishment of correspondence served as a preliminary contact that might possibly lead to some new formal Liberal involvement. Certainly, as the prime minister gradually became aware of the difficulty of Willison's situation, he proved ready to help his friend, while remaining mindful of the interests of the Liberal party.

On the subject of party interests, Willison by this time was well aware that the Conservatives, especially the Whitney government at Queen's Park, were hunting for a dependable and popular newspaper in the cheap afternoon market in Toronto. Evidently, the *Mail and Empire* in the more exclusive morning market was not sufficient in political terms. In late January, he told the readers of the *News* just what he thought of party organ journalism: "Elections are decided by the thinking, reasoning independent voters, and to these the organ seldom makes an effective appeal." Clearly then, his ideal remained to be the editor of an important newspaper that was *not* a partisan organ. This had been so before he had been able to extricate himself from the *Globe*. But how could it be possible now, with Flavelle withdrawing his support and no other "independent" source of financing apparent?

Willison confided to Sifton in mid-February the "absolutely confidential" nature of his dilemma. He wanted to see the *News* or some other independently inclined paper financed by some new syndicate of backers. Sifton warned that in recession times this could be "very difficult" and, even if success were achieved, the "worst feature" would be that Willison would "necessarily be to some extent under obligation to those who helped to find the money...." Could not Willison "preserve the status quo for the present?"[19]

Progress on resolving the situation with the *News* was slow, often non-existent through the spring. Willison continued to fret, and Sifton came down from Ottawa for a huddle over dinner in mid-April. Charlie Hamilton reported that the Ottawa rumour mills were alive with the conviction that the *News* was about to be the new Tory organ. In fact, the effort was being made, under the mandate of Premier Whitney. As of April 22, however, the premier was recording sadly that Frank Cochrane, the minister of mines, whom he had put in charge of the project, "could not get anybody to help him," and that "a considerable sum would be needed for working capital…." The premier's determination that the effort succeed probably kept it going. By mid-May, Hamilton was picking up signals in Ottawa that a Cochrane-led Tory syndicate would be putting $150,000 of fresh capital into the *News* and buying control from Flavelle. Willison told him to discount the stories, but the details must have seemed disquietingly precise.[20]

Exploration of whether such arrangements might be feasible probably was stalled by the Ontario general election campaign, held on June 8. Throughout the contest the *News* was at pains to be positive about the Whitney government, at least seemingly, as if "warming up" for an impending connection. The paper dismissed the earlier fight with the Tories over the power issue as settled, characterizing the government's general purposes in provision of cheap power for the people as "entirely praiseworthy." Whitney was lauded for his school and university reforms, his freedom from electoral wrongdoing and his careful financial management. The *News* judged the premier's integrity to be "beyond question" and warned its independent readers that his defeat would constitute "an invitation to politicians to return to the methods which prevailed from 1900 to 1905."[21]

So absolute a pro-Tory line prompted not a few of the independent readers to rebel. A.E.M. Thomson of Woodside complained that "you have descended from your high ideals of 'independence' to being a mere party sheet, as partisan as the chief organ of that party…." R.H. Smith of Toronto asked if Willison was "merely a chattel in the hands of others; or are you playing the double role of the small politician that you have for years been condemning?" Another critic wrote to demand that Willison drop the word "independent" from the heading of his editorial columns. Willison retorted that he had now put five or six years "in the attempt to conduct an absolutely independent newspaper," but that it was "heartbreaking" to work with "the independent element generally" because they "will not accept any opinion as honest unless it agrees with their own."

The conclusion of so many of his independent readers that he had turned to Toryism during the provincial campaign was not unreasonable.

But, at the same time, there is little ground for doubting that he meant it when he stressed to one of his critics at that time: "The News does not state the arguments for the Government's re-election as strongly as I feel them."[22] The Ontario Liberals in 1908 were weak and unimpressive, with no clear alternative approaches to Whitney's vigorous new government. For Willison to have opposed the Tories or to have been neutral would have run counter to his convictions.

As the months passed into summer, no other purchase arrangement for Flavelle's control of the paper than by a Conservative syndicate seemed feasible. Meanwhile, Willison's own situation was defined at last, following an extraordinary attempt all through June by several of his old Liberal friends to get him back to his former party, even to his old newspaper, the *Globe*. It was federal Liberals, in Ontario and Ottawa, who made the attempt. It began even as the provincial Liberals were receiving their expected election drubbing by Whitney, 86 to 19. It was hardly to be expected that they would have either the time or the slightest inclination to recruit one of their chief tormenters.

The author and master strategist of this "Liberal option" for Willison's future was none other than the prime minister. Sir Wilfrid met Robert Jaffray, the *Globe*'s proprietor and now a senator, in late May or early June, to find that Jaffray had remained friendly to Willison and enthusiastic about seeing if he could be brought back to the Liberal paper. The prime minister worried to George Lindsey about Willison's "very painful" situation. "He never was made to be a Tory editor," Laurier remarked, and his "personal friends" should try to make sure this did not happen.

There was also a Liberal interest. Laurier stressed to Jaffray that Willison was "so able a man that we should not lose an opportunity of enrolling him again into the active ranks of the party." The next federal election was only months, possibly weeks, away. Willison's pen on the Liberal side — or, at least, not on the Conservative one — was worth working for.

Lindsey saw Willison the next day, to show him Laurier's letter, as well as a proposed communication to Jaffray setting out terms for a proposed Willison return to the *Globe*. Lindsey reported that Willison was "non-committal and declined to permit delivery of your letter to Senator Jaffray till he had given the matter more consideration."

The proposed terms were almost certainly one cause for hesitation. Laurier knew already from Jaffray that it would not be possible for Willison to go back at this point to his former position as editor-in-chief. The existing editor, Rev. J.A. Macdonald, was an enthusiastic partisan supporter of the provincial Liberals, and attempting to dislodge him in favour of the recently pro-Whitney Willison likely would have been a highly divisive move in party terms. However, Jaffray believed he could get his board of directors to take Willison back in some other capacity. Accordingly, Laurier's proposal was that Willison "openly resign" from the *News* and declare that he "cannot be a Tory." He should then return to the *Globe*, writing from home, "and gradually work up to his former position." If Willison found that unsatisfactory, there might be another "position" elsewhere which the prime minister could make available. Two government posts were possibilities: as a member of the Civil Service Board and as a deputy minister.

By June 23, Lindsey had met with Willison several times. He reported to Laurier that the editor now believed he could "do well with his paper as a Tory organ: and he does not fear its financial success as such." Willison did admit, however, "his natural setting to be among the Liberals and would if it were possible on fair terms prefer to be with his old friends." Nevertheless, Lindsey was certain, Willison could "on no condition" work under Macdonald at the *Globe* and was not attracted by either the pay or scope of the civil service positions offered. On June 24, Lindsey urged Laurier to see Willison personally, which the prime minister promised to do as soon as the summer parliamentary recess began.[23]

That very day, an editorial in the *Globe* may have written *finis* once and for all to any lingering prospects of any Liberal arrangement for Willison. The editorial referred sarcastically to "a certain young newspaper gentleman in Toronto" who "has been for sale for some time." Lindsey told Laurier at once that he believed this had been a deliberate slur on Willison, although a *Globe* sub-editor claimed to him that it had been meant to apply to the *News* rather than its editor. Lindsey remarked that the incident "must in any event do a lot of harm." Laurier recognized with regret that there was "a breach between W. and the 'Globe' which our joint efforts could never overcome. The matter is very unfortunate." It seemed clear that the only slim chance of Willison returning to the

Liberals lay in Rev. J.A. Macdonald being removed as editor-in-chief. This neither Laurier nor any one else was prepared to attempt. Willison's own record of the whole episode is brief and categorical, that the negotiations had been opened by Lindsey, at Laurier's instance, adding: "Nothing was done at my instance. I refused to go back to *The Globe*. I would not go to Ottawa to meet Sir Wilfrid."[24]

There now was only one avenue left for Willison to follow: to accept a new more Conservative order at the *News*. Premier Whitney discussed some of the details with his cabinet colleague Frank Cochrane in early July as the last components of financing to buy out Flavelle were put together. Whitney told Cochrane that Willison was "a little uneasy," but that "I told him first of all that we considered the best asset in the 'News' to be himself...." The public announcement of the purchase came in a *News* editorial on August 4, and had a surprising twist:

> In order to set rumours at rest, and to contradict many false statements, it may be worthwhile to say that Mr. J.W. Flavelle has disposed of his interest in The News Publishing Company. In the new company Mr. Willison becomes president and is also the chief stockholder. There will be no change in the paper's editorial or business management. The direction of editorial policy, as hitherto, will be absolutely in the hands of the editor.

The masthead still contained the words AN INDEPENDENT JOURNAL. It may be that Willison now was "the chief stockholder," but even this carefully crafted wording did not claim that he had a *controlling* interest, as had been the case for Flavelle. Clearly, whatever the words in a masthead, that had passed to other men, to the Tories organized by Cochrane and Whitney. Whitney proudly told a friend that the *News* now would be "a straight Conservative organ."[25]

If there were any doubts about how loyally Tory the new *News* and the new Willison could be, they were dispelled during the federal general election that autumn, leading up to voting day on October 26. Amid Tory corruption charges against the government over the construction of the National Transcontinental and Liberal denunciations of the personal financial dealings of prominent Conservatives, especially Robert Borden's chief lieutenant George Foster, there was little room for neutrality. As well, Willison was able to find at last something at least approaching an emotional commitment to the Conservative cause. For some time he had been expressing increasing admiration for Borden's intelligence, energy, and progressive inclinations. "Like Sir Wilfrid Laurier," the *News* remarked in April 1907, "Mr. Borden stands out above and apart from his party." In the summer of 1907, Borden released his so-called "Halifax Platform." Willison was one of a select group of men the Conservative leader consulted on the terms, and he responded enthusiastically that "the main planks ... quite carry my judgment."[26]

Borden promised honest appropriation and expenditure of public funds; appointment of public servants on the merit principle; effective punishment of election fraud and bribery; an independent Civil Service Commission selecting personnel through competitive examinations; reform of the Senate; a more selective immigration policy; management of public lands for public benefit; operation of government railways by an independent non-partisan commission; improvement of national transportation links; re-organization of the Railway Commission into a Public Utilities Commission to regulate all corporations "owning or operating public utilities or invested with franchises of a national character"; a national system of telephones and telegraphs; rural free mail delivery; protection of industrial and commodity development; mutual preferential trade within the Empire; the restoration of the public lands of Alberta and Saskatchewan to those provinces; and the "unimpaired maintenance of provincial rights."[27]

Willison had a few caveats about the details of the platform. He thought Borden would have to give some meaningful guarantees to "a sceptical public" that his pledges about action against graft, election bribery, and undue partisanship in appointments actually would be carried out. He himself favoured a more open immigration policy, believing that "certain continental immigrants make for better citizens than the lower type of English." On transportation he was opposed to any extension of the Intercolonial or any addition to transcontinental railway assistance. He thought the Railway Commission overworked already, and thus was against expansion of its mandate into the broader utilities area. He argued that the provinces could "more satisfactorily" look after telephones. Nevertheless, in broad generalities it was clear that Borden's platform spelled out the kind of reformist politics with which Willison could identify. The *News* pronounced the platform "sound, prudent and progressive but the country demands evidence that it is accepted by the Conservative party…."[28] After all, Borden's policy of 1904, of public ownership of the new transcontinental, had been disdainfully rejected or ignored by many party candidates.

Over the year that ensued before the 1908 fight began, Borden stuck to his platform, but he warned Willison at the outset of the campaign that he emphasize the "boodling [corruption] and the bungling of the administration…."[29] As charge followed counter-charge in the weeks that followed, it was rare that a return to the positive planks of the platform as the leading edge of the campaign proved possible. The *News*, with its now altered and re-defined orientation, was as bitter in its pursuit of the wrongdoing of the Liberals as any other anti-government paper. The Laurier regime was depicted as "exhausted and reactionary," as "in league with corporate interests, subservient to the selfish demands of hungry partisans, and generally contemptuous of the social and industrial reforms which should be the natural concerns of Liberal Ministers." It also lashed out as the campaign progressed at what it called the "racial appeal" of Laurier and the Liberals for a solid vote from French-speaking and Catholic voters. Yet on election eve, the *News* forecast a Tory majority of fifty in Ontario, enough to carry the country.[30]

The actual result on October 26 was a virtually unchanged 58–37 Conservative edge in Ontario, not enough to prevent another, albeit reduced, Liberal majority nationally. At once, Willison reacted with indignation to what he considered the success of the Liberals' "race cry," even claiming that they had swept every seat in which there was a considerable French-Canadian vote. In an editorial entitled PARTY, MONEY, RACE AND RAILWAY Willison bitterly assailed what he saw as this unholy alliance of pro-government influences. To the "race cry" had been added the voice of the Grand Trunk Railway, chief beneficiary of Laurier's transcontinental largesse, and the call of the petty distributors of party rewards and favours in the form of public appropriations. Clearly the paper was most worried by the French and Catholic voters aspect and warned that calls for national unity and tolerance would be "in vain ... if racial considerations determine the issue of national contests...."[31]

Willison knew, however, that Borden had been held back in Ontario by more than the evil influences the *News* had listed. One great weakness had been a paucity of able lieutenants in the province. Willison even briefly entertained the idea of taking a parliamentary seat and had Charlie Hamilton sound out Borden, who seemed favourable. Willison then met Borden personally. However, the editor told Hamilton that he was "not at all clear ... that I cannot do as good service here as I should in Parliament." He was now "resolutely determined" to defeat the Laurier government through work in "the field in which I can be most useful...." He claimed to another friend that "I never was as comfortable since I was in journalism as I am now," and that he had "as free a hand as I had with Mr. Flavelle ... while I hope to on many occasions to work with a party." He was now "pretty well convinced" that "no newspaper can do its best work except in association with a powerful organization, political or social...." As for himself, he saw "nothing for me but the course I am now taking and in that course I am singularly comfortable."[32] He also was much less naïve than when he had moved originally to the *News*.

Incredibly, the list of his major career decisions and changes in 1908 was not yet complete. An important new involvement in British journalism and imperialist circles developed. For three years his involvement with the *Morning Post* had been agreeable, and its editors had been pleased with his Canadian letters. Of course, throughout the Empire there was *one* newspaper that was thought to speak for Britain and to the British governing elite: the *Times*. By an extraordinary combination of events, personal connections, and plain luck in the waning weeks of 1908, the opportunity to supply Canadian articles for the *Times* came Willison's way.

In January 1908, the *Times* was in deep financial distress and moves were afoot to sell to men who were rumoured to wish it to be conducted as a mass circulation daily and a propaganda sheet for imperialist preferential trade. Willison learned of the deal at a stage when it seemed unstoppable. He had long been an admirer of the *Times*' reputation for independent and intellectually distinguished journalism, and he sorrowfully crafted an almost poetic editorial, AS WHEN A GIANT FALLS, regretting that "vandal hands were laid upon one of the great institutions of Britain and its glory sacrificed for a price" and that it had been "dragged into the common ruck of commercial journalism...."

Astonishingly, the editors of the *Times*, in secret association with Lord Northcliffe, manoeuvred successfully to block the impending sale. Northcliffe himself arranged to buy control, on the basis of assurances that he would respect the political independence and journalistic traditions of the *Times*. Alfred Harmsworth, Lord Northcliffe, was then the *enfant terrible* and dynamo of the British newspaper world. He was only forty-three in 1908, but had established or won control of over thirty newspapers, most notably the mass circulation populist *Daily Mail* and the pioneering cheap illustrated *Daily Mirror*. By early December 1908, his rescue mission for the *Times* was so clearly a success that the *News* could write a new editorial titled THE TIMES STILL ITSELF, concluding that it "remains the greatest newspaper in the world."[33]

A month before, Willison had received a commendatory letter from Lord Northcliffe on his earlier editorial: "I have read and re-read it with the greatest pleasure, none the less because the article embodies my own ideals of that paper." Governor General Lord Grey had passed him the clipping. Grey reported, as Willison heard from their mutual friend, the Canadian MP at Westminster, Hamar Greenwood, that Northcliffe "looks upon the *News* as the highest type of our Press and speaks in glowing terms of yourself."

In the last months of 1908, Northcliffe was visiting Canada and the U.S. in connection with several of his numerous business concerns. Grey met with Northcliffe, as did Lord Milner, the British imperialist theorist and leader, then on a Canadian tour. Grey had sent Milner the Willison editorial as well. Milner in turn then had spent an evening in Toronto in what he regarded as "a long ... very interesting talk" with Willison. One immediate result, for Willison as well as others who met with Milner, was the creation of a small private Toronto imperialist discussion club that would work to "influence" influential Canadians to further the cause of imperial consolidation. In effect, these were the real Canadian beginnings of the later much more visible and Empire-wide Round Table movement.[34]

While Northcliffe was in Montreal, he saw Willison's early December editorial. He wrote at once to say that he was "much gratified" by it and was "forwarding it to the London staff." On December 12, he followed this with an urgent telegram inviting Willison to meet him in New York to discuss "regular contributions" to the *Times*. The two met on December 21. The conversation must have gone very well, as a few days later Willison reported to Lord Grey that he had "formed a connection with the London *Times*." He supposed Grey to be largely responsible for the appointment and was "grateful." He asked the governor general to tell Sir Wilfrid Laurier that, as to Canadian politics, he would in the *Times* be "abstaining from utterances that would bear a partisan interpretation...." In his view, the *Times* "should be a firm understanding friend of Canada and should not be in conflict with its Government."[35]

Lord Grey's reply must have been a bombshell to Willison. After expressing his delight at the news and indicating that Northcliffe had been in touch with him about it, Grey added:

> ... I wish, however, to disabuse your mind of the idea that you owe your connection with the *Times* to me. You have to thank Sir Wilfrid Laurier. He has never wavered from the conviction that you are the first of Canadian journalists. His language to me on this point has been consistent from the first days after my arrival, right through your autonomy attacks upon him, to the day after Lord Northcliffe's arrival. Sir Wilfrid wanted you to be the Blowitz of Canada, and I sincerely hope it may be possible for you before long to fill that part. I entirely concur with Sir Wilfrid Laurier that such an arrangement would fall in with the best interests of Canada and of the Empire. I was greatly pleased to find Northcliffe as positive as Chatham was at the beginning of the 7 years war that the key to England's future lay on this side of the Atlantic....
>
> ... It is the excellence of your own work and Sir Wilfrid's recommendation that must jointly bear the responsibility of the new arrangement.[36]

And so the pivotal year of 1908 closed for Willison. He was quite definitely launched again as a party journalist in Canada, as fully Conservative an "independent" as he had once been a Liberal one. His public antagonism in the *News* to the Laurier government was almost as intense as in 1905, but the personal estrangement from Laurier had been undercut severely. Wonderfully, the old Laurier connection continued to serve him, as the opportunity with the *Times* demonstrated. The journalistic viability of the *News*, Willison's influence with the Conservatives, and the scope of his role with the *Times* remained to be defined. Interesting times lay ahead.

Crusades for Nation and Empire, 1909–1911

A LMOST AT ONCE IN 1909, THE FRESHLY CONSERVATIVE *News* AND the mint-new *Times* correspondent were drawn into comment on two major national and imperial issues: Canadian–American trade relations and naval defence. Through almost three years, they dominated Canadian political journalism; and, for Willison, they were the kind of "great" — and potentially pivotal — controversies he so loved to write about and participate in.

Late in January, he reported in the *Times* on "a movement for reciprocity which seems to be taking form in the United States." President William Howard Taft, trying to assuage lower-tariff pressures in even his own Republican ranks, was urging downward revisions on many raw material imports, including several Canadian ones. Republican protectionists in Congress responded with tough new proposals of their own. On August 5, the resultant Payne–Aldrich tariff invited other nations to agree on mutual reductions in duties but, ominously, would impose special maximum rates, 25 per cent higher than the general levels, on imports from any country that "unduly discriminates against the United States or the products thereof." The *News* warned Canadians that the events in Washington "threatened to raise grave issues for Canada and to change the face of Canadian politics."

Canada's three-tier tariff of 1907, a Franco-Canadian trade pact under it in 1909 and the long-standing British preference tariff seemed to make application of the sky-high Payne–Aldrich penalties inevitable. To avoid them, would Canada have to throw over these existing policies, weaken the British connection, and perhaps even lay an axe to the historic National Policy of industrial protection? Willison was at once sure where he stood. "Canada should strive to build up its own industrial fabric ... and should be slow to enter into engagements which will operate against inter-Imperial tariffs, and an advantage for Canadian products in British markets," he had the *News* argue.[1]

The impending trade crisis would take some time to come to a head. More dramatic, and seemingly more urgent in March 1909, was the great "naval scare." In London, the First Lord of the Admiralty announced that Germany could be on the verge of overtaking Britain in construction of the strategically crucial "dreadnought." battleships. The resultant parliamentary and press furor concerning an accelerated Royal Navy build-up touched off a major debate in Canada as well. For the first time since 1899, there was an intense focus on an "imperial" issue by the press and politicians. This was about no far-off petty colonial squabble, no fine point of imperial constitutional practice, or no complicated trade question. The Canadian people simply refused to be excited about such things. However, with control of world trade and the safety of Canada's coasts possibly threatened, there was no such aloofness. Even the normally anti-militarist *Globe* immediately urged the country to "fling the smug maxims of commercial prudence to the winds and to do more than her share in the game of turning dreadnoughts from the stocks."[2]

Willison never entertained the slightest doubt that the German naval threat was grave and that Canada should act. The *News* affirmed: "... we should at once let Germany know that Britain does not stand alone... that we will at once build a navy to protect our own shores and that our vessels, under all proper circumstances, will be at the call of the British Admiralty." In the *Times* Willison characterized initial Canadian reaction to the crisis as "disorganized and chaotic," but "the hard shell of our indifference has been penetrated...." In his early editorials in the *News* on the subject, he seemed as "disorganized and chaotic" as anyone else, both describing the "clear" need for dreadnoughts and calling on Canada to "take the lead" in building up "reasonable naval forces" of her own.[3]

He and other Canadian commentators on the question were soon given a lead by a special parliamentary debate in Ottawa. On March 29, George Foster, Conservative MP for North Toronto, moved that Canada, with her "great and varied resources," her "geographical position and national environment" and "that spirit of self-help and self-respect which alone befits a strong and growing people," should "no longer delay in assuming her proper share" in the "suitable protection of her exposed coast-line and great sea ports." Foster opposed regular money contributions to the Royal Navy as like "hiring somebody else to do what we ourselves ought to do." He preferred the gradual development of a Canadian naval force — something "grafted on the soil of Canada's nationhood." He feared, however, that there might be an early grave crisis over dreadnought supremacy, and that if the prime minister were to believe that a gift of money or dreadnoughts to Britain was necessary, the Conservatives would "stand beside him in thus vindicating Canada's honour and strengthening the Empire's defence."

Laurier was wary in his response, well aware that many of his Quebecois, agrarian, and labour supporters recoiled from that "vortex of European militarism" he himself had condemned so often. He agreed in the House that Canada certainly should "close around the mother land" if British supremacy were really threatened — but he doubted the danger was "imminent." He would not compromise Canadian autonomy by a direct contribution to the Royal Navy; instead he would "promote the organization of a Canadian naval service in co-operation with and in close relation to the imperial navy."

The two federal party leaders did their best to find common ground. Robert Borden agreed that "the proper line" should be "a Canadian naval force of our own." He added, however, that this must be commenced "promptly," and he wanted no specific prohibition of some emergency contribution to the British. Laurier accepted the word "speedy" into resolution language on the issue, promising organization of a Canadian naval service, and, although he continued to object in principle to direct contributions, he was ready to restrict prohibition of such to "regular and periodic ones." On that compromise basis, the House agreed to passage of the resolution without dissent.[4]

Robert L. Borden, 1912. Library and Archives Canada, C-018632

In his immediate reaction, Willison had the *News* express satisfaction with the "admirable" resolutions but insisted that the government move rapidly and not "relapse into its old attitude of lethargy, indifference and inactivity." To British readers, in a three-column special article for the *Times*, he asked for understanding of the Laurier government's sensitivity to anti-militarist feeling, especially in Quebec. Canadians, he asserted, should "respect the sentiment of Quebec and … endeavour to maintain unity and harmony in our own household."[5] It was all very statesmanlike, very much the kind of thing the *Times* expected of him and he had promised.

But back in Canadian politics and political journalism, the possibly emergency character of the German dreadnought threat and the certainly volatile nature of Conservative and imperialist opinion — as well as of his own — quickly produced a rather different emphasis in the *News*. "Britain's need is our need," it proclaimed on April 8. "Then why not make an interim appropriation before our navy slides down the ways?" Two weeks later, in a lead editorial titled THE NEED FOR ACTION, the call was for "throwing two Dreadnoughts into the scales of Europe" as the only "manly" way for Canada to proceed while getting her own naval program under way.[6]

Just how much a journalistic split personality he was at this point was illustrated by his almost contemporaneous column in the *Times* about the "serious cross-currents" in Canadian opinion on the naval issue. He noted that "many English-Canadians" were in agreement with the developing French-Canadian opposition to naval expenditures, but that "the great mass of the people recognize the necessity.…" The measured, judicial tone for the *Times* seemed just right to its manager, Moberly Bell, who thanked him "very warmly" for the excellent articles.… They are of immense value to the interests we all have at heart." Willison's more aggressive line in the *News*, meanwhile, was winning the approval of Canadian Tory imperialists like the ex-MP Alex McNeil, who wrote: "Thank you, thank you a thousand times. Keep at it hammer and tongs, and perhaps our people may be roused from their lethargy."[7]

At heart for Willison, the issue was only incidentally about naval security. As he explained to the *Times*, the crisis had occasioned "a remarkable revival of Imperial sentiment in Canada, or perhaps the existence of a sentiment deep-seated in the Canadian people." Laurier, he remarked, had "infinite patience to resist a minority and an unerring ear for the voice of a majority." Even the prime minister's home naval defence approach would be "Imperial in its scope and purpose," he explained to

British readers. But in Canada he clearly thought it was time to have public opinion push Laurier further. To Premier Whitney, he enthused: "The whole fight for Canadian participation in Imperial Defence is on and I think it must be fought stoutly." He was sure that "the country generally, outside of Quebec, is just about as British as Toronto."[8]

From within Quebec, *La Presse* believed it knew where this call of the *News* for "manly" action was leading. In late June it printed with approval a vicious letter to the editor damning the *News* as "*ce vil journal … foncièrement anti-catholique et anti-français et … animé par une personnelle aiguë contre sir Wilfrid Laurier.*" The *News* responded by denouncing "the determination of *La Presse* … to suppress free discussion and to destroy one of the great political parties of Canada by baseless and frenzied appeal to racial and sectarian prejudices." To the *Times* he reported: "The attitude of the Conservative party towards Quebec is grossly misrepresented and, a more serious matter, the true objects of British imperialists are obscured and perverted."[9]

In mid-July an Imperial Defence Conference convened in London. The Canadian representatives met with British ministers and admirals and rejected suggestions for a direct Canadian contribution to a united imperial fleet. They also turned back the request that Canada build a distinct "Fleet unit," including one dreadnought, for each of her coasts, as more expensive than they desired as a beginning of naval development. The delegates returned home with the Admiralty's cost estimates and advice on construction of a more modest collection of cruisers and destroyers.

Robert Borden and his party awaited the details of the Laurier naval policy in a state of growing disunity. The *News* still called for "immediate action" on a direct contribution, even though progress on a Canadian navy was desired as well. "If Mr. Borden and his supporters … face the Government with this policy they will find no lack of friends in the constituencies," it pronounced on November 5. But three days later, the federal Quebec Conservative leader, Frederick Monk, told an audience in Lachine that he completely opposed *both* a Canadian navy and a direct contribution to Britain. He demanded a national plebiscite on the naval question.[10] Whether or not there was an emergency for the British Empire on the high seas, there was undoubtedly a very grave one developing for the unity of the Canadian Conservative party.

Willison reacted icily to Monk's announcement, with the *News* commenting: "If Mr. Monk is a Conservative he must conform to the views of his leader or else 'plow a lonely furrow'.... The country has had enough of double-jointed policies and opportunistic politicians." Borden and his party, the paper stressed, would have to "deserve" the people's confidence through urging the building of two dreadnoughts, to "belong to Canada but available for Imperial purposes," and the beginning of construction of smaller ships and facilities.[11]

The precise details of the government's policy were to be unveiled early in January, and the Conservatives had to be ready with their reaction. Borden's discussions with his ranking parliamentary colleagues were supplemented by consultations with a select group of party men from provincial governments, business, and the press.[12] Willison was one, receiving a long letter containing Borden's contemplated approach. The Tory leader had concluded that a modest beginning on a national navy — such as Laurier would undoubtedly propose — would "entirely fail to meet the present emergency," which he believed would be bound to come to a head long before a Canadian force could be of any use. Accordingly, he wanted "a sufficient and generous emergency contribution" repeated until the Canadian navy could be "an effective fighting force." All Canadian ships must be "to all intents and purposes ... an integral part of a great Imperial fleet." However, Laurier's entirely different policy would require a parliamentary response. Borden either could accept it under protest, as an "exceedingly inadequate installment of what might have been expected," or boldly oppose it through the only parliamentary device available on a government expenditure bill, the six-months' hoist [delay of consideration].[13]

Willison, like almost all the English-Canadians Borden queried, was flatly opposed to the six-months' hoist. "I fear," he told Borden, "that such a proceeding would give an aspect of insincerity to your whole position. It is clear to me that you ought to move to supplement the Government's programme by an offer of Dreadnoughts or an immediate cash contribution." Borden responded that parliamentary rules did not permit this on the bill directly, but he promised that discussions on the party's stance would continue until the precise details of Laurier's legislation were known, in early January.[14]

By then, however, Willison had put himself out of the reach of regular party consultation for some time: on December 15, he sailed from New York to Liverpool on the Cunarder RMS *Campania*, arriving on December 23.[15] Journalism and imperialism drew him to England, as they had twelve years before. He delightedly accepted an invitation from the *Times*, which offered full expenses for a lengthy visit. He could become familiar with all the leading men of the *Times*, and become better known to them. As well, he could further develop his links with major figures in the imperialist movement in Britain and report back to Canada for the *News* on what was going on there.

Willison was welcomed to the centre of the Empire as no mere journalist or *Times* employee, but as the principal Canadian colleague of the British imperialists. Just before leaving Toronto, he was sought out by three of that group, Lionel Curtis, Philip Kerr, and William Marris, who were visiting Canada. He learned from them that the London imperialists around Lord Milner now definitely aimed at creating an elite behind-the-scenes movement across the Empire to develop maximum support for closer imperial unity. A new imperialist quarterly was planned. Willison agreed with Kerr that "you want some organ for the expression of common imperial sentiment," and readily offered to write the Canadian articles, to his visitors' delight.[16]

He arrived in Britain at an extraordinarily interesting time. On December 1, the Liberal government's radical Lloyd George Budget had been thrown out, in an action unprecedented in democratic times, by the Unionist (Conservative) majority in the hereditary House of Lords. The governing Liberals at once had called a general election for mid-January. The Liberals' demand to "amend or end" the Lords' veto power and their refusal to countenance a pro-Empire modification of free trade were countered by the Unionists' defence of the traditional "balance" of the British Constitution and their championing of "tariff reform," within an imperial preferential system. There would be obvious implications for Canada in what happened, as there would be for Britain if the terms for Canadian–American trade were to be drastically altered. It was a pivotal moment for both countries. Willison, the *Times* men and the British imperialists would have much to talk about. Just before he sailed, his friend Sir Edmund Walker of the Bank of Commerce in Toronto wished him "every possible success in your mission which I regard as most important in the interests of Canada."[17]

From Liverpool he caught the train to Goring-on-Thames, near Oxford, for Christmas with his old Toronto friends George and Annie Parkin. There were a few quiet days for sifting through a flurry of invitations. Lord Milner, in the midst of electioneering, yet wanted "luncheon-only ourselves" on December 29 in London. That had to be put off until January 16, when Milner delighted in their "long talk." Before the end of December, however, Willison lunched with his old friend Fabian Ware of the *Morning Post*, was made a temporary member of the Royal Colonial Institute, and spoke at the official opening of the British Empire Club for visiting "colonials." He told his audience that the "determination" had come upon Canadians "that they had not done, and from this time they must do, their duty towards the defence of the British dominions." In the further future he still hoped for some sort of "great Imperial Council" of the self-governing Empire — by which Britain would gain "fresh strength from overseas" and the dominions the maturity of international adulthood.[18]

For a few days in early January, he was off to the country house of Lionel Curtis, at Uplands, Ledbury, to continue their discussions about that Empire-wide imperialist organization and quarterly they had talked about in Toronto the month before. A few days later, Curtis had his closest English associates to Uplands for final planning. Decisions were finalized to publish the first issue of *The Round Table* in November, including an anonymous Willison article on Canada.[19]

Willison could not be on hand for the group meeting at the Curtis home, as Lord and Lady Northcliffe had invited him to spend the election night of January 15 in London. That followed several glorious days as their guest at the Hotel Majestic in Paris. He also met with Lord Crewe, the Colonial Secretary, in London, and had several lengthy discussions with G.E. Buckle, the editor of the *Times*. Shortly before he sailed for Canada at the end of January, he was invited up for an overnight stay with the Unionist leader and former prime minister, Arthur Balfour, at Whittinghame, Prestonkirk, in Scotland.[20] It was an invaluable post-election opportunity for a *tour d'horizon* of the British and imperial scenes from a matchless authority.

Willison had covered the British election campaign exhaustively for the *News*. Few of the people with whom he was associating in Britain were sympathetic to the Liberal denunciations of the House of Lords, and Willison seemed to share at least some of their attitudes. He explained to Canadians in early January that the Lords had sought to defend the right of the people to be consulted electorally on a radical change in national financial policy. He noted that Liberal leaders such as Lloyd George and Winston Churchill "play with deadly skill upon class feeling.... The flame of popular wrath against the House of Lords rises slowly. It is not certain that it will rise at all." Joseph Flavelle wrote him that it was "the first time" that Canadians had been given a case for the House of Lords "in a strong way."[21]

Willison's chief purpose in his articles for the *News* was to get beyond the mire of "Lords versus People" to his chosen high ground of imperialism. It was the Unionist program of imperial preference or "tariff reform" that he was interested in most intensely. He judged that the Unionists had made some progress in recent years with the public on that issue, but that this clearly was being "checked" to some degree by the Lords and Budget issues. He also thought that "something still is needed" to give the Unionist party "closer and more sympathetic identification with the people and a more intimate relation to social reform." He also lamented the extraordinary concentration of Westminster politicians on domestic issues. "It is vital," he wrote, "that all the genius of Imperial statesmen, whether in Great Britain or in the colonies, should be employed to find the natural point of separation between domestic and Imperial interests, and to leave the central Parliament free to guard the security and secure the solidity of Empire." He repeated the call he had made in his British Empire Club speech for "a great Common Council of Empire." These signed front-page articles were not just reports; they constituted a very personal imperialist manifesto. Some measure of the interest they were stirring back in Canada came with word from a *News* staffer in Toronto that the editor of the Montreal *Star* was seeking simultaneous publication rights for them in his paper.[22]

The polls closed on the evening of January 15. The Liberals were severely weakened, losing 116 seats. Nevertheless, with 275 they remained marginally ahead of the 273 Unionists and could form a minority government with the normal support of 41 Labour and 71 Irish MPs.[23] It could not be foreseen when any British government would have the time or the mandate to turn its attention to imperial trade preferences, still less to anything like "a Great Common Council of Empire."

Willison's British sojourn ended with a significant upgrading of his status with the *Times*. After a year as "Our Correspondent Toronto," he learned from Moberly Bell, the manager of the *Times*, that he now would be "Our Canadian Correspondent." All other writers for the paper in Canada would report to and be paid by him. He would travel to any part of the country "when expedient" and would be paid the princely sum of 1,200 pounds a year "to include all expenses except telegraphy." He would continue to be "at liberty to do other work for newspapers outside of the United Kingdom." At the 1910 exchange of almost $5 to a pound he could expect the bulk of an extra $6,000 to be added to his income and buttress his personal independence. He had come a very long way from Hills Green "Corners."[24]

Edward Grigg of the *Times* at once wrote Sir Wilfrid Laurier, who had been so influential in establishing Willison's initial connection with the paper, to say that the work the Torontonian had done thus far for them "assures us that we could look nowhere for a more balanced, authoritative and judicial account of Canadian affairs than he will supply." Of course, he conceded, Willison's Canadian Conservative connections "may to some extent impair, on the Liberal side, the confidence which we should desire to be felt in our correspondent by both the great political parties in Canada." Grigg emphasized, however, that Editor Buckle believed that "no truly experienced Canadian journalist could be free of all political connection, and no Englishman could … possibly have the thorough knowledge of Canadian views which we most particularly desire in the Canadian correspondent of The Times."[25]

Mackenzie King, the minister of labour, recorded in his diary in January 1910 the prime minister's judgment that "the Times could have no better man than Willison…W's articles in the Times had been fair, very fair." To Grigg, Laurier wrote that Willison's work for the *Times* had been "most acceptable to all sections of Canadian opinion." Still, ever the political tactician, he urged the *Times* to prevail upon Willison "to withdraw altogether" from the *News* and give the whole of his energy and great ability as a journalist in the broader field which the 'Times' opens before him." He was sure this would be "more congenial" work for his friend. It certainly would make for more congenial daily Canadian reading for Laurier and his Liberal party. Governor General Lord Grey agreed with the prime minister that "the sooner he [Willison] cuts the painter from the shore of Canadian journalism the better."[26]

It was a vain hope. Willison returned on the *Mauretania* to "the shore of Canadian journalism" just following the beginning of a particularly intense partisan battle after Laurier finally had unveiled the details of his naval policy to the House of Commons on January 12. The prime minister announced a plan for a volunteer naval service starting with five cruisers and six destroyers. The Cabinet could place the force on active service, including with the Royal Navy, but Parliament would have to sanction this within fifteen days. Imperialist Liberals were told that a *national* navy would be a fresh centre of strength for Britain in war emergencies. Voters in Quebec, farmers, trade unionists, and other anti-militarists were to be encouraged to see the modesty of the effort as far less a contribution to the arms race than a gift of deadly dreadnoughts.

Robert Borden's initial response was to bless the prime minister's going on "slowly, cautiously and surely" with a Canadian navy, giving the people "if necessary an opportunity to be heard"; but he urged him not to ignore "an emergency which may render this Empire asunder before the proposed service is worthy of the name." Then on February 3 he offered an amendment that constituted a frontal assault on Laurier's policy. He charged that the Laurier navy, while very expensive, would give "no immediate or effective aid to the Empire and no adequate or satisfactory results to Canada." Tilting momentarily towards Monk and his Quebec *nationaliste* friends, he opposed *any* permanent policy "until it has been submitted to the people and received their approval." Meanwhile, Canada should, "without delay," give Britain the funds for the construction of two dreadnoughts.[27]

Willison's ship did not reach New York until the day of Borden's amendment. He did not direct early *News* editorials on it, or on the Laurier proposals. By the time he was able to send his first comment to the *Times*, it had hailed on January 13 the "lively sense of responsibility" the prime minister was showing. Three days later, he wired off his own assessment, in his usual studiously non-partisan *Times* manner. Conservative disunity was acknowledged, as was the unity Laurier had achieved among Liberals with his persuasive and eloquent case. While there was "strong feeling in favour of an immediate contribution to the Admiralty, public opinion is not unfavourable to the ultimate Canadian Navy." He also noted "some curious features" to Borden's amendment: the lack of express support for a Canadian navy and the pro-Monk tilt about consultation of the people before commitment to a permanent policy. He added that the Conservative leader was showing himself "soundly imperial." Privately, however, he criticized to Lionel Curtis in England "the mess made by the Opposition over the Navy proposals."[28]

Very soon it was the Opposition itself that was in a mess. The Monk Conservatives were furious about Borden's claim that there was a naval emergency, and many imperialist Tories were fed up with what they saw as Borden's weakness and vacillation in dealing with the Quebec dissidents. Premier Richard McBride of British Columbia was rumoured as the leader's replacement. Amid the rumours and rancour, Willison wrote sadly to Grigg of the *Times* that, though Borden probably would stay on as leader, a planned Conservative national policy convention had been shelved, and it was evident that "Bourassa and Monk will lead the attack on the Government in Quebec." This would give Laurier "the usual majority" there and keep him firmly in the Ottawa saddle. Publicly in the *News* there could be no such pessimism about Borden and his party. Monk was denounced as "merely an ambitious man," and it was hoped that Quebec Conservatives could be freed from his "impotent leadership." In early April, Willison learned from his Ottawa correspondents that Borden was so discouraged, he was about to give up, and that, as Frank Smith reported, some of the "old guard" were complaining bitterly about "the Toronto Clique (no doubt Messrs. Willison and Kemp [Edward Kemp, MP for East Toronto]) trying to run the party."[29]

On April 7, Willison launched in the *News* a blistering attack on the rebels, urging "farseeing Conservatives" at Ottawa and elsewhere to "lop off the mouldering branches" of "reactionary" elements in the party. The "need of the hour" was for the party to "rally around Mr. Borden." Thus would they "develop greatly increased effectiveness" and in "due time … cross the floor of the House…."

Frank Smith, Willison's sub-editor, reported on April 11 from Ottawa that "the courage displayed by The News had cleared the air and done much good." Borden was given firm support as well by Premiers McBride, Roblin, Whitney, and Hazen. On April 12 there was a caucus showdown, and Borden won a strong vote of confidence. The final House approval of the Laurier Naval Bill was already history, and some of the internal party strains now would lessen, at least for a time. Willison had all too much understanding of the divisions, jealousies, and frustrations that inevitably haunted an opposition party and its leader, especially when the leader's and the party's exclusion from power was of long duration. Laurier had known nine years of that misery before his 1896 triumph. Borden was now nine years into his leadership, and power must have seemed as far away as ever. Nevertheless, for all his sympathy for the Conservative leader, Willison could not help lamenting to Philip Kerr that Borden had made his naval position "farcical" by objecting to a Laurier policy "of which he had been one of the original advocates."[30] As an imperialist and a Conservative, he was doubly disgusted.

Other emotions were being stirred too. He had to be pleased to hear in April from Joseph Flavelle, visiting in London, who advised him that he had received "unsolicited or unsuggested by me, unqualified expression of the satisfaction of all the Times people in the character of your work for them." Interestingly, Flavelle also reported that the London imperialists were especially fascinated to read in his recent columns about a major developing story concerning potential revolutionary trade negotiations between Canada and the United States. They were, he said, "extraordinarily interested in what Canada and the United States will agree to do, and what effect it may have on their [Canadians'] views of Empire."[31]

So too was Willison. On March 3, an American delegation had arrived in Ottawa to explore possible reciprocal tariff reductions that might forestall the impending application of the prohibitive Payne–Aldrich tariff penalties to Canada. Subsequently, on March 19, Finance Minister Fielding met President Taft at Albany, N.Y. Six days later, Fielding gleefully reported to the House of Commons that Canadian tariffs would need to be lowered on only a small list of minor American imports to prevent application of the penalties. Even more important, however, was

President Taft's invitation to Canada to resume the trade negotiations — this time on a far more comprehensive basis.[32]

Willison reported to Philip Kerr in mid-April that he thought the Laurier government "came fairly well" out of the initial bargaining round with Washington and that to wish for a trade war with the Americans would be "irresponsible." Still, he feared what could come next, and expressed the belief that some blame for the drift of events lay with the British:

> If any wide treaty is effected we shall be turned again towards the policy of commercial continentalism. Failing a preference in British markets, this policy must become steadily more acceptable to Canadians and we must drift far from the position that would have been created if better pledges had been made in inter-imperial preferences. To be frank, I am more uneasy about the outlook than I have been before, for I have a good deal of sympathy with my fellow-Canadians who insist that if Britain will adhere to free trade there is no reason why we should continue to give a preference to a country which, notwithstanding our preference, gives as favourable terms to the United States as to us.[33]

Edward Grigg at the *Times* asked Willison for "a full review" of the whole trade and preference issue in a special mammoth Canadian article for the Empire Day edition. Willison promptly threw himself into a protracted preparation process, peppering friends on both sides of the Atlantic with outlines and drafts. Grigg was "delighted" with an early version and Flavelle thought a later one "magnificent." Lord Northcliffe urged him on: "The average self complacent well fed John Bull's notion is that Canada is a nicely behaved Colony occupying a highly favoured position for which she ought to be very grateful. I have not met that view in Canada." In his opinion, Willison "could do more to awaken <u>our</u> people than you know. The Times has immense influence at the top." Lord Milner wanted him to know how "very anxious" British imperialists were about Canada because of "the tide wh. seems to be running strongly for Continentalism & against Imperial Union…. It is Canadians & Canadians alone who can help their country on lines making for the Imperial zeal." He had just attended King George V's accession ceremonies, on the death of his father, Edward VII, and he "could not help wondering ... whether the New Reign would see the consolidation of this vast Empire, or its disruption....[34]

The Empire Day article was titled IMPERIAL UNION AND CANADIAN IDEALS: AN ARGUMENTATIVE REVIEW, and it covered two full pages of the *Times*. Willison opened with the contention that Canada and the Empire were "at the parting of the ways." He realized that many in Britain retained "the old distrust of the material bond as a sound basis of Empire." Yet he wanted them to understand that, for colonial imperialists, "the prospect of material advantage from mutual fiscal preferences is a very secondary consideration." Canada in particular, he explained, had "various and complex elements" that were non-British to convince that an imperial and not just a Canadian national future was worth striving for. How then could this be done? He was convinced that a policy of imperial trade preferences "would contribute materially towards the unity of the Empire...." For the British especially, the stakes would be very high — "a British Empire spread far across the earth and secure on every sea, or two islands in the Atlantic mourning the power and the glory that have passed."

He stressed that Canadian industrial ambition did not permit complete free trade with Britain, but the day would come when population growth and the maturing of the Dominion's industries allowed an "approach more nearly to Free Trade within the Empire." He reminded Britons that, if British leaders kept on blocking an imperial preferential arrangement for Canada, there was always the American alternative, stressing that it was "doubtful if Canadians will be permanently convinced that they should give exceptional treatment to British imports or should hesitate to enter into advantageous fiscal agreements with other countries...."

Beyond the imperial preference issue, what of the Empire's future? "The light on the way falls dimly," Willison conceded. "There will be halting and stumbling before a definite goal appears" but "with concentration for purposes of trade and enlarging communication, and the assumption of definite obligations for sea defence, some common centre of responsibility and power beyond the loose periodical advisory conferences of Imperial statesmen will become a practical necessity." This could not be, he argued, through some meaningless and minimal representation in the existing British Parliament. A truly "Imperial Parliament," resting "directly upon popular suffrage across the Empire must take over responsibility for foreign, defence and imperial affairs, leaving domestic British concerns to a domestic British parliament or parliaments with powers analogous to those of Canada, Australia, New Zealand and South Africa." Among other things, such "federalization" would open the way to giving Ireland 'practical control of its own affairs, and heal the running sore of centuries." He closed: "Thus would we strengthen the great wall of British power, which guards the security of free nations and loyal dependencies on every continent, and secures the inestimable blessings of peace, freedom and independence to millions of mankind."[35]

This was likely the lengthiest and most comprehensive statement on the future of the Empire that any Canadian or other non-Briton had published since George Parkin's book *Imperial Federation* eighteen years before. Willison believed that a conjuncture of events and pressures — in British politics, Canadian-American relations and the Anglo-German naval race — required the Empire countries to come together for objects its various peoples clearly could identify as meaningful and necessary. He had written not so much a report as a program for action.

There was much positive response. Lord Northcliffe thought it "splendid." L.J. Maxse of the *National Review* in London called it "invaluable and illuminating." Charles Mair, the poet and Canada Firster, enthused to Colonel Denison that it was "the best review of the Imperial question, in all its essential bearings, which has yet appeared." Arthur Willert, the *Times* correspondent in Washington, was just as complimentary. "As a contribution to Imperial literature it seems to me unequalled," he enthused to Willison. "As a contribution from Canada it should do much to disabuse England of her many misconceptions and to awaken her to what Canada and the Empire mean." Historian George Wrong congratulated him on "a first rate piece of work."[36]

However, as 1910 wore on into the summer and fall, the focus of political, press, and public attention in Canada came to be almost exclusively on one specific issue: the future of Canadian-American trade relations. The new comprehensive negotiations between the two countries were set to begin in Ottawa in November. Meanwhile, Sir Wilfrid Laurier toured the West, where he was bombarded with farmers' demands for a reciprocity agreement with the U.S. Willison predicted in the *Times* that, with so much of the American Taft administration's determination and prestige involved, "a treaty of some sort will be negotiated, but any deep study of the situation suggests that Canadian ministers will tread on dangerous ground." He was certain that "the whole [Canadian] manufacturing interest will be resolutely hostile to lower duties on American manufacturers." He was equally sure that any wide measure of reciprocity would be a "revolutionary disturbance of conditions." In a partisan vein, the *News* had fun with some of the prime minister's sympathetic musings about freer trade to the grain growers in the West while his government continued to cozy up to the manufacturers in the East, describing the manoeuvring as a "farce." By the end of the summer, examining for the *Times* the caution of Laurier's language in the West and what news could be gleaned out of Washington, he could see "no likelihood of any revolutionary trade arrangement." And the *News* described Canadians generally as "just as likely to consider the adoption of free trade as they are to jump over the moon."[37]

It was not only trade issues which commanded public and editorial attention that fall. On November 3, only a day before the Canadian and American negotiators opened their detailed discussions in Parliament's East Block, there was an astounding political development in Quebec. The hitherto "safe" Liberal constituency of Drummond-Arthabaska, where the prime minister had his summer home, fell in a by-election to a *nationaliste* anti-navy candidate who had been supported by Frederick Monk and Henri Bourassa. The *News* at once described the result as "a staggering blow" to the Laurier administration, but professed confidence that "Conservatives in the rest of Canada will remain loyal to the great ideal of the founders of the party, a united Canada within a united Empire, a common sharer in the Imperial patrimony and in Imperial responsibilities." It called on Borden and his colleagues to work for so strong a majority outside Quebec in the next election that any *nationaliste–Monk* combination from that province would be "over-ruled." Later that month, in the Speech from the Throne debate in Ottawa, Borden explicitly repudiated any alliance on naval policy with the *nationalistes* in an address Willison characterized for the *Times* as "one of the most brilliant he has ever delivered." He concluded: "Altogether, a situation has developed in our politics full of complexities and difficulties."[38] His confidence that Robert Borden might be able to deal with it all seemed to be growing.

The opening phase of the Canadian-American talks in Ottawa made the U.S. side fully aware that Canadian industrialist pressure ruled out a treaty that would include any wide list of manufactured products. When the negotiators resumed their work in Washington early in January, 1911, after a Christmas break, the eagerness, even desperation, of the Americans to produce some tangible low-tariff victory for their own public opinion rapidly pushed the process to a conclusion. Announcement of the terms of an agreement would be simultaneously in Washington and Ottawa on Thursday, January 26. The *News* reported a few days beforehand that "whatever understanding has been come to … will not be on any extensive line…."[39]

The speech of Finance Minister Fielding that Thursday afternoon in the House of Commons was an even more staggering surprise to Canadians than the Drummond-Arthabaska by-election result had been. There was to be complete reciprocal free trade in farm animals, grain, fruit and vegetables, dairy products, salt, and rough lumber. There would be markedly lower duties on some food products, agricultural implements, motor vehicles, and building materials, plus some minor reductions on a very small list of manufactures. Implementation by the two countries would be by concurrent legislation. As if by magic, for reasons of domestic American politics, the objectives of both Canadian farmers and manufacturers appeared to have been met. The political circle had been squared, and the fifteen-year-old Laurier government seemed to have given itself a new lease on life and power.

Robert Borden recorded that night "the deepest dejection" on his party's benches as the terms were unveiled. The next morning Willison surveyed the wreckage in the *News*. The changes brought by the "revolutionary" agreement would be "sweeping and far reaching" for the Canadian economy. The north–south flow of natural products doubtless would provide some important new income for Canadian producers, but at what cost? American railways, distribution centres, and credit-granting institutions would be certain to dominate the new trade. It was "sound policy" that the National Policy tariff on industry essentially would not be touched. Overall, in its "wider bearings," however, the *News* saw the agreement as "decidedly anti-national and anti-imperial." It would "probably wreck the whole movement for inter-imperial preferences." Yet, pessimistically, the *News* assumed that Washington's terms had to be so tempting in the short term that they would be "difficult for Canada to reject." Indeed, Willison at once wired the *Times*: "It cannot be doubted that the Agreement will pass the Canadian Parliament...." He soon followed that prediction with the judgment that reports of determined Conservative opposition were "not to be trusted." The Liberals, he believed, would be "positive almost to a man," and "many Conservatives, especially those representing constituencies the chief industries of which are agricultural, fishing or lumbering, admit that they cannot take a negative stand."[40]

Yet even that first day after the Fielding announcement, he told his *Times* readers that he could feel in Toronto "an undercurrent of unrest and dissatisfaction in financial and business circles." Then hour by hour and day by day over the weekend, his conversations in person and on the telephone with so many of his eminent Torontonian friends and acquaintances, of either or no party, began to confirm that the "undercurrent" had become a torrent. By Tuesday the 31st he had come to believe that there was a point, in both party and press terms, in declaring outright war on the agreement. There would be a constituency to support him, and he was coming to believe rapidly that at stake might be all the imperialist and nationalist causes he had been making his own since the early 1890s.

His mammoth editorial in the *News* that day was titled AN ATTEMPT AT NATIONAL SUICIDE, and began:

> The country is slowly awakening to the immense significance of what is involved in the tariff agreement with Washington.... We are plunging into a revolution without thought and without knowledge. None of us at first saw all that was involved in the agreement.... The issue transcends all party considerations and as the days pass the objections ... rise in ever increasing magnitude. The News does not believe that all the patriotism of Canada is vested in one party and it is convinced that when all the facts and all the bearings of the bargain with Washington are considered and understood no Government can afford to give it ratification.

For possibly illusory markets, which the U.S. could take away at any time,

> ... we are to imperil our whole national experiment, cause immense loss to other interests, increase the cost of living to the workmen, artisans and clerks of the towns and cities....
>
> Under the present policy we have made immense progress.... No community of six or seven millions ever created such a transportation system as Canada possesses. We have laid out hundreds of millions in order to connect East and West and create a vigorous, throbbing commonwealth....

With the reciprocity pact, the *News* asked, what would happen to the developing rail line to Prince Rupert? Why would it make sense to go forward with a Hudson Bay route? What point would there be in a Canadian Northern section above Lake Superior? "We surely imperil millions of British capital ... and we reduce Confederation to a string of independent Provinces. Practically ... we commercially annex the Canadian West to the United States." The pact would "destroy much of our inter-provincial trade and paralyze the forces and influences which make for Canadian nationality.... With our trade settled in American channels and with a vast new population with no reverence for British institutions we strengthen all the influences towards continentalism and risk the sacrifice both of a young nation and an ancient Empire." The *News* found it "impossible to believe that the Government has fully considered all the consequences ... and difficult to think that Parliament will risk national suicide and all the impacts upon the Imperial connection...."

This was exactly the kind of issue in which Willison gloried. It was one of those "great" causes he could argue above minor details, on a plane of high principle. His close friend Arthur Colquhoun would write that Willison was "a pillar of strength in a storm," with "an acute - almost uncanny — insight into current opinion, and the courage that rises in a crisis." It was a measure of that courage that he went on with this fight now, even while admitting while doing his more dispassionate work for the *Times*, that "I have no reason to think that the opposition can succeed...."[41]

Nevertheless, in his *News* editorials over the next weeks, he tried to encourage and accentuate anti-Reciprocity tendencies among Liberals. Of all Conservative journalists and political activists he was the best situated to do this, given his many continuing friendships and associations across the partisan barrier. "The News does not believe," it emphasized on January 31, "that the Government deliberately designs to check Canadian industry, to prejudice Canadian investments or to endanger Canadian nationality." They merely had stumbled into the arms of the Americans, and now there was "little or nothing of party in the feeling that has been aroused...." Joe Flavelle, still a close friend after his financial withdrawal from the *News*, liked this "loftiness of tone, a sense of the fair and the rational which always characterizes your best work, and which puts you by yourself in your own craft in Canada."[42]

Willison was not just shooting in the dark. Weeks before the unveiling of Reciprocity, he had learned from a *Times* aide in Ottawa, Fred Cook, that Clifford Sifton, Laurier's former interior minister and still a Liberal MP, was convinced "the Parlt[sic] of Canada would never ratify any convention." On February 2, a prominent Toronto business supporter of the government, Sir Edmund Walker, president of the Bank of Commerce, confided to an associate that Willison's editorial two days earlier "fairly states the views of almost all in eastern Canada who are Imperialists and who would view the merging of this country with the United States as the greatest of all calamities, no matter what such a destiny might mean financially." Four days later, Willison alerted Walker that Sifton wanted to see them both in Toronto "this afternoon." With necessary vagueness, Willison wired the *Times* on February 13 that in both Toronto and Montreal "movements are afoot to resist the Agreement which wholly disregard party connection."[43]

Two days later, Flavelle reported to Willison that another leading Toronto Liberal, Zebulon A. Lash, chief counsel for the Canadian Bankers Association and with major involvements with the Canadian Bank of Commerce and the Canadian Northern Railway, had phoned "asking me for names upon whom I would call tomorrow. I knew so few liberals [sic] that I hardly knew where to commence. Can you suggest any to Lash[?] I hardly know where to begin. You know Who's Who." The canvassing was of Liberal members of the Toronto Board of Trade, which on February 16 damned Reciprocity by a vote of 289 to 13, on a motion moved by Sir Edmund Walker and seconded by Flavelle. Even W.K. George, only recently the president of the Toronto Liberal Association, voted for it.[44]

The single most significant incident of the Toronto phase of the agitation occurred on February 20, when eighteen city Liberals, all leaders in business and finance, recorded their opposition. They included Lash and Walker, J.C. Eaton, president of T. Eaton Co. and a fellow member with Willison of the National Club; R.J. Christie of Christie, Brown and Co., the milling and biscuit concern; G.A. Somerville, managing director of Manufacturers Life; and W.D. Matthews, vice-president of the Dominion Bank and a director of Canadian Pacific. The others came from a broad range of banks and insurance companies. Their manifesto seemed to take its lead from Willison's editorial of January 31, with emphasis on the threats that Reciprocity posed to East–West transportation as well as "trade between the various parts of Canada and the various parts of the Empire." They were sure Canada faced a grave crisis — "that Canadian nationality is threatened with a more serious blow than any it has heretofore met with" — and that country must take precedence over party."[45]

Eight days later, it was Clifford Sifton's turn. Before packed galleries in the House of Commons, he ripped into his former colleagues' accord. His arguments followed closely the earlier criticisms, though with special emphasis on his westerner's concerns for the impending domination of Chicago over his region. "These resolutions in my judgment," he thundered, "spell retrogression, commercial subordination, the destruction of our national ideals and displacement from our position as the rising hope of the British Empire." To his friend John Dafoe he added: "... Since I have been old enough to speak nothing has ever happened which has created such a spontaneous outburst.... For myself if I never made another speech, or gave another vote, or sat in another representative assembly, I would have taken the course that I did."[46]

It was time for the Liberal renegades to draw the obvious political conclusion: Laurier's refusal to turn away from Reciprocity meant that they would have to swallow their party feelings and join forces, at least temporarily, with the federal Conservatives. Here again Willison was a crucial go-between. Sifton invited him and Sir Edmund Walker to meet in Ottawa on March 1 for "a conference which will finally close matters & put them in shape." Walker had to send Z.A. Lash in his stead, but the meeting went ahead as scheduled. Willison and Lash met first with Sifton and Lloyd Harris, the Liberal MP from Brantford. Willison recorded that they came together to "consider the best steps to be taken to resist ratification of the Reciprocity Agreement with Washington, to influence opinion in the country, to accomplish the defeat of the Government and to arrange a basis of co-operation with Mr. Borden, Leader of the Conservative party." The four then went to Borden's office and asked him to agree on a series of points.

They asked that a future government, while being fair to Quebec and Roman Catholics, "should not be subservient" to those interests in public policy or patronage. They were all English-speaking Protestants with long memories! More to the immediate point, they sought resistance to American pressures on fiscal policy, natural resources, and political relations in order to "preserve and strengthen Canadian nationality and the connection with the Mother Country." They requested that Borden consult with Walker, Lash, and Willison when he constructed his ministry, and that there should be "reasonable representation therein" of the views of rebel Liberals as well as the inclusion of "men of outstanding national reputation and influence in order to give confidence to the progressive elements of the country, and strength and stability to the Government." Further, they wanted commitments to civil service reform, enhanced export support, and the appointment of an expert tariff commission. Borden, Willison noted in his record of the meeting, was "in sympathy with all these representations, [and] freely pledged himself to use every possible endeavor to give them effect…." Accordingly, "the Committee pledged itself to cooperate with Mr. Borden and to proceed at one to organize for the next general election."[47]

There was a brief pause in those preparations, as several of the Conservative party's parliamentary "old guard," furious at Borden's manoeuvrings with Liberal enemies, tried once more to force him out of the leadership. But Borden stood firm, stiffened by the provincial Tory premiers and all but a handful of his MPs. For Willison in the *Times* there was now no doubt that Borden was "immensely strong," and that "rightly or wrongly" he and his caucus "entertain the opinion that the Government will be forced ultimately to abandon the Agreement and go to the country."[48]

Planning the 1911 Victory. Robert Borden on left, Frank Cochrane in centre, and Premier Sir James Whitney on right. Library and Archives Canada, C-017945

Emboldened now, the Conservatives began openly filibustering the Reciprocity Agreement in the Commons as April came and went. On May 5, Laurier, due in London later that month for the Imperial Conference and King George V's Coronation, agreed to adjournment of the House for two months. Willison described the move in the *News* as Laurier's "first public humiliation ... since 1896 and they [the Liberals] understand the moral effect of a surrender to Mr. Borden in face of the country."[49] When Laurier returned from London, he knew that already he had let the anti-Reciprocity agitation build for too long. He called a general election for September 21.

No one needed to tell John Willison what to do in an election campaign, not least one as pivotal as that of 1911. It was like 1896 all over again. He had the ear of the aspiring leader and a newspaper to wield as an effective propaganda instrument. As in 1896, he was on a rising tide, and this time his own city of Toronto was on the crest. Borden and Sifton were quick to enlist him to work on the leader's campaign manifesto.

Borden alerted Premier Whitney that it was "rather important that he [Willison] should be called in this way, for reasons which I shall explain when I meet you." The reference likely was to the March 1 pact with the rebel Liberals, for which Willison seems to have been serving as some sort of guarantor.

Whitney, Willison, Flavelle, and some others in Toronto responded to an early Borden draft as "too long," with too many detailed economic arguments. They recommended wording "more in the nature of an inspiring appeal...." The final product was tight and effective, even occasionally eloquent. The main anti-Reciprocity arguments were pretty familiar by now, but a phrase or two promised to stick in people's minds — especially that Canada was now at "the parting of the ways." Beyond the trade issue, and along the lines of both Borden's Halifax Platform of 1907 and the March 1 agreement, there were commitments to civil service reform, a permanent tariff commission, a government railway to Hudson's Bay, and improved control of public expenditures. A number of the Conservative leader's pledges to the West during his recent summer tour were repeated, such as return of natural resources to the prairie provinces, government terminal elevators, and assistance to the provinces for agricultural education and improvement.[50] It was the kind of electoral program Willison had been calling for, from both Liberals and Conservatives, since his "Programme for Parliament" in 1900. He had welcomed such enlightened reform proposals when Borden had championed national ownership of the Grand Trunk Pacific-National Transcontinental in 1904 and then had unveiled his Halifax Platform in 1907. As well, of course, there remained that critically important pledge in the March 1 accord that Borden would bring into a new federal cabinet "a number of men of outstanding national reputation and influence in order to give confidence to the progressive elements of the country...."

After the campaign was over, Willison would tell Sifton: "Never before have I felt that so much was at stake or felt so strongly that the fight was worthwhile." In one of his last editorials, A DAY OF DESTINY, he wrote:

> ... As a sovereign people within the British Empire we have a glorious future. Some day we may become the dominant force in that marvelous alliance that owes

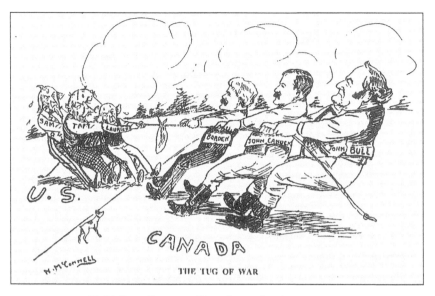

THE TUG OF WAR, *N. McConnell cartoon, News, September 21, 1911, p. 1.*

allegiance to the clustered crosses. This Dominion is the keystone of the Imperial fabric. Let us not place its security in pawn.

"A thousand years scarce serve to form a state. An hour may lay it in the dust."[51]

The results on September 21 were everything he could have wished for. This was in spite of impressive pro-free trade Liberal triumphs in Alberta and Saskatchewan and the usual even party split in the Maritimes. Elsewhere, however, results were disastrous for Laurier and his party. In Quebec, the Monk–*nationaliste* combination took 27 of Quebec's 65 seats. In Ontario, Manitoba, B.C., and Ontario it was a Conservative landslide. Above all, Ontario was the key. The province of Whitney, the Toronto 18, and John Willison buried the Laurier regime forever, with 73 seats to 16 and over 56 per cent of the vote. Overall, the Liberal majority of 50 in 1908 was now a Conservative one of 47.[52]

Toronto on election night resounded to blaring bands and glowed with torch-light and victory. As Arthur Glazebrook reported to Lord Milner: "… the whole city had the aspect of a triumph." At the *News* two huge screens, set up on the other side of Bay Street, featured projected returns, and two hired bands celebrated the victories. Five thousand revellers crowded round the building in late evening, when the dramatic scope of the result was clear. The chant for "Willison, Willison" would not be stilled, and at last he stepped out on the balcony, congratulating them on the victory they had won for Canada. He was modest then, and always would be, about his own role. Joseph Flavelle, however, continued to believe, as he had put it to Willison early in the campaign: "... the subsequent opposition to reciprocity but enlarged upon the points you made." Edward Kemp would assert to his colleagues in the new Borden cabinet that Willison "probably did more than any other newspaper man in Canada to assist in putting the present government in power."[53]

Fifteen years before he had been at the heart of another great national triumph, and at the right hand of the chief victor. As before, his pen, his position and his network of associations made him a key figure around a new prime minister. "Very important I see you tomorrow," read the telegraphed summons from Borden in Ottawa on October 3.[54] After 1896, his own prestige and the power of his newspaper had continued to grow, ever stronger, for several years. Eventually, however, in his sense of things at any rate, he had no longer really been listened to, and he had found the dictates of petty partisanship unbearable. Could he this time taste the sweet without the bitter?

XII

Fortune and Frustration, 1911–1914

THE PEACE-TIME BORDEN YEARS, FROM SEPTEMBER 1911 UNTIL THE
outbreak of world war in August, 1914, opened in high promise
for John Willison, but at length became a time of trouble for his career
and for many of the causes that were closest to his heart. In part, his
frustrations and difficulties sprang from complex disagreements in
Canada and Britain over imperial and national objectives. They also
related to the dependent and increasingly desperate situation in which
he found himself at the Toronto *News*.

As promised, he was thoroughly consulted by Robert Borden on
the formation of the new federal cabinet. Clifford Sifton came from
Ottawa to show Willison, Z.A. Lash, and Sir Edmund Walker the pro-
visional list. There was delight, and a sense of pledges kept, when the
anti-reciprocity Toronto 18 Liberal, Thomas White of the National Trust
Company, was given the finance portfolio. Willison made a personal and
successful plea, over Sifton's objections, for his fellow Torontonian, Edward Kemp, who had been a key directing influence in the campaign in
Ontario. He noted the inclusion of the controversial Manitoba Tory organizer, Robert Rogers, but wrote Borden that he would "not, however,
bring over to you certain elements in the West that you should have,"

suggesting instead Charles Magrath, the reformist Tory from Medicine Hat, Alberta. "While I believe we should deal generously with Quebec," he added, "surely it is in the West that the party must chiefly build for the future." But Rogers was appointed and Magrath was not. Willison accepted that philosophically. "I have learned," he told a friend, "that I cannot always have my own way and that sometimes I must work with men of whom I may not absolutely approve if the things which I value are to be advanced."[1]

Clearly, he wanted the new government to succeed. However, he would not be taken for granted by it, nor by its blood relation at Queen's Park. One early move was to emphasize that the *News* would be no mere propaganda sheet. As the new session of Parliament began, he requested Charlie Hamilton in Ottawa to send him "much more of a report with perhaps less comment," as he worried "if readers of the *News* can be persuaded that our Ottawa report is anything more than an editorial."

That attempt at fairness in parliamentary press coverage rebounded a few weeks later. In December, J.H. Burnham, a Conservative MP, complained to him that "yr. man Hamilton" was "clearly pro-Laurier. I believe him to be a danger to the party." Shades of the Roden Kingsmill experience with Liberal backbenchers in Willison's *Globe* days! Willison also smarted at the failure of the new government to allow his paper anything like the share of government advertising it was feeding to Tory morning papers. "I want to say that this is a position I will not accept," he exploded to Edward Kemp. "If I am to remain an active ally of the Ottawa government we must at least get as good treatment as the other papers." Kemp circularized his cabinet colleagues that the matter be "put right."

In Toronto, a really vicious confrontation occurred in October 1912 with Premier Whitney. A *News* reporter claimed that a provincial commissioner had refused certain information with curt words about it being "none of the public's business." When the premier backed the commissioner's denial of the story, the *News* retorted that the reporter was "just as honest and straightforward" as the commissioner or the premier. Whitney vented his fury to Frank Cochrane, complaining that "Willison has broken out again," and that he was "done with Willison" and would give the *News* no more government advertising.[2] The threat was not carried out, and amicable relations were restored.

Sir Robert Borden and Sir Wilfrid Laurier, 1913. Library and Archives Canada, PA-051531

The chief tensions Willison was experiencing in 1912 were not with Conservative politicians. Alarmingly, there were growing difficulties with the financing and competitiveness of the *News*. In November he went to Ottawa to inform Frank Cochrane, now a Borden minister but still the key figure in the *News* syndicate, that new "pool" stock would have to be sold if the paper was to be an effective competitor for circulation and advertising in the tough Toronto market. He recalled from earlier discussions that "I had the notion that it would not be so difficult to raise money for necessary plant when we had overcome the period of deficits." Circulation and revenue increases had dealt with the deficit for the time being, and now the *News* needed to be able to operate on a level playing field with its evening competitors like the *Star* if it was to survive. He was disappointed that he could not seem to get Cochrane to share his sense of urgency and returned to Toronto for, as he put it, "much thinking."

He did not take long to reach a conclusion. On Wednesday, November 20, eleven days after his fifty-sixth birthday, he wrote Cochrane, insisting the *News* simply had to have significant additional financing to be properly competitive and creditable. He added that he had decided "that shall be a problem for other people." He looked back on spending seventeen of the previous twenty-two years trying to save newspapers from bankruptcy. "To that sort of thing an end must come," he concluded, "and so somewhat unexpectedly to myself I have decided to withdraw from *The News* and from active journalism in Canada at the end of December." He said that he had contemplated the step "for a good while" but had felt unable to take it while the paper actually was losing money.[3]

Cochrane was bewildered, asking "what in the world is the matter? Was it because I did not express myself clearly, or that you expected me to sell this stock, or what has brought you to such a conclusion? ... We cannot afford to lose you off the News, nor from the direction of that paper in the interests of the country at large or the party...." He begged Willison not to decide his future finally until they could meet, "and if it is necessary to take up the stock I will have to get it done. We cannot spare you and are not going to."[4]

Willison responded that there *might* be some chance of his changing his mind after Cochrane's "considerate and generous" letter. He was "absolutely unwilling to continue ... with an inadequate plant," but was prepared to meet with the minister to "determine finally whether or not I should give effect finally and absolutely to my decision." Clearly he was torn. He told Cochrane that he could "live in such comfort as I have not known for many years" by dropping the *News* for his *Times* and other writing opportunities hitherto impossible to accept. He had just returned from a fascinating special assignment for the *Times* in the western U.S., covering the exciting Teddy Roosevelt–William Howard Taft–Woodrow Wilson presidential election fight, and that must have been like a holiday experience in comparison with the responsibility for keeping the *News* afloat. He stressed that his "first desire" was to continue as editor, but only with "an adequate equipment" so that he could be freed from the paper's financial strain to make "a decent showing" with his competitors.[5] Cochrane replied at once that he would have the stock matter "worked out." By mid-December, Willison wrote Prime Minister Borden that he expected to get the desired new plant and equipment to "produce the newspaper I am anxious to produce ... a far better News than we have ever had." The prime minister invited him to visit Ottawa "from time to time for a few days as I think it would be of mutual advantage that you should do so."[6]

Left: Sir John Willison, Kt. L.L.D. (facing title page of A.H.U. Colquhoun, The Life and Letters of Sir John Willison. Toronto: Macmillan, 1935)
Right: Lady Rachel Willison, 1913. (with permission from great-grandson Colonel Peter Mackenzie)

Shortly there was a far more striking demonstration of the esteem in which he was held by the new order in Ottawa. A week before Christmas, the postman delivered to the Willison residence a beautiful large buff envelope bearing the red crest of Rideau Hall. Inside, to the astonishment of both John and Rachel Willison, was a communication from the military secretary to the governor general, Lord Connaught, asking "whether it would be agreeable to you that he should submit your name to His Majesty the King for the honour of knighthood."[7]

Friday evening, January 31, 1913 was probably the proudest occasion of Sir John Willison's life. A large testimonial dinner group at the National Club brought together friends and admirers, old and new, Liberal, Tory, and independent. Accompanied by his sons Walter and Bill, the guest of honour sat down to a sumptuous gourmet meal. There were oysters, filet of sole, mignon of tenderloins and roast squab *au jus* – all accompanied by the appropriate fine French wines. The boy from the

Hills Green Good Templars Lodge had been transformed! The company that evening was reminded of Sir John's humble origins by the picture on the inside cover of the beautiful brown ribbon-tied program. There was a smiling young boy sitting on a general store's sugar barrel. On the next page a mature Sir John, watch chain, balding head, and slight paunch in place, was smiling just as broadly. Glasses were raised to toast "A Scholar and a Gentleman."[8]

Joseph Atkinson of the Liberal Toronto *Star*, long ago one of Willison's reporters on the *Globe*, put aside their contemporary circulation rivalry and political differences to voice his affectionate congratulations. No lover of titles, and very definitely an anti-imperialist, he nonetheless was wonderfully generous in his praise of this knight:

> The best part of a newspaper is its heart and conscience and some years ago I said that Mr. (now Sir John) Willison represented the conscience upon which journalism depended. In all the annals of knighthood there was one knight who was ever pure in heart and true and loyal, who never turned his back on friend or foe, and if there is a man in Canada to-day to whom I could apply the virtues of heart and loyalty it would be to our guest himself.

The chief testimonial was Joseph Flavelle's. He quoted Willison's remark to him on learning of the knighthood, that he would regard the honour "chiefly as a fresh obligation to public service." For Flavelle, that approach "possesses him and friend or opponent who fails to appreciate this misses that which alone leads to an understanding of his life and work." He spoke of the extraordinary trust in his confidentiality that "drew saint and sinner, Catholic and Protestant, capital and labour, judge and commoner, Tory and Radical … to his office or to his home…." Very likely Flavelle knew how nearly Willison had come to abandoning Canadian daily journalism when he begged him that night to display in future "more continuous evidence of his handiwork in his own paper. When he is at his best there is a note of authority which commands respect and compels attention." It was fine that so much of his energy was wanted by "the great daily across the sea," but "there are too few men of distinction in journalism in Canada to lightly permit the temptation to rest upon the leader among them to give an undue share of his best work to readers outside Canada."[9] Willison told Flavelle privately afterwards that he was "very grateful" for the tribute and for "the personal relation behind it and of associations which to me were very valuable even if all did not turn out as we desired." Flavelle responded: "If you are successful in making The News an efficient instrument for the public good it is a mere incident that I should fall out along the way."[10]

In his own speech that evening, Willison opened by joking that he could not discover any likeness between himself and the "interesting mythological figure" described by Atkinson and Flavelle. He shared with his amused audience the words on an unsigned postcard he had received after the knighthood was announced, bearing the words: "Just for a handful of silver he left us, just for a riband to stick in his coat." He mused that "the writer meant to be uncomplimentary, but each of us must take his share of praise and of dispraise, and when all is said, life is good and men are kind." He had not sought a title, he stated, or any other reward "outside of my own pursuit;" he was simply the "medium" for the Crown's honouring Canadian journalism. He firmly believed that "a title does not make one the servant of a class or faction, and ... the bravest scorner of titles may be an incurable Tory and a natural tyrant."

Talk of titles led him to his main theme — imperialism and its relationship to Canadian interests. He protested "every assumption that we are not an empire but a group of suspicious, restless and naturally hostile communities playing a farce before the nations, waiting until we are strong to pull down the whole structure, but in the meantime without courage enough to be independent citizens of the Dominions, and without vision enough to be citizens of an Empire...." He turned to his own very clear vision of how he looked forward to a fully matured adult Canada as in no sense a dependent colony but rather an equal partner in a world Empire. He argued that

> ... to limit the political authority of Canada in any degree is to reject the whole theory of equal citizenship under the Crown, to suggest that a lesser sovereignty is

reposed in the Dominions, and to deny to the overseas portion of the Empire the free play of national feeling and the proud sense of Imperial citizenship which constitute the real glory of the British Islands....

If the thirteen colonies had not separated from Great Britain — and under the organization of the Empire which has since developed there would have been no separation — would an American to-day have a citizenship in the Empire inferior to that of the Englishman? Is it inconceivable that in the years to come the British Canadian may speak with an authority as great or greater than any other citizen of the world will possess? In Canada, Australia, New Zealand and South Africa there is potential power as great as any that will centre at Washington, and a political relationship with Great Britain established in simple national equality that only criminal folly will ever disturb or destroy....

To the host of friends who had been expressing their warm feelings about him, he emotionally offered his thanks and looked back on the long working life that had led to this wonderful night:

For nearly thirty years, I have been a working journalist in Toronto. It has been my fortune to have had a share in the confidence of both political parties, but unfortunately not simultaneously. I have often blundered. I have often misjudged men and their motives. I have supported causes which deserved to succeed and did not. I have advocated causes which deserved to fail and did not. I have written some sense and much rubbish. I have been censured when I deserved praise and praised when I deserved censure. So it will be to the end of the chapter. A great Scottish editor once said that the 'life of a journalist is a warfare upon earth,' and all I have to say in my own defence is that I do not believe I have written from a sense of personal grievance or have cherished personal ill will towards any public man in Canada, or have adhered to the iron law of the fathers that to admit a mistake was unpardonable weakness and to correct an error a shameful revelation of moral and physical cowardice....

Arthur Colquhoun was Willison's oldest and closest friend. In his later biography of Sir John, he followed an account of the joy and optimism on the night of the dinner with the observation that "the other side of the picture presents a different aspect." Likely that dark despair that had been displayed to Frank Cochrane had been revealed to him too. As Colquhoun put it,

> Willison must have been assailed at this period by many misgivings. Could independent journalism be closely linked to either party? Would the newspapers identified with his beliefs ever pay? Was not the obligation to the interests of hearth and home as binding on the individual as his ideals and principles? He must have discovered that one group of politicians were very like another in preferring the independence that could be counted upon.... The question which Willison could have asked himself at twenty, if his knowledge of the world had been equal to his practical insight at fifty, would have been this: "In daily journalism is absolute freedom a possibility, lacking an inexhaustible endowment?"

Colquhoun would look back on this period of Willison's life as "these anxious years."[11] At the time he assured his friend that "you are one of the few Canadians who have been honoured on merit alone. In no quarter is a doubt of this suggested and this I think should be a source of unfeigned satisfaction for your family."[12]

Certainly, his family and personal life were very happy. Rachel was still his devoted helpmate and very active in community and women's organizations. He himself greatly enjoyed his lawn bowling and in 1914 added the York Club to his many other social networking sites. Bill and

Walter were grown now, at twenty-four. They both had gone through Upper Canada College, Bill by the skin of his teeth and much tutoring. Both loved sports, especially boxing, ending up as competing finalists for the school championship in their senior year. Then it was on to University College at the University of Toronto for Arts. Bill stuck it for only one year, in 1908–09, but Walter finished his degree and won an intercollegiate boxing title. Both sons looked for journalistic careers. Walter early took a position in the news department of the *News*. In October 1913 he married Vivyan Boulton, with Bill as his best man, and the next year took up duties in England as correspondent for the *News*. Meanwhile, Bill had stints with the Montreal *Witness*, the Regina *Province* and the Fort William *Herald* before returning to Toronto by 1914 to write editorial notes as "W.T.W." in the *News*.[13]

The challenge of keeping the *News* afloat remained. Whatever the progress through Cochrane on new plant and equipment, other expenditures could not be allowed to grow. In March 1913 the paper's managers agreed to "make the best of the material presently available" and to condense news coverage, focusing on "its interest to the man on the street." The business office was instructed to "eliminate to a very large extent the typographical errors that have been appearing."[14] Still, without new resources the *News* seemed unable to put a more saleable product on the street. W.B. Hay, the frustrated news editor, resigned in July.

In November, Willison received a bitter complaint from one reader about the "numerous and outrageous" typographical confusions in the paper. "No wonder so many Conservatives who like your editorials take the 'Star' in preference to the 'News,'" he remarked. Edward Kemp, now a Borden minister and still a member of the paper's board, looked at the year-end accounts for 1913 and was distressed to see that the situation was "$19,578.68 worse than 1912…. Can you improve on this for 1914?" The hard fact was that Canada's extraordinary boom years since the mid-1890s had given way in 1913 to a marked recession, bringing an inevitable contraction in the supply of available capital for re-financing any sort of enterprise and depressing both advertising and newspaper buying. The *News* kept afloat, thanks to monthly income supplements from Frank Cochrane, but the days of deficits and a hand-to-mouth existence continued.[15] A new crisis for the paper and its editor could not be far off.

Ironically, in spite of its financial difficulties, the *News* and its editor were at the forefront of Toronto's municipal progressive movement. In 1911 the paper went all-out for a "yes" vote in a referendum on a downtown subway system and for an extension of the city's municipally owned electric system, and the next year it fervently supported the pro-public ownership Horatio Hocken, once one of its reporters, for city board of control. When Controller Tommy Church, a right-wing Conservative opponent of public ownership, ran for mayor in 1913, it won his bitter enmity by declaring war on "politicians of the Church type" and made it clear that "in civic politics it recognizes no obligation to any party and declines to support any candidate because of the political camp to which he belongs."[16]

Premier James Whitney's Ontario government was both popular and moderately progressive. The *News* enthusiastically endorsed Whitney's reforms, such as provincial compensation for workmen's injuries, increased support for primary and secondary education, enhanced aid for the University of Toronto, and the continued expansion of public electric ownership.[17]

Willison had a personal and especially gratifying success in 1913 with the Whitney administration on housing policy. He joined with other community leaders to respond to a growing crisis in housing availability for lower-income Torontonians. To his longtime Liberal friend, Frank Beer, a leading activist on the issue, he wrote that "there are few things in our modern civilization that are more vital than the conditions under which men live and that a supreme object should be to continue the home as our best institution and in so far as possible to give each family a home to itself." He then pressed Ontario's Provincial Secretary, William John Hanna, for "legislation providing for ... guarantee of municipal bonds for this purpose." Willison had to be pleased when the government went along with his proposal, but then had to lobby again when its draft bill required approval in each municipality by ratepayers' votes. He told Premier Whitney: "Immigrants are coming by the thousands and conditions will grow worse instead of better" unless "exceptional measures" were taken. Whitney backed down, replacing the approval by ratepayers with a requirement of a two thirds municipal council vote. Beer and his fellow directors of the Ontario Housing Authority expressed to

Willison their "warmest thanks for all your kindness and help, without which our efforts might have entirely failed." Willison's concerns about the social future of urban life were deepening, and he was developing a major new theme as a journalist and public man.[18]

In September 1913 the *News* called for "security of employment" as being every bit as essential to the ordinary Canadian as an adequate supply of affordable shelter. Early in the new year the paper issued an urgent call for both governments of all levels and the private sector to respond meaningfully to sharply increasing unemployment. Firms were urged not to reduce staff, the city was advised to set up a labour exchange and workmen's relief office, and all governments were asked to put maximum funding into job creation. That winter Willison told an evening meeting at St. Giles Presbyterian Church that Canadians were faced with "New Times and New Problems." He stressed that there was "no greater problem than unemployment" and supported old-age insurance, a minimum wage, a thorough investigation of labour conditions and a profit-sharing system. He asked his middle-class audience to "think a little more sympathetically of the population which lives a hard life."[19]

Willison's initial expectations and assumptions about the prospects for progress towards imperial unity in the new Borden era for Canada were strongly optimistic. In the *News*, the *Times* and the new imperialist quarterly *The Round Table* he made that very clear. His bullish imperialist nationalist mood was never better expressed than in his Empire Day articles for the *Times* in 1912, the largest single collection of reports on Canada he ever sent to the London paper. He sought to explain to the British Canada's rejection of reciprocity with the United States, define her economic prospects in glowing terms, and set forth an unapologetically Canadian perspective on priorities for the future of the Empire.

He began by stressing that the dramatic defeat of Reciprocity in 1911 had been far more than an endorsement of protectionism. Canadians, he stressed, had "declared as decisively for an independent Canadian nationality and for continuance of the Imperial connection." He was sure that the "loyalty" of the "farms and villages" of English Canada "was a faith and a passion and that the appeal to British sentiment was as powerful as any appeal to personal interest or national feeling," that "there were considerations beyond commercialism and even beyond nationalism, and that the strain of Imperialism was in the blood of the English-speaking population of older Canada." He linked tightly the imperial preference and naval issues, arguing that both British failures to move towards a trade arrangement and Canadian hesitations about taking on a fair share of sea defence "impeded" the consolidation of the Empire. He was confident that "sooner or later" trade, communications, and naval co-operation would expand and that "the slow orderly processes of British history" would lead at last to "a powerful and enduring political federation."

Willison was fully aware that in the dangerous international context of 1912, especially given the bellicose nature of Kaiser Wilhelm's Germany, one of the principal aims of British diplomacy was to ensure friendship, even alliance, with the United States. Canadians understood, he stressed, "the overwhelming importance" of all that, and the Canadian defeat of reciprocity had not been aimed in any way at poisoning Anglo-American relations.

He knew that there was much British interest in the boom in western Canada. It was important, for settlement and investment reasons, for this interest to become an enthusiasm. He cited with approval recent estimates that the Western wheat acreage was likely to expand eventually by three to four times and that the use of the gasoline tractor and the coming of a multitude of new railway outlets pointed to an exceptionally productive future. But he had another purpose as well — to impress upon imperialists in Britain the ethnic heterogeneity of the region and that hundreds of thousands of new Canadians there "can have no active sympathy with our loyal devotion to the Crown and sense of obligation to the Empire." For the West particularly, then, there would be a need for demonstrating that there would be concrete material advantages in imperial unity.

Beyond the imperial issue, he depicted Canada in 1912 as extraordinarily prosperous and fully capable of much further advance as a united, progressive, and stable society. Canadians generally, he wrote, understood that their continuing need for massive outside investment made "confiscatory attacks" on "capital legitimately invested and fairly employed" undesirable. On the labour scene, he affirmed that the Laurier government's Industrial Disputes Investigation Act and Mackenzie King's leadership in that policy area had done much to improve relations between labour and management. On problems between East and West, there needed to be a "generous attitude" to the younger region. With the "sympathetic and adequate" consideration of the new Borden government to Western needs in freight rates and transportation outlets, "it should be far from impossible to have a tariff equal to the legitimate protection of Canadian industries. On Quebec, he expressed confidence that, with advancing modernization, an industrial explosion and political reform, there was a "restoration of the national spirit" that promised an abatement of provincialism there.[20]

In writing this extraordinary collection of special articles for the *Times* Willison was, as he explained to Flavelle, "very greatly concerned to do a service for Canada." He did not hurt his own interests either. The veteran editor-in-chief, G.E. Buckle, wrote to praise the articles as "really masterly.... You have caught, as it seems to me, the essential features of the Dominion at a critical phase of her career, and deftly photographed them for the instruction of the Mother Country & the other nations of the Empire.... Your articles, by themselves, justify the Empire number; and they are conceived in the traditional spirit of The Times, which as you know, you have made your own." Buckle was then in his last days as editor, but his designated successor, Geoffrey Robinson, was equally delighted. He wrote: "It is exactly what I hoped you would produce.... I have never read anything which gave me such a clear idea of its [Canada's] conditions and problems." Robinson arranged for the articles to be grouped together as *The New Canada*, published by the *Times* in handy book form. By August the book was out, and Lord Northcliffe delightedly reported to Willison that it was "much admired" in London.[21]

In Canada, among those who knew that he was the Canadian Correspondent of the *Times*, there was much positive comment too. A good deal of it was from Liberals. Sir George Ross, the former Liberal premier of Ontario and the Leader of the Opposition in the Senate, whom Willison had done so much to hound out of office in 1905, found the book "a splendid summary of our national outfit ... impartial, and the matter well classified." O.D. Skelton, a pro-Laurier Queen's professor of political economy, was even more complimentary, describing the account as "the most comprehensive, balanced and far-seeing discussion of Canadian problems I have read for many a day."[22]

The writer for the far-off *Times* always did his best to accentuate the positive, on the highest plane. Yet the daily journalist and behind-the-scenes political strategist in Canada had to face the imperfections and frustrations of reality, even contribute to them. His greatest frustration during the pre-war Borden era was that no measurable progress was made towards his ideal of imperial unity."

Prime Minister Borden moved very slowly indeed on the naval issue. He told the House of Commons in November 1911 that he wanted to find out "what are the conditions that confront the Empire." In March 1912, he announced that the modest Laurier approach of a national naval force of small ships would not be continued and that any permanent policy would be submitted to the people and would be tied to "a greater voice in the councils of the Empire...."[23] Further details would have to await his trip to Britain that summer.

Meanwhile, there took place what Willison described to Professor George Wrong, the University of Toronto historian, as "an amazing development of public opinion on Imperial relations...." By that, he meant that English Canadians wanted a truly effective action by Canada to contribute to Britain's strategic naval power — now! In mid-June, shortly before Borden left for Britain, Willison wrote him that "delay in determining upon a definite course may be dangerous." A detailed discussion with the prime minister very likely then took place, because when Borden reached London in early July, Willison's seemingly authoritative dispatch preceded him with the prediction that "the Dominion will offer two or three Dreadnoughts to be constructed at a cost of 20 to 30 million dollars.... This will be both partial discharge of an immediate duty and will clear the way for consideration of the details of a permanent policy...." The details of that, he added, would be settled after consultation with Admiralty experts, but "much will depend on what form of Imperial representation is devised ... Canada must establish its position as the chief Dominion of the Empire...."[24]

There were no quick decisions. Borden went to London fully aware that Frederick Monk and many of the *nationaliste* Conservatives from Quebec opposed any naval defence action or expenditure without a direct consultation of the people. The First Lord of the Admiralty, Winston Churchill, supplied the Canadian leader with suitable "proof" of a strategic naval "emergency," but Borden could not win a cautious Prime Minister Herbert Asquith's agreement that a direct contribution by Canada would win a real voice in imperial foreign policy. Borden was left to make the most he could before the Canadian public of the British government's readiness to have a Canadian representative in London attend meetings of the advisory Committee of Imperial Defence when Canadian "interests" were being discussed. Borden accepted this as a "temporary measure."[25]

Back in Canada, Borden won his cabinet's agreement to the "emergency" contribution, and this immediately prompted Frederick Monk's resignation from the cabinet. Most of the other Quebec Conservative MPs and ministers stayed in line, either convinced by the Admiralty's "proof" of crisis at sea, or won over by Borden's promise of eventual fat naval construction contracts for Quebec. Willison had been worried that there might be a wholesale desertion of the prime minister by the Quebec Conservatives in the House, and he had feared this "would mean an immediate general election" if Laurier and the Liberals decided to oppose Borden's proposals. Willison did not want the prime minister to back down before Monk, but he was interested in seeing what could be done to put together a bipartisan common front in English Canada. Accordingly, he warned the government publicly in *The Round Table* — and no doubt privately too — that it should not repeal the Laurier Naval Service Act, that this "would be at best a political concession to the extreme critics of the Liberal policy, and possibly among its undesirable results would be an aggravation of domestic party feeling over an issue which many Canadian Imperialists of both parties desire to exclude from the area of party conflict."[26]

A bipartisan movement in journalism and business, principally in Toronto and Winnipeg, did come together to call for a navy "worthy of our national aspirations," coupled with such emergency aid to Britain as justified by "official information." The *News* hailed this "remarkable movement" of opinion and made much of the prominent Liberals, such as the editors of the Toronto *Globe* and *Star* and the Manitoba *Free Press*, who were part of it. However, without the agreement of Borden and Laurier such a compromise was pointless. The two party leaders had their own priorities — both in imperialist and nationalist objectives and in politics.

Borden was not ready yet to decide on a permanent naval policy and had become highly doubtful, as he came to explain to Parliament, that a strictly national naval policy could be "effective" in defence terms "within a quarter or perhaps half a century." Laurier absolutely declined any other course for Canada and worried lest Borden's search for a voice in imperial foreign policy "would bring us into the intricacies of European diplomacy with all its consequences."[27] As well, the aggressive imperialism of so many English-Canadian Conservatives, coupled with the Quebec base and desire for return to office of the recently deposed Liberals, pushed the two parties towards confrontation rather than coalescence.

Borden presented his Naval Aid Bill to the House of Commons on December 5, 1912. The Laurier Naval Service Act was not to be repealed, but there would be no ship construction under it until Canada's "permanent" naval policy had been determined, related to a proper role in the formation of imperial foreign policy. Just about as Willison had predicted, an "emergency" contribution of $35,000,000 to build three dreadnoughts would be given to Britain. Borden declared fervently: "... in the urgency of the moment we come to her [Britain] ... in token of our determination to protect and ensure the safety and integrity of this Empire...."[28]

Willison commented in *The Round Table* that Borden "has made no greater speech in the course of his public career." He took at face value the prime minister's assurance that the Canadian sometime consultative role on the Committee of Imperial Defence was "a real voice in imperial foreign policy." Actually, the British did not so regard it at all, and made haste to ensure Borden knew this. They had not in any way to this point conceded to Canada any serious role in foreign policy formation. That was for private dispatches, however, and Willison very likely had no knowledge of the Anglo-Canadian differences on this point. In any event, Borden was delighted with Willison's enthusiasm, writing: "I cannot tell you how highly I value such words of commendation from one who is able to speak with your authority and with your experience."[29]

Partisan politics engulfed the Naval Aid Bill. Laurier boldly strengthened his earlier policy as prime minister by proposing two major "fleet units," each containing a dreadnought, for the two Canadian coasts. All ships were to be built in Canada, manned by Canadians and under Canadian control. From a nationalist but pro-defence position, the Liberal leader could damn Tory "tribute" to London. Willison's non-partisan characterization of Laurier's move for *The Round Table* was that it "commands respect." Behind the scenes, he remarked to Borden that the Laurier strategy, "in face of his own record … is rather farcical."[30] Weeks and then months of debate over the Borden bill turned farce into bitterness. First, the Liberals successfully filibustered the legislation, seeking either to stop or force an election over it, as the Tories had done with Reciprocity in 1911.

On March 13, Willison rumbled to Edward Grigg in England that the Liberals "have no considerable public support behind them, that the party has lost its head and is going to destruction." The *News* proclaimed savagely that Laurier's "plain object" was "to unite the French population of older Canada, the American communities of the West and generally the 'foreign' elements against the Government, against Great Britain and against the Empire…."[31] The partisan shrillness further increased on April 9, when Borden introduced a motion in the House for the passage of rules permitting the use of closure in debate. By a procedural manoeuvre, the Conservatives managed to have debate on these new rules limited to one speech by each MP, and passage followed on April 23. The Naval Aid Bill, with closure applied, was approved by the House on May 15.[32]

That delivered the bill to the Senate, with its huge Liberal majority. Earlier, before the struggle in the House had become so bitter, Willison had discussed the measure thoroughly with his old friend and former political adversary, Sir George Ross, the Liberal leader in the Senate, and was optimistic of eventual passage by the upper house. By mid-April, however, with the closure issue freshly accentuating partisan anger, he reported to Edward Grigg of the *Times* that he had learned from Ross that "the Liberal majority in the Senate now has been affected by the bitter quarrel in the House of Commons and that even Sir George Ross is afraid the Upper Chamber will reject the naval bill." He added a month later: "I am not sure that the Government can permit a bill of such vital importance to be defeated and not appeal to the country." He told the prime minister: "The supreme thing to do is to defeat Laurier in the next election." On Borden's request, he had the *News* issue a blunt editorial warning that if the Senate were to defeat or seriously alter the bill, the upper house as then constituted would have to perish.[33]

The Senate Liberals would not be bluffed, sending the Naval Aid Bill back to the House with the amendment that it must be "submitted to the judgement of the country." There was no election call from Borden, who apparently believed that he should await redistribution of constituency boundaries and that he needed time to put together a credible record on domestic issues before facing the electorate. When Willison published his *Reminiscences* six years later, he looked back sorrowfully on the deterioration from the unanimity on the naval issue in 1909 to the partisan squabbling of 1913, and judged that "a great issue was enmeshed in party strategy and that neither party is to be congratulated upon the result to which they mutually contributed."[34]

That was written in the calm of much later. At the time, Willison put his emphasis on seeing the Liberal–Conservative squabbling over the navy as part of a much larger issue, with what he saw as profound implications for the future course of Canadian nationality and imperialism. In November 1913, the *News* carried a long, reflective editorial on the threat to Canada's imperial connection:

> The signs of a separatist movement in Canada become very manifest. For the moment the leaders conceal their purposes and avow their British sympathies....
>
> The movement is deftly fostered by some of the chief journals of the Liberal party. They recognize that the appeal to British feeling was influential in defeating the trade agreement with Washington. Sullen and revengeful, they create the impression that Imperial feeling is something to be feared and distrusted. Associated with these journals is a group of sincere opponents of the Imperial movement.... They deny any obligation to the Empire. They jeer at any 'emergency'.... Within the Liberal party their influence is great and they aim to make it paramount. They know what they want, and unless they are strongly resisted they may seriously impair the good relations which now exist between Canada and Great Britain....[35]

It was not only the Canadian Liberals whom he believed to be holding up progress towards greater imperial unity. The British Unionists (Conservatives), for a decade the champions of imperial preferential trade, were tiring of their lack of electoral success with it. In the late autumn of 1912 there was a rebellion in party ranks against continuing to support "food taxes" as part of a preferential system. In January 1913, with the support of Geoffrey Robinson, the editor of the *Times*, the party disavowed "food taxes" and committed itself to a preference "upon manufactures and luxuries alone." Robinson had several English Round Tabler friends, including Lionel Curtis and Philip Kerr, who agreed that the preference policy had to be altered if the larger cause of imperial consolidation was not to be discredited with the British electorate. Lord Northcliffe, the proprietor of the *Times*, concurred, telling his editor: "I am sure that your opinion about Food Taxes is the right one...."

Willison most definitely did not agree. As the story developed, he fired off to London what Lord Northcliffe characterized to Robinson as a "remarkable" cable on imperial preference, warning that the contemplated Unionist manoeuvre would be ruinous to imperialism in Canada. Northcliffe doubted Willison was correct, but warned Robinson that Willison, whom he described as "the father of the [imperialist] movement in Canada," could not be ignored. "I am very sure that it would be well for you to see him or get him over here before 'The Times' commits itself to the food tax policy."[36]

Willison stayed home but repeatedly told Northcliffe that the Unionist moves gave him "intense concern," as he was sure that "essentially the question of Empire is a question of trade." For Canadians, he stressed, preference had "no meaning" if it did not apply to their foodstuff exports to Great Britain, and if there was to be no progress in this quarter, the movement for cooperation in defence will be substantially checked." He grimly asked Edward Grigg: "Could we possibly resist again free trade proposals from Washington, if it is definitely understood that we are to have no trade preference in the Mother Country?"[37]

There would be no Willison compromises with the Curtis–Kerr group in London. He was annoyed early in 1913 by a favourable article in *The Round Table* on the Unionist food tax strategy. It may be that the quarterly's decision to print it, re-emphasizing the ignoring of major

Canadian concerns, only confirmed his decision to cease his regular Canadian contribution for them. He had written that faithfully since the first issue in November 1910. He would remain a member of the Round Table group in Canada, and he would write on occasions for the magazine, but often in the future there would be no easy coalescence between his nationalist Canadian imperialism and the views of the Londoners. While he remained an imperialist as 1914 dawned, it must have been hard for him to know just how the trend towards imperialist enthusiasm and greater imperial unity, which he had felt roused in Canada in 1909–12 over the naval and reciprocity issues, was to be revived. In May 1914 he pleaded in the *News* that "the Old Country should understand tendencies and conditions here, and should know the strength of Canadian feeling, and should consider the Imperial problem from the standpoint of this country...."[38]

Meanwhile in Canada, the old linguistic and sectarian controversies were flaring, in fresh forms. The most serious involved both separate schools and the French language in Ontario. The French-speaking population, especially in the eastern and northern districts, had expanded rapidly since the turn of the century and, by 1910, had come to number close to ten per cent of the provincial population. The pressure of their numbers and their demands for French-language schooling heavily affected the hitherto English-language Catholic separate schools in the districts where they had settled. The English-speaking, mainly Irish, Catholic community feared for its identity. Monsignor Fallon, Bishop of London from 1910, rallied the English-speaking Catholic prelates of the province to press the Whitney government to prevent "French domination." It was claimed that in many areas, and without legal sanction, the language of instruction was French and the quality of English instruction dubious. In the fall of 1910, the Whitney government set up a provincial commission, under Dr. F.W. Merchant, to study conditions in these so-called "bilingual" schools.

In the 1911 session of the Legislature, a unanimous resolution declared that English must be "the language of instruction and of all communication with the pupils in the public and separate schools ... except where, in the opinion of the department [of education], it is impracticable by reason of the pupils not understanding English." The *News* declared:

"The schools must be efficient. And on this continent, in this Dominion, in this Province a pupil's knowledge of English is one of the most important tests of efficiency." For the *News* and its editor the issue was not merely "efficiency." The paper declared firmly: "The pressures from Franco-Ontarians and their allies in Quebec for bilingual rights must be resisted.... In Ontario and in the Western Provinces English must be the common language of the schools and of the people." That this was the case south of the border "greatly explains the success of the United States in infusing many nationalities into a common citizenship.... It is a national duty ... in so far as we are not restricted by constitutional guarantees to make English the language of the schools, to resist separation in education, and to oppose every new demand of racial or religious minorities."[39]

In these years there was tension as well in Ontario and throughout Canada over the *Ne Temere* question. This involved the Vatican's decree ruling invalid Protestant–Catholic marriages not performed by Catholic priests under special permission. The Borden government was put under heavy Protestant pressure to enact federal marriage and divorce provisions, to protect such marriages. Its response was to refer to the courts the question of its jurisdiction. Willison agreed with the "reasonableness" of this position, but the *News* emphasized that a favourable court ruling should be followed by quick action, proclaiming that the "arrogant pretensions of any ecclesiastical authority ... cannot be accepted for a moment."[40]

On March 6, 1912 the Merchant Report on bilingual schools was presented to the Ontario Legislature. It found that in eighty per cent of the separate schools of eastern Ontario and ninety per cent of the public and rural separate schools in the north, French was used generally for the teaching of all subjects but English. Few teachers could teach English effectively. In mid-April, Premier Whitney announced that the government would insist on proper knowledge of English in all schools, and additional inspectors were to be provided to ensure this. Then, in the core of what would be known as Regulation 17, it was declared that instruction in English was to begin on school entry and that French instruction was to vary with local conditions "but in no case to continue beyond the end of the first form [first two grades]." The *News* expressed its approval that "no section of Ontario is to be Gallicized."[41]

Nevertheless, the Franco-Ontarian agitation for French-language instruction in the schools merely intensified. Senator N.A. Belcourt proclaimed that there was a constitutional "right" to the equality of the English and French languages in the treatment of Canada-wide concerns. The *News* in October 1913 bluntly and absolutely rejected official bilingualism in Canada, arguing that outside of the existing constitutional provisions for protection of French in parliament, the federal courts and Quebec, it had "no stronger position than Welsh or Japanese, and any attempt to create new privileges cannot be permitted to succeed."[42]

In June 1914, an Ontario general election took place. The Liberal leader, Sir John's personal friend Newton Rowell, described the teaching to a child in his or her mother tongue as being quite compatible with efficient English-language schools. The *News* immediately charged that there was a "close understanding between the Opposition leader and the extreme advocates of French schools in this Province." It went on to claim that Rowell had "failed to give the electors any pledge that he would enforce Regulation 17...." That was a gross exaggeration, since Rowell's chief criticism of the Whitney government on the schools issue was that it had not done *enough* for English-language efficiency.[43] In any event, the sentiments, convictions, and partisan loyalty of the man who commanded the editorial page of the *News* were very clear.

Willison was not at all uncharacteristic of his time, generation, and community in his utter rejection of any kind of bilingual or denominational rights beyond those already constitutionally guaranteed. In fact, he did not go far enough for some of his readers. In July 1914 one accused him of being "weak on bilingualism" because the *News* would not denounce the bilingual postcards recently printed by the federal government. He replied that "under the constitution the right to have both languages on postcards is unassailable. I am sure we both agree that the Constitution should be faithfully observed...."[44]

Far from Canada, another majority-minority issue was brewing which touched profoundly upon both his convictions and his emotions. The British Liberal government was preparing to grant "Home Rule" autonomy to a new all-Ireland parliament at Dublin. Protestants in northern Ireland were vehemently opposed to being subjected to a Catholic majority and wished to continue to live in a fully integral part of the

United Kingdom. In February 1912, Willison, along with Mayor Hocken, addressed a protest rally of 3,000 at Massey Hall and denounced the plan to "impose upon the loyal Protestant minority [of Ireland] conditions and restrictions to which we would not submit."

The controversy in Britain became protracted and very bitter, and by the spring of 1914, as many Protestant Ulstermen were arming to resist Home Rule, the *News* pronounced that it was "as certain as the shining of the sun that the United Kingdom must choose between revolution and withdrawal of the Home Rule Bill." Again Willison was a main speaker at an anti-Home Rule rally, this time a monster one in Queen's Park in May. He condemned the attempt to "take away from Ulster its full citizenship in the Empire…." In the *Times* he linked the Home Rule issue to the very future of the Empire. "The mass of active and aggressive Imperialists in Canada sympathize with Ulster," he claimed. "It is they who have 'kept the flag flying' in North America. Will they be as active if Ulster is forced under a Dublin Parliament by Imperial Ministers? Do British statesmen and British journalists fully understand the Canadian aspect of the Imperial problem, and how vitally careless handling would affect the whole structure and future of the Empire?"[45] In so many ways then, by the summer of 1914, he clearly was feeling that his kind of Canada and his kind of Empire were under siege. No one could doubt his readiness to mount the battlements.

Still, could he fight everywhere and on and on? Geoffrey Robinson in London was alarmed to hear from a visiting Arthur Glazebrook that Willison was "finding the double demand of The Times and the News rather a heavy burden." He himself wrote Robinson that he was "quite in despair as to what The Times wants." The business office had been ordering him to cut cabling costs, while Lord Northcliffe and various sub-editors had been demanding more news. Meanwhile, his longer reflective articles often were being set aside. He must have wondered if his candid critiques of the economic positions of British Unionists and imperialists had become unpalatable in London. He was finding it all, he commented to Robinson, "embarrassing and unsatisfactory." Robinson advised him, a little curtly perhaps, to "just meet our miscellaneous wishes as best you can" on the news side; he would see that "you have no cause in future to complain that your mailed articles are set aside."[46]

By late June, however, Willison informed Robinson that he wanted to end his connection with the *Times*. He may not have been fully serious. Perhaps, as to an extent had been the case in 1912 when he had threatened to leave the *News*, his core purpose was to have his concerns and dissatisfactions taken more seriously. Once again, he succeeded. Robinson hastened to respond that "I should deplore most bitterly any decision which confined your work to the <u>News</u> and caused you to give up <u>The Times</u>." He would "try to arrange something a little less arduous for you.... I think, besides, that your work for <u>The Times</u> is of real imperial importance at the present juncture."[47]

Willison, mollified, wrote back in mid-July that he would agree to carry on. Robinson was "much relieved.... I feel, as you do, that our relations with Canada during the next few years are going to be so vitally important that I am simply in despair at the very thought of losing your guidance from the other side."[48] He was wanted and valued. He would carry on. By the time he received that latest letter from Robinson, he knew from the newswires that he now absolutely had to put aside any thought of abandoning his highly important and unique role of interpreting Canada to the British. It was August 1914, and the guns of war were sounding across Europe.

XIII

Battles Lost and Won, 1914–1917

THE YEARS OF WHAT PEOPLE IN WILLISON'S TIME CALLED THE GREAT War were for him and his family, as for so many other Canadians, a time of unprecedented trial, tension, and sacrifice. The war brought private sorrow, and a new intensity of conflict characterized the political and journalistic worlds in which he moved. Meanwhile, he doggedly kept up his long battle to keep the *News* alive, in the face of the terrible pressures of wartime newspaper economics — until he was obliged to face at last a decisive turning point in his career. Well before the war was over, by the end of 1917, both his life and Canada's had been vastly changed.

The *News* barely noticed the assassination in late June 1914 by a Serbian of Archduke Francis Ferdinand, heir to the Austro-Hungarian throne. Then on Saturday, July 25th, a small sub-heading alerted readers to "the danger of a general European war" in Austria-Hungary's threatening ultimatum to the Balkan kingdom of Serbia, which it held responsible for the murder. By Monday, Serbian defiance pointed toward hostilities and the *News* expressed its "fear … that all the great continental nations may be drawn into the conflict as allies of the principals." And so it happened, as Russia pledged to aid Serbia, Germany promised to aid Austria-Hungary and France said she would stand by her Russian ally. At first the

News saw Britain as the "powerful pacifist," but by July 31, it expressed the "grave fear that Britain cannot remain neutral" in the face of possible French defeat. Britain's belligerency was clinched by Germany's attack on British-guaranteed Belgium. On Tuesday, August 4, Britain declared war on Germany, automatically bringing all the Empire in with her.[1]

"Not for a hundred years have the people of Toronto been so stirred … talking only of war," the *News* reported on August 1. The hunger for news swamped press capacity, and occasioned the first Sunday extra in the publication's history on August 2. On August 5 it put this perspective on the coming struggle:

> … we face a conflict without parallel in human history. None of us can forsee the issue. Either Britain will again destroy despotism or the map of the world will be remade….
>
> It is for the British people in a quarrel which they have not made, to keep their house inviolate and to prove if they must that the blood still runs red in the veins of the race.

"The British people," for Willison and the *News*, most certainly included Canadians. "The restless tide of feeling which sweeps across the Dominion," it intoned, is nothing more than a revelation of the real heart of the Canadian people." It warned as well that there would be "an awful price in blood and treasure for Canadians to pay, and called for "a truce to all meaner prejudices and partisan bitterness and vainglorious clamour."[2] As to forswearing partisan political wrangling, the editorial page columnist J.E. Middleton put it best in his poem "Brothers All" on August 6:

> *We have a Hansard, all complete,*
> *And if we cared to look*
> *Some funny speeches could be found*
> *In every single book*
> *But NO. The book-case door is locked*
> *The key is in the Bay*
> *And we have bought a picture of*
> *Sir Wilfrid Laurier.*

For his part, Laurier himself stimulated this kind of mood by his declaration in Parliament of wholehearted support for war measures and his pledge to "offer no criticism so long as there is danger at the front."[3]

In that same non-partisan spirit, but also on personal grounds, Willison wrote a special *News* editorial in October praising the recent appointment by the American-based Rockefeller Foundation of the former Liberal labour minister, Mackenzie King, as head of its Department of Industrial Relations. "The relation between capital and labor constitutes the supreme problem of the twentieth century," he observed. "No Canadian has devoted himself more closely to the study of these questions than Hon. Mackenzie King. He has the sympathies and the attachments which peculiarly qualify him for the work he is to do...." As Sir John put it to King's father, he was declaring his "admiration" for his son's "character and attainments, and our sense of his fitness for the position...."

Mackenzie King, at last beginning to restore the career progress that had been interrupted by his loss of ministerial office and his parliamentary seat in 1911, wrote his first employer to "thank you for the more than generous and kind personal references to myself," adding: "I have never doubted your feelings of kindly interest in all the members of our family, including myself...." He also expressed his thanks at learning that "you had been canvassing my name among friends as one which might be considered in connection with the Presidency of Queen's University."[4]

The Middleton poem referring to Laurier and the Willison tribute to King were, however, about the only non-partisan themes in the *News* in the early war months. Even before the end of August, Willison was cabling confidentially to the editor of the *Times* that he expected the Borden government to call a federal general election for November. Frank Cochrane was telling him that most cabinet ministers thought the public's war spirit presented a "golden opportunity" for a triumphant new majority. Initially and instinctively, Willison was opposed to the opportunism of the idea. However, by late September, as he explained to his Ottawa correspondent, Arthur Ford, he had "rather changed my mind," musing that "a constructive program could be framed now that would go far to justify an election." He had come to conclude, he remarked, that the "war-made imperialists" of the Liberal party — "with all their teaching discredited" — fully deserved an election trouncing. On October 17, the *News* publicly called for an election. However, Sir Robert Borden finally decided, as he would recall, that the "intense discussion and fierce controversy of an election "was not justified on patriotic grounds."[5]

Willison did not complain about that decision but was galled by the negative reaction to the election idea expressed to him by some of his imperialist Round Table Toronto friends like Arthur Glazebrook and the young U of T historian, Edward Kylie, who claimed that such a move would have "destroyed" their non-partisan missionary work in Canada for Imperialism. Willison acidly retorted that "the objects of the Round Table will be accomplished only through political conflict, and probably party conflict...."[6]

He still favoured an election as soon as possible in 1915, but became annoyed when he came to feel that Canadian ministers, to keep their calendar free for that, opposed the convocation of a special imperial conference. Willison wanted to see the early reshaping of the decision-making processes of the Empire, to match its coming together in emergency wartime action. "Not for a long time can we hope to have again a condition of opinion so favourable to material advances," he argued to the governor general, the Duke of Connaught, in January 1915.[7]

In March he had a welcome opportunity to come out in public forcefully on the issue in a luncheon address to the Canadian Club of Ottawa on "The War and the Empire." From his place at the head table in the gilt ballroom of the Chateau Laurier, he had to be gratified as he looked out at the overflow crowd, agreeably sprinkled with cabinet ministers. Incredibly, touchingly, his old mentor and idol, Sir Wilfrid, was there too, smiling at him warmly across the gulf of a decade's political estrangement. Willison began his speech by equating the British cause in the war with humanity's struggle for freedom, because from all over the Empire men were "freely" offering to risk their lives to defend justice. After the war, for the same reason, there must be a strong and united Empire as "a great factor for permanent world peace.... Let us resolve that out of the ruin and agony of war, there shall emerge an Empire that will outlast the centuries."

There was time after the speech to mingle with many members of his audience, including Laurier. Later, he sat down and wrote Sir Wilfrid to say how delighted he had been to see his old friend again and have the chance to re-establish that personal connection that once had meant so much to him. Laurier wrote back to say "how deeply touched I was by your letter. For I cannot disguise from you that one of the sorrows of my life was the estrangement which gradually crept up between us. Our relationship had been so close & so intimate that it was most painful one day, to realise that we had drifted into irreconcilable positions...." He congratulated Willison on his "brilliant address" which, however, "did not convince me," as he could not believe that imperial federation was a realistic future option for Britain, Canada, and the other self-governing Dominions. He added: "Let me avow that even if the old relations cannot be resumed, I will accrue it a favour, if the old friendship can be restored, & if you will, on this or any other questions ... frankly let me have your views & criticisms." Willison replied that he was "very grateful" for Laurier's words. "It is important to me to keep your personal regard."[8]

If he was to contribute meaningfully in Canada to the imperial cause, he needed more than an occasional speaking engagement. He had played large policy and political roles in the past from his editorial platforms. Now his *News* was sicker than ever. The 1913 recession had restrained advertising and circulation revenues for all papers.[9] Now wartime inflation, especially in newsprint prices, added alarmingly to financial pressures. In September 1914, the paper had been forced to raise its new subscription price from $1.50 to $2.00 yearly. But years of cutting costs and paring personnel had only put it at a heavy competitive disadvantage with its Toronto rivals. Frank Cochrane's regular monthly supplemental financing was ever more necessary. To make matters worse, as the news editor complained in November, the paper's city coverage had become "very weak and very radical improvement is essential...."[10]

By January 1915, Willison was deeply worried. He knew the *News* urgently needed much more permanent capital investment. For some time, the Toronto publisher and newsprint magnate C. Lesslie Wilson and others in his family had been angling for a major stock interest, on the condition of taking over the financial management. That would mean the exit of Charles Pearce, manager since 1903. Willison now abandoned Pearce, claiming to Frank Cochrane that Pearce had been too diffident in seeking advertisers while engaging in penny-pinching economies in operating expenses and preferring the hiring of "cheap men in responsible positions." Astonishingly, Willison claimed that "outside the editorial page since 1904 until the last three months the News had expressed Mr. Pearce rather than myself." Years later, while preparing his biography of Willison, his friend Arthur Colquhoun lamented this "detachment from all financial dealings" which he saw "reflected in the fate of the News and other undertakings."[11]

Undeniably, the need was for more capital. Frank Cochrane agreed to supply up to $50,000 or even $60,000 in exchange for stock at fifty cents on the dollar "to cover any advances I have made or may make." Lesslie Wilson would replace Pearce, buying from him $10,000 worth of stock at fifty cents on the dollar. And Willison henceforth would have, as Cochrane put it, "absolute control upstairs [all but the printing department]." Cochrane angrily vetoed Lesslie Wilson's proposal, endorsed by Willison, that the Wilson family be given an option to repurchase stock Cochrane might have to take through the year. The minister exploded that "Wilson expects somebody to put up all the money to keep the News running and at the same time hand out an option on the stock so that if it is a success he can take up the stock."[12] Lesslie Wilson's name was added to the News masthead on March 23, but on Cochrane's terms. The omens for a smooth Cochrane–Wilson relationship were not propitious.

Nevertheless, Willison was soon gushing to Cochrane that the new manager "has the sort of genius necessary to make this business a success" and that there was a "natural combination between this paper and the newsprint business of the Wilson Publishing Company." He had been told that the Wilsons were "ready to provide" a new building and "we could all look forward to a prosperous future and this could become what it ought to be, the first Conservative newspaper in the Dominion." Cochrane remained "greatly disappointed," he made clear to his editor, in Wilson's "no risk" approach to stock, and his financial analysis that, to make the plant viable, up to $150,000 in new funding would be required. "I do not like the manager's idea that whatever money is wanted, it must come out of me," he added angrily.[13]

Dutifully, Willison drew back, remarking in May that "the machinery immediately necessary" was some new stereotyping equipment for just under $20,000. "When the Wilsons are ready to risk money we can consider what stock they are to have," he conceded but enthused: "We are making such progress as we have never made before" and claimed that street sales were "nearly double as heavy as they were down to a few months ago," with total circulation up by three to four thousand. Ominously, Cochrane responded that "the time must come, and come very shortly, when I will be relieved from the necessity of finding further money in this connection."[14]

For Willison, the war was increasingly his chief concern. His sons were twenty-six, and both were finding their own roles in it. Walter had been the *News* correspondent in London when hostilities broke out. He and his wife Vivyan remained there now with their baby son, named after brother Bill. Walt's dispatches from the British capital and on the Canadian troops flooding overseas were the most popular feature of the wartime *News*. Sir John's longtime veteran journalist friend, Arthur Ford, congratulated him in November on Walter's "splendid work. He is giving the best service of any paper in the country."

Meanwhile, Bill Willison, married early that year to Marjorie Hoskins, had volunteered for the army. Sir John told Frank Cochrane in May: "Bill has been drilling all winter and is now looking for a commission. He has, however, had a bad foot ever since his school days and I do not believe will be taken. But he intends to keep his mouth shut, take the medical examination and abide by the results." The commission was secured, and in November Sir John could report to Sir Robert Borden that Bill was in Britain awaiting departure for the front. His wife Marjory had accompanied him, to engage in voluntary aid work.[15]

In April 1915, the war first began to have a direct and brutal impact on Canadians. The First Contingent made its heroic stand in Belgian Flanders against poison gas and massed German attacks, thrilling the home front. The cost was appalling. Out of a front-line infantry force of about 10,000, 1850 were killed, 341 wounded, and 776 taken prisoner. The British commander-in-chief said that the Canadians had "undoubtedly saved the situation." Willison reported to the *Times* that the heavy Canadian losses in the crucial battle had caused in Canada "a deepening of the Imperial spirit and an increase in the contributions to hospital and patriotic funds." Armageddon was now a reality for thousands of Canadian families, and this was only the beginning. The *News* remarked, however: "If war destroys life … it may also breed national feeling of high order."[16]

The same old partisan political wrangling kept on, in spite of any idealistic wishes for national unity. The normal four years of a legal five-year federal Parliamentary mandate were up in the fall. Willison's *News* detailed a steady escalation of Liberal partisan attacks on the Borden government and concluded that "if the Liberals insist on controversy it might be better for the country and the great cause which the vast majority of Canadians have at heart to have the contest over once and for all and thus be done with it...."

The *News* worried about the danger for Canada of having its post-war imperial policy decided by a Liberal government. "No studied system of mutual defence will be satisfactory to these statesmen," it warned. Aside from their "pretended fear that our Autonomy will be invaded," it warned acidly, "they believe that the Empire has no concern with Foreign Policy and that North America is a separated garden of the gods, where nations dwell together in unity, selling soap."

Willison told a Toronto friend that he was "ready" for a general election so that a fully enthusiastic war effort could be mandated and a post-war Liberal separatist policy on the Empire forestalled.[17] Partisanship could run both ways. Once again, however, Prime Minister Borden, weighing non-partisan negative reactions to a wartime election fight, stepped back from the electoral brink. The chance for a an undoubtedly opportunistic but likely decisive wartime mandate for a still-popular Conservative government passed once more — for the last time.

During the early war years, Sir John was caught up intensely and prominently in a non-partisan crusade to fight unemployment and the shortage of affordable housing in Ontario. Even in 1913 he had become deeply worried about how recession times were impacting ordinary Canadians. In the early weeks of the war he came to chair a committee of community, business, and labour leaders petitioning Prime Minister Borden to set up a commission to find jobs and accommodation for the unemployed. There was no early action from Ottawa — ministers were too preoccupied with military mobilization — but Willison, in alliance with Mayor Hocken of Toronto and the Leader of the Liberal Opposition at Queen's Park, Newton Rowell, worked to bring about provincial action. He successfully lobbied William Hearst, who recently had succeeded as premier on the death of Sir James Whitney, to set up a full-fledged Ontario Commission on Unemployment in November 1914. Sir John was named chairman and other members were: W.P. Gundy, president of the Toronto Board of Trade; Archbishop Neil McNeil of the Catholic archdiocese of Toronto; Archdeacon Henry J. Cody of St. Paul's Anglican Church in Toronto; Reverend Daniel Strachan, a Presbyterian cleric; W.K McNaught, manufacturer and former Conservative MLA; W.L. Best of the Locomotive Engineers Union; Professor A.T. DeLury, mathematician from the University of Toronto; and Joseph Gibbons of London. Gilbert Jackson, an economist from the University of Toronto, and Miss Marjorie McMurchy, women's editor of the *News*, were named joint secretaries.[18]

It was soon very clear that Willison wanted the commission to see the problems it was dealing with in surprisingly radical terms. In an editorial on unemployment in January 1915 the *News*, while conceding that profit was "one of the rightful purposes of industry," insisted also that "consumption and labor are of equal status. When the consumer and the worker receive as much consideration from industry as the stockholder we shall be on the road to remedy not only unemployment but many other ills of our civilization." As the commission's work progressed that winter, Willison warned Premier Hearst that "we shall have a long period of reconstruction and a very trying period if we do not look ahead."[19]

In a March editorial titled A NEW CANADA, the *News* noted the pre-war background of irresponsible overbuilding of railways and factory capacity, and reckless borrowing and expenditures. With the pre-war recession, and then the cutting off by the war of immigration, capital inflow, and normal exports, this "wildest orgy of speculation in history had ended in collapse." For a time, Allied purchases of foodstuffs and war supplies would take up much of the slack, but "with the termination of the war ... this special industrial activity will suddenly cease." Then there likely would be confusion and delay in conversion to peacetime production while disbanded soldiers would be seeking employment. The *News* argued that "subventions from the public treasury should go directly to the stimulation of the agricultural industry." Land settlement should be "greatly increased," to swell farm production, "to keep the railways busy, furnish a home market for Canadian factory products and to meet our foreign debt and interest obligations...."

Both provincial and federal governments, in Willison's view, had much to do in all employment-related fields. The *News* was sure that "New Ontario is capable of supporting a large population in comfort. The thing is to get people on the land." It wanted provincial loans for home building and the acquisition of equipment and stock. More attractive farm labour conditions would have to be legislated and research on labour-saving productivity advances furthered. But, as Willison put it to Sir Robert Borden, "the future depends greatly upon production and immigration and these are national rather than provincial questions." He proposed that the prime minister convene a conference of provincial premiers as well as major industrial, transportation, farm, and labour leaders to plan concerted action and perhaps spawn a federal advisory commission on social and economic strategy for during the war and its immediate aftermath. He was "certain that we are facing a tremendous problem that will require heroic treatment."

Borden promised to consider the "several important suggestions," but he and his government were slow to move. The prime minister cautioned him that the federal government needed to keep its legislation "restricted to such measures as necessarily result from the War or from conditions arising from the War." Nevertheless, the *News* continued to press for a special conference and wanted as well a royal commission to follow that up. In May 1915, Sir John accompanied a delegation of the unemployed to Ottawa, and wired Borden in advance: "Believe radical action necessary and think chief effort should be to put people on land thus relieving municipalities and increasing settlement and production.... If people want land and land wants people why not Dominion, Provinces and municipalities unite to effect union? Sooner or later action imperative so better act quickly." The *News* remarked: "We have no fear for the people. The danger is that the representatives of the people will fall short of the high duty to which they are called. The time is not for craven plodding in the old paths...."

Willison learned all too quickly that those "old paths" were all too crowded. He found that Thomas White, the federal minister of finance, was strongly opposed to a royal commission, believing the problems the editor was concerned with would be dealt with best during the war by other levels of government, with any early federal financial outlays slight.[20] And Premier Hearst warned him against proposals that would be "impossible of action" by the provincial government. Hearst wanted no part of any soldiers' insurance scheme and had "grave doubts" about the likely success of any attempt to settle city unemployed as farmers in northern Ontario.[21]

There was an inevitable collision. The commission's final report in January 1916 stressed that it had "no faith in the ordinary palliatives of unemployment" — emergency relief and make-work projects. It called for a co-operative governments–labour-management effort to "avert the recurrence of seasonal and periodic lack of employment." It wanted a provincial labour commission and local offices to facilitate employment contacts and worker mobility. Export activities should be stimulated through improved credit, tariff agreements with foreign countries, and better language training for Canadians. Major urban centres should have cheap and rapid transportation links to surrounding districts, where workers could live cheaply and even be involved in growing some of their own food. Reformed methods of land taxation should free urban and suburban building lots from the grasp of speculators. The province should press for an Imperial Migration Board to channel post-war British immigration to Ontario. There should be improved conditions for women's employment and a protection for boys and girls just out of school from being landed in "blind-alley" employment. As well, the government should educate young people for employment in fields for which they were fitted. Finally, the commission "strongly recommended" government insurance against unemployment and expressed the hope that its report could be "influential" in improving social and industrial conditions throughout Ontario and beyond."[22]

A month later, the Hearst government's speech from the throne promised that a Trade and Labour Branch of the Public Works Department would be created. The News expressed "no doubt" that local labour offices soon would follow and declared: "The old political economy will not avail, and a press or pulpit which preaches only smooth things will not be influential." It called for profit-sharing with workers, public operation or control of electric, water, and transportation systems, and urged that slums be "cleansed" and "the adequate housing of the poor secured by state or municipal action." Joseph Flavelle congratulated him on the "good reading" in the editorial but added: "I wonder if we have many leaders who will accept its challenge?"[23] It soon was evident that the straightened financial circumstances of provincial governments in wartime, as well as Premier Hearst's cautious nature, did not open the way to any more than gradual and partial implementation of the kinds of social reforms which the Commission and the *News* were proposing. As the war went on, the immediate unemployment problem Willison had seen as urgent before the war and in its early stages was alleviated considerably as army recruitment, the expansion of munitions, and other war industries and the development of a farm labour shortage had their effects. Still, he would continue to believe that Canada would be terribly vulnerable to post-war conditions.

Meanwhile, it was his newspaper that was in very deep trouble. In September 1915 he had passed on to Cochrane and his group Lesslie Wilson's latest financial demands, including — most alarmingly — monthly transfusions of $10,000 into the foreseeable future. Cochrane promised to meet his existing obligations but to the new plea for major monthly support, he replied simply that "this I cannot do."

Willison responded that the paper had "gained over ten thousand of circulation" while "The Telegram has lost five thousand and The Star ten thousand according to their own figures just published. If we have to stop again for want of money all that has been spent is lost."[24] By late October the situation had become grave and he wrote Cochrane despairingly: "We badly need a cheque for $10,000 by Friday [two days later]. We have no resources of our own that are of any value at the bank." Reluctantly, grudgingly, Cochrane made sure, in late October and again a month later, that the paper could meet its financial commitments. Just before the end of the year, a stockholders' meeting authorized an extra issue of bonds.[25]

The strain was beginning to tell on Willison. He had a severe cold through most of the winter months of 1915–16 and confided to Flavelle in early April that "I have had a pretty heavy year and lately have felt the pressure more than usual." His friend George Creelman tried to coax him south for a vacation, but had to report sadly to Frank Beer: "He says if he went there would be so many things on his mind that he would not enjoy the holiday at all." In fact, he already had decided he could not go on through any more of these financial crises. Frank Cochrane was ill, so it was to his ministerial colleague, J.D. Reid, that he wrote:

I do not want to put pressure on any one. I make no claim. I have no grievance. But I cannot go on as I have gone on for twelve years. We have never been able to fight for any length of time, for want of money. We have wasted tens of thousands of dollars by producing a poor paper.

The war has been disastrous. I do not speculate as to who is at fault and I make no claim of immunity for myself. But I cannot stand the strain of daily worry and of a humiliating relation with the banks any longer. It is hard to go on and hard to let go. But one or the other I must do.

I would far rather face the future empty-handed than continue under present conditions. I do not need to explain that I prefer to go on and that with adequate and continuous support I have no doubt we would save all that has been invested in this property. But that has been said before and the situation is still unsatisfactory. I can only promise to do my best if we can continue. But I am writing today simply to say that I have reached the point where continuance under present conditions is impossible and that I am ready to go out if that is the judgment of my friends and to go without any sense of grievance."[26]

Reid begged Willison to delay any move until Cochrane's return to work and indicated that Lesslie Wilson had been in touch, to say that "it would take $100,000 a year until the war was over (he might do it for $84,000) to keep the News alive — for six months after it would have to be assisted."[27]

Cochrane was back at work at the end of April. On May 4th, the nature of his response to the situation was indicated when he sent to the News offices a certain A.T. Wilgress, whom he described as "an excellent man to take Wilson's place if he can be induced to do so." Sir John was stunned and worried to his friend and a News board member, C.S. McInnes, about "the ugly situation…. Mr. Cochrane and his associates are not willing to go on with Mr. Lesslie Wilson. I do not agree with their judgment. I think whoever takes his place will have to pursue the policy that he had followed and until the war is over will have to make expenditures just as heavy as he has made."

He knew his own "ultimate obligation" was to the Cochrane-Kemp-Reid group, but "I would rather go out than continue to be connected with a newspaper which is not reasonably equal to its competitors...." Briefly, he toyed with quitting at once, perhaps with the *News* closing down, stinging Frank Cochrane into the icy response that the Wilson matter "has nothing to do with whether the News should go on or whether it should not."[28] Willison never changed his mind about the need for a Lesslie Wilson-style approach to making the *News* a competitive newspaper, but he came to see that Wilson had been less than candid with him on actual circulation and advertising statistics. And he agreed to co-operate with Cochrane's forced removal of the manager, whose resignation was accepted by a directors' meeting on June 14.[29] Cochrane now insisted on the strictest accounting. "The matter is too serious to go on in this way," he warned. Just how serious was clear from the loss figure for June of $10,433 and the need for a cheque from Cochrane of $12,000 in July. As J.D. Reid put it to Willison: "....if it is to be continued that way I cannot see how it can be carried on...."[30]

The editor did not carry through at this point with his threatened resignation. He told Geoffrey Robinson of the *Times* that "national and imperial reasons" kept him going, "when my disposition would be to step out and endeavour for the rest of my days to find time to live." To an audience in neutral America in February 1916 he explained:

> We believe that we battle for free men, free seas, a free world and that the cause is worth the sacrifice.... History has no record of any great political experiment quite like that in which we are engaged ... and if we should be overcome the British Empire, now spread across the earth and secure on every sea, may shrink into two islands on the Atlantic, mourning the power and glory that have passed. But we shall not fail, however long may be the struggle or whatever the sum of the sacrifice....[31]

Partisan politics kept heating up more and more, and Willison saw them as inextricably related to the war cause. In May 1916, the Laurier Liberals moved the so-called Lapointe Resolution in the House of Commons, calling on the Ontario Legislature not to interfere with the French-language instruction of French-speaking children. Willison considered this proof of Laurier's willingness to make common cause with Henri Bourassa's ultra-*nationaliste*, clericalist, and anti-war forces in Quebec, and he warned Arthur Meighen, the federal solicitor general, that the Borden government "can live only by appeal to the English-speaking population. I hope this fact will be recognized and that we will fight boldly for only in boldness is there safety." The year before he had observed to Geoffrey Robinson: "My own view as strengthened by this war is that we must have a federated Empire or separation.... Laurier argues that Nation and Imperialism are incompatible terms. In saying this I am not guessing at his views. If he is right, what of the future? I grow ever more anxious that reconstruction in Canada after the war shall not take place under a Government dominated by Quebec."[32]

As 1916 wore on and the burden of protracted war weighed ever more heavily on Canadians, support for the Conservative administration at Ottawa was waning. One particularly wasting reason was the minister of Militia and Defence, Sir Sam Hughes, with his questionable associations with rich friends such as Colonel J. Wesley Allison, who were suspected of fattening on war contracts. In March 1916, the Liberal Opposition made specific allegations of profiteering, triggering the appointment of a royal commission inquiry. Willison warned the prime minister that he needed to be "more of an autocrat" in dealing with discreditable colleagues, but the *News* kept silent, prompting Joseph Flavelle to write Willison heatedly, damning "selfish party allegiance.... If in these surroundings, we cannot appeal to ideals when will we?"

In July, the commission formally exonerated Hughes but questioned his administrative competence and censured Allison. Willison's friend Arthur Glazebrook begged him to "kill" Hughes with an open assault in the *News*. But as Glazebrook explained to Lord Milner, "Willison has had a good deal of fighting and doesn't at present feel like rushing into a new battle...." Still, Sir John admitted to Geoffrey Robinson at the *Times* that "the Government cannot live if Hughes remains a member of it...."[33]

There was a crisis too in 1916 within the Canadian imperialist movement. Early in the year, Lionel Curtis in England had published his *The Problem of the Commonwealth*, detailing formidable taxing powers and functions for a proposed central parliament of a federated Empire. Curtis specified that the proposal was a purely personal one, but inevitably his prominence in the Round Table movement prompted significant nationalist backlash against the Canadian Round Tablers. The Toronto Round Table Committee, led by Willison, Sir Edmund Walker, Professor George Wrong, Arthur Glazebrook, and the young manufacturer, Vincent Massey, worked out what they thought a more palatable and prudent statement of Canadian imperialist objectives. In their "Memorandum," which eventually was made public, they claimed that the war contributions of Canada and the other Dominions to the preservation of the Empire and the establishment of "a lasting and honourable peace" entitled them to a "share" in determining the policy by which that peace was kept. They believed the "effective organization of the Empire must not involve any sacrifice of responsible government in domestic affairs or the surrender of control over fiscal policy by any portion of the Empire." They contended that a "proportionate share" in defence and foreign policy was "an inevitable development of responsible government" and they called for a meeting of political leaders throughout the Empire irrespective of party" as soon as circumstances permitted.[34]

It was an imperialist message, far more "nationalist" as far as the future roles of Dominions than Curtis wished to see; but it was also full of ambiguities. This was just as true of a very similar statement by the Imperial War Conference in April 1917. Sir Robert Borden was instrumental in devising Resolution IX which committed Britain and the Dominions to a special post-war imperial conference to undertake a "readjustment" of constitutional relations respecting "all existing powers of self-government" and regarding the Dominions as "autonomous nations of an Imperial Commonwealth" with "an adequate voice in foreign relations" through consultation.[35] The difficulties of defining at last the nature of a matured Canada's status in the Empire-Commonwealth lay ahead, for Borden, Willison, and Canadians. Meanwhile, there was the war, with victory far from certain.

In September 1916, the Willison family was plunged into intense tragedy. Canadian troops readied themselves early in the month for a key battle role in Field Marshal Sir Douglas Haig's major offensive in the region of the French river Somme. Lieutenant W.T. Willison was there, and in the *Times* his father wrote: "Probably we are nearer more solemn days than we have known since the war began. The roll of casualties lengthens. Day by day and week by week death strikes at many households." At 6:20 a.m., (local time), Friday, September 15, the Canadian Corps smashed against the German lines near Courcelette. After bloody fighting, that village and the neighbouring hamlet of Pozières were captured. By evening in far-off Toronto, the *News* was printing its first excited reports and warning that "Ontario units are hard hit."

In that battle, Bill Willison, while leading his men of the Fifth Canadian Mounted Rifles to attack fleeing Germans a thousand yards north-west of Pozières, was killed instantly by shell fire. His comrades buried him where he had fallen. In the confusion of battle, it took a week for the news to reach London, where Walter Willison on the 19th knew only, as he cabled the *News*, that "Canadians took a splendid part in the great British successes....." By Friday the 22nd, the casualty list for the 15th was published in the *Times*, and the next day in the *News*. By then, Sir John and Lady Rachel in Toronto and Bill's wife Marjory, in England, had received their dreaded telegrams. On the same front page as the article about "Lieut. W.T. Willison, Toronto Daily News," the paper ran Walter's proud and sorrowing article detailing the Canadians' bloody victory — DROVE ENEMY IN DISORDER. SWEPT THROUGH COURCELETTE.[36]

The condolences poured into 10 Elmsley Place. "We are only one among so many families that have had to make the sacrifice," Willison wrote to Geoffrey Robinson. "But this is a bad time for his mother and for me. We were comrades, never like father and son. I cannot remember that ever a word passed between us that either of us would now wish to recall...." To William Grant, Bill's favourite teacher at UCC and wounded himself in France, he wrote: "I will not deny that we have needed sympathy. Bill's mother grieves very much and at best her health is not good.... I had a sad conviction that he would not come back but with this become a certainty I fear no thought even of the cause for which the boy died counts for much…. It is hard to keep any faith in the things we once believed, or thought we believed…."[37]

Unfortunately, his work could not be ignored. The clamour for conscription was rising, as voluntary enlistment figures dipped yet further and the casualties mounted. The *News* believed the call was coming particularly "from many of those who have lost their sons in France and Flanders," but reasoned that "when we consider the various elements which constitute our population, the problems which will face us when peace comes, and the long international boundary, conscription for a war in Europe is difficult." The comment followed a long talk Sir John had with Borden in Ottawa, after which he reported to Geoffrey Robinson that he and the prime minister were absolutely agreed that conscription would be neither a politically feasible nor practically effective way of getting needed replacements.[38]

In November, the prime minister finally fired Sir Sam Hughes, the minister of militia and defence, following a bitter clash over Borden's creation of a minister of overseas services. "As you know we have had two governments in Canada, one headed by Hughes, the other by Borden," Willison told Geoffrey Robinson. "It is a wonder that the thing went on as long as it did." However, when Robinson suggested that the Hughes affair had cast grave doubt on the prime minister's leadership abilities, Willison urged him to "not be too certain about Borden…. he is the ablest man at Ottawa. I agree that he bore with Hughes much too long but we all admit that Lincoln was great and yet bore with intriguing if not with incapable colleagues just as Borden has done. Somehow or other I think Borden has passed through a phase and will never be submissive to a Hughes again…." Though Borden could be "slow," he conceded, he "has in a crisis no lack of resolution or decision."[39]

As it happened, a crisis of potentially fatal proportions was looming for the prime minister, his government, and the war effort. More and more, demands for conscription of men and wealth for the war were being linked with pressure for an end to party government, especially under a weak leader such as Borden was widely believed to be. Parliament's term had been extended once already, with bipartisan agreement. If an election, at the latest in the fall of 1917, was to be avoided, such an agreement would be required again. Willison, however, wrote in the *Times* in

December 1916 that he was sure Sir Wilfrid Laurier, sensing the swelling unpopularity of the Conservatives, would agree to neither a further extension of Parliament nor the formation of a coalition or "national" government. That being so, the Liberal leader, in the inevitable party fight that was coming, would aim for a solid Liberal Quebec. The *News* began to run a daily slogan: A VOTE FOR LAURIER IS A VOTE FOR BOURASSA, counting on the widespread hatred of the Quebec *nationaliste* anti-war leader to be a Conservative vote-catcher in English Canada.[40]

There were many English-Canadian Liberals who truly wanted a non-partisan government to better prosecute the war and inspire the country. One was D. Macgillivray of Halifax, who raged to Sir Edmund Walker: "Can anything be more irritating to Liberals than its [the *News*'] daily jibe?" John Dafoe of the Manitoba *Free Press* observed to Professor George Wrong that the *News* was "now the most mischievous paper in Canada" in its savage partisanship, and traced this attitude to a "junta" or "gang" of cabinet ministers, including Cochrane and Reid, who were anti-coalition "because they know they would not be in such a Government...." Wrong replied: "I agree with what you say about the Toronto News.... It is pathetic to see Willison the editor of such a paper...." All through the winter of 1916–17 the "national government" movement became more and more widespread. Joseph Atkinson of the *Star* was a strong supporter, along with fellow Liberals A.W. Ames and W.E. Rundle.[41]

Even the normally pro-Conservative Joseph Flavelle, in spite of his post as head of the Imperial Munitions Board, gave a speech in mid-December in favour of a government "chosen ... not by party guidance or by party methods." Willison responded bitterly to his friend that a "national government" would mean a compromise with Quebec on the war effort and "bow to Quebec I will not.... I am not willing to have my son killed in France to make a French triumph in the Dominion." The *News* in January 1917 was just as blunt about where it believed all the agitation was heading:

> Unquestionably the chief object is to get rid of the Prime
> Minister. We believe, however, that while the war lasts
> it is absolutely in the interests of Canadian unity, in
> the interests of a common Empire, and in the interests

of the cause for which Canadians are making such exertions and sacrifices, that he should remain at the head of the Government.... His withdrawal or defeat would cause rejoicing chiefly among those who believe not that Canada has done too little, but that it has done too much, in the war upon which the future of Canada, the Empire and the world depend.

He wanted Borden to hold his ground. "My strong disposition is not to concede at all to the national government movement," he advised Sir Robert on January 26. The prime minister responded by asking him to see him in Ottawa before he sailed for England and key war planning meetings.[42]

That conversation seemed to change things dramatically for Willison. He was still against any coalition that would include Laurier and the existing official Liberal leadership in Ottawa. Yet many readers who picked up their *News* on February 8 must have wondered if they were reading some kind of Borden-inspired hint that the way just might be open for another kind of "national" government in the near future. The *News* emphasized its undying confidence in the prime minister but added:

He [Borden] will not hesitate at any step necessary to give effective representation in the cabinet to all the elements of the people and all sections of the country. He will endeavour to utilize for the public advantage all that there is of public spirit and disinterested patriotism for the movement of coalition and national government so that we may be strong for the prosecution of the war, and strong and united for the solution of other great problems which have become onerous and urgent....

This at once prompted an excited response from Joseph Flavelle. "If you have made this statement by authority," he wrote Willison, "it is important and heartening. If you are stating it without authority, it is as valueless as expressions of a similar character made by myself and other friends of the Government during the past two years...." In his view, a wait-and-see approach by Borden until his return from Europe would not do. "The war does not wait," he chided. In March, with Borden gone and nothing changing, Flavelle was fed up, and exploded to Willison:

> If the country grows to believe — and it is growing that way — it can get nothing from Sir Robert it may turn to even Sir Wilfrid.... I am sorry we take opposite sides. Your powerful pen would have accomplished much. As it is, you are a voice crying in the wilderness — and the work will have to be done by less able men.... What is the use of your platitudes concerning the Government?

Willison was unapologetic, musing to Flavelle that a general election might come very soon and predicting Borden would win it. To Geoffrey Robinson he remarked: "Everything waits until Borden's return."[43]

Unfortunately, not everything. The burden of the *News* on Willison was becoming worse than ever. In September 1916 he had negotiated a personal overdraft of $15,000 to put into the paper, supposedly only until the end of the year, when he expected further funding aid from Cochrane's group. By March, as part of a new financing arrangement, his note was re-negotiated to $20,000 to the credit of the *News*, secured by warehouse receipts for the paper's newsprint and by Willison's depositing with the bank his life insurance and other personal securities.[44]

The prime minister returned to Canada on May 15. During his absence, he would record in his memoirs, he "had kept closely in touch with conditions in Canada and, greatly to my disappointment, I was obliged to conclude that any further effort for voluntary enlistment would provide very meagre and wholly inadequate results." Willison was coming to exactly the same conclusion. On May 10, the *News* had predicted that conscription would have to be adopted:

> If, as seems certain, the voluntary system has been exhausted, other methods must be taken to secure the reinforcements.... The war runs longer than we thought it would. The demand upon Canada is great beyond all expectations. Public opinion will support the Govern-

ment in any measure necessary to make the Dominion still more effective in the tremendous struggle in which we are involved.[45]

Neither Borden nor Willison had wanted conscription. They knew the national divisions — particularly French–English — which would be enflamed. But for them, as for so many Canadians in 1917, the war came first. Russia, overwhelmed by revolution, was on her way out of the conflict, with a vastly strengthened and possibly decisive German thrust on the Western Front against the exhausted British and French armies an impending certainty. Even the entry in April of the United States on the Allied side could do little for some time, as American mobilization for significant battlefield readiness would be slow. Germany's resumption of unrestricted submarine warfare, meanwhile, threatened to cut the Allied lifeline to North America. It was not the time for Canada to slacken her contribution to the struggle, and casualties now were vastly outnumbering voluntary enlistments.

As soon as Borden was back in Ottawa, Willison advised him "frankly" about the political situation:

> I think you must authorize a form of conscription or frankly tell the country that Great Britain requires us to concentrate on the production of food and munitions. It is of the first importance that there should be a few changes in the Government. As you know, I am not animated by personal hostility to any Minister and I speak only what I conceive to be in your interest and in the interest of the country. Public opinion is getting out of hand. You can restore it and in a day create a revolution in your favour.

He did not think the prime minister needed to go "the length of a Coalition or National Government." The addition of a couple of Westerners "who could speak for the West rather than for either party" would be "all that needs to be done to make yourself supremely strong and to capture the imagination of the country."[46]

The day after Willison's letter was sent, and probably before it could be read, Borden secured his cabinet's approval for conscription. On the following afternoon, May 18, he announced it to the House. As yet, nothing was decided on whether some kind of coalition would be sought, but within days, Willison's Ottawa correspondent, Arthur Ford, was reporting that Tory caucus support was building for a conscriptionist "union government" with "the patriotic wing" of the Liberal party. Increasingly, many prominent English Canadian Liberals, in Parliament and out, wanted Sir Wilfrid Laurier to agree. They included Newton Rowell, the Ontario provincial Liberal leader and long a close personal friend of Willison's. On May 25, the prime minister proposed that the two leaders join in a new government, with equal numbers from each party, aside from Borden as prime minister.[47]

Before the outcome of the ensuing negotiations became clear, Willison made one final attempt to resolve his dilemma with the *News*. On May 28 he approached his original backer, Flavelle, with one last plea. "I am very hopeful that with $50,000 we could succeed," he argued, requesting that "if additional money is raised," Flavelle make him a personal loan of $25,000. He wondered if "the best thing for myself would be to withdraw now. As to that I cannot be clear. I have not been clear for a good while." He added that it was "grievously hard to give up what I have fought for for 14 years" and "not easy to have one's life hope go to pieces and at 60 a precarious outlook ahead."

It was clear that the Cochrane group was prepared to put no more money into the paper. They wanted substantial economies instead. To Strachan Johnston, lawyer for the *News* and a faithful Cochrane supporter, Willison patiently explained: "No possible organization of this business will reduce the cost of management and operation, nor is there any possibility that you will get a staff of more capable and energetic young men." He estimated that "half the staff is doing its work for from 15 to 40 per cent lower than is paid on other papers." Further, it was already the case that the *Star*'s staff was "one-third larger than that of the News' and the Telegram's twice its size."[48] His message was clear: no more economies — there had been too many already! Flavelle, in Ottawa on business, did not absolutely refuse Willison's desperate plea. However, he was "not clear that the course you suggest is the one you ought to take. I fear it ventures too much upon a single throw."

Even before Willison had that reply, however, he had received an urgent message from the prime minister "not to take any precip[it]ate action until at a little later date I can discuss the situation with you and advance some considerations which in my judgment would make your proposed course inadvisable in the public interest." He counselled that Willison's voice and interest "may be even more necessary in the future than they have been in the past for the welfare of the nation."[49]

The Borden–Laurier discussions over coalition stretched out over a week. Willison heard from his Ottawa correspondent, Arthur Ford, that Arthur Meighen believed Laurier "likely" would refuse to participate in a union government pledging conscription and that then approaches were to be made to Western and Ontario Liberals. On the weekend of June 2–3, Flavelle came back from the capital for a thorough talk with Willison about both politics and the *News*. It became clear that no general refinancing scheme was going to materialize, to which a Flavelle personal loan to Willison might have been related. There would be no further agonizing over money for the paper nor about Willison staying on as editor. Flavelle returned to Ottawa, saw the prime minister and proposed a senatorship for Willison, which would free him to concentrate on helping to put a comprehensive Conservative–Liberal alliance together. The days at the *News* were about to end.[50]

On June 6, Laurier finally declined to enter a coalition government, on the ground that he could not support conscription. Willison reported to Geoffrey Robinson at the *Times* that he had been "very close to the Prime Minister" throughout and "had never believed that Sir Wilfrid Laurier would support any such step.... He [Borden] will still struggle to establish a national Government. He knows that a party Government cannot make much headway with conscription. I am not very certain that any Government can."

Laurier's decision turned the pressure on conscriptionist English-Canadian Liberals. Willison retained close links, through personal friendships, to several prominent Ontario Liberals. Two were pivotal figures. He had known Newton Rowell, the provincial Liberal leader, since Young Men's Liberal days. Frank Beer, a key Liberal activist, was a fellow parishioner with him at St. Paul's Church. On June 8 he wired the prime minister: "Understand Rowell would enter coalition and active organiza-

tion begun among Liberals against Sir Wilfrid and favor conscription."
That same day, he cabled the *Times* about "a formidable revolt" among
Liberals in the province and that the party's two leading English-lan-
guage papers, the *Globe* and the *Star*, were part of it.[51]

Willison kept Borden advised daily of the latest Toronto Liberal developments. On June 12, a mass public meeting of Liberals at Massey
Hall, under Rowell's leadership, heartily endorsed conscription. Willison
told the prime minister:

> From the first I have been very much inside the Lib-
> eral revolt in Toronto. I have been consulted as to every
> step that was taken and possibly may have been useful.
> This does not mean that I attempted to speak for the
> Government but only that I was asked to advise as to
> the best course to be taken in the national interest. No
> doubt many of those Liberals who appeared at Massey
> Hall will go back to the party. It is just as certain, how-
> ever, that some of them will not and that such a man
> as Mr. Frank Beer, who was more responsible for the
> revolt and the public protest than anyone else, will not
> support Sir Wilfrid or compromise over conscription....
> What I want to say, however, is that there is a serious
> breach in the Liberal ranks and that some of those most
> active in organizing the Massey Hall meeting have fi-
> nally separated from the Liberal leader. I write this only
> to yourself as it is most undesirable that any connection
> of mine with recent events here should be disclosed.[52]

It was hardly desirable that wavering Liberals should be scared off
from conscription and union government by some "Tory conspiracy"
scare associated in any way with Willison.

It was time now for him to cut his ties with the *News*. In that way at
least he could distance himself somewhat from the ultra-partisan Tory aspect of his recent past. Further, there could be no logical reason any longer
for believing that the situation at the paper could be saved. As for his own
future he had only a shadowy promise from Borden, through Flavelle, of a

senatorship. On June 5, Flavelle had reported that the prime minister had said: "I never thought of Sir John in that capacity. If coalition goes through it will be difficult, as the other side will claim appointments, if it does not I ought to be able to do it. There are many pressing for appointment and 3 out of the 5 vacancies have been almost promised, but I would like to do this."

It was clear that Willison's personal interest in being a senator lay in there being no coalition, but that was not his priority. He was absolutely committed now to working for a union of parties. On June 15, Frank Beer begged him and the Liberal Winnipeg journalist John Dafoe "to find a way out of the present impasse…. Those whom you could unite would command the overwhelming confidence and support of the Canadian people." True to that spirit, he made sure on Saturday, June 16, that the final copy of the *News* he edited carried a firm plea to Canadians: "The time has come for English-speaking people of both parties to get together and stand together. If no element of the English Provinces lend … encouragement to the reactionaries of Quebec the most critical period in the life of Canada will be safely passed."[53]

That night a special messenger from the prime minister arrived at 10 Elmsley Place, direct from the Ottawa train. There was work to do and no time to waste. The next day, June 17, was a Sunday, and in the quiet of the afternoon he walked across Queen's Park to call on Newton Rowell. He had been instructed by Borden to invite the Ontario Liberal leader to enter a coalition government, of which one half were to be Liberals. Rowell later recorded Willison's assurance that "Sir Robert was extremely anxious to bring about an understanding and create a truly National Government" and would give entering Liberals "an equal voice." Rowell objected that such an offer, after Laurier's refusal, should have gone first to the chief federal Liberal from Ontario, George Graham. Sir John responded that he thought it had, but he would check. He and Rowell agreed absolutely on two fundamental objectives: "putting forth our utmost efforts to help win the war and … to preserve our national unity."

Willison grimly told Rowell that the Quebec situation was "very difficult," that conscription likely could not be enforced there, and that it would be "extremely difficult" to carry on a stable government without influential Quebec participation. They agreed that any Liberal members of a coalition should "really represent the Liberal Party in their own province" and should be "able to command parliamentary support." Rowell would consult with George Graham and Fred Pardee, the chief Liberal whip in the House of Commons, as well as "await events" during the parliamentary debate on conscription, "before taking any action."[54]

The next morning, June 18, the *News* announced that Willison had resigned its editorship "to devote more of his attention to the service of the London Times." He had not warned any of the Cochrane group in Ottawa, even a now-shocked Edward Kemp. The secret had been kept so well that even Arthur Colquhoun only found out when he read the paper. In a quick note, he commented that he was sure that the step was "a wise one & sets you free from anxieties and labour that brought you no real satisfaction.... What you have done for honourable journalism during the past fifteen years & for clear political thinking in this country cannot be forgotten." To Geoffrey Robinson, Willison remarked: "Party journalism in Canada under existing conditions is impossible. I went on as long as I could." The *News* survived for two more years, changed its name to the *Times*, and then expired. Before it did so, Sir John managed to free his life insurance policy and personal securities from the bank.[55]

Newton Rowell soon was back to Willison for "definite information" on two points: first, whether Rogers, the minister of public works and political master-manipulator, was being promised the post of high commissioner to London; and, second, whether or not a coalition offer had been made to George Graham. Rogers symbolized to Liberals all the worst suspicions of Tory graft and corruption. There could be no coalition if he was to be rewarded, to Willison's express agreement. He soon was able to pass on to Rowell the prime minister's promise that there would be no such appointment to Rogers and the information that a coalition offer had been tendered to conscriptionist Liberals in the House, but through Fred Pardee rather than George Graham.[56] Willison advised Borden that there was little chance of movement in Liberal ranks towards coalition until the vote in the House on conscription, likely still some time off. However, he judged Rowell's attitude now "better and I believe ... he will go far to help in a difficult situation." The prime minister then invited Rowell to Ottawa for a face-to-face meeting.[57] For now, Willison had done all he could. If union government were to come about, it would be Borden and the conscriptionist Liberals who would make it happen.

For three frustrating months it seemed as if it never would. Sir Wilfrid Laurier, drawing on the enormous reserves of respect and affection that Liberals across Canada had for him, very nearly blocked coalition and forced a straight party election fight in the fall. Delegates to party conventions over the summer in both Ontario and the West proved immensely loyal to him, in spite of his implacable opposition to conscription, which many of them supported. Yet Sir Robert Borden did not give up his efforts to form a truly "national" administration, and within the Liberal party he was supported by Rowell, Sir Clifford Sifton, and John Dafoe, the editor of the Manitoba *Free Press*.

The Conservatives, after successfully winning a majority of English-Canadian Liberal MPs to vote for conscription, then pushed through the Wartime Elections Act disenfranchising for the coming election thousands of generally Liberal-inclined voters of recent enemy origin and giving the vote to the female relatives of soldiers. The electoral danger to Liberals outside a coalition became all too apparent. Even the insistence of many of their Western leaders on Borden's leaving the prime ministership broke on the determination of the Conservative caucus that they would accept no other leader. Finally, on October 12, the Union government was formed — with twelve Conservatives and nine Liberals, including Thomas Crerar, the leader of the Manitoba Grain Growers, and one labour representative.[58]

Throughout the protracted crisis, Willison was in touch with all the main principals — Borden, Sifton, Rowell, and Dafoe — in the drive for union. Arthur Ford, with Willison continuing to employ him in Ottawa on assignment for the *Times*, was an invaluable source of inside intelligence. After many discussions with Rowell, Willison told Borden in late July, that he was "not hopeful" of progress there, adding that a coalition with western Liberals and the organized grain growers' movement would be "far more important." By the end of August he advised Geoffrey Dawson — Geoffrey Robinson with a new surname for inheritance reasons — of the *Times*, that "we are so close to a general election and Laurier is so confident of victory that Liberals are persuaded at the eleventh hour to refuse coalition. I am somewhat disappointed in Rowell. He has been too cautious." When the Conservative caucus defied the Western Liberals on their demand that Borden step aside, Willison was deeply moved, writing Borden:

GEOFFREY DAWSON
Editor, *The Times*
From a drawing in Grillion's Club, London

Geoffrey Dawson (formerly Robinson), editor of the Times of London. (From Colquhoun, Willison, opposite p. 262.)

Believe me under any other Leader than yourself Laurier will come into office and reinforcements for the army in France will not be secured. On National and Imperial grounds it is most undesirable that Laurier should be in office during the war or during reconstruction. If I write you from time to time on public questions you must not suspect me of any double motive. Please forget that I ever thought of a Senate seat....

Meanwhile, the *Times*, as Geoffrey Dawson put it, "greedily published Sir John's exceptionally well informed articles on the union government drama as fast as they could cross the water."[59]

In the last days before the new administration was formed, Willison once more played a direct and influential role. He was anxious that his friend Rowell not be left off Borden's team once it became clear that a truly bipartisan list at last was being put together. He assured Borden that Rowell had never been unfavourable to him personally and that the sole source of his earlier demurring had been related to an insistence on a real coalition and not merely the addition to a Conservative government of an insignificant number of Liberals. He won his point, and then hailed in the *Times* Rowell's appointment as president of the Privy Council and his evident status as the leading Liberal Unionist minister.[60]

A general election was called for December 17. Hard on the heels of that announcement was an urgent wire to Willison from the prime minister to come to Ottawa at once. He and Borden talked at length and then he saw Sifton before returning to Toronto to prepare a draft of the prime minister's election appeal to Canadians. His Ottawa discussions with Borden also had addressed the senatorship issue, and he wrote the next day to the prime minister that Sifton, who also was interested in a Senate seat, now "understood that I was to be appointed and that as between us he would insist on second place.... Meeting you yesterday was a very great pleasure and the talk profitable to me." Borden responded that Willison's information about Sifton's position "makes the situation much clearer. You may have every confidence that I shall not overlook the considerations which you placed before me at our interview."

As the unionist organization began to fall into place, Willison now took up the task of coordinating the new government's publicity overall. His joy at both his present and future roles was shared with Arthur Colquhoun who told him: "By dropping the <u>News</u> you have found yourself again & I rejoice thereat exceedingly…. Can you think of anyone better than myself to agree with you that resentments do not pay?…. It gives me great satisfaction to know that you & Sir Robert Borden are on satisfactory terms & that you feel as you do towards events past & present…."[61]

In one of the longest personal letters Willison ever wrote, penned to Geoffrey Dawson, the editor of the *Times*, in late October, he set forth how he viewed his own role, not just in 1917 but for years beforehand:

> During these last weeks I have often thought that I would like to talk to you as one talks to an old and intimate friend. In what has happened in Canada I greatly rejoice. I had not much to do with the actual organization of the Coalition Government. I did bring Rowell and the Prime Minister together at the Prime Minister's request and at the eleventh hour I intervened to some advantage. But I did nothing of great account in the actual negotiations…. I do feel, however, that I did more than any other man to produce the situation which made coalition possible. For years I fought Laurier because I thought he was nationally and Imperially dangerous. Today I find tens of thousands of Liberals who thought I was acting out of personal feeling taking my position and many many tell me now that I was right all the time but that they did not understand. One of these is Dafoe…. In any event I felt that Laurier was a danger to the Empire and I fought to prevent his return to office and to destroy the ascendancy of Quebec in Canadian affairs. That has been done but Quebec will be well treated….
>
> May I say, too, that for 25 years I have fought against the evil of party patronage. For years I fought almost single-handed. I have made scores of speeches all over

Canada for Civil Service Reform and I think with some effect. I take peculiar satisfaction, therefore, in the determination of the new government to destroy the old patronage system. There could be no greater gain for decent politics in Canada. Of course the union of Eastern Conservatives with Western Liberals in the Cabinet is of all things the best that could have happened for the war, for national unity and for a good understanding with Quebec in the early future.

I am sending this letter in the assurance that you will understand. You will not think I am a mere egotist. I have lived long enough to know that pretension is the sum of human folly. But I did want you to know how I feel about what has happened here and just how I am personally affected. I am to go to the Senate shortly but I am in no hurry. The appointment may come very soon and perhaps not for some months. The Prime Minister assures me it will be soon but of course I am not "lobbying." A place in the Senate, however, will keep me in close touch with public affairs....[62]

It was time to turn, with all his old enthusiasm, to the political fray. He was delighted with the new government's program, announced to the press on October 18, and congratulated Borden on its "impressive" nature. "The Union Government has been formed," it began, "with a desire to give representation to all elements of the population supporting the purpose and effort of Canada in the War." He was especially delighted with the second item, the abolition of patronage — "to make appointments upon the sole standard of merit." Other promises in domestic policy were in directions he had favoured for years: enfranchisement of women, effective employment, and settlement aid to demobilized soldiers, adequate pensions to the disabled and to dependents of the fallen, a vigorous attack on war profiteering, the opening up of new lands for colonization, and the improvement of labour-management relations.[63]

The politicians had agreed on the program and a general election was set for December 17. In early November, at Borden's request, Willison wrote a draft of the follow-up — for the prime minister's personal election address to Canadians. The text was made public on November 12 and very much had a Willison stamp on it, particularly in a stirring passage about what the Union Government and its conscription policy were all about:

> Three hundred and fifty thousand Canadian soldiers have gone overseas to service and sacrifice on the seared fields of France and Flanders. Many thousands of them lie in graves hallowed by their own blood and glorified by their sacrifice. Pride in their valor and their achievements mitigate the sorrow which possesses so many of our homes. Through what they have done we have a new revelation of patriotism. The nation is clothed with new dignity. But how meanly we shall stand at the bar of history if, through any neglect or failure of ours the cause for which they fell does not prevail. By the test which they met so steadily and bravely we shall be judged. If their living comrades in the trenches are not supported, shame and humiliation will be our position. They will have paid a price for us beyond our deserts. What they have saved in honour we shall reap in dishonour.[64]

There was more, much more, but those words summed up what had driven both Borden and Willison to their objectives.

Sir John worked tirelessly through the rest of November and into December, sensing and trying to help fix the weak points in Unionist rhetoric, sending off suggested copy to friendly newspapers and keeping up his *Times* work. The Toronto *World* gave over its front page to him on November 20 for a lengthy review of why union government had become essential. He was available too, at the shortest of notice, to fill in for Borden, Rowell, and other Unionist leaders on Ontario platforms. On the last weekend he was rushed to London and then Hamilton for such rallies. At least one Liberal Unionist, John Harold of Brant, felt that he owed his election, placed in jeopardy by an unofficial straight Tory candidate, to Willison's telegraphed endorsement and then a campaign speech on his behalf.[65]

As the contest wore on he worried more and more about the result. He warned Geoffrey Dawson about the "formidable slacker element," allied to Quebec and "the German and other foreign elements." He was getting "only bad news from the constituencies. I do not believe the election can go wrong but those who are out speaking and canvassing are greatly alarmed. The alarm is over the draft and cost of living." As to Quebec he reported grimly: "You cannot know how close we are to riots — if not civil war. Quebec is a closed door to Unionists...." A week into December, the election only nine days away, he worried to Flavelle: "I have refused to even think that the election will go wrong but disturbing reports persist and even my confidence is almost shaken at times." Whatever he was encouraging Unionist propagandists to say as a bitter fight deteriorated too often into diatribe and denunciation, he kept his *Times* reports scrupulously fair, including, astonishingly, a moving tribute to the embattled Sir Wilfrid Laurier that "he makes no lament, utters no reproach, shows no lack of resource or courage. There is still a great body of feeling behind him."[66]

Nevertheless, the election result on December 17 was a Unionist triumph, even before the massively pro-government overseas soldiers' vote could be counted. The final tallies gave them 153 seats and 57 percent of the vote and the Liberals 62 seats with 39.9 percent of the ballots. Quebec went for Laurier overwhelmingly, 62 seats to 3, with 72.7 percent. In the Maritimes, old party lines held more strongly, although the Unionists held an edge except in Prince Edward Island. The Unionist percentages elsewhere rivalled or even surpassed Laurier's in Quebec: Ontario, 62.7; Manitoba, 79.7; Saskatchewan, 72.0; Alberta, 61.0; and British Columbia, 68.4.[67]

From Ottawa, the victory complete, Sir Robert Borden sent Sir John his "warmest thanks" for "your untiring efforts on behalf of the causes which triumphed so magnificently." Newton Rowell thanked him for "the assistance you gave in the recent campaign to the cause of union Government, both in connection with the publicity and also on the platform. The result exceeded our expectations."[68] For his part, Willison found a special way of conveying to the prime minister what the victory meant to him, through a message sent to him by his son Walter, covering the troops at the front:

The Canadian election results are glorious. Men over here are over-joyed. Really it would have been a calamity had something else happened, and you have no idea how greatly pleased all ranks are that the Union Government was returned without any necessity of appealing to the Soldiers' vote. The soldiers wanted Canada to support them without the necessity of their vote....[69]

For Willison and Borden, as for men like Rowell, Sifton, Dafoe, and many, many others, the conviction that they had kept faith with the boys at the front and those who lay beneath its mud was the greatest source of satisfaction in December 1917. John Willison had done his duty for his son Bill. The war was still to be won in Europe, but the battle for a maximum war effort, for Canada and the Empire, had been won at home. He could look forward now confidently to a whole new dimension of service in the war cause and in the peace that was coming, for his country and his Empire. At sixty-one, the agony of the *News* and the worst personal tragedy he ever had known behind him, he was sure he would soon be in the Senate, the friends and causes he espoused in triumph. He had every reason to look with fresh confidence and enthusiasm to the future.

Reconstruction and Reflection, 1918–1921

AFTER THIRTY-SIX YEARS OF FRONT-RANK DAILY JOURNALISM, Willison now needed a new career base for a continuing role in public affairs. There was a war to win, an Empire to unite and a nation to reconstruct. It was no time to be a spectator.

In February 1918, he heard rumours from Ottawa that his senatorial appointment was imminent. However, a few weeks later he learned directly from the prime minister that it "did not prove possible," owing to "the difficulties and complexities which surround such a situation." In all likelihood, the problem was a coalition government's obligation to share patronage. Sir John had once been anxious — even a bit pathetically perhaps — for the upper house post. Now he guarded his dignity, replying to the prime minister that he had "no complaint to make and no grievance to cherish. I hope I may never become a mere office-seeker...."[1]

In fact, a possibly far more important office was seeking him. He had been asked to meet that winter with several Toronto business leaders looking to influence post-war Canadian reconstruction policy. A number had been active in the old Canadian Home Manufacturers' Association anti-reciprocity drive of 1911. A key participant in the CHMA, really an offshoot of the Canadian Manufacturers' Association (CMA), was

W.K. George, a former president of the Toronto Liberal Association and an old friend of Willison. By the first week in March, George and his associate John Ellis had convinced Sir John to play an active role and were arranging offices and staff. At a blue-ribbon organizing dinner of this new Canadian Industrial Reconstruction Association's Montreal Committee at the Mount Royal Club on April 19, Willison was the chief speaker. When a similar affair finalized the Toronto and overall organizations at the York Club on May 3, he was named the CIRA's national president.[2]

The members of his executive were a who's who of Canadian manufacturing, transport, and finance. Lord Shaughnessy, the retiring president of the CPR, was honorary president. There were four national vice-presidents: George and Ellis from Toronto; W.J. Bulman, the president of the CMA, from Winnipeg; and Huntley R. Drummond of Montreal. The national executive committee included: Edward W. Beatty, president of the CPR; D.B. Hanna of the Canadian Northern, T.A. Russell, the auto maker; S.R. Parsons of British American Oil Company; Frederick Nicholls, the utilities and financial magnate; and the Toronto manufacturer W.K. McNaught. The Association's principal objectives were circularized to prospective corporate subscribers as: "(1) To maintain industrial stability, and (2) to secure wise consideration and prudent treatment of problems of reconstruction." Moreover, the CIRA would work to spread "accurate knowledge of … actual conditions in the country and the probable effects of new legislation." Investigations would be launched of the competitive market and cost situations in particular industries and there would be promotion of technical and general education, land settlement, fair labour relations, and an improved position for women in industry.[3]

In June, yet another new public role came Willison's way. Premier Sir William Hearst gratefully remembered Willison's energetic leadership of the Ontario Commission on Unemployment in 1914–15. Now Hearst worried about a severe post-war housing crisis and on June 7 appointed him Chairman of an Ontario Housing Committee. Another one of his long-time Liberal friends, Frank Beer, of the low-profit Toronto Housing Company, was a member, joined by: Reverend Peter Bryce, a clerical reformer; a Toronto alderman; a labour unionist; and representatives of war veterans, manufacturers, real estate brokers, bankers, and insurers.

The premier wanted early recommendations, and Sir John accordingly convened the group for numerous protracted summer meetings.[4]

His obvious priority, however, was to establish firmly a positive profile for the CIRA. On June 12 he told the CMA's annual meeting in Montreal that he was an "optimist" about manufacturers and organized farmers reaching a reasonable compromise on the tariff and other issues which traditionally had divided them.[5] On July 17, at Galt, Ontario, he unveiled "A National Policy" for the CIRA. He warned of foreign nations systematically organizing their economies for postwar competitiveness and of the "immense problems" Canada was certain to face. Almost 700,000 people would be released at war's end from the military and war industries. With dependents they would approach two million, desperate for new jobs and housing on a vast scale. Agriculture could absorb only modest numbers; for the rest, a huge industrial expansion was essential. Government indebtedness for military pensions had soared. "If we are to bear this load," he counselled, "it is vital that the production of farm and fishery should be increased, new industries expanded, home markets enlarged and exports of manufactures and farm products multiplied."

He warned farmers that the once-capacious British market had dwindled with Britain's war-induced improvement in agricultural self-sufficiency and that the slack would have to be taken up by an expanding industrial sector in Canada. For maximum export effectiveness, large-scale combinations of enterprises would be needed, as well as effective government assistance through a Canadian trade corporation. In the face of difficult competition, especially American, there would be unprecedented opportunities for growth and efficiency, requiring enhanced government and university research assistance.

As for labour, he warned it would be "vain to contest the validity of its right to organize, to deny the necessity for collective action, or to minimize the benefits which thorough organization have accrued to the working population." But in light of the chaos of revolutions such as the Bolshevik one in Russia, he was sure that "no one can believe that human nature will change its character, that progress will appear except through individual initiative, that organized society can exist except upon the basis of private property…." It would be "only by methods of conciliation, sympathetic appeal and laborious effort toward a better understanding that the class war will be abated, and more satisfactory relations between labour and capital established." He called for industries to "call their workmen into council and establish so far as is practicable the co-operative but mutually dependent relation which will be necessary if we are to have unity, stability and prosperity during the difficult period of reconstruction ... a greater and happier postwar Canada." Sir John had absolutely no doubt that a major campaign to awaken Canadians and their governments to the post-war challenges was required, telling Frank Beer: "We are drifting in Canada and the curious fact is that no one seems to know that we are drifting...."[6]

There was widespread praise from across the country for the Galt speech and his several subsequent addresses in the West during an extraordinary September tour. Even W.J. Healey, associate editor of the farmers' often radical organ, the *Grain Growers' Guide* in Winnipeg, was very impressed with the Galt message and asked for a special follow-up article. S.R. Parsons of B.A. Oil was delighted that Willison had outlined "a broad and generous platform which ought to appeal to Canadians everywhere." Professor George Wrong congratulated him on a "noble address," and Principal W.L. Grant of Upper Canada College praised "so comprehensive and dignified a statement of policy."

On September 5, Sir John sought before the Winnipeg Canadian Club to establish a definitely favourable CIRA image with organized farmers and the labour movement in a region where both were especially militant. He argued that Canadians would have to "forget that there is an East or a West ... and subject all our economic proposals and legislative measures to the crucial test of the common national welfare.... We will meet the test of peace far less nobly than we met the test of war if those who seek employment seek in vain; if we fail in adequate preparation for the conditions and problems which we cannot escape when peace is restored....'Jerusalem is builded as a city that is compact together.'" He spoke similarly at Regina, Calgary, Lethbridge, Moose Jaw, and Vancouver. The Moose Jaw *Daily News* praised him as "a pioneer with a propaganda of no mere theorems, but with sound business for its basis," and judged that his message "went home deeply." The Vancouver *Sun* called him "an optimist, with reservations" and the Vancouver *Province* described him as "one of the preachers of the day of preparation."[7]

Inevitably, the praise was not universal. Words, however sincere and well crafted, were one thing. Effective, workable national reconciliation of interests and divergent priorities was another. After all, wasn't the CIRA a *business* organization, pursuing *business* interests? John Dafoe's Manitoba *Free Press* review of Willison's Winnipeg Canadian Club speech was personally friendly but pointedly skeptical about the supposed disinterestedness of the CIRA and its purposes. For Dafoe, the speech was "shrewd, conciliatory, plausible and skilful, but it left the most interesting part of the story untold.... The import ... was that this highly desirable 'after the war' status, which he drew in such roseate colours, can be obtained — at a price. But Sir John did not tell us what the price was to be." Dafoe was sure that the industrialists and financiers of the CIRA had "some very definite ideas as to the policy which should be followed by Canada after the war; and it should put them before the public." He added: "Sir John as the expounder and defender of a definite policy of tariff protection will have a part more in keeping with his talents and temperament than his present role of keeper of the candy in which the pill is to be hidden." [8]

The Willisons returned east via Winnipeg, and Sir John took the opportunity to answer Dafoe in a speech before the Kiwanis Club there on October 1. Yes, he conceded, the CIRA was a business organization, but he argued that it could play a beneficial role in national reconstruction "not less desirable or less legitimate" than, say, the organized farmers. He believed "conflict ... justifiable only when co-operation has failed and agreement is impossible." There were "overwhelming reasons for co-operation instead of conflict in Canada...." In that spirit, he had done his best throughout his western tour to have a wide range of lengthy discussions, negotiations really, with regional leaders representing a wide range of particular interests, including: Henry Wise Wood, president of the United Farmers of Alberta; J.G. Rutherford, president of the Western Canada Livestock Association; and G.R. Marnoch, president of the Lethbridge Board of Trade. [9]

The result was that Sir John, following his return home, was able to write the prime minister on October 15, on behalf of them all, asking for the early convening of a national reconstruction conference "representing all interests in Canada." They wanted Borden to name a small mixed businessman–trade, unionist–farmer nominating committee to invite delegates. "We reached the natural conclusion that it was infinitely desirable to establish a better understanding between east and west and between Western Grain Growers and Eastern industrial and financial interests," he explained, adding that the westerners desired the meeting be called by the PM, so that "all would go to Ottawa with the national interest in mind and free from any suspicion of personal or party motives." He hoped for a conference by February 1919 and believed it would be of supreme national importance." But he warned that "the wisdom of such a conference may be doubted by the extremists of every type and faction."[10]

He already believed that one such "extremist" was W.J. Bulman of Winnipeg, a CIRA vice-president and the president of the CMA. Bulman was furious with Willison for not including him in his western negotiations and told Sir John before the approach was made to Borden that the federal government would not want to "burn their fingers" with a conference. Willison briefed another CIRA vice-president, Huntley Drummond of Montreal, about Bulman's negativism, classifying him as a hard-line Unionist partisan. "No leader among grain growers or low tariff element in the West will co-operate with Bulman," he observed. "His only idea is conflict, while I believe that co-operation is the only policy which this Association can wisely pursue until it is convinced that co-operation will produce no results." Ominously, W.G. Cates of the Canadian Press warned Sir John that his correspondents in the West were reporting "the impression … that the CIRA is a branch of the CMA. I think it might be well to correct this. The CMA is not in very good odour with the public."[11]

There would be no early conference. The government proved reluctant to sponsor it. Willison reported to J.G. Rutherford in Alberta in late October that he supposed ministers might be worried about being charged with breaking the "tariff truce" agreed to at the time of formation of the Unionist alliance in 1917. He also judged that the government was "so overburdened by war problems that as yet it is hardly looking beyond the end of the war." He managed to get a promise from the prime minister that if the various farm, business, and labour organizations themselves would get a conference process going, the government would assist financially. Rutherford and Henry Wise Wood were to take this idea to the Canadian Council of Agriculture (CCA) meeting in late

November. As it turned out, however, the CCA preferred conflict to co-operation. It seemed not only the CMA had "extremists." The CCA's "New National Policy" platform featured an utter rejection of tariff protection and a blunt call for free trade with both Britain and the U.S. Marnoch of Lethbridge warned Willison that the CIRA and Canadian business generally could anticipate "a trial of strength." Reconstruction, it now seemed clear to a doubtless alarmed and disappointed Willison, would be a messy, quarrelsome affair.[12]

Progress with the Ontario Housing Committee was much more heartening. After two meetings with his colleagues, Sir John pressed on Premier Hearst a one-year, one million dollar provincial loan program to municipalities, for the construction of houses to a maximum value of $2,500 or for rental at up to $25 monthly. The premier agreed, even doubling the fund's total. He also accepted, after initial protest, Willison's view that municipalities must not be obliged to have their plans approved by ratepayers' votes, owing to the "emergency situation" being faced by the average citizen.

After three months of study, the committee concluded that Ontario's housing emergency only could be solved "by co-operation with the Federal authorities." In a memorandum to the federal cabinet in mid-October, it argued forcefully that "the war and federal action resulting from the war is mainly responsible for the diversion of private capital from the building of inexpensive homes," and that there was "a growing recognition of the final responsibility of the state for the housing of its people." The war effort had required "large services of its citizens," they stressed, and the government "owes in return to these citizens and their families the assurance that they will not lack decent shelter and an opportunity to enjoy home life...." The federal government was asked to make available to the provinces not less than $10,000,000 for the improvement of rural and urban housing. Willison did not make the request public but had reason to be delighted on December 3 when the federal finance minister, Sir Thomas White, informed Premier Hearst that a low-interest federal loan fund of $25,000,000 — more than twice the amount the OHC had asked for — would be made available to the provinces for their housing programs. Hearst at once removed Ontario's $2,000,000 ceiling on its own emergency loan fund.[13]

In February and March, 1919 the OHC's final report was published, and Premier Hearst, introducing a comprehensive housing bill to the Legislature, termed the committee's work "a valuable contribution to public thought." As recommended, the province would take up its proportionate share of $8,500,000 of the federal loan funding. The province would distribute it through non-profit municipal housing commissions for the construction of homes up to $3,000 in value. Willison, on behalf of a powerful group on the committee, had urged Hearst beforehand to permit private low-profit housing companies to participate, in localities where municipal action was blocked by developers. When the premier had ruled that out, Willison dropped the proposal. In mid-March the bill was given all-party approval by the Legislature, and Sir John proudly told his friend T.A. Russell of the CIRA board: "If the money now being appropriated ... is wisely expended we will immensely improve the whole character of housing...."[14] He had ample cause to be proud of the part he had played in the OHC's widely praised work.

Likely his chief source of contentment, satisfaction, and pride in 1918–19 was found once more in a literary role, through work on what became his serialized memoirs, eventually published in 1919 as *Reminiscences: Political and Personal*. In the wake of the December 1917 election and before he became enmeshed in the CIRA, he had put on paper a few chapters on his boyhood, youth, and early days in journalism. He showed them privately to Arthur Colquhoun, who pronounced them "all delightful.... If you go on in this vein we shall have nothing like it in our books." Now he pushed onwards, and Newton MacTavish of the *Canadian Magazine* delightedly agreed to monthly serialization, which began in the issue of May, 1918, on his pre-journalism years. MacTavish pronounced the piece "really a fine piece of writing" and S.P. Gundy gushed to him when he read the chapter that "memories undisturbed for over thirty years ... came to life when you touched the chords." As the story advanced in each monthly issue through Sir John's newspaper and political careers, John Nelson, one of his former reporters, wrote from Vancouver:

> You will not mind my saying what delight your sketches
> are offering one to whom many of the men whom you

treat as intimates loomed like great crags against my boyish horizon....

Where the truth has to be told it is done so skilfully as almost to be palatable; when appreciation is expressed it is with a reserve which is most delightful....

I have two hopes — one that the series may never come to an end and the other that as they progress they may be incorporated in book form so that they may always be near to entertain and to cheer.

If your withdrawal from active journalism is what has made this possible it was a fortunate calamity.[15]

The last of the magazine articles appeared in March 1919. That November McClelland and Stewart published the book version, and it immediately won wide praise. Sir Edmund Walker marvelled to the author: "I am so full of your book that I must write to you before I lose any of the flavour. I remember nothing compared with it." Sir Joseph Flavelle passed on Sir Thomas White's praise of the book's "literary merit and its richness in memories full of fine qualities...." Principal Bill Grant of UCC told him: "It is given to few to be reserved and yet picturesque, moderate and yet definite, but you have achieved it, and with a distinction and a kindliness of phrase which set a fine example."

The professional reviewers were as kind. Arthur Colquhoun in the *Canadian Historical Review* was naturally enthusiastic, pronouncing that the work "lifts the curtain upon Canadian public policy of the past forty years as it has not been lifted before...." "Xanthias," the book reviewer for the *Queen's Quarterly*, praised "the remarkable gallery of portraits both of the famous and the obscure." But almost certainly the appreciation and praise that must have pleased Sir John the most came from Sir Wilfrid Laurier. His old chief and long-time idol died shortly before the book's publication, but Senator Laurent Olivier David had reported to Willison just beforehand, in December 1918, that Sir Wilfrid had read avidly the magazine series of articles dealing with him and "has been pleased with your kind and impartial appreciation of his political career." David himself observed that "it is impossible to better characterize the moral and intellectual faculties of our most eminent political men."[16]

"If it be said that only great men may write Reminiscences," Sir John observed early in his volume, "it may be pleaded that a close, even if accidental relation to great men or great events may give equal or better qualifications...." He defended memoir history, believing that he was "less hampered by reticence than will be the writer of fifty years hence by ignorance...." He would observe "a decent discretion" about others in memoirs "frank and open, but, I trust, free from temper or malice, from detraction or adulation."

He started from his boyhood and then his instant birth into politics at sixteen, mesmerized by his first election debate. Since then, he remarked, he had experienced "no interest in life comparable to the study and discussion of public questions.... From that hour I saw the way along which I must go." It was political journalism, not candidacy, that had attracted him. He believed "the true journalist ... most happy in the promotion of movements which assail privilege and diffuse social blessings. If he thought chiefly of wealth or position he would not plant his ladder upon any such unstable foundation." His humble origins, the dreary years as a store clerk, and then his meteoric climb to prominence at the *Globe*, must have astounded readers who thought of him as a titled publicist for the powerful.

His story was an agreeable blend of the events of his own public life with fascinating portraits of the politicians and other opinion leaders he had known so well. Probably his most sophisticated and historically valuable analysis was of the former Liberal leader, Edward Blake. He contended that Blake was "as great a man as ever was born in Canada if the mind is the test and the standard." However, he

> ... was sensitive to every kind of criticism, blow it ever so softly. He was so mortally afraid he would be misunderstood that he never fully understood himself. Disabled by temperamental defects this man of whom giants might be afraid let his soul be harried by insects and to the gnats gave victories which belonged to the gods.

Blake's condemnation in 1886 of Louis Riel's execution Willison still found "embarrassing" on grounds of political opportunism, and he believed that the anti-Unrestricted Reciprocity West Durham Letter of

1891 "closed forever ... any prospect of union or co-operation between Blake and the Canadian party he had done so much to create and destroy."[17]

Probably the most charming and delightful chapters centred on Sir John A. Macdonald. "Around no other name in Canadian history gathers so much of praise and detraction, of confidence and distrust, of story and legend," he remarked. Macdonald, in his view, had been "a man with his feet on the earth and his head not so far above it. He seldom sought to climb to moral elevations where the footing might be insecure." These words harked back to Willison's attitudes in young manhood, when his inherited Tory faith had been dashed in Macdonald's Pacific Scandal embarrassment and then his Liberalism affronted in Sir John's hyper-partisan and anti-*Globe* "treason" campaign in 1891. Then he had been unable to manage a good word for the Conservative chief on the day after his passing, but time had gone a long way to heal those old wounds. Brushing aside now the traditional Liberal view of Macdonald as an unprincipled opportunist, he was happy to argue that his "supreme objects were to unify Canada and maintain the connection with the Empire.... The substantial consistency of Sir John Macdonald's career is good evidence that he directed while he managed and that he abandoned none of his essential convictions for office...." He recalled the "universal sorrow which bound all Canadians together" when Macdonald died, and judged that "it was no common man who so touched a nation's heart and as time passes we see his stature more clearly and forget the way in which some things were done in gratitude for all that was achieved."[18]

Blake and Macdonald were long in their graves when Willison's *Reminiscences* appeared. But Sir Wilfrid Laurier was very much alive at the time of the initial magazine serialization. Willison's treatment of him was notably generous. There was little in the book of the two men's later, often bitter, differences, even over conscription and union government scant months before. There was far more on their earlier alliance and friendship. Willison mused at the common impression early in Laurier's party leadership that "at best he would be an ornamental figure, obedient to the commands of stronger men in the party." He recalled the intense French–English and Catholic–Protestant divisions of the 1880s and 1890s, concluding that "the leadership of a Federal party was a delicate and difficult undertaking for a Frenchman, a Roman Catholic and a citizen of Quebec."

Readers probably were far more interested in his treatment of Laurier's role in the Manitoba Schools issue. Since his last published account, in *Sir Wilfrid Laurier and the Liberal Party* in 1903, he had split with Sir Wilfrid over what he had interpreted as a betrayal by Laurier of his 1896 pro-provincial rights position for a later pro-separate schools stand for Alberta and Saskatchewan. Willison restated his own antagonism to separate schools but now remarked admiringly that Laurier in 1896 had been "wonderfully dextrous but neither uncandid nor dishonest."

Even on Laurier's relationship to imperialism, Willison was restrained and gentle, evidently determined to pen a scrupulously fair, even detached account. "No one who knew Laurier could believe he was Imperialist," he commented. "Economically he was a continentalist and politically he was an autonomist.... Looking into the future he probably saw an independent Canada, not separated from Great Britain in interest and sentiment, but politically dissociated from problems which are the necessary condition and inheritance of an Empire...." Still, he contended, Laurier "made no quarrel between Great Britain and Canada, he established the British fiscal preference, he first sanctioned the organization of Canadian regiments for Imperial service abroad, and he first committed Canada to a definite obligation for naval defence. It may be that he answered to public opinion but he did answer and that was something."[19]

In the magazine articles and published book, he did not choose to add anything on the very last of his major and bitter conflicts with Laurier, only a few months before – over conscription and union government. On Sir Wilfrid's death in February, 1919, the anonymous obituary in the *Times* was obviously Willison's, concluding movingly:

> History will pronounce judgment on this decision of his, to which he clung in spite of every inducement, not to join Sir Robert Borden in a Union cabinet. It is too soon as yet for a fair judgment; but there is this to be said for the line which Laurier took — that it was consistent with the principles to which he had been faithful all his life, that he was then a very old man, and that consistency has been the rock on which many younger men have split, consistency too, with principles far less vital than

resistance to conscription must have seemed to Laurier. In the General Election of 1917 he was at the greatest pains so to fight his battle that no hurt should be done to the cause of the Empire — no easy task, as he must have known that it was a losing battle.

Laurier's career, as a whole, presents many occasions for easy criticism. What career of a great man does not? And even his most hostile critics will agree that he was a great man, who served his Dominion and the Empire well....[20]

Naturally, there were observations in *Reminiscences* about the craft and calling of journalism. He recalled the conditions of partisan reporting that had so often grated on him as a young man. He claimed proudly that "a revolution was effected" by his insistence as an editor on carrying fair and full reports of public meetings without reference to party and that "the example was influential with other public journals.... That, I believe, was my best contribution to Canadian journalism."

Recalling how he had rebelled so often against partisan allies and superiors insisting he defend dubious patronage behaviour, he rejoiced that the press "now generally revolts against such unhappy servitude, and nothing is more certain than that administrative and electoral corruption become less common if evil practices go undefended." But as the grip of party had loosened on the press, he asserted, that of certain other forces had increased. "A generation ago," he reflected, "it required courage for a newspaper to attack a great railway or a group of capitalists. Now it requires even greater courage to defend corporate and financial interests even when these are assailed by mercenaries and demagogues...." On the whole, however, he was sure the press had become more influential as its readership had become the masses rather than a small elite:

There may be loss of prestige with the few, but there is increase of authority with the many.... Now the newspaper enters every household. It thinks for those who do not think for themselves. It reaches the multitude who are not instructed in social, economic or political

science, who have meagre knowledge of the experiences
of other generations, who have faith in the omnipotence
of statutes and the power of governments over natural
laws and inevitable human tendencies....[21]

He left unanswered, for future generations of journalists, the
question as to whether this new broader influence would be for good or
ill. Memoirs, after all, are supposed to look backward.

Meanwhile, his old familiar concern for Canada's imperial future
kept surfacing. The war in Europe wound to its wearying end in the
last months of 1918, with sweeping Allied victories in the fall replacing
the near triumph of the Germans in April and May. On November 11,
Torontonians went mad with joy at the news that a dictated armistice
had been accepted by Germany. Willison had done his best over the four
years of the conflict's agony to support a maximum Canadian effort at
Britain's side. He had espoused conscription and union government,
though originally opposed to both, for that end. He had to know too
that the very strength of the Canadian role on the battle fronts had
stimulated a huge increase among Canadians of a sense of a distinct
Canadian nationalism. As well, the huge cost in war casualties and
national dislocation inevitably was breeding a growing public distancing
from too close an involvement with the kind of clash of empires which
had triggered the conflict. B.K. Long of the *Times*, meeting Sir Robert
Borden in London late that same November, reported to Willison
that the prime minister was "strongly of opinion that anything like an
Imperial Parliament runs quite counter to the present current of public
opinion...." Earlier in the year, Willison had conceded to Zebulon Lash
that any move of that sort was "for the present ... out of the question." As
Arthur Glazebrook advised Lord Milner in December 1918: "The sense
of Canadian nationalism has grown very fast."[22]

Early in 1919, Sir John was disturbed by Prime Minister Borden's
insistence on a distinct diplomatic role for Canada at the Versailles Peace
Conference and in subsequent international arrangements, fretting to
Arthur Glazebrook in March: "I wonder if we are not moving directly
and somewhat swiftly towards independence." That summer he tried in
the *Times* to put the bravest face possible on developments, remarking:

"Unquestionably the war has accentuated national feeling in the Dominions. More and more the emphasis is laid upon nationality rather than upon Empire.... It demands more exact and more responsible machinery for consultation and cooperation between the Dominions and the Empire and a more definite expression of the Dominions in Imperial policy." More candidly, he told Lord Milner that December: "There is a point at which we will turn either towards organic union or separation. If we put all the emphasis on the theory of equal nations the turning may not be in the direction we would like to go...." Early in 1920 he observed to Principal J.O. Miller of Ridley College: "The political, commercial and social leaders of Canada ... are indifferent and uninformed. If you point out the danger you are likely to be regarded as an alarmist, a feeble Canadian, or a Jingo Imperialist...." He confided in May that year to Hume Cronyn, a Liberal Unionist MP: "I sometimes fear that our new status is a long step towards separation from Great Britain."[23]

In August 1920, he was afforded a welcome opportunity to air his deeply felt views on imperialism and Canadian nationalism to a prestigious audience, the delegates to the Imperial Press Conference in Montreal. He at once won their rapt attention with a delightfully humorous opening, explaining that he had come by train to the wine-loving "metropolitan dignity" of Montreal from the anti-liquor "rural simplicity of Toronto," adding: "If I am dull or dry you will remember that there are long arid stretches between Toronto and Montreal and if one comes in a crowded Pullman what is a flask among so many?" Then, moving on to his central and very serious theme, he affirmed:

> ... when skies are clear and winds gentle and seas smooth we put the emphasis on nationality, when storms appear and waters are turbulent we forget that we are a nation and remember only that we are an Empire....
>
> Let us not worry over much about the theory of equal nations or the designs and projects of suspected and imaginary centralists in London. Let us say to the emotional autonomists and the Jingo Imperialists "a plague on both your houses." British statesmen, we are convinced, have no other desire than that the

Dominions shall express themselves within the Empire and the people of the Dominions would make short shrift of statesmen who would attempt to lead them outside of the Empire. That is enough for the time and ... if the necessity for more definite constitutional machinery develops the genius of British statesmen in the Dominions and the Mother Country, supported by the common will of the British peoples, will forge new bonds of union and establish more firmly and securely the foundations of the Imperial Commonwealth....[24]

Nevertheless, throughout the early 1920s the steady development of Canada's autonomous status in the Empire and world affairs continued to cause him grief, and the status quo position he had praised at the Imperial Press Conference proved not to be "enough for the time." An added frustration was that, unlike his previous position of often significant influence over Canadian policy-making on imperial matters during the Laurier and early Borden administrations, he no longer had the entrée of a powerful editorship and the advantage of a close relationship with a prime minister to sustain such a role. The Sir Robert Borden of autonomist policies and almost perpetual absence from Canada and his office in 1919 and 1920 — because of peacemaking and illness — was a stranger to him. It remained to be seen whether Borden's successors would be more amenable and approachable.

A way was made open late in 1918 for him to return to daily newspaper editing when he was invited to Montreal by Lord Atholston, proprietor of the mighty *Star*, and tendered its editorship. He was tempted but finally replied to Atholston that "agreement just now is difficult if not impossible." He was then in the very midst of his delicate negotiations with farm leaders and the prime minister over a reconstruction conference and could hardly quit the CIRA until that issue was resolved. His hesitations were related as well, as he confided later to Arthur Colquhoun, to his view that the *Star*'s editorial page had lacked "character" for some time, as its editors were expected to be "docile" under Atholston's dictation. As well, he told his friend, he preferred "the old associations ... in this populous but petty village on Lake Ontario" to residence in Montreal.[25]

The idea of his return to some kind of journalism, however, kept coming up. In February 1919, Arthur Glazebrook sounded out Huntley Drummond on the idea of a Willison-edited weekly. Sir John himself approached Edward Beatty of the CPR later that year for support, estimating that an initial capital of $60,000, with a reserve of $15,000, advanced for five years, could start up "a National Weekly for Canada," on the model of the American *New Republic* magazine, which would speak with greater deliberation, greater knowledge and greater authority than its daily contemporaries...." He stressed to friends that such a publication "should be in a position to declare its independence of control by financial interests" and that "to do its best would have to be much more than a class organ...." In that spirit, he rebuffed a CMA proposal that he edit their *Industrial Canada* publication as a weekly.[26]

When Edward Beatty organized a dinner discussion in Montreal in December 1919 for some prospective backers for the kind of magazine Willison sought to edit, he reported back that they doubted a weekly could effectively influence public opinion. The role of influential weekly analyst on national affairs was not to be, at least for the foreseeable future. He certainly had no intention of trying himself to raise the capital required. He still spoke occasionally and — for Canadians — distantly in the *Times*. Subject to the whims and wishes of Lord Atholston, his views appeared irregularly in the Montreal *Star*. As well, since April 1919, Newton MacTavish's *Canadian Magazine* carried his four pages of comment in each issue, entitled "Month to Month," on the understanding that he was "not to publish anything that could be established as an expression of any purpose as to either politics or religion."[27]

His principal focus remained his presidency of what now was styled simply the Canadian Reconstruction Association. He was far more than merely a paid publicist. To his decades of experience in politics, across party lines, he now added an extraordinary set of acquaintanceships and associations among leaders of manufacturing, transportation, and finance. His sense of what the CRA and its president should do was related intimately to his understanding of the evolution of an unprecedently volatile Canadian political scene. At war's end he told W.J. Bulman of the CMA that it was "the wise policy in the interests of industrial Canada to strengthen Borden's hands." He warned in the Montreal *Star* that the "test" for the Union government "will be the wisdom with which ... [it] handles the problems of reconstruction and the courage which it displays in policy and in administration."

By January 1919 he worried in the *Times* that the Unionists' policy inclinations, particularly on the tariff, were "curiously unsettled." He commented in March and April that year to Bulman on the "disturbing readiness" of many western Unionist MPs to agree with the organized farmers' low tariff campaigns. He had some cause for relief when the government rejected that pressure in its budget that year, but at the cost of Thomas Crerar's resignation of his portfolio in June and his leading of eight other renegade western Unionists into outright opposition.[28]

The seeds of what would be a fiercely anti-protectionist farmers' Progressive Party were being sown, and the harvest promised to be rich indeed. In the face of the gathering storm from both farmers and organized labour, the CRA did not shrink from an activist propaganda effort. By April 1919, Willison had given sixty speeches, all well covered in the press and several reprinted in pamphlet form, widely distributed to subscribers and politicians. Now the bimonthly bulletin became weekly. But to the urgings of some of the CRA's backers that it should mount a frontal assault on labour and the organized farmers in the West — as classes — Sir John was absolutely opposed, responding that May to one demand: "For my own part, I have always insisted that to fight Labour or to fight the West would be suicide...."[29]

Within a few short days that spring, the polarization of Canadians escalated alarmingly. Momentarily forgotten were the fulminations of the farmers. Radical trade unionism boiled over through six tense weeks in Winnipeg beginning in mid-May, reaching the proportions of a general strike. Eventually, the economic cost to workers, federal police action, and the arrest of strike leaders brought the struggle to a bitter end. Meanwhile charges about "Bolshevism" and "tyranny" were traded by polarized partisans of labour and business. Willison warned in the Montreal *Star* that "no excesses of the Red element should be allowed to prevail against the legitimate claims of organized Labour." He firmly supported the right to strike, form unions, and federate nationally and internationally but equally strongly opposed efforts to "erect upon the principle of the sympathetic strike an autocracy which defies

Governments and forces ... civil conflicts." He was sure that "prevention of Bolshevism does not lie in repression but in its exposure to air and sunlight, in improving social and industrial conditions and in a greater sympathy between employers and employed."

That kind of counsel drew warm thanks and praise from Henry Wise Wood of Alberta, one of the chief radical farmers' leaders, who wrote him that "I may not agree with all your viewpoints, but I am sure that the time is here when all the thinking people of Canada will have to do their very best thinking. We have already got so far apart that the future of Canada is in doubt."[30]

The CRA did its best to encourage more moderate trade unionists open to at least some tariff protection. It pledged $50,000 in June 1919 to George Pierce, a leader of railway unionists, and his colleagues if they would try to encourage the Trades and Labour Congress to endorse the appointment of a federal expert or "scientific" tariff commission. The idea had been pushed by men like Beatty of the CPR and W.A. Black of Ogilvie Flour. Willison had been dubious about the likelihood of success and in October was furious when the TLC unanimously shelved a resolution favourable to a scientific tariff commission, and the Canadian Brotherwood of Railway Workers explicitly rejected the idea. Willison demanded "open fighting" by Pierce and others in the TLC getting CRA money. It was bad enough that their arguments for a commission were "completely without publicity, although publicity is what we want above all things," and none of these co-called labour "allies" of the government and the CRA dared go so far as to endorse protection itself. Eventually, by late in 1920, the last payments to the Pierce group went out, in return for a pro-commission testimony to federal tariff committee hearings.[31]

The more militant side of labour was in the ascendant, in Ontario and nationally. This was starting to have major political impact. After the provincial election of October 1919, 43 winning candidates of the United Farmers of Ontario joined 12 Labour MLAs in a new governing coalition at Queen's Park. Willison had helped Premier Hearst of the Conservatives draw up a socially progressive election platform, including the activist housing program that his own Ontario Housing Committee had recommended. "If we lose Labour the industrial system of this country cannot survive," he warned Bulman of the CMA.[32]

Nationally, the mighty Unionist political strength of two years before had become an empty shell. Even in January 1919, Willison had reported to the *Times* that the Borden coalition might not survive the session. In May he asserted for that paper that reorganization of the government in both personnel and policy had become "imperative," adding: "Uncertainty over the tariff, combined with labour unrest, is affecting public confidence and tending to decrease industrial activity...." He worried that Sir Robert Borden "would not be as thorough as desired" in giving that lead to his government."[33]

In August the federal Liberals held their national leadership convention to select a successor to Sir Wilfrid Laurier, who had died in February. Willison's employee and young friend of years before, William Lyon Mackenzie King, who had been a Laurier loyalist in 1917, was the winner. The platform included a tariff plank which Willison described to Sir William Hearst as "largely identical with that of the organized Grain Growers." To Bulman he now despaired that the Unionists, in the face of all this, were "committing suicide. [How] in the name of Heaven can you hold a position without fighting or with two aggressively low tariff parties fail to declare?" His fading faith in Sir Robert Borden was now gone completely. As he confided to the governor general, the Duke of Devonshire, that December, the prime minister "lacks constructive quality. Twice he has been carried into office by a situation which other people created ... but one doubts if he could of himself create a situation through which he could obtain power or retain power...."[34]

He hoped the Unionist coalition would not simply wither away. In September he urged the Liberal Unionist Newton Rowell to remain in the cabinet, as "there is no position you may not attain if you remain in public life." Then in mid-December, he informed Sir Edward Beatty that "a group of representative Toronto citizens are moving to effect a revolutionary reorganization of the Government at Ottawa" starting with "a change at the head." He had "good reason to believe," he told Beatty, that the former minister of finance, Sir Thomas White, recently returned from Ottawa to Toronto business, "could be induced to become Prime Minister." He was sure that "nothing short of a change in leader and a revolutionary change of the personnel of the cabinet would impress the country...."

He informed W.S. Steed of the *Times* that "White is the only available man...." His chief potential rival, Arthur Meighen, he explained, was "not popular in Quebec and it is most desirable that Quebec should be considered." But to Willison's disgust that winter, an ailing Sir Robert Borden was persuaded by cabinet colleagues to hang on as prime minister, while attempting to rebuild his health by an extended holiday. "I am so convinced that a sound industrial and national policy can prevail in Canada, fumed Willison to T.A. Russell, "that I am impatient over the indecision of so-called leaders and the want of aggressive political direction...."

By May he reported to Campbell Stuart of the *Times* that Sir Thomas White "thinks it is too late now to save the Unionists and that a Farmer-Liberal Government must come into office after the next general election...." In June he told readers of the *Times* that there was "still the utmost uncertainty in Unionist ranks," but that Borden's resignation was now generally desired, with his likely successor Arthur Meighen, the solicitor general and MP for Portage La Prairie, Manitoba.[35] In a matter of days that speculation was reality.

There was one last reminder for Willison of how cool his once-warm relationship with Borden and the Conservatives had turned. Newton Rowell, also about to leave the government, reminded Sir Robert that Sir John's appointment to the Senate ought not to be "overlooked," both because of his "eminent qualifications and ... the conversations which have taken place with him...." Borden replied wearily that it would "not be possible" to arrange the appointment before he left office, but he passed on the plea to Meighen. Rowell still believed, as he asked Borden to stress to Meighen, that the appointment was "one of the duties of Union Government which had not been performed...." For his part, Willison declined to lobby for the post, commenting icily there was "nothing that I value so much as my political freedom.... One cannot be quite free if he is looking and hoping for recognition by Government." To Huntley Drummond he confided: "My own view is to advocate steadily a sound national protectionist policy and so far as may be avoid direct complications with parties."[36]

In spite of that view, he was briefly highly enthusiastic about the early performance of Prime Minister Meighen. In the *Times* he hailed Meighen's "straightforward style," and when the government unexpectedly won two by-elections, he delightedly sent the prime minister his congratulations. He rejoiced to Lord Northcliffe at the difference between the "indecisive" leadership of Borden and Meighen's "great energy."[37] However, he had to know full well as 1920 wound to its close that, in a very changed and radicalized Canadian political environment, Meighen's party still faced daunting odds with a general election looming ever closer.

In particular, he explained to Sir Campbell Stuart of the *Times*, the new government had to go slow on the imperial front because of the political necessity to "cultivate Quebec." The province still bitterly resented the imposition of conscription in 1917, and Meighen understandably was anxious not to raise anti-Empire tensions there once more. There would be an imperial prime ministers' conference in London in the summer of 1921, with future political, military and naval relations bound to be prominent on the agenda. In the *Times* Willison explained in January 1921 that "Canada must not be blamed if the disposition of the people is to refuse to take over seriously problems which may excite differences and add new uncertainties to the political situation." In April he even went so far as to urge Meighen to try and have the London meeting cancelled. He worried to the prime minister that he would forfeit such political momentum as he had achieved by leaving Canada for several weeks and that mere discussion by a conference of naval defence would give Liberals "a cry against you in Quebec.... As you know, I believe we should take a greater share in the defence of the Empire, but there are times when it is wise to act and times when action is unwise."[38]

However, as Willison saw things, Meighen sometimes was ready to go rather too far in an overtly nationalist direction. When in the spring of 1921 the prime minister proposed appointing a Canadian ambassador in Washington, Sir John complained to W.F. Cockshutt, a Conservative Unionist MP, that "the whole movement for separate diplomatic representation at foreign capitals and separate representation in the League of Nations goes directly towards separation...." He damned the "loose and frothy" autonomist teachings of "travelling political evangelists" such as Borden and Rowell for influencing Meighen in such a direction.[39] He then was disturbed when Meighen at the June Imperial Conference in London opposed initially the renewal of the Anglo-

Japanese Alliance of 1902 because of concerns this would antagonize the United States. Willison complained bitterly to B.K. Long at the *Times* that Meighen "expresses the feeling which prevails among extreme Liberals in Canada, if not among actual opponents of British connection...."

His anger eventually cooled, as an Anglo-American-Japanese diplomatic rapprochement took shape, in preparation for an international conference on naval armaments and the Far East. Meighen now could be seen as a statesman of imperial and Anglo-American reconciliation, and Willison readily dropped his antagonism, even enthusiastically describing to Sir Campbell Stuart a Toronto speech on the Empire Meighen gave on his return from London as "admirable in spirit and outlook." But as Willison had advised some months before, Meighen and his party sensibly played down Empire issues in the ensuing election campaign.[40]

For all the prominence Willison's presidency of the CRA had brought him, the future of the organization was uncertain. Organized labour, farmers' organizations, and progressive reformers mostly regarded it, not unjustly, as essentially a "pro-business" organization. Yet the Canadian Bankers' Association, and most of its member banks, never joined it. Huntley Drummond in Montreal regretted to Willison in March 1920 that "we have never at any time ... got very close to the Manufacturers' Association" and warned that the CMA was itching to go off on a full-scale propaganda campaign of its own on the tariff as the federal general election campaign approached. Willison told the CPR's Sir Edward Beatty in April that the CRA "should ... cease at the end of the year or there should be a definite decision very soon that its work should continue." If it was to go on, he contended, it "should be supported as a distinct national organization putting the national interest first, regardless of any sectional or class interest.... I think, too, that it cannot afford to have too intimate relations with any party or Government." However, as he told Huntley Drummond that July, "we must take a more aggressive attitude towards the fiscal platform of the Farmers and the wing of the Liberal party which acts with the Farmers...." The competition for corporate funding among the several national business organizations had become very difficult by the time of the CRA's annual meeting in October, when the budget was cut severely.[41] Very clearly, the future for the organization and its president was uncertain.

Willison understood all too well that the CPR and very many others among the Montreal business and financial leadership were at least as concerned about the future of private transportation in post-war Canada as they were about the tariff. He was invited to address the Canadian Club there in January 1921, and he welcomed the opportunity to speak principally about that issue. For years he had been an advocate of the public ownership of railways and generally had supported the Borden–Meighen policy during and after the war of taking over the bankrupt Canadian Northern and Grand Trunk railways. As he went to Montreal, he knew that a board of arbitration was considering the price to be paid by the government for Grand Trunk stock and that the CPR and related interests were deeply concerned about the potential competitive threat from a giant competitor supported by the federal treasury.

He began his speech by reminding his largely private interest audience that, in the pre-war craze for transcontinentals, "we became as polygamous as the pioneer Mormons...." The federal government, he stressed, effectively had been obliged in the public interest to take over the lines when wartime economics ruined them as private investments and he boldly asserted: "All Canadian patriots must desire that success shall attend the great experiment upon which we have entered, and that neither the Government nor the Board to which the control of the National Railways has been committed shall be embarrassed by intemperate criticism or interested attack."

That likely was not something many in his audience wanted to hear, but he won far more applause when he warned against the "ravages of political patronage and of excessive political pressure on rate structures." Warm approval certainly was evident when he opposed "any legislation" which would deprive the CPR of "adequate revenues to maintain its position as perhaps the most efficient public carrier in the world," arguing that this "would react disastrously upon all the interests and communities which it serves, and would damage the credit of Canada." He closed with a plea: "For the difficult situation which exists most of us have some responsibility, and while one emphasizes the obligation of the Government and the people to be just to the private company, it is just as necessary that the Government should have public sympathy in its handling of an onerous and complex problem...."[42]

Willison told Flavelle afterward that the audience had given him "extraordinarily close attention but not a great deal of applause. I could not go far enough to meet the opponents of public ownership and went too far to suit its advocates." In any event, he had cause to be pleased when the Montreal *Gazette*'s Robert White reported to him that his thoughtful speech had been "appreciated by a serious audience."[43]

It is likely that Willison had hoped his address would do something to revive flagging support for the CRA among Montreal's business and financial elite. Yet the Association's national executive, meeting immediately after the speech, resolved to close both the Winnipeg and Montreal offices and trim staff at the Toronto headquarters. However, there was then a delay in closing the Montreal office, and when Beatty of the CPR was sent details on the still-impressive circulation statistics for the Association's pamphlets, and on Sir John's continuing average of three or four well-received major speeches monthly, he convinced the railway's board to approve a further year's subscription of $10,000. Willison delightedly exulted to Huntley Drummond that "apparently the undercurrent of hostility to us in certain quarters seems to have almost disappeared." For his part, Drummond warned him that, as time went on, "it is going to be extremely difficult to get the money." Willison was philosophic in response: "As you know I never offer any argument as to how long this Association should continue."[44]

As 1921 wore on, he came to the conclusion that his time with the CRA should end. On November 8 he informed the board that he had "very definitely decided to withdraw in the very near future." The federal election campaign was then at its mid-point, and he took much satisfaction in observing that the actual words all three party leaders were using on the tariff was "not far from the platform of the Reconstruction Association" and that "we may have had a little to do with it." He was particularly pleased, he wrote in the *Times*, that "the most striking fact ... is that the Liberal candidates in the Province of Quebec are unanimously declaring in favour of an adequate protectionist tariff...."

As the 1921 federal general election campaign commenced, he wrote the Ontario Unionist Liberal John Harold, for whom he had campaigned in 1917, to "regret" that he was not running to keep his seat. "My own view," he commented sadly, "has always been that the only people who made any sacrifices in 1917 were Liberal Unionists. They gave up the associations of a lifetime in order to support a Conservative leader in a national emergency. Among Conservatives in Toronto I have not found much recognition of the sacrifices Liberal Unionists made...."

On election day in December, Mackenzie King's Liberals won 116 seats, to 50 for Meighen's Conservatives and 64 for the farmers' Progressive party. As soon as the votes were counted, he wrote to congratulate Mackenzie King, whose intelligence and abilities he never had doubted:

> I have said for some time that I believed the country was quite safe in the hands of the Liberals and that even on the subject of the tariff I did not fear a revision by a Liberal government. For that reason I did not take any personal part in the election and even the literature of the Reconstruction Association was strictly confined to the industrial question....

As he put it in the *Times* on December 8, "A Protectionist Government has been defeated, but the result cannot be regarded as a defeat for Protection." Four days later, his resignation from the CRA presidency was accepted, with complimentary references, as the minutes put it, "to the work that has been done for nearly four years." The CRA's general purpose — to help shape Canada's overall reconstruction after the war — largely had proven beyond its big-business grasp in a time of widespread social and sectional clash. But unquestionably on the protective tariff issue, on which it had come to put its chief focus, there was some cause for satisfaction.[45]

"My future is somewhat indefinite," he admitted to Sir Edward Beatty that December, "but not to the extent of causing any anxiety. I have the London Times correspondence and certain other connections which give me what Sir Frank Smith used to call 'a livin.'" He had his minor roles with the Montreal *Star* and the *Canadian Magazine*. More important monetarily, it was to be hoped, was the lengthening list of private business contacts his CRA connection had entailed. As he put it to Joseph Flavelle: "Serve and starve, if you will not take me too seriously, is the condition prescribed for journalists in Canada." On December 31, 1920, the press had carried an announcement that he was to be president of a new firm, Mortgage, Discount and Finance Limited. In September 1921 he had alerted Sir Campbell Stuart of the *Times* that "possibly I could be useful to any group of British capitalists who may think of negotiations in connection with the Canadian railways." In October 1921 he had become a director of the Canadian Bond Corporation of New York.[46]

In all likelihood, he expected business now to be the prime focus of the rest of his working life. At sixty-five he was no longer pursuing actively his dream of editing a weekly magazine, and notwithstanding his part-time writing for publications at home and abroad, he believed, as he had told Flavelle in January 1921, that he was "out of journalism in this country and there is no prospect that I will ever return to that field." The financial world beckoned him. He could not take much expertise or capital into it, only his reputation for probity, his capacity for lucid argument, and his associations with the great and near-great in public and private life.

It remained to be seen whether all this would be, or could be, the basis for a last career phase worthy of what had gone before. Shortly before he departed the CRA, there had been a startling appeal to him in Augustus Bridle's book *The Masques of Ottawa*. Writing anonymously as "Domino" but leaving aside that character's normally humorous tone, Bridle admiringly recalled Willison's "big Canadianism in all its forms." He urged Sir John now to "do something of more value to the country, so that the older enthusiasm of men who used to think he was Canada's greatest editor may not altogether die."[47]

XV

Free at Last, 1922–1927

"I am more comfortable than I ever was in my life," Willison told Sir Edward Beatty in 1922. He had welcome fresh income from his new business involvements, and there was a novel personal independence to savour. The old partisan ties and antagonisms had little appeal to him any more, and he wrote Prime Minister Mackenzie King that summer to say that he was "convinced that you have an opportunity to create a very strong National Liberal Party, and to consolidate behind you many of the vital influences in this country." He also no longer had to tailor his words to the views of the CRA money men and exulted to King: "I never was quite so free as I am now to express my own views."[1]

Not surprisingly, his new business involvements did not really give him much personal satisfaction. He now held the presidencies of Mortgage, Discount and Finance Limited and the Municipal Bankers' Corporation in Toronto and a directorship in the Canadian Bond Corporation of New York City. To one colleague he lamented in 1924 that "the chief business of some of us is to prevent the dissipation of trust funds by crooks and rascals." Quarrels over investments and gruelling proxy fights for corporate control were regular trials, but he succeeded in keeping his two Toronto companies solvent and in his hands throughout the period. Both, thankfully, proved reasonably prosperous, though he stressed wearily in 1923 to a collaborator in one of them that he was "not going through another struggle of a year or two for this company or any other."[2] He never really could be fully comfortable in a life devoted to making money.

As always, he needed "causes." Not surprisingly, a new one came his way. The Western Canada Colonization Association had been set up in Alberta in 1920 to link local businessmen, governments, and the railways in settling unoccupied prairie lands. Willison was appointed to the Eastern Advisory Board in 1921, involved principally with gaining private subscriptions. He told Beatty of the CPR in May that year that he wanted to see a "progressive and aggressive" immigration policy to re-ignite the pre-war prairie boom.[3] Pressure grew on him, with his excellent Ottawa, London, and railway connections, to accept the presidency. Prime Minister King assured him of his co-operation, but in a time of government financial and administrative retrenchment, it was clear that CPR support mattered even more. The CPR had done its own immigration organizing in pre-war days, and its participation in the new venture would be essential. Sir John told Beatty in June that he was prepared to accept the presidency, but only if the WCCA "would have your confidence and support."[4] Beatty expressed delight but was "somewhat dubious" of the organization's prospects for success "in view of its personnel." Specifically, he worried about the role of M.A. Brown of Medicine Hat, whose "hucksterism" he distrusted. To protect CPR interests, he insisted on getting his aide, Colonel Dennis, and a leading Winnipeg financier, Sir August Nanton, on the executive.[5] On that basis Willison accepted the presidency that summer.

Months of frustration lay ahead. The British government's Empire Settlement Board held up a loan, pending concrete assurances of adequate Canadian funding. Mackenzie King remained encouraging, but Sir Augustus Nanton, whom Beatty insisted on as chairman of the Operating Committee, would not agree even to serve until M.A. Brown was ousted. In November, Sir Edmund Osler of the Dominion Bank and Joseph Shenstone of the Massey-Harris farm implements company, warning Willison that they spoke for "a good many subscribers," insisted on a full financial accounting and an explanation of the long delay in actually starting settlement work. Willison quickly ordered financial statements for all subscribers and convened an Operating Committee for Winnipeg in mid-December. He complained bitterly to an English friend that the CPR had "made constant trouble" but confided to Joseph Flavelle that M.A. Brown now had to "disappear" from the WCCA if it were to live. At Winnipeg Brown agreed to go — but not before the following May. When the CPR's Beatty reacted that therefore the Association "cannot, I think, go on," Sir John threw up his hands and resigned, explaining to the minister of agriculture that he had "done all that I can do to reconcile conflicting interests."[6]

He still wanted a strong immigration policy, but he did not now believe that it could come from a mixed public-private organization. In a Montreal *Star* editorial in January 1923, he called for "action, immediate and practical, and a frank recognition by the authorities at Ottawa that the responsibility lies chiefly upon their shoulders and cannot be placed elsewhere." By April, however, he had concluded sadly to Flavelle that the King administration "lacked aggressive quality on immigration.[7]

In May, a re-named Canada Colonization Association, with some very modest support from the CPR, Canadian National Railways, and the federal government, actually was set up, with Sir Augustus Nanton as president. Willison lamented to a former WCCA colleague that "what has now been done … could as easily have been done a year and a half ago…." That August he wrote again in the *Star* that the federal government had been "so fearful and so cautious, so much afraid of certain elements, that nothing effective has been accomplished." One of those "elements," he had to know, was the anti-immigration group among the farmer Progressives, on whose parliamentary support the minority King government depended for survival. So low would be the level of activity on immigration, he regretted, that the conclusion could be drawn reasonably in Britain that Canada did not really want settlers.[8]

The 1920s also held many frustrations for him in the area of imperial relations, so long one of his most intense interests. He continued to be dismayed at the steady drift of all Canadian political parties towards "autonomy" — which he saw as virtual independence within the Empire. Also, he was outside the formal imperialist movement, after ending his contributions to the *Round Table* quarterly rather than have them vetted by a new Canadian editorial committee and finding that he was being ignored in policy planning by Lionel Curtis in London. Arthur Glazebrook regretted to Lord Milner that for a decade Curtis had been "more or less anti-Willison" and that Willison had known this. Their past quarrels over what Sir John had thought the insensitive rigidity of Curtis's federation scheme in *The Problem of the Commonwealth* (1916) and what Curtis had believed to be the handicap to imperialist success in Canada of Willison's partisan associations no doubt had been prime factors in that divergence. Distressingly, there was new tension too for him with the *Times*.

Geoffrey Dawson had quit as editor in 1919 after a quarrel with Lord Northcliffe. Northcliffe himself died in 1922. H. Wickham Steed was briefly editor, and his right-hand man in London as "managing director" was the Anglo-Montrealer Sir Campbell Stuart. Stuart was cultivating a close personal connection with Mackenzie King, even spending a weekend with the new prime minister in the Adirondacks in the summer of 1922, telling Willison that he had "become a convert" to the King idea of a separate Canadian ambassador in Washington.[9]

Sir John tried to be as optimistic as possible. In the *Times* Empire Day Supplement for 1922 he wrote that "if the Empire were in danger, no body of Constitutionalists could prevail against the British sentiment in Canada." In June he spoke at a Toronto memorial service for his fellow imperialist, Sir George Parkin. "No project of organic federation yet commands the general support of the British peoples," he admitted. "It may be that the conception of Empire which attracted the early federationists will never be embodied in an Imperial Constitution…." Parkin, he claimed, understanding this, yet saw "the fact of Empire realized in common effort and common sacrifice and he was content…."[10]

Willison was not. For the July 1922 English review *The Nineteenth Century and After* he wrote a major article denouncing "this feverish haste to refashion the Empire" of Canadians such as Borden, Meighen, Sifton, Dafoe, and the Queen's University political scientist, Oscar Skelton. He warned that "if we do not set ourselves to methods and projects of co-operation who can deny that there is a danger of separation and dissolution?" He would not pine for some possibly unrealizable federationist goal, but stressed the "indissoluble" character of what he called for the first time in print, the "British Commonwealth." He asked: "Can we think of a world without a British Empire? … Through connection with Great Britain and co-operation with Great Britain, Canada has greater power to serve all the good ends of civilization than can be had through any autonomous nationality…."

To Flavelle later that year he concluded that "ultimately the Empire will be federated or will break into a group of separate and independent nations."[11] In correspondence with Sir Robert Borden early in 1923, he argued that separate diplomatic representation and failure to share defence responsibilities was "not distinguishable in my judgment from full political independence.... I think we ought to have a common diplomacy and assist in maintaining the unity and integrity of the Empire or go out frankly in favor of complete independence." To John Dafoe he stated that "I am an imperialist chiefly because I want some full citizenship in some country." If that could not be found in an "organized Empire," he stressed, "then I want an independent Canada." To Horatio Hocken, the former mayor of Toronto, he lamented: "The trouble is that those who hold my view seem to have been deserted by all their old leaders."[12]

Even by the men of the *Times*! Sir Campbell Stuart, the managing director, came out publicly in *The Empire Review* early in 1923 for a separate Canadian embassy in Washington and an independent signature on a halibut fisheries treaty with the U.S. When Willison tried to take a more critical line in his *Times* contributions, Franklin Peterson, the foreign and imperial editor, pointedly warned him "against pursuing this subject too strenuously," prompting a reply that "I cannot go as far with the extreme Autonomists as I fear the Times goes." When Peterson protested that the paper merely wished not to "stiffen Mackenzie King's back" at the coming Imperial Conference, Sir John retorted that the *Times* and other British papers were wrong to "encourage" the autonomist movement in Canada by "seeming to accept its leaders as the authoritative exponents of Canadian opinion."[13]

But there was no delaying the triumph of that movement. The Imperial Conference of 1923, at Mackenzie King's insistence, definitively abandoned the concept of a common imperial foreign policy with its declaration that the conference was a meeting of governments, not an imperial cabinet, and that all decisions were subject to ratification by the individual parliaments. Willison calmly cabled the *Times* the comment that this decision was "much what was expected." And he hailed Britain's first tentative steps, at the accompanying Economic Conference, to open selected preferences in her market to the Dominions. However, when later in the year, the British Baldwin government's trade policies were lashed by the Labour and Liberal oppositions, Willison wrote in the Montreal *Star* that "we may be at the 'parting of the ways,' not politically, but commercially, and in these next few pregnant weeks the Mother Country may make decisions which will have consequences and reactions of profound significance to the future of the British Commonwealth." To Flavelle he observed: "I think sometimes that if the British Empire is ever destroyed it will be destroyed in Great Britain...."[14]

It had been fourteen years since he had been in Britain, and he was eager to explore more directly just how British attitudes on imperial relations and trade were evolving. Geoffrey Dawson had come back as editor of the *Times* in 1923, and it would be particularly interesting to discuss it all with him. He and Rachel planned at first to go for two or three months in early May, 1924, as they both badly needed a long, refreshing holiday. She was eager to go and they could hope that she would be up to it. Since Bill's death she had aged visibly, and Sir John had worried to a friend that "at best her health is not good." In the fall of 1921, just before they were to leave for a trip to New York, Washington and points south, she had fainted on a Toronto street while shopping, and in falling had struck her head. Convalescence had been slow and worrying. He had been very busy since then, and now his schedule and her strength perhaps would coincide. Besides, they had a grave to visit in a French village on the Somme.[15]

He also had a biographer's reason for the trip. He had accepted Lady Parkin's request to write a life of the late Sir George. "Aside from other considerations," he explained to Flavelle, "it will enable me to deal with the whole problem of Empire." The "other considerations" no doubt included a promised fee of $4,000, with the first quarter payable on July 1, 1924 and the others at six-month intervals thereafter. Completion was projected in two years. What the family, very much led by the widow, wanted was a short sketch giving the flavour of Parkin's personality and some clear insights into his work and its meaning. Bill Grant, Parkin's son-in-law, had known Willison since his boyhood and had taught Bill and Walter at Upper Canada College. He made it clear to Sir John that he had pressed his selection on Lady Parkin "from the first," and would give all possible help.[16] Sir John eagerly got to work, and through January and February he sifted through a pile of boxes of Parkin letters and notes and arranged for Lady Parkin and Bill Grant to put together a list of Sir

George's closest confederates in Britain in the old Imperial Federation League. A first draft chapter was worked up and he felt well started in meeting this new and fascinating literary and intellectual challenge.[17]

The Empire was much on his mind. In the last days of 1923 he had sent Lord Milner a copy of a recently printed volume of speeches he had given since 1905 under the title *Partners in Peace*. Milner naturally was in "very great sympathy" with the imperialist faith therein expressed but wondered if Willison still cherished the hope of a common parliament at Westminster, fearing now himself that "of late years we seem to be moving away from it." Willison confessed that he now had "small hope of a federal Parliament of Empire in my time.... But such representation must come eventually or the Empire will not last. I believe as firmly as I ever did that the Empire will last and that the true and lasting feeling of its peoples was expressed during the war."[18]

His imperialism, far broader than an approach to political structures, was a faith, not a program. It could not die. Suddenly, irresistibly, there came that winter an extraordinarily attractive opportunity for him to see far more of the Empire than he had ever seen before, or likely ever had expected to see. In mid-March, Edward Beck, the Secretary of the Canadian Pulp and Paper Association, pressed to see him on a mysterious matter "you may find extremely interesting." The CPPA wanted Willison to undertake a major lobbying mission to Australia in favour of that country extending its British preference on paper to Canadian products. He at first declined, but within days, as he explained to Geoffrey Dawson, the proposal was "renewed on terms which a decent regard for my own interests practically compelled me to accept." The first offer had been for $10,000 including expenses, the second for $15,000 including expenses, and an additional $5,000 for "satisfactory" results. The England and France trip would have to be delayed until he and Rachel, who would accompany him to Australia, could return that way in July and August.

Within days he was in Montreal, so he could huddle with the CPPA leaders at a Ritz Carlton luncheon. He had only time after that for the briefest of meetings in Ottawa with J.A. Robb, the Acting Minister of Finance, to get the federal government's perspective on Australian trade. Then he and Rachel left April 4 on the transcontinental CPR for Vancouver. They arrived there on the morning of April 9, and sailed that after-

Sir George Parkin, circa 1920 (facing title page of J.S. Willison, Sir George Parkin. Toronto: Macmillan, 1929*)*

noon on RMS *Niagara* of the Canada-Australian line. From Honolulu a week later he sent an enthusiastic note to Flavelle that "I am moving towards conditions and problems in which I will be profoundly interested and we ought to get benefit out of the experience...." The warming sun, the sea air, the shipboard life in first class, the time to read and chat — it all must have helped him leave far behind the memories of tensions past, of the *News*, the war, the CRA, the WCCA, and the ups and downs of business life. From Suva in Fiji they followed the Union Jack to Auckland, New Zealand, and thence across the Tasman Sea in early May to Sydney harbour and a first glimpse of Australia where, as he would record, "five or six millions of free, adventurous confident British people are holding a continent for Throne and Empire."[19]

In the Australian capital of Melbourne he received a warm welcome from political, business, and press leaders, as well as, astonishingly, a telegram from Mackenzie King in Ottawa who advised that Australia might favourably consider a recent Canadian offer of fairly broad reciprocal preference and "the next move should come from Australia." He saw Prime Minister Bruce on the broad preference and narrower paper issues and sought every opportunity to lobby cabinet ministers, importers, exporters, and editors on potential benefits for Australia, visiting Brisbane and then Sydney before sailing westward at the end of June for more than two thousand miles along the continent's southern shore to Perth. It would be a year before a major Canada–Australia trade agreement, including paper, was finalized, but long before then the CPPA executive in Montreal had judged that he had succeeded brilliantly with his mission and should have his full $20,000 fee.

Neither the money nor the mission to Australia seemed as important to Willison as what he saw on the global tour that took him there and back. He would write: "One who goes round the world with open ears and seeing eyes must be impressed, as it seems to me, not so much by the power and majesty of the British Empire, as by the tremendous responsibilities and obligations which lie upon its people." From Perth to Ceylon and then across the Arabian Sea to the Gulf of Aden to the Red Sea to the Suez Canal, Sir John and Lady Rachel saw the outposts and lifelines of the Empire. "One cannot make such a journey," he would remark, "without a wider and deeper conception of Empire, and, as it seems to me — a conception to which there is less of arrogance and jingoism and more of gratitude and reverence...." Given the "vast burdens ... infinite difficulties, perplexities and anxieties" of Britain's tutelary and defence responsibilities as "the legatary trustee of mankind" for so many dependent peoples and dominions facing potential anarchy and aggression, he wondered "if the extreme autonomists ... are not nagging the Foreign Office into a state of futility." Arthur Colquhoun would comment that when Willison reached home he talked of how "the sight of the flag at so many varied outposts of British rule ... stirred his emotions to their depths. Looking beyond the present, he could see a permanent purpose in the partnership."[20]

On their way to London from Paris in August, where they had come after docking at Naples, the Willisons stopped in Amiens. A car and driver met them at the station for a scorchingly hot day of battlefield touring. Pozières was only twenty-two miles up the straight, dusty road to the north-east, and Courcelette less than two more. In the sunlight, with the birds, the rolling farmland, and the tranquillity, it must have been scarcely possible to imagine the horrors that had been seen in the area just a few years before, except that one still could spot many shattered buildings in the villages and the surrounding fields. Lines from Robert Louis Stevenson came to him:

> *We traveled in the print of olden wars,*
> *Yet all the land was green'*
> *And love we found, and peace,*
> *Where fire and war had been.*
> *They pass and smile, the children of the sword –*
> *No more the sword they wield;*
> *And O, how deep the corn*
> *Along the battlefield!*

Beside Bill's grave in Courcelette cemetery they stood quietly, snapped photographs and drove away, their memories in agony.[21]

Work on the Parkin project and a close study of British politics and imperial policy should have kept him some weeks in England. However, he and Rachel had been nearly five months in their travels and, as he explained to Bill Grant, they "had no other thought than to get home as soon as possible." Also, it was distinctly the off-season in London, with few prominent figures to be found. The Geoffrey Dawsons had just left for Canada, but Sir Campbell Stuart entertained the Willisons for dinner, and there was a chance to visit the *Times*. Early passages for Canada allowed them gratefully to reach Toronto by the end of August.[22]

Willison promised Bill Grant that he would make the Parkin book "the first consideration until it is completed." It was not easy. Ten Elmsley Place was overrun with decorators — long overdue — until late September. In November, Walter was rushed to hospital for a serious operation, followed by a touch-and-go recovery. Both older Willisons were exhausted by their travels, and the strain brought on by worry about Walter just made things worse. Sir John himself was laid up most of November and admitted afterwards to Geoffrey Dawson that his condition had been "somewhat serious." Then Lady Rachel caught a chill before Christmas and grew so weak that a private nurse was engaged. Pneumonia set in early in January, and she did not have the strength to resist it. She died on January 25, 1925.[23]

Willison was devastated. Rachel had often been in poor health in recent years, but he told Frank Beer that she "never was more buoyant and happy than since we got back from Australia and every day of our long journey she enjoyed." To another friend he sorrowed: "We had a long journey together and a happy journey. We know that finally such companionships must be broken but when that day comes surely a good deal of the zest in life goes forever."[24] A legion of friends offered such consolation as they could.

Only work really helped. Lady Parkin found him in late February "very full of the book but feels it may take longer than he thought...." She repeatedly urged him to go to Europe that summer, but he planned instead a visit to the New Brunswick places of Sir George's youth and early career. By October he had completed two chapters, after consulting almost all of the thousands of letters, clippings, and documents he could find in Canada on Parkin. Throughout 1926, he made steady progress, reporting to Lady Parkin that summer that "one easily sees the end."[25] His progress was as fast as so busy a man could manage. In addition to his regular responsibilities, he seemed more determined than ever to take on new challenges. In March 1925 he proposed to George Morang, publisher of his two-volume Laurier biography in 1903, that there be a re-issue, with three new chapters on his old chief's later career. The new one-volume edition appeared in December, 1926, under the imprint of Oxford University Press in their Makers of Canada Series. As in his *Reminiscences* and in his *Times* obituary in 1919, he was more than kind to his old chief's memory, so there was no angry outburst from aggrieved Liberals.

Conservatives had reason to be pleased too when he linked together the lasting legacies of Laurier and Sir John A. Macdonald: "In personal distinction and in genius for popular and parliamentary leadership they are the outstanding figures in the history of the Canadian Confederation." He deliberately placed Laurier even higher by recalling with evident emotion and personal conviction that leader's oft-confirmed determination not to hate and his extraordinary ability not to inspire hatred:

> There are those who insist that the capacity of a political leader is measured by the degree of hatred he inspires among his opponents. But they were few who hated Laurier and few towards whom he cherished animosity. Resolute, unyielding, uncompromising he could be in pursuit of his objects, and to win he could wound, but the desire to wound was seldom a dominating motive and there was not much of malice or envy in his disposition.[26]

A far more major consumption of his time was represented by his decision in the early months of 1925 to try to make a long held journalistic dream come true. The special windfall money from his Australian mission had improved his financial situation agreeably, and in February he revealed to Sir Edward Beatty that he and his son Walter were going to launch "a sound monthly ... or weekly publication for Canada." He cut his last links to the *Canadian Magazine* and began searching out contributors to what he and Walter decided by the end of March would be called *Willison's Monthly*. "Nothing effective can be done unless the policy of the magazine is continuously directed to definite industrial and national objects," he told one of his old CRA backers, John Ellis. For the first time in nearly a decade he would have a regular platform of his own for his unapologetically protectionist nationalism and his ineradicable imperialism. This time he was beholden to no proprietor, moneyed sponsor, politician, or party. Mackenzie King enthusiastically subscribed, expressing the hope that the magazine would be "unbiased" on controversial matters. Arthur Colquhoun joked to another Willison friend, John Dafoe, that he anticipated rather "a deadly moderation" from a conservative Willison absolutely free at last to speak his own mind.[27]

Willison's Monthly had by-lines for most of its contributors, but Sir John and his son adopted *Times*-style anonymity. His own all too recognizable "From Month to Month" section headed each forty-page issue. He opened in June 1925 with four pages calling for reform of parliamentary rules for more efficiency, recommending ratification of the Australian trade treaty, calling for lowered taxation on investment and enterprise to stimulate job creation, celebrating the growing role of women in politics, literature, and social services, and demanding a more aggressive federal immigration policy. A special additional article stoutly defended the protective tariff as *the* essential foundation for national development. These initial pages of extended editorial comment always were the heart of the magazine and gave it its special character. After the first couple of issues John Dafoe marvelled to Arthur Colquhoun: "What a shrewd old boy Sir John is! Nothing could be gentler or more deferential than Sir John's treatment of the various heresies which he combats; but in essentials he is as unyielding as the stiffest Tory of them all." Dafoe thought he knew all too well where the magazine's principal readership was to be found. "I have no doubt," he joked to Colquhoun, "Sir John's monthly will become a veritable bible to the tired old men who assemble in the club after a hard day cutting coupons."[28]

The rest of that first issue was typical of what would follow. Marjory MacMurchy, Willison's former women's editor at the *News* and later a colleague at the CRA, reviewed books. J.E. Middleton, a former staffer at the *News*, offered a page of light, humorous verse and chit-chat in "On The Side." Charles Eaton, once a *Globe* writer and a minister at Toronto's Bloor Street Baptist Church, was now an American congressman, and reported from Washington. Frank Beer pushed a buy-Canadian campaign, and an anonymous "English MP" covered the London political scene.

Advertisements were from prestige companies, often for prestige tastes. Canadian Pacific took a full page for its world tour package, the Robert Simpson Company trumpeted that its stores constituted "An International Exposition," and there were large stylish ads from T. Eaton Company, Good Year Tire, Canadian General Electric, British-American and Imperial Oil Companies, and the like. With a talented band of contributors, the wealthy advertisers, and the modest, controllable expenses of a monthly, Sir John had found in the twilight of his journalistic career a viable vehicle for his craft. Dafoe was pleased to hear from Frank Smith of the Montreal *Star* that "Sir John is pretty well insured against loss," and Willison himself happily told Sir Robert Borden after the first year of operation: "Success has been better than we hoped for." However conservative his views and the positions of the *Monthly* might be, he had long had his fill of partisanship in politics. "I have ceased to have any acute interest in any political party," he emphasized to Flavelle, "and feel that the most useful work I can do will be done without too close association with party...."[29]

He still had strong views on imperial relations, but, as he lamented to Geoffrey Dawson in 1925, "practically no political journal or political leader touches imperial questions except to warn against entanglement in Imperial and foreign policy." He speculated that most Canadians "want to remain and mean to remain in the Empire but they feel that the war has left them with obligations almost too heavy to be borne and that any movement towards even a common Imperial foreign policy means ultimately new obligations for Canadian taxpayers."

A year later, he conceded in the *Times* that the issues of an autonomous status and an independent foreign policy for Canada were "settled," but added: "There are also in history moments, which may never be exactly defined in codes or predetermined in any constitution, when the Empire must act as one in the face of all the world." He reinforced this point in the text he was developing for his biography of Parkin, where he acknowledged that there was now "no movement towards federation either in the Mother Country or in the Dominions" but he argued that the "Imperial spirit" that had captured Parkin — and, of course, himself — had "found its utmost expression in the common exertions and sacrifices of the armies of the Empire in the greatest crisis in human history" and that such an emotion would not die. He was remembering 1914–18 and places like Courcelette. He might have been predicting 1939–45.[30] He and other Canadians of his viewpoint had lost their fight for a vital *imperial* partnership with Britain, but there was as yet in Canada no evident appetite for abandoning a meaningful *connection* that still had emotional resonance and the potential to influence foreign and military policy in truly crisis times.

The years 1925 and 1926 saw two bitterly contested federal election campaigns. In the first, Mackenzie King's Liberals lost seats heavily outside Quebec and finished second to Arthur Meighen's Conservatives, but managed to continue to cling to office with the help of the Progressives. Before the second election, a brief Conservative minority took power because Governor General Lord Byng refused dissolution to King when his government was threatened by revelations about a customs scandal. But then the Tories were toppled in a Commons vote, and King went on to win a triumphant majority victory in 1926. Willison's comments on the rapidly changing political scene were necessarily non-partisan in the *Times*, and the monthly nature of his magazine tended to rule out quick judgments and predictions about a wildly turbulent and unpredictable political scene. Also, as he explained to Sir Campbell Stuart of the *Times* that year, he was loathe to join in what he described as the "incurable contempt" for Mackenzie King that was so common among his Toronto friends, "for one's judgment is worth nothing when one develops that kind of spirit." For his part, he thought King's personal standing in the country as a whole had "greatly improved" since he had taken power. On King, he told readers of the *Times* just before the election: "It is doubtful if either his friends or his opponents have ever fully realized with what skill, despite a suggestion of heaviness, he plays the great game of politics."

When the prime minister clung to office after losing so many seats in the 1925 election Sir John commented to Flavelle that King was "almost done no matter what may happen…." King's 1926 campaign attacks on Lord Byng for refusing him dissolution and granting power to the Conservatives he reported factually in the *Times* but privately damned as "irresponsible." But when King's majority victory was won, largely through attracting former Progressives and their voters to the Liberals, he recorded in the *Monthly* that the restored King government was "one of the best that has come into office since the first Laurier administration," especially as it was "nationally well balanced" from all parts of the country. "One has always thought," he remarked, "that Conservatives were too contemptuous of Mr. King's leadership."[31] Sir John had known Mackenzie King since he was a young student employee and family friend and long ago had measured his ample capabilities.

He never could really warm to Arthur Meighen. As he put it to his Australian friend, Sir Mark Sheldon, "his mind is purely destructive." In the 1925 election, he remarked to Joseph Flavelle that the Conservative leader's failure to attract capable new candidates was "pitiful" and the party's organization was "badly handled." When Meighen tried after that campaign to win support in Quebec by pledging that if he were in power and war broke out involving the Empire, he would seek parliamentary and electoral approval before sending Canadian troops overseas, Sir John wrote in the *Times* that such a pledge was "unacceptable to the great body of English-speaking Conservatives." He told Flavelle that the objective was worthwhile but the means "impracticable and impossible." To Geoffrey Dawson he lamented Meighen's "temper, unsteadiness and … impulsive radicalism." Later, after Meighen's heavy losses to King in Ontario and the West in 1926, he told Dawson that the Conservative leader had been "hopelessly out-generalled" by King.[32]

In his own personal life there was occasion for renewed happiness. On Saturday, April 10, 1926, surprising even his closest friends, he married again, to Marjory MacMurchy, a close associate at the *Globe*, the *News*, with the CRA, and in the *Monthly*. She was a leading feminist and author of *The Woman – Bless Her* (1916), *The Canadian Girl at Work* (1919), and *The Child's House* (1923). "We are old friends," he related to Geoffrey Dawson from his honeymoon hotel in Atlantic City, New Jersey. Sir Robert Borden and Mackenzie King were only two of the many who wired and wrote congratulations. His friend Dr. Herbert Bruce praised Marjory as "such a charming clever woman," probably touching correctly on the combination of attributes that had attracted Sir John.[33] No doubt he believed he had much to be thankful for, with a new marital happiness and an enjoyable, manageable editorial role at last.

That peace and contentment did not last very long. On the night of the September 1926 federal election, he felt for the first time a pain in his right side. Minor to begin with, it would not go away. By March 1927, he was suffering terribly, entering the Toronto General Hospital at month's end. The diagnosis, after a multitude of tests and X-rays, was that he was suffering from pressure on the sciatic nerve in his hip. He was discharged in mid-April with the assurance of his doctors that he would be, as he happily wrote Geoffrey Dawson, "as well as ever in the near future." Through all but his two hospital weeks he had kept up with his *Times* and *Monthly* responsibilities. Page by painful page, he struggled too to complete the Parkin biography. By late February he had written all but five thousand of the 75,000 words he had set as his target, and he had fought through March to finish it off, without quite succeeding. Now, home once more at 10 Elmsley Place, he tried again, but it was no use.

He had thirteen of sixteen chapters done and extensive notes existed for the others, but the pain would let him write no more. He went back to the doctors, and on April 28 an X-ray showed for the first time a cancerous growth on the hipbone socket. Even more shocking was a larger malignancy in his shoulder area, which had not yet given him any trouble. He re-entered the Toronto General to begin treatments, but over the following month he only grew steadily weaker. On May 27, with Lady Marjory, Walter, and his niece Hazel at his bedside, he died.

To the end of consciousness he said he would recover. He was almost halfway through his seventy-first year. His published words just a few months earlier, as he had looked back on Laurier's passing, may be said to describe superbly his own as well: "He died as he had lived with serenity and dignity. He had often said that he could think of nothing more pitiful than an old age encumbered by physical debility and turning towards mental decay. When he was spared that a prayer was answered." His long-time Liberal friend John Dafoe perhaps had those very lines in mind in his emotional Manitoba *Free Press* obituary: "Sir John lived the full term of years as fixed by the Psalmist; but there was nothing about him which suggested age or infirmity; and his death will bring to his friends a sense of powers cut off too soon and a race that fell short of its goal."[34]

The funeral was at his parish church, St. Paul's Anglican, Bloor Street, three days later. His old friend Canon Henry Cody took the service and briefly sketched the story of Sir John's life, influence, and ideals to the overflowing congregation before he was interred beside Lady Rachel at Mount Pleasant Cemetery. A year later a charming stained-glass window to his memory was unveiled at the church, the gift of thirty Torontonians eminent in the press, politics, and business. There was the fitting depiction of a printing press, and an inscription he would have loved:

> *The Times*
> *1785*
> *In honoured memory of Sir John Willison, Kt.*
> *Journalist, Publicist, Patriot. Was erected*
> *By some of his friends in 1928*
> *He was a very perfect gentle knight.*[35]

Of course, there had been nothing "perfect" about his career. He had achieved a towering success as a political journalist and counsellor through his first quarter-century of work. By 1905 he was, as B.K. Sandwell of *Saturday Night* accurately would judge, "by far the most influential English-speaking journalist in Canada and had been so for a number of years." He had saved the *Globe* and, astonishingly, had come very near to making Tory Protestant Ontario a Laurierite Liberal province. He had been a major influence in giving the Liberals at least a moderate imperialist reputation that was politically helpful. It was during this time too that he led a largely successful fight for respectable standards of fairness and professionalism within party journalism.[36]

His early views he once described as those of "a democrat, a free trader and a moderate social radical," but long before he changed party colours he became philosophically conservative — particularly in a firm protectionism and a romantic imperialism very much in tune with the interests, values, and attitudes of the Toronto milieu he had made his own. That kind of evolution came to differentiate him dramatically from a Liberal party which came to support a more flexible view on tariff policy and an antagonism to imperialist naval and conscriptionist policies. That no doubt helped his anti-protectionist and anti-imperialist friend John Dafoe to muse privately several years after his death, when the Liberal party's triumphant dominance of Canadian politics seemed virtually insurmountable, that the later Willison could be seen as "one of our most distinguished failures...."

For his part, Mackenzie King, remembering Laurier's travails with Willison and in spite of his own generally harmonious relationship with him, told his diary that the Toronto man had been "a tory snob in his behaviour, tho' he had within him qualities that might have made him a truly great man."[37] Not being a consistently loyal Liberal could leave a man vulnerable to much criticism in some quarters. As well, there doubtless were undeviating Tories who could not understand his youthful radical Liberalism, his gradual disillusionment with Sir Robert Borden and post-1918 Unionism and Conservatism, and his continuing comfortableness with Liberal friends and networks.

Such criticisms would not have surprised Willison. He had seen the often self-serving and hypocritical behaviour of both major parties.

When he had turned against the federal Liberals, it was not only because of separate schools for Alberta and Saskatchewan but also because he had found them in office to be disturbingly laissez-faire on social and transportation issues and as self-serving as their Tory predecessors on patronage and greed. He had had just reason to damn the provincial Liberals for their lack of vision for the social needs of industrial society and their employment of electoral fraud. He had embraced the federal Conservatives as a potential governing alternative and had done much to contribute creatively to their historic national victory in 1911 through bringing them into alliance with rebel Liberals over the Reciprocity issue. He had found a strong progressive commonality in policy terms with successive Conservative governments at Queen's Park. The war and needing to see it through successfully had brought him to a Unionist pro-conscriptionist allegiance in 1917, even as he had been unable to find financial viability for the *News* in the unforgiving economics of that time. But it had not taken him long to see the Borden coalition in Ottawa as an ineffectual post-war instrument for national reconstruction. His frustration after 1918 as an imperialist was directed at all the national parties and their leaders. More generally, he made clear to his Liberal Unionist friend Newton Rowell in 1919 just how far his weariness with traditional partisan definitions and loyalties had progressed: "Of course, I am not impressed by the notion that the word 'Liberal,' as distinguished from 'Conservative,' has any meaning in Canada. Laurier was a Tory. Borden is a Liberal. I do agree with you however that 'Conservative' is not a good name for this country."[38]

Willison's career was astonishingly creative, triumphal, and influential over more than four decades. In 1917 he added a major influential role in the construction of Union Government and the winning of the 1917 election for the Unionists to his previous key political advisory and political journalistic contributions to the epochal Laurier Liberal and Borden Conservative victories in 1896 and 1911.

Undoubtedly, the last decade of his career was somewhat frustrating for him. Little by little, as he failed to achieve financial viability for the *News*, as his relationship and sense of common purpose with Sir Robert Borden soured, as he became a publicist for pay, and as Canadians largely abandoned the key tenets of his imperialist faith, he drifted away from centre stage in Canadian life. At the end, he was, as the irreverent Augustus Bridle put it, "the clear thinking high priest of the elect and the inner temple." He remained until his death, in Arthur Colquhoun's words, "a formidable antagonist and a pillar of strength in the storm. So men of all sorts sought his counsel in an emergency, trusting to his balanced judgment, his unique experience and his incorruptible integrity."[39] No other Canadian political journalist or politician ever has had so prolonged an insider involvement with and perspective on both major political parties and their key leaders. That the leaders involved were arguably three of the four most significant of all the nation's prime ministers, Laurier, Borden, and Mackenzie King, reinforces the point. That he was able to measure the three of them against what he had been able to observe directly of the fourth — Macdonald — only makes his insights even more historically valuable.

At the end, with *Willison's Monthly*, he found the journalistic vehicle and market that perfectly suited the viewpoints and sensibility that had come to be his. Its evident success by 1927 likely would have carried on and been reinforced if he had been spared for more years of vitality and creativity. It was undeniable too that through his nineteen years with his beloved *Times* he had interpreted brilliantly the Canada he knew so well and loved so intensely to the British elites. The charm and history he left behind in his *Laurier* and *Reminiscences* constituted a major literary and scholarly achievement.

Controversial, sometimes tragic and certainly flawed, his career was yet that of a very considerable Canadian, and it touched and reflected much of the story of Canada's developing nationhood in the later nineteenth and early twentieth centuries. His ability to forge and sustain close and trusting friendships and intellectual relationships across major partisan and ideological divides had contributed enormously to his impact and influence on his times. In John Dafoe's admiring obituary he commented that Sir John had

> passed across the whole political stage — from combative radicalism to serene acceptance of the Conservative scheme of things, without losing a friend or raising a single doubt in the mind of a single friend of his

sincerity and honesty of purpose. That is to say, he was an honest man with a generous and kindly mind, bound to follow where the light seemed to lead him, but capable of appreciating the point and honouring the motives of those who, unable to travel with him, took other roads.

In 1924, the *Dalhousie Review* had published his poem "The Alien." Many details did not match his own life, but others did — the rural poverty of boyhood, the pioneer schoolhouse of youth, the books that liberated him from "the stark loneliness of fallow minds," the "curious ease and certainty" of his rise to prominence, and, just perhaps at least the core of the final verse:

> *But through the great adventure he was still*
> *As lonely as when from his father's door*
> *He saw the rugged fields fade into night;*
> *As lonely as the shaft that at the cross road*
> *Stands in memory of a youth obscure,*
> *Who challenged fate and won the heights and died.*[40]

Notes

FOREWORD

1. J.S. Willison, *Reminiscences Political and Personal* (Toronto: McClelland & Stewart, 1919), 188–89.

CHAPTER ONE

1. *Illustrated Historical Atlas of the County of Huron* (Toronto, 1897), xviii; R.W. Hermon, *New Map of the County of Huron* (Toronto, 1862); OA, WP, W.J. Jarrott to Lady MW, February 3, 1928 and Lady MW memoir, 1; UWOL, Clerk of the Peace, Huron County, *Voter Lists: Stanley Twp.*, Box 1, 1860, no. 594; *County of Huron Gazeteer and General Business Directory for 1863-'64* (Ingersoll, 1863), 89; and, JSW, *Reminiscences Political and Personal* (Toronto, 1919), 9.

2. OA, Canada, *Census Returns, 1871*, Huron County, Stanley Township, District 2, page 5; Lady MW memoir, page 1; AO, Province of Canada, *Census Returns, 1861*, Huron County, Stanley Twp., 4, Folio 48; WP, J.E. Elliott to F.D. L, Smith, June 27, 1932; *Reminiscences*, page 9; interviews with Mrs. M. Madge and Mr. Jack Schwartz, Hillsgreen, September 1979.

3. *Census Returns, 1871*, *op.cit.*; Lady MW memoir, 21–22; AO, WP, W.J. Jarrott to Lady MW, September 19, 1927; JSW, "The Spirit of Canada," in *Partners in Peace: The Dominion, The Empire and The Republic* (Toronto, 1923), 85–86; and, Hillsgreen School Register (fragment) in possession of Mrs. M. Madge, listing William Willison as a pupil.

4. *Reminiscences*, 9–10; Observer, "Swimming," *Globe*, August 3, 1889, 16.

5. Observer, "Sugaring Off," *Globe*, May 11, 1889.

6. Observer, "The Hired Man," *Globe*, September 28, 1889.

7. OA, WP, Mrs. Mary Richards to Lady MW, n.d., reprinted in Lady MW memoir, 37; *Reminiscences*, 21–23; A.H.U. Colquhoun, *Press, Politics and People: The Life and Letters of Sir John Willison, Journalist and Correspondent of THE TIMES* (Toronto, 1935), 6.

8. *Census Returns, 1871, op. cit.*; Lady MW memoir, 22–25; and LAC, WP, vol.117, a fragment of autobiography, n.d.

9. *Reminiscences*, 13–15.

10. "Observations," *Globe*, June 28, 1888.

11. *Reminiscences*, 24–27, 33–34; OA, Levi Mackey to Lady MW, January 31, 1928 and J.E. Middleton to Lady MW, n.d.

12. Lady MW memoir, "Notes"; OA, Levi Mackey to Lady MW, January 31, 1928; Irven McLean and Beatrice McLean, *Greenwood Through the Years* (n.p., 1960), 7, 26.

13. *Reminiscences*, 41–42; OA, WP, Mackey to Lady MW, January 31, 1928 and Lady MW memoir, 27.

14. Lady MW memoir, 42–43; LAC, WP, John A. Love to JSW, March 18, 1880.

15. *Reminiscences*, 52–54.

16. Lady MW memoir, 25–26, 11 and 16; OA, Lady MW memorandum on a trip to Tiverton in 1931; W.S. Wallace, ed., *The Macmillan Dictionary of Canadian Biography* (3rd edition, Toronto, 1963), 803; *Reminiscences*, 55; *Globe*, September 10, 1887.

17. WP, John Cameron to JSW, May 31 and October 24, 1881.

18. *Reminiscences*, 56; WP, Cameron to JSW, October 24, 1881 and Rev. N.D. McKinnon to JSW, April 6, 1904.

19. JSW, "The Spirit of Canada," in *Partners in Peace*, 85–86; Lady MW memoir, 21–22.

CHAPTER TWO

1. *Reminiscences*, 56–58; London *Advertiser*, November 5, 1881.

2. *Reminiscences*, 58–59; *Advertiser*, March 24, 1882.

3. *Reminiscences*, 89.

4. *Reminiscences*, 89; WP, agreement between Cameron and Willison, November 23, 1883; Lady MW memoir, 29.

5. J.M.S, Careless, *Brown of the Globe*, II (Toronto, 1963), 372–73; H. Charlesworth and M.O. Hammond, *History of the Globe*, incomplete manuscript in the possession of the Toronto *Globe and Mail*, 111–30; *Reminiscences*, 81.

6. Arthur Wallis, "The Press of Ontario," in J.R. Bone, J.T. Clark et. al., *A History of Canadian Journalism* (Toronto, 1908), 169–71; *N.W. Ayer and Son's*

American Newspaper Annual, 1884 (Philadephia, 1884), 362; R. Harkness, *J.E. Atkinson of the Star* (Toronto, 1963), 28.

7. *The Toronto City Directory for 1883* (Toronto, 1883), 823–24; H.J. Morgan, ed., *The Dominion Annual Register and Review, 1883* (Toronto, 1884), 217.

8. W.S. Wallace, ed., *Macmillan Dictionary of Canadian Biography*, 195, 284, 474,636, 686.

9. *Reminiscences*, 111.

10. *Globe*, January31, 1884, "Assembly Notes."

11. *Globe*, March 21, 1884.

12. *Globe*, July 23 and September 1, 1884.

13. *Globe*, September 5, 8, 17, and 18, 1884.

14. *Globe*, February 24, 1885; DLQU, W.D. Gregory Papers, autobiography, 87–88.

15. Lady MW memoir, 11–13; Lady MW Tiverton memorandum.

16. *The Toronto City Directory for 1887* (Toronto, 1887), 947.

17. *Globe*, October 6, 1885.

18. *Globe*, October 13, August 31, September 14 and 17, 1885.

19. *Globe*, January 22, 1897, 22.

20. *Globe*, November 2, 1889.

21. *Globe*, November 24 and December 9, 1885, and January 20, 1886.

22. *Reminiscences*, 113; Christopher Andreae, *Lines of Country: Atlas of Railway and Waterway History in Canada* (Erin, 1997), 150ff.

23. *Globe*, March 18, 1886.

24. R. Cook, *The Politics of John W. Dafoe and the Free Press* (Toronto, 1963); J.W. Dafoe, *Laurier: A Study in Canadian Politics* (Toronto, originally 1922), page 27 of the 1963 edition.

25. Cited, O.D. Skelton, *Life and Letters of Sir Wilfrid Laurier,* Volume I, *1841–1896* (Toronto, 1921), page 95 of the 1965 edition.

26. Dafoe, *op.cit.*, 24.

27. U. Barthe, *Wilfrid Laurier on the Platform* (Quebec, 1890), 303ff.

28. W.D. Gregory autobiography, 96; J.S. Willison, *Sir Wilfrid Laurier and the Liberal Party* I (Toronto, 1903), 467–68.

29. Willison, *Laurier* I, 349.

30. *Reminiscences*, 113–20; Dafoe, *Laurier*, 27; L. LaPierre, *Sir Wilfrid Laurier and the Romance of Canada* (Toronto, 1996), 118–19; *Macmillan Dictionary of Canadian Biography* (Toronto, 1963), 101, 150, 670, 794.

31. A.HU.C. [Colquhoun], The New Era of the Toronto Globe," *The Printer and Publisher* (July 1895), 8; *Reminiscences*, 123; *Globe*, June 4, 1887, "Gallery Notes."

32. *Reminiscences*, 188–89.

33. OA, Blake Papers, Blake to M.P's (circular), March 5, 1887; Margaret A. Banks, "The Change in the Liberal Leadership, 1887," *CHR*, XXXVIII (June 1957), 110–15; Blake Papers, Blake to M.P.s, March 28, 1887.

34. *Globe*, March 17, 1887.
35. *Reminiscences*, 160.
36. *Globe*, "Gallery Notes" June 8, 1887.
37. *Globe*, June 24, 1887.
38. *Globe*, February 22, 1888.
39. *Reminiscences*, 162.
40. D.G. Creighton, *John A. Macdonald* II (Toronto, 1955), 452, 454.
41. e.g., *Globe*, August 31, 1885, June 12, 1886.
42. Blake Papers, Cameron to Blake, January 28, 1887.
43. *Globe*, March 3, 1887.
44. Blake Papers, WL to Blake, June 30 and July 14, 1887; LAC, Laurier Papers (LP),Cartwright to WL, July 8, 26 and August 12, 1887.
45. *Globe*, October 4 and 18, November 29, 1887, and January 17, 1888.
46. *Globe*, February 29 and April 6, 1888.
47. *Globe*, April 6, 1888, "From the Capital."
48. *University of Toronto, Roll of Service, 1914–1918* (Toronto, 1921), 149; E.Q.V., "Canadian Celebrities, No. XXXIX, Mr. J.S. Willison," *Canadian Magazine*, XX, No. 3 (June 1903), 222–24.
49. LP, JSW to WL, July 19, 1888.
50. *Globe*, August 4 and 29, 1888; *Reminiscences*, 164.
51. LP, JSW to WL, September 6, 1888.
52. *Globe*, October 12, 1888.
53. *Globe*, November 15, 1888.
54. *Globe*, November 26, 1888, "Observations."
55. *Globe*, January 15, 1889.
56. *Mail*, March 30, 1889.
57. Blake Papers, Thomson to Blake, March 18, 1889, Jaffray to Blake, March 10, 1889 and Blake to Jaffray, March 19, 1889 (copy).
58. *Globe*, June 30, 1890; Harkness, *Atkinson*, 10.
59. A.H. Young, *The Roll of Pupils of Upper Canada College, Toronto, January 1830 to June 1916* (Kingston, 1917), 629; Lady MW memoir, 13–16.
60. *Reminiscences*, 170–71.
61. *Globe*, February 12 and May 1, 1889.
62. LP, JSW to WL, April 26 and June 17, 1889.
63. WP, Canon A.W. MacNab to JSW, n.d., but by context, 1902.
64. *Globe*, August 24, 1889, "Observations."
65. LP, JSW to WL, June 17 and July 16, 1889.
66. *Ibid.*, Edgar to WL, July 30, 1889, Preston to WL, August 1, 1889 and Cartwright to WL, August 19, 1889.
67. *Reminiscences*, 169.
68. *Globe*, October 1, 1889; *Reminiscences*, 170–74.

69. *Reminiscences*, 170–71.

70. Hammond and Charlesworth, *History of the Globe*, 167–68; OA, J.D. Edgar Papers, Cartwright to Edgar, August 9, 1886; LP, Cartwright to WL, August 8, 1889; Edgar Papers, Edgar to Cartwright, November 29, 1889.

71. Cartwright Papers, Preston to Cartwright, November 20, 1889; *Reminiscences*, 201; WP, WL to JSW, June 26, 1890.

72. *Reminiscences*, 202–05.

73. LP, JSW to WL, April 17, 1890.

74. LP, JSW to WL, May 5, 1890.

75. *Globe*, June 7, 12, 14, and 16, 1890.

76. WP, White to JSW, June 19, 1890.

77. WP, Dryden to JSW, June 9, 1890; LP, Blake to WL, June 15, 1890; WP, WL to JSW, June 26, 1890.

78. *Globe*, June 17, 1890; *Reminiscences*, 204–06.

79. LP, JSW to WL, June 23, 1890; WP, JSW to WL, June 26, 1890 (copy).

CHAPTER THREE

1. *Saturday Night*, July 5, 1890.

2. WP, WL to JSW, June 18, 1890.

3. LP, JSW to WL, June 23, 1890; WP, WL to JSW, June 26, 1890.

4. WP, WL to JSW, June 26, 1890; LP, JSW to WL, June 30, 1890.

5. *Globe*, July 3, 1890; LP, JSW to WL, July 9, 1890.

6. W.T.R. Preston, *My Generation of Politics and Politicians* (Toronto, 1927), 134–37; LP, Preston to WL, July 11, 1890.

7. LP, Cartwright to WL, July 7 and 10, 1890; *L'Électeur*, July 7, 1890; *Globe*, July 17, 1890.

8. Toronto *Empire*, February 18, 1891.

9. *Reminiscences*, 209. See also Carman Cumming, *Secret Craft: The Journalism of Edward Farrer* (Toronto, 1992), 1–11.

10. *Globe*, February 18, 1891.

11. *Reminiscences*, 228; Blake Papers, Blake to D.B. Simpson, January 28, 1891 (copy); WP, Blake to JSW, Janurary 28, 1891.

12. UTL, John Charlton Papers, Diary, April 14, 1892; Blake Papers, JSW to Blake, January 28, 1891; *Reminiscences*, 230–33.

13. Blake Papers, WL to Blake, February 2, 1891.

14. J. Dafoe, "Review Article: Press, Politics and People," *CHR*, XVII (March 1936), 61; Blake Papers, JSW to Blake, February 12, 1891.

15. P. Magnus, *Gladstone* (London, 1963), 269–73.

16. LP, JSW to WL, March 11, 1891.

17. *Globe*, March 6, 1891.

18. Cited, *Globe*, March 12, 1891; Blake Papers, Blake to WL, July 24, 1891 (copy).

19. *Reminiscences*, 239–44.
20. *Globe*, June 9 and 8, 1891.
21. JSW, *Sir Wilfrid Laurier and the Liberal Party* (Toronto, 1903), I, 27.
22. *Globe*, August 1, 1891.
23. *Globe*, August 1, 6, and 17, 1891; *L'Électeur*, August 10, 1891; *Globe*, October 27, 1891.
24. *Reminiscences*, 217–18; Lady MW memoir, 27.
25. LP, JSW to WL, October 29, 1891 and Gregory to WL, November 11, 1891.
26. *Globe*, March 9, 1892; LP, Tarte to WL, February 8, 1892.
27. *Globe*, February 6, 1892; *Le Canadien*, January 26, 1892.
28. *Globe*, September 26 and December 14, 1891.
29. *Ibid.*, October 5 and 7 and November 21, 1891.
30. Ibid., December 14, 1891.
31. LP, Mowat to WL, December 26 and 31, 1891.
32. Gregory autobiography, p. 105.
33. Blake Papers, JSW to Blake, December 22, 1891.
34. *Reminiscences*, 244.
35. *Grip*, March 26, 1892.
36. *Globe*, April 26, 1892.
37. *Globe*, July 27, 1892; *Macmillan D.C.B., op. cit.*, 535.
38. LP, Smith to WL, August 2, 1892, JSW to WL, August 4 and September 2, 1892, and Farrer to WL, August 16, 1892.
39. LP, JSW to WL, August 4, 1892.
40. *Globe*, August 8 and 10, 1892.
41. *Globe*, March 2, 1891, October 31, and November 26, 1892; LP, Power to WL, December 9, 1892; OL-CU, Goldwin Smith Papers, Smith to J.H. Wilson, December 1, 1892 (copy).
42. LP, JSW to WL, December 6, 1892.
43. *Ibid.*
44. *Globe*, March 27, 28, and May 12, 1893.
45. *Official Report of the Liberal Convention* (Toronto, 1893), 71, 81._
46. *Globe*, September 13, 1890.
47. Hammond and Charlesworth, *History of the Globe*, 154, 175: Macmillan *D.C.B.*, 221, 413, 812; H. Charlesworth, *Candid Chronicles: Leaves from the Note Book of a Canadian* Journalist (Toronto, 1925), 135–75.
48. Toronto *Star*, September 28, 1927, cited, Colquhoun, *Press, Politics and People*, 21–2.

CHAPTER FOUR

1. *Statutes of Canada*, 38 Vict., C-49, S-11, 110; 33 Vict., c-3, S-22.
2. C.B. Sissons, *Church and State in Canadian Education* (Toronto, 1959), 256–58.

3. *Mail*, July 15, 1889; *Globe*, August 1, 1889; *Empire*, August 7, 1889.

4. *Manitoba Statutes*, 53 Vict., C-38, S-178ff; W.L. Morton, *Manitoba: A History* (Toronto, 1957), 247–48.

5. Canada, Parliament, *Sessional Papers*, 1893, no. 332; 1895, no. 20.

6. LP, Cartwright to WL, August 9, 1889.

7. LAC, U. Barthe Papers, WL to Barthe, August 17, 1889.

8. H.C. *Debates*, March 6, 1893, 1878ff.

9. LP, WL to McDonnell, July 14, 1893 (copy).

10. *Le Canadien*, January 17 and July 1, 1892.

11. *Globe*, February 3, 1891, March 21, and August 1, 1892, July 14, 1893.

12. LP, JSW to WL, April 1, 1895; WP, WL to JSW, April 9, 1895.

13. LP, Tarte to WL, October 11, 1893 and January 17, 1894.

14. *Globe*, January 22, 1894; LP, JSW to WL, January 29, 1894.

15. *Globe*, September 20, 1893, June 25, July 17, August 8, 11, 20, and September 14, 1894.

16. WP, Ross to WL, February 27, 1895 (copy) and WL to Ross, March 2, 1895 (copy).

17. WP, JSW to WL, January 7, 1895 (copy).

18. *Globe*, January 7, 1895.

19. *Mail and Empire*, March 8, 1895.

20. WP, JSW to WL, March 5, 1895 (copy); *Globe*, March 4, 1895.

21. WP, WL to JSW, March 7, 1895 (copy).

22. LP, Mills to WL, March 18, 1895; *Reminiscences*, 248; WP, Grant to JSW, March 18, 1895; *Globe*, March 1 and 11, 1895.

23. *Sessional Papers*, 1895, no. 20, 189.

24. Dafoe, *Laurier*, 36.

25. *Globe*, March 23, 1895.

26. LP, JSW to WL, March 22, 1895.

27. *Ibid.*, WL to C. Hyman, March 28, 1895 (copy).

28. WP, WL to JSW, March 30, 1895.

29. WP, JSW to WL, April 1, 1895 (copy).

30. WP, WL to JSW, April 9, 1895.

31. LP, WL to Anglin, April 2, 1895 (copy); WP, JSW to WL, April 1, 1895 (copy).

32. WP, WL to JSW, May 6, 1895.

33. Globe, April 20, 1895.

34. *Sessional Papers*, 1895, no. 20; *Globe*, June 15, 1895.

35. J.T. Saywell, "Introduction," to *The Canadian Journal of Lady Aberdeen* (Toronto, 1960), li–liii.

36. *Orange Sentinel*, July 13, 1895; *Mail and Empire*, July 31, 1895.

37. LP, JSW to WL, July 7, 1895.

38. *Globe*, July 17, 1895.

39. WP, WL to JSW, July 17, 1895.

40. LP, JSW to WL, July 20, [1895], misfiled with 1900 correspondence, 47619–624.

41. WP, WL to JSW, July 24, 1895.

42. WP, Lavergne to JSW, July 4, 1895.

43. Charlton Papers, autobiography, 739; Dafoe, *Laurier*, 36.

44. *Globe*, July 20, September 5, 10, 12, 18, 25, 28, and October 9, 1895; *Le Cultivateur*, October 26, 1895.

45. WP, WL to JSW, December 26, 1895; LP, JSW to WL, December 27 and 29, 1895.

46. WP, WL to JSW, December 30, 1895.

47. Saywell, "Introduction," lix–lxv; *Globe*, January 16, 1896.

48. Commons, *Bills*, 1896, Bill 58; *Globe*, January 16, 1896.

49. House of Commons, *Debates*, March 3, 1896, 2736ff and March 20, 1896, 4250–251.

50. L.J.L. LaPierre, *Politics, Race and Religion in French Canada: Joseph Israel Tarte* (unpublished Ph.D. thesis, University of Toronto, 1962), 301, 338.

51. WP, Tarte to JSW, May 17, 1896; WL to JSW, May 25, 1896.

52. *Globe*, May 18, 21, and June 6, 1896.

53. *Globe*, especially the issues of May 21, 23, 26, 29, 30, and June 4, 11, and 19, 1896.

54. *Globe*, January 1, February 1, April 1, July 1, 1896, and January 1, 1897; *American Newspaper Directory, September 1897* (New York, 1897), 972; OA, WP, J.E. Middleton to Lady MW, October 16, 1928; *Globe*, June 13, 1896.

55. Saywell, "Introduction," lxxvi; J.M. Beck, *Pendulum of Power: Canada's Federal Elections* (Scarborough, 1968), 86; LP, A. Smith to WL, June 23, 1896 and JSW to WL, June 25, 1896; WP, WL to JSW, June 29, 1896.

56. *Globe*, June 24 and 25, 1896; WP, Brown to JSW, June 27, 189, McPherson to JSW, June 24, 1896; LP, Anglin to WL, June 25, 1896; and WP, Mrs. O'Brien to JSW, June 28, 1896.

57. *Sessional Papers*, 1897, no. 35, 2; *Manitoba Statutes*, 60 Vict., C-26.

58. *Globe*, November 21, 1896.

59. WP, JSW to Dafoe, March 7, 1923 (copy) and WL to JSW, April 9, 1895.

CHAPTER FIVE

1. LP, WL to JSW, January 7, 1895.

2. Average daily circulation as of January 1, 1895 was 20,075; as of July 1, 1896, it was 33,100; as of January 1, 1897, with the abnormal sales of election times over, it was 29,091.

3. WP, Caswell to JSW, July 24, 1896, Patteson to JSW, December 9, 1895 and Cameron to JSW, November 12, 1896.

4. *Ibid.*, Wilson to JSW, August 26, 1889 and Cameron to JSW, August 29, 1889, Edgar to JSW, June 13, 1895; *Macmillan D.C.B.*, 213; WP, Lavergne to JSW, June 24, July 22, and August 4, 1895 and WL to JSW, July 29, 1895.

5. *Globe*, January 7, 1895.

6. Lady MW memoir, interview with R.H. Coats, 31.

7. *Ibid.*, 66.

8. R.M. Dawson, *William Lyon Mackenzie King: A Political Biography, I, 1874–1923* (Toronto, 1958), 31, 51–53; Charlotte Gray, *The Life and Times of Isabel Mackenzie King* (Toronto, 1997), 97; LAC, W.L.M. King Papers, Harper to King, November 21, 1895; LAC, W.L.M. King Diary, May 7, August 16, and July 31, 1896; *Globe*, January 16, 1897, and November 19, 1898.

9. J. Mavor, "Goldwin Smith," *MacLean's Magazine*, XXXIV (March 1921), 12–13, 47–49; National Club, membership records; F. Yeigh, "Goldwin Smith and the Round Table Club," *Willison's Monthly*, III (January 1928), 302–11; G.P. de T. Glazebrook, *Sir Edmund Walker* (London, 1933), 55–56; *Macmillan D.C.B.*, 30, 306, 330, 335, 778, and 815.

10. C.F. Klinck, *Wilfrid Campbell: A Study in Late Provincial Victorianism* (Toronto, 1942), 49; C.Y. Connor, *Archibald Lampman: Canadian Poet of Nature* (Montreal, 1929), 113–14: *Globe*, January 18, 1892.

11. WP, Johnson to JSW, August 20, 1895 and Roberts to JSW, January 2, 1897.

12. WP, Parker to JSW, December 20, 1896, February 19 and June 8, 1897; *Globe*, April 7, 1896, 1 and 4.

13. Speech to Canadian Club, Boston, December 4, 1905, cited Toronto *News*, December 4, 1905.

14. *Globe*, December 3, 1892.

15. WP, JSW to Cleveland, n.d., but by context, June 1892.

16. A.E. Campbell, *Great Britain and the United States, 1895–1903* (London, 1960), 11–47.

17. *Globe*, December 23, 1895, December 8, 1896, 2.

18. *Globe*, December 8, 1896, 2; *Official Report of the Liberal Convention* (Toronto, 1893), 71, 81.

19. JSW, "A Survey: Position of Affairs and the Capital," *Globe*, June 11, 1895, 1–2.

20. G.M. Grant, *Ocean to Ocean: Sanford Fleming's Expedition through Canada in 1872* (revised edition, Toronto, 1925), 410–11.

21. Goldwin Smith Papers, Grant to Smith, January 17, 1896.

22. cited, W.L. Grant and C.F. Hamilton, *Principal Grant* (Toronto, 1904), 353–54, 359.

23. *Globe*, May 23, 1894.

24. cited, Grant and Hamilton, 352–53, 365–67.

25. WP, Grant to JSW, July 26, 1895.

26. *Globe*, September 5, 12, 18, 21, and 25, 1895. Editorial reaction is in the issues of September 5 and 18.

27. *Reminiscences*, 338–39; LP, JSW to WL, December 29, 1895.

28. cited, Grant and Hamilton, 349–50; *Globe*, May 17, 1902.

29. G.T. Denison, *The Struggle for Imperial Unity* (Toronto, 1909), 156–93; *Empire*, October 30, 1888.

30. Denison, 163–64; LAC, Denison Papers, Denison to Salisbury, Dec 19, 1891, May 7, 1892, August 12, 1893, and December 14, 1894 (copies)

31. Denison Papers, Colquhoun to Denison, June 16, 1896, Denison to WL, February 1, 1896 (copy), Denison to Salisbury, May 22, 1896 (copy) and Diary, May 25, 1896.

32. Denison, p. 219; Denison Papers, Mowat to Denison, May 22, 1896 and Diary, May 25, 1896.

33. WP, JSW to Sifton, August 17, 1896 (copy).

34. A.H.U. Colquhoun, "The New Era of the Toronto Globe," *The Printer and Publisher* (July, 1895), 8.

35. *Globe*, December 8, 1896, 1; Denison Papers, Denison to Salisbury, December 15, 1896 (copy).

36. WP, JSW to Van Horne, December 15, 1895 (copy).

37. WP, Van Horne to D. McNicoll, October 5, 1895 (copy) and A.M. Burgess to JSW, October 16, 1895.

38. *The Saturday Globe*, October 19, 1895, 1–4.

39. Lady MW memoir, 13–17, 29, 38, 90–91, 121; King Diary, August 26, 1896.

CHAPTER SIX

1. LP, JSW to WL, November 29,1894; *Globe*, June 3 and 19, 1896.

2. LP, JSW to WL, June 25, 1896; WP, MacLean to JSW, July 30, 1896.

3. LP, JSW to WL, November 3, 1896.

4. *Globe*, December 19, 1896.

5. *Reminiscences*, 299–300.

6. LAC, Pope Papers, Diary, April 26, 1897; *Globe*, April 26, 1897.

7. *Times*, April 28, 1897; Denison Papers, Salisbury to Denison, May 22, 1897; *Globe*, May 7, 1897.

8. LAC, Rodolphe Lemieux papers, WL to Lemieux, December 1, 1892 (author's translation); *Times*, June 14, 1897, 4–5; cited, LP, WL to Ernest Pacaud, April 12, 1900 (copy).

9. *Globe*, December 1, 1897, 1.

10. *Globe*, August 9, 1897.

11. LP, Smith to WL, May 30, 1896; Smith Papers, Smith to J.H. Wilson, July 15, 1897 (copy).

12. *Globe*, August 9, 1897; LP, JSW to WL, May 10, 1897; Colquhoun, *Willison*, 55–56.

13. *Globe*, April 24 1902, p. 4; WP, Atkinson to JSW, October 28, 1897.

14. JSW, "Temples and Monuments," *Globe*, October 23, 1897, 18.

15. JSW, The New Imperialism," *Globe*, October 4, 1897, 18.

16. JSW, "Canada and Laurier," *Globe*, October 13, 1897, 4.
17. JSW, "Canadian Affairs in London," *Globe*, October 15, 1897, 4.
18. WP, Sifton to JSW, July 11, 1897.
19. JSW, "Lessons from the Old World," *Globe*, October 30, 1897, 18.
20. JSW, "Liberalism and Labor," *Globe*, October 8, 1897, 4.
21. WP, Denton to JSW, October 19, 1897, Wilson to JSW, October 24, 1897 and Parker to JSW, November 11, 1897; Colquhoun, *Willison*, 55–56.
22. JSW, "Lessons from the New World," *Globe*, October 30, 1897, 18; *Globe*, November1, 1897.
23. *Globe*, May 7, April 20 and June 2, 1898.
24. *Ibid.*, June 3 and 22, 1898.
25. WP, WL to JSW, July 13, 1898; LP, JSW to WL, July 25, 1898.
26. LP, JSW to WL, December 15, 1898 and January 16, 1899; WP, WL to JSW, January 10, 1899; Lady MW memoir, 116.
27. JSW, "Relations between Britain and America," *Globe*, February 24, 1899, 1–2.
28. *Globe*, February 7, 1899.
29. *Globe*, January 27, 1899.
30. *Globe*, December 6, 1898, 9.
31. LP, WL to H. Borden, September 5, 1899 (copy).
32. *N. Penlington, Canada and Imperialism, 1896–1899* (Toronto, 1965), 252; WP, WL to JSW, October 5, 1899.
33. *Globe*, October3, 1899; LAC, Sifton Papers, JSW to Sifton, October 3, 1899; WP, Sifton to JSW, October 4, 1899 (telegram); *Reminiscences*, 303.
34. WP, WL to JSW, October 5, 1899; *Reminiscences*, 303–05.
35. LP, Cameron to WL, October 13, 1899; LAC, Lord Minto Papers, Volume I, South African memorandum, 23; Dafoe, *Laurier*,.
36. *Reminiscences*, 303–04.
37. LP, JSW to WL, October 14, 1899; *Globe*, October 16 and 18, 1899.
38. J.L. Garvin, *The Life of Joseph Chamberlain*, III (London, 1934), 489–92.
39. *Globe*, October 16, 23, 30 and November 6, 1899.
40. Sifton Papers, JSW to Sifton, November 1, 1899; Garvin, *Chamberlain*, 519–20.
41. *Globe*, December 9, 1899, 18.
42. Garvin, 523–24.
43. *Globe*, December 15 and 19, 1899 and January 9, 1900; WP, WL to JSW, January 15 and 19, 1900; LP, JSW to WL, January 20 and 25, 1900.
44. J. Schull, *Laurier:The First Canadian* (Toronto, 1965), 387; LP, JSW to WL, January 17, 1900 and October 25, 1901.
45. LAC, Campbell Papers, JSW to Campbell, November 6, 1899; *Globe*, October 14, 1899; WP, Bourassa to JSW, November 3, 1899; *Globe*, November 20, 1899.
46. EQV, "Canadian Celebrities: Messrs Ewan and Hamilton," *Canadian Magazine*, XV (October 1900), 495–96; WP, Biggar to JSW, March 2, 1900;

American Newspapers Directory (New York, 1900), 1164–66, and *Rowell's American Newspaper Directory* (New York, 1907), 1294–96. See also *Globe*, 1899 and 1900 for end-of-month computation of daily averages as basis for yearly figures.

47. *Globe*, February 21 and June 4, 1900.
48. W.D. Gregory Papers, Smith to Gregory, May 2, 1900.
49. Cited, L. LaPierre, *Politics, Race and Religion in French Canada: Joseph Israel Tarte.* Ph.D. (University of Toronto, 1962), 392–94.
50. *Mail and Empire*, November 3, 1900; *World*, November 5, 1900.
51. LP, JSW to WL, November 11, 1901; WP, JSW to Parkin, June 2, 1902 (copy).
52. *Globe*, October 26 and November 9, 1899.
53. *Globe*, March 9, 1901.
54. *Globe*, January 27, 1900, March 14, and May 16, 1901.
55. *Globe*, April 9, 1900 and April 6, 1901.
56. Cited, *Globe*, May 3, 1902.
57. J. Amery, *The Life of Joseph Chamberlain*, IV (London, 1951), 417–47; J.E. Kendle, *The Colonial and Imperial Conferences 1887–1911* (London, 1967), 39–54; *CAR, 1902*, 112–14.
58. *Globe*, April 24, 1902, 4.
59. Denison Papers, JSW to Denison, May 14, 1902; *Globe*, May 3, 1902; Denison Papers, Parkin to Denison, May 16, 1902 and Colquhoun to Denison, June 13, 1902.
60. WP, WL to JSW, June 12, 1902; Denison Papers, JSW to Denison, February 21, 1902; *Globe*, March 17, 1902.
61. LP, WL to Ross, January 14, 1902 (copy) and JSW to WL, June 20, 2002; WP, JSW to Parkin, June 2, 1902 (copy).
62. LP, JSW to WL, June 10, 1902.
63. Kendle, *op. cit.*, 39–54.
64. Cited, *Globe*, November 7, 2002.
65. Denison Papers, Denison to Chamberlain, April 18, 1903 (copy).
66. *Globe*, May 3, 1902.

CHAPTER SEVEN
1. UTL, G. M. Wrong Papers, JSW to Wrong, October 24, 1913; WP, Hardy to JSW, July 11, 1896.
2. LP, JSW to WL, September 9 and November 12, 1896; WP, WL to JSW, November 6, 1896.
3. *Globe*, November 12, 1892 and November 16, 1895, 13-14; WP, WL to JSW, November 16, 1895 and Van Horne to JSW, April 11, 1896.
4. WP, Jaffray to JSW, August 1, 1896.
5. *Globe*, August 24, 27, 28, 31, and September 2 and 5, 1896.

6. LP, T.G. Shaughnessy to WL, September 12 and November 12, 1896; *Globe*, November 11, 1896.

7. Victoria *Daily Times*, December 31, 1896, 4; LP, S.H. Janes to WL, November 19, 1896.

8. Manitoba *Free Press*, January 15, 1897.

9. *Globe*, January 19, 1896.

10. Victoria *Times*, February 24, 1897; LP, Shields to WL, February 23, 1897, Armstrong to WL, February 25, 1897 and WL to A.T. Wood, February 26, 1897; *World*, February 27, 1897.

11. Sifton Papers, JSW to Sifton, March 4, 1897; WP, Sifton to JSW, March 10, 1897.

12. *Debates*, April 15, 1897, 493–516; *Globe*, April 8, 1897; WP, WL to JSW, April 8, 1897; *Debates*, April 9, 1897, 709–17.

13. H. Charlesworth, *More Candid Chronicles: Further Leaves from the Note Book of a Canadian Journalist* (Toronto, 1928), 162.

14. The full title is *The Railway Question in Canada with an Examination of the Railway Law of Iowa* (Toronto, n.p., n.d. [1897]).

15. WP, Lyon to JSW, May 15, 1897, Atkinson to JSW, May 17, 1897, Hardy to JSW, May 12, 1897 and Walker to JSW, May 17, 1897.

16. *Debates*, June 11, 1897, 3780–82 and June 18, 1897, 4525, 4527.

17. *Globe*, June 5, 1897 and April 15, 1898; *Debates*, April 15, 1898, 3552–53; WP, Sifton to JSW and WL to JSW, April 21, 1898; Sifton Papers, JSW to Sifton, April 25, 1898.

18. *Globe*, November 21, 1898.

19. WP, Van Horne to JSW, November 29, 1898, JSW to Van Horne, November 30, 1898 (copy).

20. WP, Van Horne to JSW, December 1, 1898 and JSW to Van Horne, December 15, 1898 (copy).

21. LP, JSW to WL, October 31, 1898; WP, WL to JSW, November 2, 1898 and Blair to JSW, November 3, 1898.

22. LP, JSW to WL, June 19, 1899; *Globe*, June 23, 1890; Sifton Papers, JSW to Sifton, May 14, 1899 and Sifton to JSW, May 16, 1899 (copy).

23. LAC, C.J. Fitzpatrick Papers, Hardy to Fitzpatrick, December 27, 1897; WP, Hardy to JSW, February 8, 1898; *Reminiscences*, 329.

24. LP, JSW to WL, April 20 and 22, 1898; WP, WL to JSW, April 21 and 24, 1898.

25. *Globe*, January 5, 1899; WP, WL to JSW, January 7, 1899; LP, JSW to WL, January 21, 1899; *Mail and Empire*, January 30, 1899.

26. *Globe*, August 4, 1899.

27. WP, Russell to JSW, August 4, 1899, WL to JSW, August 4, 1899, Kingsmill to JSW, August 4, 1899 and Richardson to JSW, August 8, 1899.

28. Sifton Papers, JSW to Sifton, July 4, 1898; WP, John Lewis to JSW, April 7, 1899 and Sifton to JSW, May 7, 1899; Sifton Papers, JSW to Sifton, May 7, 1899.

29. Sifton Papers, JSW to Sifton, October 1 and 3, 1899.

30. JSW, *Journalism: An address delivered before the Political Science Club of Toronto University* (Toronto, [1899]).

31. Harkness, *Atkinson*, 19–23; LP, Atkinson to WL, December 1, 1899.

32. WP, WL to JSW, January 11, 1900 and JSW to Col. Hugh Clark, March 12, 1919 (copy).

33. LP, JSW to WL, January 11, 1900; WP, WL to JSW, January 15, 1900.

34. WP, Workman to JSW, March 6, 1900, Wallace to JSW, March 22, 1900, Bourinot to JSW, May 30, 1900, Campbell to JSW, June 5, 1900 and Bourinot to JSW, June 5, 1900.

35. WP, Dunbar to JSW. March 11, 1900 and Sifton to JSW, July 7, 1900; Sifton Papers, JSW to Sifton, July 5, 1900.

36. LP, Ross to WL, August 7, 1900; WP, Ross to JSW, September 11, 1900; *Globe*, September 14 and 17, 1900.

37. WP, Hunter to JSW, September 18, 1900 and Black to JSW, September 20, 1900.

38. *Globe*, September 20 and October 7, 1900.

39. A copy of the "bogus *Globe*" was a supplement of the Goderich *Star*, October 26, 1900; *Globe*, October 31 and November 2, 1900.

40. WP, MacLean to JSW, November 7, 1900 and Tarte to JSW, November 7, 1900.

41. Sifton Papers, JSW to Sifton, January 29, 1901.

42. WP, Sifton to JSW, February 7, 1901.

43. Sifton Papers, JSW to Sifton, February 10, 1901.

44. *Globe*, January 4, 10, 12, 14, and 15, 1901; *CAR, 1901*, 381–84; LP, Shaughnessy to WL, January 14, 1901;

45. *Saturday Night*, January 19, 1901; WP, "An Old Subscriber" to JSW, April 17, 1901; *Globe*, February 13, 1901.

46. See e.g., *Globe*, May 30, 1901; *CAR,* 1902, p. 214; *Globe*, April 10, 1902; WP, WL to JSW, May 19, 1902.

47. LP, Hays *et al.* to WL, November 3, 1902; WP, WL to JSW, November 3, 1902.

48. LP, JSW to WL, November 2, 1902.

49. *CAR*, 1901, 337–38; WP, Ross to JSW, March 30, 1901.

50. M. Denison, *The People's Power: The History of Ontario* (Toronto, 1960), 29–30; C.W. Humphries, "The Sources of Ontario Progressive Conservatism, 1900–1914," *CHARs, 1967*, 119–21; *CAR*, 1902, 46; *Globe*, February 1 and March 7, 1902.

51. LP, JSW to WL, April 11, 1902; *CAR,*1902, 47; *Globe*, April 22, 1902; Sifton Papers, JSW to Sifton, May 11, 1902; C.W. Humphries, *The Political Career of Sir James P. Whitney* (unpublished Ph.D. dissertation, University of Toronto, 1966), 281–83; LP, R. Cartwright to WL, July 31, 1902.

52. *Reminiscences*, 321–22; *Globe*, September 1, 1902; *CAR*, 1902, 53.

53. *Mail and Empire*, September 13, 1902; *CAR*, 1902, 53–54.

54. *Globe*, November 28, 1902; WP, Ross to JSW, November 28, 1902.

55. WP, JSW to P.S. Armstrong, January 30, 1905 (copy); J.W. Dafoe, "Press, Politics and People: A Review Article," *CHR*, XXVII (March 1936), 61.

56. JSW, "The Function of Journalism in Democracy," *Queen's Quarterly*, VII (April 1901), 313–14.

CHAPTER EIGHT

1. WP, Hopkins to JSW, June 5, 1900; PAO, WP, Memorandum of Agreement between George N. Morang Co. Ltd. and J.S. Willison, July 3, 1901; LP, JSW to WL, November 11, 1901.

2. *Canadian Magazine* X (November 1897), 16–31; WP, Colquhoun to JSW, July 4, 1897.

3. LP, JSW to WL, November 11, 1901.

4. WP, Morang to JSW, August 29, 1902.

5. WP, WL to JSW, November 8, 1901 and May 19, 1902.

6. LP, JSW to WL, November 11, 1901.

7. *Laurier*, II, 355.

8. LP, JSW to WL, November 11, 1901.

9. *Laurier*, I, 40, 42, 51–52, 49, 254.

10. *Ibid.*, 253–84, 287–313.

11. *Ibid.*, 253–322, 318, 322–24, 326.

12. *Ibid.*, 30–31, 96–97, 191, 328.

13. *Laurier*, II, 355–56; *Laurier*, I, 113–15, 112.

14. *Laurier*, I, 138–39, 421; *Laurier*, II, 44–51.

15. *Laurier*, II, 215–16, 238–41.

16. *Laurier*, II, 241, 244, 257, 275–76.

17. WP, WL to JSW, March 7 and 30, 1895, JSW to WL, April 1, 1895 (copy), WL to JSW, April 9, 1895 and JSW to Dafoe, March 7, 1923 (copy).

18. *Laurier*, I, 30–31, 39, 134–35, 467; *Laurier*, II, 297–98.

19. *Laurier*, II, 317–22, 327–28.

20. *Ibid.*, 217–20, 363-67; *Laurier*, II, 120, 149, 160, 181–83, 187, 358.

21. WP, George N. Morang to JSW, August 29, 1902. The "Author's Note" at the beginning of Vol. II is dated June, 1902.

22. *Globe*, February 16, 1903; *Advertiser*, Marc 24, 1903; *Free Press*, February 21, 1903; *Le Soleil*, February 21, 1903.

23. *Mail and Empire*, February 17, 1903; *Gazette*, March 18, 1903; *La Presse*, October 17, 1903.

24. *Canadian Magazine*, XX (March 1903), 474; *Saturday Night*, n.d. (WP, volume 116); *Journal*, February 21, 1903; WP, JSW to Ross, March 26, 1903 (copy).

25. *Times Literary Supplement*, October 30, 1903; *Spectator*, October 31, 1903; *Morning Post*, October 31, 1903; *Yorkshire Daily Post*, December 16, 1903;

Daily Chronicle, October 7, 1903.

26. DLQU, FP, JWF to JSW, April 25, 1903.

27. *Laurier*, II, 389.

28. WP, Canon A.W. Macnab to JSW, n.d., but by context 1902, Cassels and Standish to JSW, May 3, 1904 and W.D. Gregory to JSW, August 2, 1904; Lady MW memoir, 29; interview with Mrs. A.M. Mackenzie (daughter of Walter Willison), November 28, 1973; Lady MW memoir, 101 and 105.

29. Lady MW memoir, 121–26; Mrs. A.M. Mackenzie interview; Dorothy Ferrier (secretary, 1918–1927) to author, February 8, 1974; obituary of Rachel Willison, *Globe*, January 20, 1925, 14; A.H. Young, *The War Book of Upper Canada College* (Toronto, 1923) has alphabetical entries on the boys.

CHAPTER NINE

1. FP, "Inventory and Biographical Summary," 1-5; Michael Bliss, *A Canadian Millionaire: The Life and Business Times of Sir Joseph Flavelle, Bart., 1858–1939* (Toronto, 1978), 1–146.

2. EQV, "Canadian Celebreties: No. XXXIX — Mr. J. S. Willison," *Canadian Magazine*, XX (January 1903), 223–24; Goldwin Smith Papers, JWF to Smith, December 13, 1904.

3. Colquhoun, *Willison*, 111; FP, JWF to JSW, August 4, 1902. Flavelle, an executor of the Willison correspondence, seems to have shifted several letters between himself and Willison to his own collection.

4. FP, JWF to JSW, October 3, November 25, December 1, 3 and November 27, 1902; WP, "Rae" to JSW, October 1, 1902.

5. FP, JWF to JSW, November 26, 1902.

6. WP, WL to JSW, November 3, 1902; Colquhoun, *Willison*, 111.

7. WP, Ross to JSW, November 28, 1902, Young to JSW, November 29 and December *n.d.*, 1902, Cooper to JSW, December 2, 1902 and Parkin to JSW, December 11, 1902; Gregory Papers, Smith to Gregory, December 11, 1902.

8. *CAR*, 1903, 126, 148–49; C.W. Humphries, "The Gamey Affair," *Ontario History*, LIX (June 1967), 104.

9. LP, Gregory to WL, March 18, 1903.

10. Humphries, "Gamey," 106; *News*, June 5 and 17, 1903; WP, Armstrong to JSW, March 27, 1903; *News*, April 6, 190, 3; LP, JSW to WL, July 11, 1903; WP, Campbell to JSW, March 23, 1903.

11. *News*, February 13, 1903

12. *CAR*, 1903, 286–88; *News*, May 1 and July 17, 1903; Minto Papers, JSW to Minto, July 18, 1903.

13. *News*, February 18, 1904.

14. Minto Papers, JSW to Minto, July 18, 1903.

15. *News*, May 26 and September 21, 1903.

16. JSW, *Laurier* (Toronto, 1926) Part II, 382.

17. WP, Ewan to JSW, April 19, 1904.

18. G.R. Stevens, *Canadian National Railways*, II, *Towards the Inevitable, 1896-1922* (Toronto, 1962), 135–36; LP,W. Mulock to WL, February 14, 1903, Blair to WL, April 9, 1903, Sifton to WL, April 9, 1903; W.S. Fielding to WL, May 19, 1903, Mulock to WL, June 7, 1903 and F.W. Borden to WL, June 24, 1903; Stevens, 138–43.

19. LP, JSW to WL, July 11, 1903; *CAR, 1903*, 430–31; *News*, May 26, 1903.

20. *Debates*, July 30, 1903, cols. 7659–60; *News*, July 31 and August 7, 1903.

21. *Debates*, July 30, 1903, cols. 7697–718; *News*, August 12 and 14, 2003.

22. *CAR*, 1903, 40–42; *News*, August 22 and 25, 1903; FP, JWF to RLB, August 16, 1903 (copy) and RLB to JWF, August 20, 1903.

23. *Debates*, April 5, 1904, cols. 710–26.

24. *News*, January 20, 1904; LP, JSW to WL, January 25, 1904; WP, WL to JSW, January 26 and 29, 1904.

25. *News*, March 8, 1904.

26. *Debates*, May 26, 1904, cols. 3540–73. The quoted portions are from cols. 3571–73.

27. *News*, May 28, 1904; LP, JSW to WL, June 9, 1904; WP, WL to JSW, June 15, 1904.

28. *News*, May 28, 1904; *CAR*, 1904, 83; JSW, *Laurier* (1926), Part II, 363; *News*, October 12 and November 4, 1904; WP, JSW to WL, December 24, 1904 (copy) and WL to JSW, December 31, 1904.

29 *CAR*, 1904, 281–85.

30. *News*, September 19, 1904; WP, McMullen to JSW, December 13, 1904; JSW to W.S. Frost, December 14, 1904 (copy); *News*, November 25, 1904.

31. JSW, "The Party System of Government," *Canadian Club of Toronto, Addresses, 1903-1904*, 70; WP, JSW to Caswell, February 2, 1904 (copy).

32. *News*, January 17, 1905; LP, JSW to WL, January 4, 1905; *News*, January 17, 1905.

33. Humphries, *Whitney*, 318–19; *CAR*, 1905, 209–10; *Rowell's American Newspaper Directory* (New York, 1907), 1294–95.

34. Canada, *Statutes*, 39 Vict., C-49, S-11 (1875); C.C. Lingard, *Territorial Government in Canada: The Autonomy Question in the Old North-West Territories* (Toronto, 1946), 155–59; *CAR*, 1905, 46.

35. Lingard, 97-125; LP, WL to Sbaretti, March 7, 1904 (copy).

36. *News*, January 22 and May 1, 1903 and May 26, 1904; WP, WL to JSW, June 7, 1904; LP, JSW to WL, June 9 and 14, 1904; WP, WL to JSW, June 11, 1904.

37. Lingard, 129-131; *Debates*, March 15, 1905, cols. 2506-07; LP, WL to Sbaretti, January 19, 1905 (copy); J. W. Dafoe, *Clifford Sifton in Relation to His Times* (Toronto, 1931), 275-81; *Debates*, March 24, 1905, col. 3105 (Sifton).

38. *Debates*, February 21, 1905, cols. 1451-52.

39. WP, JSW to Beer, November 29, 1912 (copy).
40. *News*, February 22, March 1, 4 and 8, 1905.
41. WP, WL to JSW, March 7, 1905; LP, JSW to WL, March 9, 1905; WP, WL to JSW, March 9, 1905.
42. LP, Ross to WL, March 9, 1905, J. McMullen to WL, March 9, 1905, L.M. Jones to WL, March 25, 1905, Rowell to WL, March 20, 1905 and Macdonald to WL, February 2, 1905; *Globe*, February 24, 1905.
43. Dafoe, *Sifton*, 188, 282; *Debates*, March 24, 1905, col. 3105; Sifton Papers, Sifton to Fielding, March 1, 1905 (copy); WP, C.F. Hamilton to JSW, March 3, 1905; LP, WL to L.A. Jetté, March 1, 1905 (copy).
44. Lingard, 184–85; *Debates*, March 22, 1905, cols. 2195–2926; LP, WL to L. Jones, March 31, 1905; Skelton, *Laurier*, II, 246 and 291; Lingard, 291; *Globe*, March 24, 1905.
45. *News*, March 27, April 5 and 10, 1905.
46. WP, LeSuer to JSW, April 7, 1905, Caswell to JSW, April 12, 1905, Lewis to JSW, April 3, 1905 and JSW to RLB, April 17, 1905 (copy); *News*, April 18, 1905.
47. WP, S. Caldecott to JSW, March 23 and 29, 1905 and JSW to RLB, April 22, 1905 (copy).
48. *News*, June 2, 1905; *CAR, 1905*, p. 103; Paul D. Stevens, *Laurier and the Liberal Party in Ontario, 1887–1911*, unpublished Ph.D. thesis, University of Toronto, 1966, 296.
49. *CAR*, 1905, 239–40, 259; JSW, *Laurier* (1926), Part II, 378–80.
50. WP, WL to JSW, February 5, 1908 and JSW to Col. Hugh Clark, March 12, 1919 (copy); AO, WP, Lady MW memoir, 114–15.

CHAPTER TEN

1. WP, Caswell to JSW, April 12, 1905, Hamilton to JSW, June 24, 1905 and JSW to P.S. Armstrong, January 30, 1905 (copy).
2. Bliss, *Flavelle*, 161–65; AO, J.P. Whitney Papers, JWF to Whitney, November 28, 1905 and Whitney to A. Brodeur, November 29, 1905 (copy); *News*, November 29, 1905; Kingston *Daily British Whig*, April 26, 1906, 2.
3. WP, JSW to Lindsey, March 8, 1906 (copy); JSW to Hamilton, April 28, 1906 (copy); *News*, July 9, 1906 and June 24, 1907; Dawson, *King*, 183-189; King Diary, June 24, 1907.
4. *Le Nationaliste*, July 30, 1905.
5. JSW, *Partners in Peace* (Toronto, 1923), 77–94.
6. WP, Campbell to JSW, January 2, 1906; University of Toronto Library, B.E. Walker Papers, J.A. Cooper to Walker, January 25, 1906; WP, Cooper to JSW, March 12, 1906.
7. WP, Parkin to JSW, July 12, 1905 and Sam Hughes to JSW, July 29, 1905; AOC, G.R. Parkin papers, Ware to Parkin, August 10, 1905; WP, Jebb to

JSW, October 3, 1905, A.F. Sladen to JSW, October 20, 1905, Ware to JSW, December 27, 1905 and *Morning Post* to JSW, 1905–1909. The *Post* was a 1½ pence paper with the *Times* at twice that price (see S. Nowell-Smith, *Edwardian England, 1901–1914* [London, 1964], 320 and 144).

8. FP, JWF to JSW, April 10, 1907.

9. *Post*, November 21, 1905, 8 and December 19, 1906, 4; WP, Jebb to JSW, January 6, 1907 and Ware to JSW, March 21, 1907. See Simon J. Potter, "Richard Jebb, John S. Ewart and the Round Table, 1898–1926," *English Historical Review*, CXXII (February 2007), 105–32 on Jebb's consistent opposition to imperial federation while favouring an imperial connection based instead upon alliance of equal autonomous states.

10. *Rowell's American Newspaper Directory, 1907* (New York, 1907), 1294–95; Harkness, *Atkinson*, 60–67; Bliss, *Flavelle*, 172–73; FP, Fifth Annual Report of the News Publishing Co., January 29, 1908.

11. *News*, August 4 and December 15, 1906; Walker Papers, JWF to Z. Lash, December 19, 1906 and JWF to Walker, December 19, 1906.

12. *CAR*, 1907, 515–17; *News*, December 16, 1907; H.V. Nelles, *The Politics of Development: Forests, Mines and Hydro-Electric Power in Ontario, 1849–1941* (Toronto, 1974), Chapter 7; Bliss, *Flavelle*, 173–74.

13. *News*, May 6, November 26, 27, and 29, December 14, 1907; Bliss, 174; *CAR*, 1907, 523; *CAR*, 1908, 299, 347.

14. Bliss, p. 175; Whitney Papers, Whitney to E.C. Whitney, December 4, 5, 26, 1907; WP, JSW to W.R. Riddell, November 28, 1907 (copy) and Saunders to JSW, January 16, 1908.

15. Walker Papers, JWF to Z.A. Lash, December 19, 1906; Minko Sotiron, *From Politics to Profit: The Commercialization of Canadian Daily Newspapers, 1890–1920* (Montreal and Kingston, 1997), 30–32.

16. FP, JWF to J. Macdonnell, September 5, 1934.

17. *Globe*, September 18, 1884; WP, Clark to JSW, June 14, 1907, Lindsey to JSW, April 13, 1908, Gibson to JSW, January 13, 1908, Sifton to JSW, July 31, 1907 and JSW to Sifton, February 21, 1908 (copy).

18. LP, JSW to WL, February 3, 1908; WP, WL to JSW, Feb, 5, 1908.

19. *News*, January 25, 1908; WP, Sifton to JSW, February 21, 1908.

20. WP, Sifton to JSW, April 16, 1908 and Hamilton to JSW, April 21, 1908; Whitney Papers, Whitney to E.C. Whitney, April 22, 1908 (copy); WP, Hamilton to JSW, May 17 and 18, 1908.

21. *News*, May 12, 1908.

22. *News*, May 12, 1908; WP, Thomson to JSW, May 21, 1908, Smith to JSW, May 9, 1908, H. Strang to JSW, May 12, 1908 and JSW to Strang, May 13, 1908 (copy).

23. LP, Lindsey to WL, June 8, 1908 and WL to Lindsey, June 5, 1908 (copy); *CAR*, 1908, 342, 344–45; LP, WL to Jaffray, June 5, 1908 and WL to Lindsey,

June 5, 1908 (copies), Lindsey to WL, June 23, 1908 and WL to Lindsey, June 24, 1908 (copy).

24. *Globe*, June 24, 1908; LP, Lindsey to WL, June 24, 1908 and WL to Lindsey, June 25, 1908; memorandum in Willison's handwriting, cited, Colquhoun, *Willison*, 154.

25. Whitney Papers, Whitney to Cochrane, July 8, 1908 (copy); *News*, August 4, 1908: Whitney Papers, Whitney to W.F. Nickle, August 4, 1908.

26. *News*, April 30, 1907; R.C. Brown, *Robert Laird Borden; A Biography*, I, *1854–1914* (Toronto, 1975), 129–34; WP, JSW to RLB, August 15, 1907 (copy).

27. *CAR*, 1907, 459–60.

28. WP, JSW to RLB, August 15, 1907 (copy); *News*, August 26, 1907.

29. WP, RLB to JSW, September 12, 1908.

30. *News*, September 18, 19 and October 15, 1908.

31. *News*, October 27 and November 2, 1908.

32. WP, Hamilton to JSW, November 1 and 10, 1908, JSW to Hamilton, November 4, 1908 (copy), Hamilton to JSW, December 1, 1908, JSW to Hamilton, November 4, 1908 (copy) and JSW to Rev. S.F. Dixon, November 6, 1908 (copy).

33. *News*, January 13, 1908; Colquhoun, 260; R. Pound and G. Harmsworth, *Northcliffe* (London, 1959), 306–20, 193ff, 277ff; *News*, December 2, 1908.

34. WP, Northcliffe to JSW, November 9, 1908 and Greenwood to JSW, August 20, 1907; WP, Grey to JSW, December 29, 1908; Pound and Harmsworth, 335–37; Bodleian Library, Oxford University, Lord Milner Papers, Diary, October 23, 24, and 26, 1908; LAC, Arthur Glazebrook Papers, Milner to Glazebrook, October 28, 1908;

35. WP, Northcliffe to JSW, December 7 and 12, 1908 and Northcliffe to desk clerk (St. Regis Hotel, New York City), December 21, 1908; LP, JSW to Grey, December 28, 1908 (copy).

36. LP, Grey to JSW, December 29, 1908 (copy). *Henri de Blowitz (1825–1903), born in Bohemia, had a brilliant journalistic career, most notably as *Times* correspondent in Paris and at key diplomatic conferences in the later 19th century (see *Encylopaedia Britannica*, Eleventh Edition (1911). Biography summarized by Wikepedia (*http://en. www.wikipedia.org/wiki/Henri_Blowitz*).

CHAPTER ELEVEN

1. FOCT (From Our Correspondent Toronto), *Times*, January 30, 1909, 7; A.S. Link, *American Epoch* (New York, 1963), 105–06; R.C. Brown and R. Cook, *Canada, 1896–1921* (Toronto, 1974), 179; *News*, August 4 and March 19, 1909.

2. *CAR*, 1909, 79–83; *Globe*, March 23, 1909.

3. *News*, March 22, 1909; FOCT, *Times*, April 12, 1909; *News*, March 23, 1909.

4. *Debates*, March 29, 1909, 3483–564; R.C. Brown, *Robert Laird Borden*, I, *1854–1914* (Toronto, 1975), 154.

5. *News*, March 30, 1909; FOCT, *Times*, April 12, 1909, 4.
6. *News*, April 8 and 21, 1909.
7. FOCT, *Times*, May 1, 1909, 6; WP, Bell to JSW, May 4, 1909 and McNeill to JSW, May 11, 1909.
8. FOCT, *Times*, June 9, 1909, 5; Whitney Papers, JSW to Whitney, June 11, 1909.
9. *La Presse*, 19 juin, 1909, 22; *News*, June 21, 1909; FOCT, *Times*, July 1, 1909, 14.
10. *CAR*, 1909, 79–83; *News*, November 5, 1909; Brown, *Borden*, I, 154–58.
11. *News*, November 12 and 15, 1909.
12. Premier Whitney (Ont.), Premier Roblin (Man.), JWF, R.B. Bennett, T.C. Casgrain, Sir Charles Hibbert Tupper, A.E. Kemp, Richard White (Montreal *Gazette*), A.F. Wallis (*Mail and Empire*) and JSW (*News*) were among those consulted (Brown, *Borden*, I, 160).
13. WP, RLB to JSW, Nov, 19, 1909.
14. WP, JSW to RLB, November 22, 1909 (copy) and RLB to JSW, November 24, 1909.
15. WP, E.W.M. Grigg to JSW, December 2, 1909; FOCT, *Times*, December 17, 1909, 12 and December 24, 1909, 10.
16. WP, Grigg to JSW, November 13, 1909; J.F. Kendle, *The Round Table Movement and Imperial Union* (Toronto, 1975), 55–56; WP, Curtis to JSW, November 3, 1909; Scottish Record Office, Lord Lothian (Philip Kerr) Papers, Diary, September-November 1909 and letter, Curtis to Kerr, July 21, 1910.
17. WP, Walker to JSW, December 13, 1909.
18. WP, Parkin to JSW, December 24, 1909; Milner Diary, January 16, 1910; WP, Ware to JSW, December 29, 1909 and J.R. Boosé to JSW, December 28, 1909; *Times*, December 31, 1909, 4.
19. WP, Curtis to JSW, December 26, 1909; Lothian Papers, Diary, January 16, 1910 and letter, Curtis to Kerr, July 21, 1910.
20. WP, Northcliffe to JSW, December 31, 1909 and January 14, 1910, Colonial Office to JSW, January 12, 1910, E.R. Peacock to JSW, January 8, 1910 and Balfour to JSW, January 25 and 27, 1910.
21. *News*, January 3, 1910, 1; WP, JWF to JSW, January 5, 1910.
22. *News*, January 12, 1910, 1, January 10, 1910, 1 and January 5, 1910, 1; WP, C.T. Pearce to JSW, January 6, 1910.
23. *News*, January 16 and 17, 1910.
24. WP, Bell to JSW, January 24, 1910.
25. LP, Grigg to WL, January 24, 1910.
26. LAC, W.L.M. King Papers, Diary, January 31, 1910; LP, WL to Grigg, February 5, 1910 (copy) and Grey to WL, February 7, 1910.
27. Brown, *Borden*, I, 162.
28. *Times*, January 13, 1910, FOCC, *Times*, January 16, 1910, 5–6; WP, cited, Curtis to JSW, April 8, 1910.

29. Brown, *Borden*, I, 165–67; WP, JSW to Grigg, March 14, 1910 (copy); *News*, March 19, 1910; WP, Smith to JSW and Hamilton to JSW, April 5, 1910.

30. WP, Smith to JSW, April 11, 1910; Brown, 167-169; Milner papers, Kerr to Milner, April 30, 1910, enclosing JSW to Kerr, April 15, 1910.

31. WP, JWF to JSW, April 24, 1910.

32. *CAR*, 1910, 621–23.

33. Milner Papers, Kerr to Milner, April 30, 1910, enclosing JSW to Kerr, April 15, 1910.

34. WP, Grigg to JSW, April 8 and 29, 1910, Flavelle to JSW, April 30, 1910, Northcliffe to JSW, May 1, 1910 and Milner to JSW, May 8, 1910.

35. FOCC, *Times*, May 24, 1910, 40–41.

36. WP, Northcliffe to JSW, May 24, 1910 and Maxse to JSW, June 16, 1910; Denison Papers, Mair to Denison, June 13, 1910; WP, Willert to JSW, June 11, 1910 and Wrong to JSW, June 24, 1910.

37. FOCC, *Times*, June 27, 1910, 7–8; *News*, July 4, 1910; FOCC, *Times*, August 13, 1910, 5; *News*, August 17, 1910.

38. *News*, November 4 and 15, 1910; FOCC, *Times*, 7.

39. *News*, January 23, 1911, 8.

40. Brown and Cook, 180; Borden, *Memoirs*, I, 303; *News*, January 27, 1911; FOCC, *Times*, January 27, 30 and February 1, 1911

41. Colquhoun, *Willison*, 294; FOCC, *Times*, February 1, 1911, 10.

42. *News*, January 31, 1911; WP, JWF to JSW, January 31, 1911.

43. WP, Cook to JSW, November 7, 1910; Walker Papers, Walker to R.A. Ramsay, February 2, 1911 and JSW to Walker, February 6, 1911; FOCC, *Times*, February 13, 1911, 8.

44. FP, JWF to JSW, February 15, 1911; *News*, February 17, 1911, p. 1; FOCC, *Times*, February 18, 1911, 8.

45 *CAR*, 1911, 48–49; National Club, membership lists.

46. *Debates*, Mach 28, 1911, 4385–409; Dafoe Papers, Sifton to Dafoe, March 2, 1911.

47. WP, Sifton to JSW, February 23, 1911 and volume 105, memorandum, undated.

48. WP, C.F. Hamilton to JSW, March 27 and 29, 1911 and F. Cook to JSW, March 19, 1911; FOCC, *Times*, April 3, 1911, 5.

49. *News*, May 6, 1911.

50. Sifton Papers, Sifton to JSW, August 3, 1911 (copy); Whitney Papers, RLB to Whitney, August 7, 1911 and Whitney to RLB, August 8, 1911 (copy); *News*, August 15, 1911, 1.

51. Sifton Papers, JSW to Sifton, September 23, 1911; *News*, September 18, 1911.

52. Beck, *Pendulum of Power*, 135.

53. Milner Papers, Glazebrook to Milner, September 22, 1911; *News*, September 22, 1911, 1–3; FP, JWF to JSW, August 25, 1911; LAC, A.E. Kemp Papers, Kemp to other ministers, November 30, 1911 (copy).

54. WP, RLB to JSW, October 3, 1911.

CHAPTER TWELVE

1. WP, Sifton to JSW, September 30, 1911; BP, JSW to RLB, October 5, 1911; WP, JSW to R.G. Scott, October 11, 1911 (copy).

2. WP, JSW to Hamilton, November 28, 1911 (copy), Burnham to JSW, December 5, 1911; Kemp Papers, Kemp to ministers, November 30, 1911; Whitney Papers, Whitney to Cochrane, October 4, 1912 (copy).

3. WP, JSW to Cochrane, November 20, 1912 (copy).

4. WP, Cochrane to JSW, November 22, 1912.

5. WP, JSW to Cochrane, November 23, 1912 (copy), Grigg to JSW, October 4, 1912 and JSW to Annie Heustis, October 18, 1912 (copy).

6. WP, Cochrane to JSW, November 25, 1912; BP, JSW to RLB, December 12, 1912; WP, RLB to JSW, December 9, 1912.

7. WP, H.C. Lowther to JSW, December 16, 1912.

8. OA, WP, *Complimentary Dinner Given by the National Club to Sir John Willison, K.B., L.L.D., January 31, 1913.*

9. Cited, Colquhoun, *Willison*, 190–93; FP, notes for speech to National Club, Toronto, January 31, 1913; *News*, February 1, 1913, 4.

10. FP, JSW to JWF, February 1, 1913 and JWF to JSW, February 1, 1913.

11. WP, Colquhoun to JSW, February 17, 1913.

12. Cited, Colquhoun, *Willison*, 194–200.

13. WP, W.P. Fraser to JSW, January 14, 1914; Rodger Manning to JSW, July 28, 1908, A.L. Cochrane to JSW, April 6, 1907, D.M. Gordon to JSW, March 16, 1910, J.B. Hay and W.A. Willison to JSW, March 31, 1913, E.W.M. Grigg to JSW, October 28, 1914 and A.R. Ford to JSW, November 6, 1914; A.H. Young, *The Roll of Pupils of Upper Canada College*, January 1830 to June 1916 (Toronto, 1917), 629; *News*, October 2, 1913, 2 and July 14, 1914.

14. WP, C/T. Pearce to JSW, April 1, 1913.

15. WP, Hay to C.T. Pearce, July 29, 1913, J. Hobson to JSW, November 25, 1913, Kemp to JSW, n.d. (by context, January 1914), p. 16811 and Cochrane to JSW, October 21, 1914.

16. *News*, December 27, 1911; WP, Hocken to JSW, December 27, 1911; *News*, October 22, 1912; WP, Hocken to JSW, October 25, 1912; *News*, April 19, December 19 and 23, 1913.

17. *News*, January 22, 1914; *Reminiscences*, 329.

18. WP, JSW to Beer, January 23, 1913 (copy), Beer to JSW, March 21, 1913, JSW to Whitney, April 11, 1913 (copy), Whitney to JSW, April 14, 1913; Whitney Papers, JSW to Whitney, April 21, 1913; WP, Beer to JSW, June 5, 1913.

19. *News*, September 2 1913 and January 6, 1914; *Globe*, March 30, 1914, 9.

20. *The New Canada: A Survey of the Conditions and Problems of the Domin-*

ion by the Canadian Correspondent of the Times (London, 1912), 8, 12–13, 16–38, and 39–118.

21. FP, JSW to JSW, June 3, 1912; WP, Buckle to JSW, May 24, 1912, Robinson to JSW, April 25, 1912 and Northcliffe to JSW, September 12, 1912.

22. FP, Ross to JSW, October 18, 1912 and Skelton to JSW, November 4, 1912.

23. *Debates*, November 20, 1911, 59–60 and March 18, 1912, 5356–57.

24. Cited, UTL, G.M. Wrong Papers, Wrong to Lord Bryce, May 22, 1912 (copy); BP, JSW to RLB, June 13, 1912; FOOC, *Times*, July 4, 1912, 9–10.

25. Brown and Cook, 205–07.

26. Brown, *Borden*, I, 238; WP, JSW to C.F. Hamilton, October 7, 1912 (copy); *The Round Table*, II, No. 4 (August 1912), 709–10.

27. *CAR*, 1912, 44–45; *News*, August 21, 1912; *Debates*, December 5, 1912, cited, *The Round Table*, III, No. 2 (February 1913), 345–46; Dafoe Papers, WL to Dafoe, September 26, 1912.

28. Cited, *The Round Table*, III, No. 2 (February 1913), 341.

29. *Ibid.*; *News*, December 6, 1912; *Debates*, December 5, 1912, 692–93; Brown and Cook, 207–08; WP, BP to JSW, December 9, 1912.

30. *The Round Table*, III, No. 2 (February 1913), 342; BP, JSW to RLB, December 19, 1912.

31. Brown and Cook, 208; NPHSP-JSW, JSW to Grigg, March 4, 1913; *News*, March 25, 1913.

32. Brown, *Borden*, I, 242.

33. NPHSP-JSW, JSW to Grigg, February 27, April 14 and May 15, 1913; BP, JSW to RLB, May 12, 1913; *News*, May 20, 1913.

34. Brown and Cook, 209, 211, and 374; FP, JWF to JSW, June 21, 1913; *Reminiscences*, 317.

35. *News*, November 12, 1913.

36. J.E. Wrench, *Geoffrey Dawson and Our Times* (London, 1955), 90; Kendle, *Round Table Movement*, 166; British Museum, Lord Northcliffe Papers, Northcliffe to Robinson, November 4 and 29, 1912 (copies).

37. WP, JSW to Northcliffe, December 26, 1912 (copy); NPHSP-JSW, JSW to Grigg, February 27, 1913.

38. NPHSP-JSW, JSW to Grigg, March 22, 1913; WP, G.L. Craik to JSW, February 21, 1913 and Grigg to JSW, November 27, 1913 (copy); *News*, May 18, 1914.

39. Brown and Cook, 253–56; *Journals of the Legislative Assembly of Ontario*, March 21, 1911, 260; *News*, November 4 and 20, 1911.

40. BP, JSW to RLB, January 24, 1912, No. 62; *News*, January 24, 1912.

41. *Ontario Sessional Papers*, 1912, No. 62; *News*, April 15, 1912.

42. Brown and Cook, 256–57; *News*, October 30, 1913.

43. *Ibid.*, June 16 and 18, 1914; M. Prang, *Newton W. Rowell: Ontario Nationalist* (Toronto, 1975), 146–47.

44. WP, JSW to J.F. Smith, July 30, 1914 (copy).
45. *News*, February 29, 1912, 10; and May 11, 1914, 3; FOOC, *Times*, May 9, 1914, 7.
46. WP, Robinson to JSW, May 31, 1914; NPHSP-JSW, JSW to Robinson, April 14, 1914; WP, Robinson to JSW, April 30, 1914.
47. WP, Robinson to JSW, June 29, 1914, citing JSW to Robinson of recent date (not surviving in either WP or NPHSP-JSW).
48. WP, July 27, 1914, citing JSW to Robinson, July 13, 1914 (not surviving).

CHAPTER THIRTEEN
1. *News*, June 29, July 27 and 31, August 5, 1914.
2. *News*, August 7, 1914.
3. *News*, August 6, 1914; *Debates*, August 19, 1914, 6.
4. Dawson, *King*, I, 230–31; "The Century's Problems," *News*, October 22, 1914; WP, JSW to J. King, October 19, 1914 (copy) and W.L.M.King to JSW, October 26 and November 14, 1914.
5. NPHSP-JSW, JSW to Robinson, August 28, 1914; WP, Cochrane to JSW, September 7, 1914 and JSW to Ford, September 29, 1914 (copy); Borden, *Memoirs*, I, 218.
6. WP, Kylie to JSW, October 16, 1914 and JSW to Kylie, October 19, 1914 (copy).
7. NPHSP-JSW, JSW to Robinson, January 4, 1915; WP, JSW to Col. Stanton (Secretary), January 5, 1915 (copy).
8. Ottawa *Journal*, March 29, 1915. The original Willison letter has not survived, but see: WP, WL to JSW, April 16, 1915 and LP, JSW to WL, May 9, 1915.
9. Paul Rutherford, *The Making of the Canadian Media* (Toronto, 1978), 51.
10. Kemp Papers, *News* to subscribers, September 11, 1914; WP, Cochrane to JSW, October 21, 1914 and S.R. Weaver to JSW, November 30, 1914.
11. WP, Wilson to JSW, January 7, 1913, February 2 and December 14, 1914, JSW to Cochrane, January 15, 1915 (copy) and Colquhoun notes on JSW's *Reminiscences*, n.d., vol. 112, 41239–340.
12. WP, Cochrane to JSW, January 30, 1915, JSW to Cochrane, February 8, 1915 (copy) and Cochrane to JSW, February 9, March 8 and May 23, 1915.
13. WP, JSW to Cochrane, April 15, 1915 (copy) and Cochrane to JSW, May 12, 1915.
14. WP, JSW to Cochrane, May 18, 1915 (copy) and Cochrane to JSW, May 22, 1915.
15. WP, Ford to JSW, November 18, 1915, JSW to Cochrane, May 18, 1915 and JSW to RLB, November 17, 1915 (copy); Toronto *Star*, September 20, 1916.
16. D.J. Goodspeed, *The Road past Vimy: The Canadian Corps, 1914–1918* (Toronto, 1969), 18–38; FOOC, *Times*, April 27, 1915, 9; *News*, April 30, 1915.
17. *News*, April 28 and May 27, 1915; WP, JSW to James George, May 14, 1915 (copy).
18. WP, JSW to RLB, August 17, 1914 (copy), Hocken to JSW, August 27, 1914, Rowell to JSW, August 29, 1914; OA, G.F. Beer Papers, Rowell to Beer, September 29 and October 16, 1914; WP, JSW to Hearst, November 25, 1914 (copy) and

JSW to RLB, February 23, 1915 (copy); Margaret Prang, *Rowell*, 162–63.

19. *News*, January 4, 1915; WP, JSW to Hearst, March 4, 1915 (copy).

20. WP, JSW to RLB, April 1, 1915 (copy) and RLB to JSW, March 2, 1915; *News*, May 25, 1915; WP, JSW to RLB, n.d., but by context, May 26, 1915 (copy); *News*, May 28, 1915; WP, JSW to RLB, May 28, 1915 (copy).

21. WP, Hearst to JSW, September 15, November 4 and 15, 1915.

22. *News*, January 19, 1916, 1.

23. *News*, March 1 and 4, 1916; FP, JWF to JSW, March 5, 1916.

24. WP, JSW to J.D. Reid, September 16 and 24, 1915 (copies), Cochrane to JSW, October 1, 1915 and JSW to Cochrane, October 14, 1915.

25. WP, JSW to Cochrane, October 27, 1915, Cochrane to JSW, October 29 and November 27, 1915, C.S. McInnes to JSW, December 11, 1915 and A.E. Kemp to JSW, December 15 and 21, 1915.

26. FP, JSW to JWF, April 6, 1916 ; OA, G.F. Beer Papers, Creelman to Beer, April 7, 1916; WP, JSW to J.D. Reid, April 4, 1916 (copy).

27. WP, Reid to JSW, April 5, 1916.

28. WP, Cochrane to JSW, May 4, 1916, JSW to McInnes, May 12, 1916 and Cochrane to JSW, May 22, 1916, citing two JSW to Cochrane letters, May 20, 1916 (not surviving).

29. FP, JSW to JWF, September 26, 1916; WP, JSW to J.D. Reid, July 21, 1916 (copy), JSW to L. Wilson, June 12, 1916 (copy) and Cochrane to JSW, June 22, 1916.

30. WP, Cochrane to JSW, June 22, 1916 and J.D. Reid to JSW, July 5 and 19, 1916.

31. NPHSP-JSW, JSW to Robinson, November 13, 1916; JSW, *Canada's Relation to the Great War: Address Before the University Club of Rochester, N.Y., February 19, 1916* (Toronto, 1916).

32. WP, JSW to RLB, June 17, 1916 (copy) and JSW to Meighen, July 27, 1916 (copy); NPHSP-JSW, JSW to Robinson, August 4, 1915.

33. Brown and Cook, 235; FP, JWF to JSW, April 28, 18, and May 29, 1916; Glazebrook Papers, Glazebrook to Milner, May 11, June 5, 20, and July11, 1916; NPHSP-JSW, JSW to Robinson, August 29, 1916.

34. NPHSP-JSW, JSW to Robinson, November 15, 1916; Glazebrook papers, Glazebrook to Milner, May 11, June 5, 20, and July 11, 1916 (copies); NPHSP-JSW, JSW to Robinson, November 15, 1916 (enclosure).

35. C.P. Stacey, *Historical Documents of Canada*, V, *The Arts of War and Peace, 1914–1945* (Toronto, 1972), 368–69.

36. FOOC, *Times*, September 13, 1916, 7; Goodspeed, *Vimy*, 73 and map, 75; *News*, September 15, 1916, 1, 15; LAC, RG 9, III, A Overseas Ministry, Series 10 — Personal (Kemp) File 10 W-156 (W.T. Willison); G.O. Smith, ed., *University of Toronto Roll of Service, 1914–1918* (Toronto, 1921), 149; *News*, September 19, 1916, 1 and September 23, 1916, 1.

37. NPHSP-JSW, JSW to Robinson, September 27, 1916; LAC, W.L. Grant Pa-

pers, JSW to Grant, November 17, 1916.

38. *News*, September 25, 1916; NPHSP-JSW, JSW to Robinson, September 27, 1916.

39. Borden, *Memoirs*, II, 16–20; NPHSP-JSW, JSW to Robinson, November 14 and 29, 1916.

40. FOOC, *Times*, December 7, 1916, 7; *News*, November 28, 1916.

41. Walker Papers, Macgillivray to Walker, November 28, 1916; Dafoe Papers, Dafoe to Wrong, December 12, 1916 (copy) and Wrong to Dafoe, December 19, 1916; Bliss, *Flavelle*, 296.

42. Cited, Bliss, *Flavelle*, 299–300; FP, JWF to JSW, January 2 and 8, 1917; *News*, January 22, 1917; BP, JSW to RLB, January 26, 1917; WP, RLB to JSW, February 2, 1917.

43. *News*, February 8, 1917; FP, JWF to JSW, February 8 and March 2, 1917 and JSW to JWF, March 22, 1917; NPHSP-JSW, JSW to Robinson, April 9, 1917.

44. WP, JSW to G. Wilson, September 5, 1916 (copy) and P. Macdonald to JSW, March 14, 1917; FP, JWF to JSW, July 20, 1917.

45. Borden, *Memoirs*, II, 77; *News*, May 10, 1917.

46. WP, JSW to RLB, May 16, 1917 (copy).

47. J. English, *The Decline of Politics: The Conservatives and the Party System, 1900-1920* (Toronto, 1975), 129–130; WP, Ford to JSW, May 23, 1917; LAC, N.W. Rowell Papers, Rowell to R. Lemieux, May 21, 1917, LP, Rowell to WL, May 29, 1917; BP, Diary, May 25, 1917, cited, English, 131; Borden, *Memoirs*, II, 90–91.

48. FP, JSW to JWF, May 28, 1917 and JSW to Johnston, May 28, 1917 (copy).

49. FP, JWF to JSW, May 30, 1917; WP, RLB to JSW, May 28, 1917.

50. WP, Ford to JSW, May 24, 1917; FP, JWF to JSW, May 30 and June 5, 1917.

51. NPHSP-JSW, JSW to Robinson, June 11, 1917; Prang, Rowell, 21; St. Paul's Pew Lists, 1911; BP, JSW to RLB, June 8, 1917; FOOC, *Times*, June 11, 1917, 6.

52. Prang, *Rowell*, 191; WP, RLB to JSW, June 8 and 11, 1917; BP, JSW to RLB, June 9 and 12, 1917.

53. FP, JWF to JSW, June 5, 1917; WP, Beer to JSW and Dafoe, June 15, 1917; *News*,

54. WP, Hugh Clark to JSW, June 16, 1917; Rowell Papers, confidential memorandum, June 18, 1917.

55. WP, C. MacInnes to JSW, June 30, 1917 and Colquhoun to JSW, June 18, 1917; NPHSP-JSW, JSW to Robinson, June 21, 1917; Rutherford, *Media*, 51–152; WP, JSW to C.F. Crandall, March 19, 1919 (copy) and JSW to E. Beatty, February 17, 1920 (copy); FP, JWF to JSW, July 20 and August 17, 1917; WP, S. Johnston to JSW, October 17, 1917.

56. Rowell Papers, confidential memorandum, June 19, 1917, Graham to Rowell, June 20, 1917 and confidential memorandum, June 23, 1917.

57. BP, JSW to RLB, June 24, 1917; Rowell Papers, RLB to Rowell, June 24, 1917 and confidential memorandum, June 25, 1917.

58. English, 136-160; Dafoe, *Sifton*, 407–37; R. Cook, *The Politics of John W. Dafoe and the Free Press* (Toronto, 1963), 76–81; Brown and Cook, 269–72; Borden, *Memoirs*, II, 93–109; Prang, *Rowell*, 194–210.

59. BP, JSW to RLB, July 22 and August 14, 1917; NPHSP-JSW, JSW to Dawson, August 29, 1917; BP, JSW to RLB, August 30, 1917; WP, Dawson to JSW, September 28, 1917.

60. BP, JSW to RLB, October 7, 1917; FOOC, *Times*, October 13, 1917, 5.

61. WP, RLB to JSW, October 17, 1917 and E.L. Newcombe to JSW, September 5 and October 8, 1917; BP, JSW to RLB, October 19, 1917; WP, RLB to JSW, October 22, 1917 and Colquhoun to JSW, October 24, 1917.

62. NPHSP-JSW, JSW to Dawson, October 25, 1917.

63. BP, JSW to RLB, October 18, 1917; *CAR, 1917*, 587.

64. WP, RLB to JSW, November 6, 1917; D.O. Carrington, ed., *Canadian Party Platforms, 1867-1968* (Toronto, 1968), 69–74.

65. WP, A.H. Birmingham to JSW, December 13, 1917 and J. Harold to JSW, March 6, 1918.

66. NPHSP-JSW, JSW to Dawson, November 28 and 30, 1917; FP, JSW to JWF, December 8, 1917; FOOC, *Times*, December 15, 1917, 5.

67. Beck, *Pendulum of Power*, 148.

68. WP, RLB to JSW, December 20, 1917 and Rowell to JSW, December 21, 1917.

69. Cited, BP, JSW to RLB, January 22, 1918.

CHAPTER FOURTEEN

1. WP, A. Ford to JSW, February 25, 1918 and RLB to JSW, March 12, 1918; Rowell Papers, RLB to Rowell, March 12, 1918; WP, JSW to RLB, March 18, 1918 (copy).

2. WP, George to JSW, February 25, 1918, A.N. Worthington to JSW, April 15, 1918; Glazebrook Papers, Glazebrook to Lord Milner, May 21, 1918 (copy).

3. Cited, WP, volume 13, JSW, *A National Policy* (CIRA pamphlet), masthead; *Canada Weekly*, XXV (August 24, 1918), 3–4.

4. WP, Hearst to JSW, May 29 and June 7, 1918; AO, W. Hearst Papers, Hearst to JSW, June 5 and 7, 1918 (copies) and JSW to Hearst, July 13, 1918; and WP, Hearst to JSW, July 17, 1918.

5. Montreal *Star*, June 13, 1918, 5.

6. *A National Policy*; WP, JSW to Beer, July 23, 1918 (copy).

7. WP, W.J. Healey to JSW, August 6, 1918, Parsons to JSW, August 30, 1918; Wrong to JSW, August 12, 1918; Grant to JSW, July 22, 1918; volume 13, JSW, *New Problems of the New Era* (CIRA pamphlet on Winnipeg Canadian Club speech, September 5, 1918); WP, newspapers' file on CRA; Vancouver *Province*, September 24, 1918.

8. Manitoba *Free Press*, September 7, 1918.

9. WP, volume 13, JSW, *East and West: Land and Industry* (CIRA pamphlet of speech to Winnipeg Kiwanis Club, October 1, 1918); JSW to Rutherford, September 21, 1918 (copy); JSW to W.J. Bulman, October 7, 1918 (copy).

10. WP, JSW to RLB, October 15, 1918 (copy).

11. WP, Bulman to JSW, October 10, 1918, JSW to Drummond, November 15, 1918 (copy) and Cates to JSW, November 15, 1918.

12. WP, JSW to Rutherford, October 28, 1918 (copy), RLB to JSW, October 25, 1918, JSW to RLB, October 26, 1918 (copy), Rutherford to JSW, November 5, 1918 and Marnoch to JSW, December 30, 1918.

13. Hearst Papers, JSW to Hearst, July 13, 1918; WP, Hearst to JSW, July 17, 1918; Hearst Papers, JSW to Hearst, August 21, 1918, OHC minutes, August 22, 1918, Premier's Office news release, December 4, 1918, Env. 4, Correspondence on Housing, 1918, OHC memorandum to federal government, October 18, 1918, JSW to Hearst, November 8, 1918, White to Hearst, December 3, 1918 and Premier's Office news release, December 4, 1918.

14. *CAR*, 1919, 638–39; WP, Hearst to JSW, January 22, 31, February 6, 13, 17, and 19, 1919; Hearst Papers, JSW to Hearst, February 18 and 28, 1919; WP, JSW to Russell, March 21, 1919 (copy).

15. WP, Colquhoun to JSW, January 20, 1918, McTavish to JSW, February 12 and March 5, 1918, Gundy to JSW, May 26, 1918 and volume 16, 22681–84, Nelson to JSW, n.d.

16. WP, Walker to JSW, December 14, 1919, JWF to JSW, January 10, 1920, Grant to JSW, May 27, 1921; *CHR*, I (March 1920), 358; *Queen's Quarterly*, XXVIII (April 1920), 449; WP, David to JSW, December 5, 1918.

17. *Reminiscences*, 12–13, 15, 40–41, 69–70, 148, 244.

18. *Ibid.*, 177–78, 197–98, 220.

19. *Ibid.*, 161, 176, 247, 307, 311–12, 320.

20. *Times*, February 18, 1919, 7.

21. *Reminiscences*, 129–30, 216, 275.

22. WP, Long to JSW, November 28, 1918 and JSW to Lash, April 29, 1918 (copy); Glazebrook Papers, Glazebrook to Milner, May 21, 1918 (copy).

23. WP, JSW to Glazebrook, March 21, 1919 (copy); FOOC, *Times*, August 16, 1919, p. 9; Milner Papers, JSW to Milner, December 5, 1919; WP, JSW to Miller, January 12, 1920 (copy); and JSW to Cronyn, May 16, 1920 (copy).

24. JSW, *Partners in Peace*, 11–23.

25. WP, Atholston to JSW, October 5 and November 13, 1918 and JSW to Colquhoun, May 10, 1921.

26. WP, Glazebrook to Drummond, February 21, 1919 (copy), JSW to Beatty, September 24, 27 and October 16, 1919 (copies), JSW to H.D. Scully, November 5, 1919 (copy), G.H. Carlisle to JSW, November 10, 1919 and JSW to Carlisle, November 13, 1919 (copy).

27. WP, Beatty to JSW, December 12, 1919 and February 16, 1920, JSW to Beatty, February 17, 1920 (copy) and JSW to Carlisle, November 13, 1919 copy).

28. WP, JSW to Bulman, November 4, 1918 (copy); *Star*, November 29, 1918 (JSW); FOOC, *Times*, January 7, 1919, 7; WP, JSW to Bulman, March 18, 1919 (copy); W.L. Morton, *The Progressive Party in Canada* (Toronto, 1967 edition), 69.

29. WP, volume 13, CRA pamphlets and JSW to B. Richey, May 6, 1919 (copy).

30. *Star*, May 28 and 29, 1919 (confirmed as JSW's in WP, C.F. Crandall to JSW, May 29, 1919); WP, Wood to JSW, July 3, 1919.

31. WP, JSW to W.A. Black, June 2, 1919 (copy); Tom Traves, "The Story That Couldn't Be Told: Big Business buys the TLC," *Ontario Report*, I (No. 6, September 1976), 27–29; WP, JSW to T.P. Howard, July 18, 23, October 9, November 12, 1919, February 2 and June 23,1920 (copies); Howard to JSW, July 21, September 22 and 23, December 12, 1919, June 24 and October 4, 1920; J.E. Walsh to JSW, August 30, 1920.

32. Morton, *The Progressive Party in Canada*, 85–86; WP, JSW to Bulman, October 27, 1919 (copy).

33. FOOC, *Times*, January 7, 1919, p. 7 and May 28, 1919, 10.

34. WP, JSW to Hearst, August 7, 1919, JSW to Bulman, October 27, 1919 and JSW to Devonshire, December 2, 1919 (copies).

35. WP, JSW to Rowell, September 23, 1919 and JSW to Beatty, December 11, 1919 (copies); NPHSP-JSW, JSW to Steed, December 23, 1919 (copy); WP, JSW to Russell, January 21, 1920 and JSW to Stuart, March 17 and May 12, 1920 (copies); FOOC, *Times*, June 30, 1920, 15.

36. BP, Rowell to RLB, July 7, 1920 and RLB to Rowell, July 8, 1920 (copy); Rowell Papers, JSW to Rowell, July 13, 1920; WP, JSW to Drummond, July 21, 1920 (copy).

37. FOOC, *Times*, August 16, 1920, 9; WP, JSW to Meighen, September 22, 1920 and JSW to Northcliffe, September 28, 1920 (copies).

38. WP, JSW to Stuart, December 15, 1920 (copy); FOOC, *Times*, January 5, 1921, 9; WP, JSW to Meighen, April 18, 1921 (copy).

39. WP, JSW to Cockshutt, April 27, 1921 (copy).

40. R. Graham, *Arthur Meighen*, II, *And Fortune Fled* (Toronto 1963), 84–109; NPHSP-JSW, JSW to Long, June 30, 1921; WP, JSW to Stuart, September 6, 1921 (copy).

41. Doug Owram, *The Government Generation: Canadian Intellectuals and the State, 1900–1945* (Toronto, 1986), 109; WP, JSW to W.A. Black, June 19, 1919 and H.A. Richardson to C.H. Godfrey, January 9, 1920 (copies), Drummond to JSW, March 25, 1920, W.J. Bulman to JSW, April 7, 1920, JSW to Beatty, April 19, 1920, JSW to J.S. Christie, December 20, 1920 and JSW to Drummond, July 15, 1920 (copies).

42. JSW, *The Railway Question in Canada* (CRA pamphlet on speech to Canadian Club of Montreal, January 31, 1921).

43. WP, JSW to JWF, February 1, 1921 (copy) and White to JSW, February 21, 1921.

44. WP, C.H. Godfrey to JSW, February 1, 1921 (copy), Beatty to JSW, February 26, 1921, JSW to Drummond, April 12, 1921 (copy), Drummond to JSW, April 13, 1921 and JSW to Drummond, April 14, 1921 (copy).

45. WP, JSW to H. D. Scully, November 8, 1921; FOOC, *Times*, October 1, 1921, 9; WP, JSW to Harold, October 13, 1921; Beck, *Pendulum of Power*, 160–61; WP, JSW to King, December 7, 1921 (copy); FOOC, *Times*, December 8, 1921, 10; WP, volume 13, Report of CRA Annual Meeting, December 12, 1921; Tom Traves, *The State and Enterprise: Canadian Manufacturers and the Federal Government, 1917–1931* (Toronto, 1979), 16–28.

46. WP, JSW to Beatty, December 9, 1921 (copy), FP, JSW to JWF, January 8, 1921, W.G. Cates to JSW, December 31, 1920; JSW to Stuart, September 8, 1921 (copy) and W.T. Stevens to JSW, October 24 and November 12, 1921.

47. (Toronto, 1921), 172.

CHAPTER FIFTEEN

1. WP, JSW to Beatty, June 16, 1922 and JSW to King, August 22 and July 16, 1922 (copies).

2. WP, JSW to Frank Carrel, March 17, 1924 and April 14, 1923 (copies).

3. WP, A.D.McRae to JSW, May 4 and 26, 1921 and JSW to Beatty, May 30, 1921 (copy).

4. WP, JSW to Beatty, June 16, 1922 (copy).

5. WP, Beatty to JSW, June 17, 1922

6. WP, D. Marshall to P.C. Larkin, June 21, 1922 and L.S. Amery to M.A. Brown, July 20, 1922 (copies), King to JSW, August 16, 1922, JSW to Nanton, October 19, 1922 (copy), cited, Beatty to JSW, November 13, 1922, Osler to JSW, November 14, 1922, Shenstone to JSW, November 15, 1922, JSW to S. Dennis, November 20, 1922 and JSW to Stuart, November 17, 1922 (copies) and JSW to JWF, December 8, 1922.

7. WP, JSW to Beatty, December 15, 1922 (copy), Beatty to JSW, December 18, 1922, JSW to Charles Stewart, December 27, 1922 (copy); *Star*, January 31, 1923 (confirmed as JSW's in WP, JSW to Charles Stewart, February 1, 1923); FP, JSW to JWF, April 3, 1923.

8. WP, cables to *Times*, May 29 and June 9, 1923, JSW to A.E. Mackenzie, July 3, 1923 (copy); *Star*, August 18, 1923; Dawson, *King*, I, p. 449.

9. LAC, Glazebrook Papers, Glazebrook to Milner, November 5, 1921; John Evelyn Wrench, *Geoffrey Dawson and Our Times* (London, 1955), 309–12; Camil Girard, *Canada: A Country Divided: The Times of London and Canada, 1908–1922* (Chicoutimi, 2001), 155–75; WP, Stuart to JSW, September 4 and July 31, 1922.

10. FOOC, "Canada: Equal Status," *Times*, May 24, 1922, Empire Day Supplement, vi; LAC, Lady Parkin Papers, volume 109, 37858–63.

11. XCII (July, 1922), 25–39; FP, JSW to JWF, November 3, 1922.

12. WP, JSW to RLB, January 31, 1923, JSW to Dafoe, March 7, 1923 and JSW to Hocken, April 3, 1922 (copies). See Simon J. Potter, *op. cit.*, 125–26.

13. WP, JSW to Stuart, February 5, 1923 (copy), Peterson to JSW, April 12 (also citing a not surviving JSW letter of March 23) and April 16, 1923; NPHSP-JSW, JSW to Peterson, April 25, 1923.

14. R. Cook, *Dafoe*, 138–45; FOOC, *Times*, November 10, 1923, 9; *Star*, December 17, 1923 (identified as JSW's in NPHSP-JSW, JSW to Dawson, December 18, 1923; WP, JSW to JWF, January 4, 1924 (copy).

15. NPHSP-JSW, JSW to Dawson, January 3, 1924; WP, Stuart to JSW, January 24, 1924; LAC, W.L. Grant Papers, JSW to Grant, November 17, 1916; WP, Hotel Belmont to JSW, October 19, 1921, George Patullo to JSW, November 4, 1921 and Pelham Edgar to JSW, December 1, 1921.

16. FP, JSW to JWF, January 9, 1924; W.L. Grant Papers, Grant to JSW, November 18, 1923 (copy); memorandum of author's conversation with Raleigh *Parkin* (Sir George's son), May 6, 1974; Grant Papers, JSW to Grant, November 17, 1916 and Grant to JSW, December 4, 1923 (copy).

17. Lady Parkin Papers, JSW to Lady Parkin, February 24, 1924.

18. (Toronto, 1923); WP, Milner to JSW, January 27, 1924; Milner Papers, JSW to Milner, March 29, 1924.

19. WP, Beck to JSW, March 13, 17, 21, 27, 29, 1924, and JSW to Beck, March 27, 1924 (copy); NPHSP-JSW, JSW to Dawson, March 31, 1924; FP, JSW to JWF, April 14, 1924; J.S. Willison, "Australia as I Saw It," *Dalhousie Review*, V (April, 1925), 51.

20. WP, King to JSW, May 6, 1924; JSW to S.M. Bruce, May 20, 1924 (copy) and E. Beck to JSW, December 5, 1924 and March 12, 1925; Willison, "Australia," 51–52; Colquhoun, "Sir John Willison," *Dalhouse Review*, VII (July 1927), 162.

21. WP, V.L. Humphreys to JSW, August 5 and 15, 1924; Willison, "Australia," 52.

22. WP, Stuart to JSW, August 8, 1924 and T.H. Blacklock to JSW, August 28, 1924.

23. W.L. Grant Papers, JSW to Grant, September 11, 1924; WP, JSW to A.L. Dawe, September 11, 1924 (copy); FP, JSW to JWF, November 12, 1924; WP, JSW to Blacklock, December 1, 1924 copy); NPHSP-JSW, JSW to Dawson, December 1, 1924; WP, Gladys McBride to JSW, January 9, 1925; G.F. Beer Papers, JSW to Beer, February 14, 1925; WP, JSW to *Times*, January 19, 1925 (copy).

24. Beer Papers, JSW to Beer, February 14, 1925; WP, JSW to W.S. Dingman, February 16, 1925 (copy).

25. Lady Parkin Papers, memorandum on talk with JSW, February 25, 1925, JSW to Lady Parkin, March 2 and October 27, 1926, December 28, 1926.

26. WP, JSW to Morang, March 10, 1925 (copy); JSW, *Sir Wilfrid Laurier* (Toronto, 1926), 355, 411.

27. WP, JSW to Beatty, February 12, 1925, JSW to T.A. Russell, March 13, 1925,

JSW to Ellis, April 23, 1925 (copies) and King to JSW, May 7, 1925; Dafoe Papers, Colquhoun to Dafoe, May 22, 1925.

28. *Willison's Monthly* (hereinafter *WM*), I (No. 1, June 1925), 1–10; Dafoe Papers, Dafoe to Colquhoun, July 25, 1925 (copy).

29. Dafoe Papers, Dafoe to Colquhoun, July 25, 1925; WP, JSW to RLB, April 20, 1926 (copy); FP, JSW to JWF, October 12, 1925.

30. NPHSP-JSW, JSW to Dawson, February 23, 1925; FOOC, *Times*, June 29, 1926, 26; *Sir George Parkin: A Biography* (Toronto, 1929), 259.

31. WP, JSW to Stuart, May 20 and June 30, 1925 (copies); FOOC, *Times*, October 29, 1925, 15; FP, JSW to JWF, November 12, 1925; WP, JSW to A.F. Sladen, August 3, 1926 (copy); *WM*, II, No. 5 (October 1926), 163–65.

32. WP, JSW to Sheldon, April 16, 1925 (copy); *Australian Dictionary of Biography* (online edition 2010); FP, JSW to JWF, September 28 and 30, 1925; FOOC, *Times*, December 1, 1925, 9; FP, JSW to JWF, November 18, 1925; NPHSP-JSW, JSW to Dawson, February 2 and August 6, 1926.

33. *Macmillan D.C.B.*, 803; NPHSP-JSW, JSW to Dawson, April 20, 1926; WP, RLB to JSW, April 20, 1926, King to JSW, April 12, 1926 and Bruce to JSW, April 28, 1926.

34. NPHSP-JSW, JSW to Dawson, April 13, 1927 and Lady M. Willison to Dawson, May 22, 1927; Lady Parkin Papers, JSW to Lady Parkin, February 21, 1927 and Lady Parkin to Hugh Eayrs, May 27, 1927 (The Parkin biography was completed by W.L. Grant and published in 1929 under Willison's name by Macmillan); NPHSP-JSW, Lady M. Willison to Dawson, July 5, 1927; *Globe*, May 28, 1927, 1; JSW, *Laurier*, 458; Manitoba *Free Press*, May 28, 1927, 13.

35. Colquhoun, *Willison*, 297–98.

36. *Saturday Night*, LI (December 7, 1935), 1.

37. *Globe*, January 22, 1897, 9; Dafoe Papers, Dafoe to George Iles, April 3, 1936; King Diary, July 17, 1927.

38. WP, JSW to Rowell, September 23, 1919 (copy).

39. Augustus Bridle, Toronto *Star*, October 26, 1935, 36; Colquhoun, "Sir John Willison," *Dalhousie Review*, VII (July 1927), 160.

40. Manitoba *Free Press*, May 28, 1927, 13; *Dalhousie Review*, IV (No. 1, April 1924), 25–28. On the poem the reflections of Lady Marjory Willison (OA, Lady MW memoir, p. 23) are interesting. She wrote: "There is no doubt that much can be learned of his early boyhood and his youth from his poem 'The Alien.' But to imagine that he wrote of himself, with entire self-revelation, in this poem is to be mistaken. Every writer knows how much material is used, and how it undergoes a transmutation in the mind and in the writing…. But he used that vivid, quick burning recollection of his early days to illustrate a type of the servants and saviours of mankind. Yet in a sense it is also autobiographical."

Bibliography

I PRIMARY SOURCES

Manuscripts

<u>Library and Archives Canada</u>
U. Barthe
R.L. Borden
G.T. Denison
C.J. Fitzpatrick
Arthur Glazebrook
G.M. Grant
W.L. Grant
A.E. Kemp
W.L.M. King
Wilfrid Laurier
Lord Minto
Annie Parkin (Lady Parkin)
G.R. Parkin
Joseph Pope
Newton W. Rowell
Clifford Sifton
J.I. Tarte

Bibliography

J.S. Willison

<u>Archives of Ontario</u>
G.F. Beer
Edward Blake
Richard J. Cartwright
J.D. Edgar
W. Hearst
T.C. Patteson
J.P. Whitney
J.S. Willison

<u>Douglas Library, Queen's University</u>
Wilfrid Campbell
J.W. Flavelle
W.D. Gregory

<u>John M. Olin Library, Cornell University</u>
Goldwin Smith

<u>University of Toronto Library</u>
John Charlton
B.E. Walker
G.M. Wrong

<u>National Club of Canada, Toronto</u>
Membership Lists

<u>Saint Paul's (Bloor Street) Anglican Church, Toronto</u>
Pew Lists

<u>New Printing House Square, London</u> *Times*
J.S. Willison

<u>Bodleian Library, Oxford University</u>
Lord Milner

<u>Scottish Record Office, Edinburgh</u>
Lord Lothian (Philip Kerr)

<u>British Museum, London</u>

Lord Northcliffe (Alfred Harmsworth)

Printed Material

American Newspaper Directories, 1890, 1892, 1895, 1897, 1898, 1900 (New York: G.P. Rowell and Co., 1890–1900).

Barthe, U. *Wilfrid Laurier on the Platform.* Quebec, 1890.

Bliss, M. *A Canadian Millionaire: The Life and Business Times of Sir Joseph Flavelle, Bart., 1858–1939.* Toronto: Macmillan, 1978.

Borden, H., ed. *Robert Laird Borden: His Memoirs,* I. Toronto: Macmillan, 1938.

Canada, *Census Returns, 1871.*

Canada, House of Commons, *Bills.*

_____. *Debates.*

Canada, Parliament, *Sessional Papers.*

Canada, *Sessional Papers.*

Canada, *Statutes.*

Canada Weekly

Canadian Club of Toronto, Addresses.

Carrington, D.O., ed. *Canadian Party Platforms, 1867–1968.* Toronto: Copp Clark, 1968.

Cartwright, R. *Reminiscences.* Toronto: Briggs, 1912.

Charlesworth, H. *Candid Chronicles: Leaves from the Note Book of a Canadian Journalist.* Toronto: Macmillan, 1925.

_____. *More Candid Chronicles; Further Leaves from the Note Book of a Canadian Journalist.* Toronto: Macmillan, 1928.

Clerk of the Peace, Huron County. Census of Huron, 1850. London, 1850.

County of Huron Gazetteer and General Business Directory for 1863–'64. Ingersoll, 1863.

Denison, George T. *The Struggle for Imperial Unity.* Toronto: University of Toronto Press, 1909.

Encyclopedia Britannica, Eleventh Edition. Cambridge: Cambridge University Press, 1911.

Grant, G.M. *Ocean to Ocean: Sanford Fleming's Expedition through Canada in 1872* rev. ed. Toronto: Radisson Society, 1925.

Hopkins, J.C., ed. *The Canadian Annual Review of Public Affairs, 1901-1927.* Toronto, 1901-1927.

Hermon, R.W. *New Map of the County of Huron.* Toronto, 1862.

Illustrated Historical Atlas of the County of Huron. Toronto, 1879.

Manitoba, *Statutes.*

McLean, I. and Mclean, B. *Greenwood Through the Years.* Toronto, n.p., 1960.

Morgan, H.J., ed. *Canadian Men and Women of the Time.* Toronto, 1898.

_____. *The Dominion Annual Register and Review, 1883*. Toronto, 1884.

_____. ed. *The Dominion Annual Register and Review, 1886*. Toronto, 1887.

_____. ed. *Official Report of the Liberal Convention, 1893*. Toronto: n.p., 1893.

N.W. Ayer and Sons American Newspaper Annual, 1884. New York: N.W. Ayer Co, 1884.

Official Report of the Liberal Convention, 1893. Toronto, 1893.

Ollivier, M., ed., *The Colonial and Imperial Conferences from 1887 to 1937*. 3 vols., Toronto, Queen's Printer, 1954.

_____. *British North America Acts and Selected Statutes, 1867–1962*. Ottawa: Queen's Printer, 1962.

Ontario, *Journals of the Legislative Assembly*.

_____. *Sessional Papers*.

Pope, J. *Correspondence of Sir John Macdonald*. Toronto: Oxford University Press, 1921.

Preston, W.T.R. *My Generation of Politics and Politicians*. Toronto: D.A. Rose Co., 1927.

Province of Canada, *Census Returns, 1861*.

Rowell's American Newspaper Directory. New York: The Printer's Ink Co., 1907.

Stacey, C.P. *Historical Documents of Canada*, V. *The Arts of War and Peace, 1914–1945*. Toronto: Macmillan, 1972.

The Canadian Newspaper Directory, 1899 Edition: A Complete List of the Newspapers and Periodicals Published in the Dominion of Canada and Newfoundland, With Full Particulars. Montreal: A. McKim and Co., 1899.

The Toronto City Directory for 1883. Toronto, 1883.

The Toronto City Directory for 1887. Toronto, 1887.

University of Toronto, *Roll of Service, 1914–1918*. Toronto: University of Toronto Press, 1921.

United Kingdom, *Statutes*.

Willison, J.S. *A National Policy*. Toronto: Canadian Industrial Reconstruction Association pamphlet, 1968.

_____. "Australia as I Saw It," *Dalhousie Review*, V (April, 1925), pp. 37–53.

_____. *Canada's Relation to the Great War: Address Before the University Club of Rochester, N.Y. Feb. 9, 1916*. Toronto, n.p., 1916.

_____. *East and West: Land and Industry*. Toronto: Canadian Industrial Reconstruction Association pamphlet, 1918.

_____. *Journalism: An Address delivered before the Political Science Club of Toronto University*. (n.p., [1899]).

_____. *New Problems of the New Era*. Toronto: Canadian Industrial Reconstruction Association pamphlet, 1918.

_____. *Partners in Peace: The Dominion, the Empire and the Republic*. Toronto: Warwick Bros. and Rutter, 1923.

_____. *Reminscences Political and Personal*. Toronto: McClelland and Stewart, 1919.

_____. *Sir Wilfrid Laurier and the Liberal Party*. 2 vols. Toronto: George N. Morang Co., 1903.

_____. *Sir Wilfrid Laurier and the Liberal Party*. Toronto: Oxford University Press, 1926.

_____. "The Function of Journalism in Democracy," *Queen's Quarterly* VII (April 1901), pp. 313–14.

_____. *The New Canada: A Survey of the Conditions and Problems of the Dominion by the Canadian Correspondent of the Times*. London: The *Times*, 1912.

_____. "The Party System of Government," *Canadian Club of Toronto, Addresses, 1903–04*, pp.70ff.

_____. *The Railway Question in Canada with an Examination of the Railway Law of Iowa*. Toronto: n.p., n.d. [1897].

Young, A.H. *The Roll of Pupils of Upper Canada College, Toronto. January 1830 to June 1916*. Kingston: Hanson, Crozier and Edgar, 1917.

_____. *The War Book of Upper Canada College*. Toronto, 1923.

Newspapers, Journals, and Magazines

Canadian Annual Review
Camadian Magazine
London *Advertiser*
Manitoba *Free Press*
Montreal *Le Cultivateur*
Montreal *Star*
Orange Sentinel
London *Morning Post*
London *Times*
Quebec *Le Canadien*
Quebec *L'Électeur*
Quebec *Le Soleil*
Queen's Quarterly
Saturday Night
The Printer and Publisher (Toronto)
The Round Table
The Week (Toronto)
Times Literary Supplement
Toronto *Empire*
Toronto *Globe*
Toronto *Mail*
Toronto *Mail and Empire*
Toronto *News*

Toronto *Star*
Vancouver *Province*
Victoria *Daily Times*
Willison's Monthly

II SECONDARY SOURCES

Books

Amery, J. *The Life of Joseph Chamberlain,* Vol. IV. London: Macmillan, 1951.

Andrae, Christopher. *Lines of Country: Atlas of Railway and Waterway History in Canada.* (Erin: Boston Mills, 1997).

Australian Dictionary of Biography. Online edition, 2010.

Beck, J.M. *Pendulum of Power: Canada's Federal Elections.* Scarborough: Prentice-Hall, 1968.

Berger, C.C. *The Sense of Power: Studies in the Ideas of Canadian Imperialism, 1867–1914.* Toronto: University of Toronto Press, 1970.

Bone, J.R., Clark, J.T. *et.al. A History of Canadian Journalism.* Toronto, 1908.

Bourinot, A.S. *At The Mermaid Inn.* Ottawa: The Editor, 1958.

Brown, R.C. and Cook, R. *Canada, 1896–1921.* Toronto: McClelland and Stewart, 1974.

Brown, R.C. *Canada's National Policy, 1883–1900: A Study in Canadian-American Relations.* Princeton: Princeton University Press, 1964.

Brown, R.C. *Robert Laird Borden: A Biography,* I. *1854–1914.* Toronto: Macmillan, 1975.

_____. *Robert Laird Borden: A Biography* II. *1914–1938.* Toronto: Macmillan, 1980.

Campbell, A.E. *Great Britain and the United States, 1895–1903.* London: Longman's, 1960.

Careless, J.M.S. *Brown of the Globe,* II. Toronto: Macmillan, 1963.

Clippingdale, R. *Laurier: His Life and World.* Toronto: McGraw-Hill Ryerson, 1979.

Colquhoun, A.H.U. *Press, Politics and People: The Life and Letters of Sir John Willison.* Toronto: Macmillan, 1935.

Connor, C.Y. *Archibald Lampman: Canadian Poet of Nature.* Montreal: Louis Corrier and Co., 1929.

Cook, R. *The Politics of John W. Dafoe and the Free Press.* Toronto: University of Toronto Press, 1963.

Creighton, D.G. *John A. Macdonald,* II. *The Old Chieftain.* Toronto: Macmillan, 1955.

_____. *The Road to Confederation: The Emergence of Canada, 1863–1867.* Toronto: Macmillan, 1964.

Cumming, Carman. *Secret Craft: The Journalism of Edward Farrer.* (Toronto: University of Toronto Press, 1992.

Dafoe, J.W. *Clifford Sifton in Relation to His Times*. Toronto: Macmillan, 1931.

_____. *Laurier: A Study in Canadian Politics*. Toronto: McClelland and Stewart, 1964.

Dawson, R.M. *William Lyon Mackenzie King: A Political Biography*, Vol. I. Toronto: University Press, 1958.

Denison, M. *The People's Power: The History of Ontario Hydro*. Toronto: McClelland and Stewart, 1960.

English, J. *Borden: His Life and World*. Toronto: McGraw-Hill Ryerson, 1977.

_____. *The Decline of Politics: The Conservatives and the Party System, 1900–1920*. Toronto: University of Toronto Press, 1975.

Evans, W.S. *The Canadian Contingents and Canadian Imperialism*. Toronto, 1901.

Ferns, H.S. and Ostry, B. *Mackenzie King: The Rise of the Leader*. London: Heinemann, 1955.

Fraser, P. *Joseph Chamberlain: Radicalism and Empire, 1868–1914*. London: Cassel, 1966.

Garvin, J.L. *The Life of Joseph Chamberlain*, III. London: Macmillan, 1934.

Gibbon, *Steel of Empire: The Romantic History of the Canadian Pacific, the Northwest Passage of Today*. Toronto: McClelland and Stewart, 1935.

Girard, C. *Canada: A Country Divided: The Times of London and Canada, 1908–1922*. Chicoutimi: Groupe de recherche et d'intervention régionales, 2001.

Glazebrook, G.P. de T. *Sir Edmund Walker*. London: Oxford Press, 1933.

Goodspeed, D.J. *The Road Past Vimy: The Canadian Corps, 1914–1918*. Toronto: Macmillan, 1969.

Graham, R. *Arthur Meighen*, II, *And Fortune Fled*. Toronto: Clarke, Irwin, 1963.

Granatstein, J.L. *Mackenzie King: His Life and World*. Toronto: McGraw-Hill Ryerson, 1977.

Grant, W.L. and Hamilton, C.F. *Principal Grant*. Toronto: George N. Morang, 1904.

Gray, Charlotte. *The Life and Times of Isabel Mackenzie King*. Toronto: Penguin, 1997.

Harkness, R. *J.E. Atkinson of the Star*. Toronto: University Press, 1964.

Innis, H.A. *A History of the Canadian Pacific Railway*. London: McClelland and Stewart, 1923.

Kendle, J.E. *The Colonial and Imperial Conferences, 1887–1911: A Study in Imperial Organization*. London: Longmans, 1967.

Kendle, J.E. *The Round Table Movement and Imperial Union*. Toronto: University of Toronto Press, 1975.

Klinck, C.F. *Literary History of Canada*. Toronto: University of Toronto Press, 1965.

Klinck, C.F. *Wilfrid Campbell: A Study in Late Provincial Victorianism*. Toronto: Ryerson, 1942.

LaPierre, L. *Sir Wilfrid Laurier and the Romance of Canada*. Toronto: Stoddart, 1996.

Lingard, C.C. *Territorial Government in Canada: The Autonomy Question in the Old North-West Territories*. Toronto: University of Toronto Press, 1946.

Link, A.S. *American Epoch: A History of the United States Since the 1890s*. New

York: Knopf, 1963.

Magnus, P. *Gladstone: A Biography*. London: John Murray, 1954.

Miller, C. *Painting the Map Red: Canada and the South African War, 1899-1902*. Montreal and Kingston: McGill-Queen's University Press, 1993.

Morton, W.L. *Manitoba: A History*. Toronto: Macmillan, 1957.

_____. *The Progressive Party in Canada*. Toronto: University of Toronto Press: 1967 edition.

Moyles, R.G. and Owram, D. *Imperial Dreams and Colonial Realities: British Views of Canada, 1880-1914*. Toronto: University of Toronto Press, 1988.

Neatby, H.B. *Laurier and a Liberal Quebec*. Toronto: McClelland and Stewart, 1973. Edited and with an Introduction by R. Clippingdale.

Nelles, H.V. *The Politics of Development: Forests, Mines and Hydro-Electric Power in Ontario, 1849-1941*. Toronto: Macmillan, 1974.

Nevins, A. *Grover Cleveland: A Study in Courage*. New York: Dodd Mead and Co., 1932.

Noel-Smith, S. *Edwardian England, 1901-1914*. London: Oxford University Press, 1964.

O'Leary, G. *Recollections of People, Press and Politics*. Toronto: Macmillan, 1977.

Owram, D. *The Government Generation: Canadian Intellectuals and the State, 1900-1945*. Toronto: University of Toronto Press, 1986.

Ormsby, M. *British Columbia: A History*. Toronto: Macmillan, 1958.

Penlington, Norman. *Canada and Imperialism, 1896-1899*. Toronto: University of Toronto Press, 1965.

Pope, J. *Memoirs of the Right Honourable Sir John Alexander Macdonald, G.C.B., First Prime Minister of Canada*, Vol. II. London: 1894.

Pound, R. and Harmsworth, G. *Northcliffe*. London: Cassell, 1959.

Prang, M. *Newton W. Rowell: Ontario Nationalist*. Toronto: University of Toronto Press, 1975.

Preston, R.A. *Canada and Imperial Defense: A Study of the Origins of the British Commonwealth's Defense Organization, 1867-1919*. Toronto: University of Toronto Press, 1967.

Rumilly, Robert. *Histoire de la Province de Québec*. IV-XII. Montréal: Editions Bernard Valiquette, n.d.

Rutherford, P. *The Making of the Canadian Media*. Toronto: McGraw-Hill Ryerson, 1978.

Saywell, J.T., ed. *The Canadian Journal of Lady Aberdeen., 1893-1898*. Toronto: Champlain Society, 1960.

Schull, Joseph. *Laurier: The First Canadian*. Toronto: Macmillan, 1965.

Sissons, C.B. *Church and State in Canadian Education*. Toronto: Ryerson, 1959.

Skelton, O.D. *Life and Letters of Sir Wilfrid Laurier*, 2 vols. Toronto: Oxford University Press, 1921.

Sotiron, Minko. *From Politics to Profit: The Commercialization of Canadian Daily Newspapers*. Montreal and Kingston: McGill-Queen's University Press, 1997.

Stevens, G.R. *Canadian National Railways, II, Towards the Inevitable, 1896–1922*. Toronto: Clarke Irwin and Co., 1962.

Storey, N. *The Oxford Companion to Canadian History and Literature*. Toronto: Oxford University Press, 1967.

Traves, T. *The State and Enterprise: Canadian Manufacturers and the Federal Government, 1917–1931*. Toronto: University of Toronto Press, 1979.

Underhill, F.H. *The Image of Confederation*. Toronto: CBC, 1964.

Waite, P.B. *Canada, 1874–1896: Arduous Destiny*. Toronto: McClelland and Stewart, 1971.

Wallace, E., ed. *The Macmillan Dictionary of Canadian Biography*, 3rd ed. Toronto: Macmillan, 1963.

Weir, G.M. *The Separate School Question in Canada*. Toronto: Ryerson, 1934.

Willison, J.S. *Sir George Parkin: A Biography*. London: Macmillan, 1929.

Wrench, J.E. *Geoffrey Dawson and Our Times*. London: Hutchinson, 1955.

Articles

Banks, Margaret A. "The Change in the Liberal Leadership, 1887." *Canadian Historical Review*, Vol. XXXVIII (June, 1957), pp. 109–28.

Berger, C.C. "The True North Strong and Free." in Russell, P., ed. *Nationalism in Canada*. Toronto: McGraw-Hill, 1966, pp. 3–26.

Brown, R.C. "Goldwin Smith and Anti-Imperialism." *Canadian Historical Review*, Vol. XLIII (June 1962), pp. 93–105.

_____. "The Commercial Unionists in Canada and the United States." *Canadian Historical Association Reports*, 1963, pp. 116–24.

Clark, L.C. "The Conservative Party in the 1890s." *Canadian Historical Association Reports*, 1961, pp. 58–74.

Clippingdale, R. "J.S. Willison and Canadian Nationalism, 1886–1902." *Canadian Historical Association Reports*, 1969, pp. 74–93.

Colvin, J.A. "Sir Wilfrid Laurier and the British Preferential Tariff System." *Canadian Historical Association Reports*, 1955, pp. 13-23.

Colquhoun, A.H.U. "Sir John Willison." *Dalhousie Review* VII (July 1927), pp. 158–62.

_____. "The Journalistic Field of 1887: Memories of the Background from which Saturday Night Sprang." *Saturday Night*, Dec. 10, 1925, p. 5.

Creighton, D.G. "The Use and Abuse of History." *Journal of Canadian Studies*, I (May, 1966), pp. 3–11.

Dafoe, J.W. "Review Article: Press, Politics and People." *Canadian Historical Review*, Vol. XVII (March 1936), pp. 59–64.

E.Q.V. "Canadian Celebreties: Messrs. Ewan and Hamilton." *Canadian Magazine*, Vol. XV (October 1900), pp. 1164–66.

_____. "Canadian Celebreties, No. XXXIX, Mr. J.S. Willison." *Canadian Magazine*, Vol. XX, No. 3 (June 1903), pp. 222–24.

Fraser, B. "The Political Career of Sir Hector Louis Langevin." *Canadian Historical Review*, Vol. XLII (June 1961), pp. 93–132.

Graham, W.R. "Sir Richard Cartwright, Wilfrid Laurier and Liberal Trade Policy, 1887." *Canadian Historical Review*, Vol. XXXIII (March 1952), pp. 1–18.

Gundy, H.P. "Sir Wilfrid Laurier and Lord Minto." *Canadian Historical Association Reports*, 1952, pp. 28–38.

Hammond, M.O. "Edward William Thomson." *Queen's Quarterly*, Vol. XXXVIII (January 1931), pp. 123–28.

Harrington, F.H. "The Anti-Imperialist Movement in the United States, 1898–1900." *Mississippi Valley Historical Review*, Vol. XXII (Sept. 1935), pp. 211–229.

Humphries, C.W. "The Gamey Affair." *Ontario History* LIX (June 1967), pp. 101–09.

_____. "The Sources of Ontario Progressive Conservatism, 1900–1914." *CHAR*, 1967, pp. 118–29.

Kerr, J.B. "Sir Oliver Mowat and the campaign of 1894." *Ontario History*, Vol. LV (March 1963), pp. 1–13.

Landon, F. "D'Alton McCarthy and the Politics of the later Eighties." *Canadian Historical Association Reports*, 1932, pp. 43–50.

Landon, F. "The Canadian Scene, 1880-1890." *Canadian Historical Association Reports*, 1942, pp. 5–18.

La Terreur, M. "Correspondence Laurier-Mme. Joseph Lavergne, 1891–1893." *Canadian Historical Association Reports*, 1964, pp. 37–51.

Lederle, J.W. "The Liberal Convention of 1893." *Canadian Journal of Economics and Political Science*, Vol. XVI (Feb. 1950), pp. 42–52.

MacKirdy, K.A. "National vs. Provincial Loyalty: The Ontario Western Boundary Dispute, 1883–1884." *Ontario History*, Vol. LI (Spring 1959), pp. 191–98.

_____. "The Loyalty Issue in 1891." *Ontario History*, Vol. LV (Sept. 1963), pp. 143–54.

Mavor, J. "Goldwin Smith." *Maclean's Magazine*, Vol. XXXIV (March 1921), pp. 12–13, 47–49.

Miller, H.O. "The History of the Newspaper Press in London, 1835–1875." *Ontario History*, Vol. XXXII (1937), pp. 114–39.

Morton, W.L. "Manitoba Schools and Canadian Nationality, 1890–1921." *Canadian Historical Association Reports*, 1951, pp. 51–9.

Neatby, H.B. "Laurier and Imperialism." *Canadian Historical Association Reports*, 1955, pp. 24–32.

Page, R.J.D. "Canada and the Imperial Idea in the Boer War Years." *Journal of Canadian Studies*, Vol. V, No. 1 (Feb.1970), pp. 33–49.

Potter, Simon J. "Richard Jebb, John S. Ewart and the Round Table, 1898–1926." *English Historical Review*, Vol. CXXII (Feb. 2007), pp. 105–32.

Prang, Margaret. "Nationalism in Canada's First Century." *Canadian Historical Association Reports*, 1968, pp. 114–25.

Sandwell, B.K. "Political Developments Around the Turn of the Century." *Canadian Historical Association Reports*, 1945, pp. 49–57.

Silver, A.I. "French Canada and the Prairie Frontier, 1870–1890." *Canadian Historical Review*, Vol. L (March, 1969), pp. 11–36.

Stamp, R.M. "J.D. Edgar and the Liberal Party, 1867–1896." *Canadian Historical Review*, Vol. XLV (June 1964), pp. 93–115.

Traves, T. "The Story That Couldn't Be Told: Big Business Buys the TLC." *Ontario Repor*, Vol. I (No. 6, Sept. 1976), pp. 27–9.

Underhill, F.H. "Laurier and Blake, 1882–1891." *Canadian Historical Review*, Vol. XX (Dec., 1939), pp. 392–408.

_____. "Laurier and Blake, 1891–1892." *Canadian Historical Review*, Vol. XXIV (June, 1943), pp. 135–56.

Wallace, W.S. "Arthur Hugh Urquhart Colquhoun." *Canadian Historical Review*, Vol. XVII (March, 1936), pp. 89–90.

Watt, J.T. "Anti-Catholic Nativism in Canada: The Protestant Protective Association." *Canadian Historical Review*, Vol. XLVIII (March 1967), pp. 45–58.

Yeigh, F. "Goldwin Smith and the Round Table Club." *Willison's Monthly*, II (January, 1928), pp. 307–11.

Unpublished Theses and Papers

Banks, M.A. *Toronto Opinion of French Canada during the Laurier Regime, 1895-1911.* M.A. (University of Toronto, 1950).

Berger, C.C. *The Vision of Grandeur: Studies in the Ideas of Canadian Imperialism, 1867-1914.* Ph.D. (University of Toronto, 1966).

Buell, J.P. *The Political Career of N. Clarke Wallace, 1872-1896.* M.A. (University of Toronto, 1961).

Charlesworth, H. and Hammond, M.O., *History of the Globe.* Unpublished manuscript in the possession of the Toronto *Globe and Mail*, n.d.

Clippingdale, Richard T. *J.S. Willison, Political Journalist, 1881-1905.* Ph.D. (University of Toronto, 1970).

Graham, R. *Sir Richard Cartwright and the Liberal Party, 1863-1896.* Ph.D. (University of Toronto, 1950).

Greening, W.E. *The Globe and Canadian Politics, 1890-1902: A Study of the Globe and its Influence on Liberal Policies.* M.A. (University of Toronto, 1939).

Harris, J.G. *The News and Canadian Politics, 1903–1914*. M.A. (University of Toronto, 1952).

Humphries, C.W. *The Political Career of Sir James P. Whitney*. Ph.D. (University of Toronto, 1966.

Jackson, E. *The Organization of the Liberal Party, 1867–1896*. M.A. (University of Toronto, 1962).

LaPierre, L.J.L. *Politics, Race and Religion in French Canada: Joseph Israel Tarte*. Ph.D. (University of Toronto, 1962).

Maclean, G.R. *The Imperial Federation Movement in Canada, 1884-1902*. Ph.D., Duke University, 1958).

McNaught, K.W. *The Globe and Canadian Liberalism, 1880-1890*. M.A. (University of Toronto, 1946).

Neatby, H.B. *Laurier and a Liberal Quebec*. Ph.D. (University of Toronto, 1956).

O'Sullivan, J.F. *D'Alton McCarthy and the Conservative Party, 1876-1896*. M.A. (University of Toronto, 1949).

Prang, M.E. *The Political Career of Newton W. Rowell*. Ph.D. (University of Toronto, 1959).

Sorely, G. *The Liberal Debacle in the Federal By-Elections in Ontario, 1891–1893*. Unpublished M.A. seminar paper (Carleton University, 1968), copy in possession of the author.

Spalding, G.L. *The Toronto Daily Star as a Liberal Advocate, 1899–1911*. M.A. (University of Toronto, 1954).

Stevens, P.D. *Laurier and the Liberal Party in Ontario, 1887–1911*. Ph.D. (University of Toronto, 1966).

Tennant, G.R. *The Policy of the Mail, 1882–1892*. M.A. (University of Toronto, 1949).

Index

More Canadian History from Dundurn

Canada 1911: The Decisive Election that Shaped the Country
by David Mackenzie and Patrice Dutil
978-1554889471
$29.99

One hundred years ago, Canadians went to the polls to decide the fate of their country in an election that raised issues vital to Canada's national independence and its place in the world. Canadians faced a clear choice between free trade with the United States and fidelity to the British Empire, and the decisions they made in September 1911 helped shape Canada's political and economic history for the rest of the century. *Canada 1911* revisits and re-examines this momentous turn in Canadian history, when Canadians truly found themselves at a parting of the ways. It was Canada's first great modern election and one of the first expressions of the birth of modern Canada. The poet Rudyard Kipling famously wrote at the time that this election was nothing less than a fight for Canada's soul. This book will explain why.

"Dutil and MacKenzie have succeeded in bringing to life the Canada of a century ago in their fascinating, well-written, and well-researched book."
Halifax Chronicle Herald

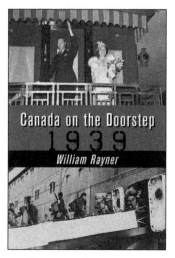

Canada on the Doorstep: 1939
by William Rayner
978-1554889921
$24.99

Some years are more spectacular than others, and 1939 was no exception. Canada was a different place: steak was twenty-nine cents a pound and a brand-new Ford coupe could be bought for just $856. It was a year when the king and queen toured Canada and wowed — to use a showbiz term — everyone from Toronto and Vancouver to Gogama and Craigellachie.

It was also a year when Canada wavered on the doorstep of a clouded future: isolation and neutrality or the continued embrace of the British Empire? The onset of war — and the Royal Visit — settled all that as Prime Minister William Lyon Mackenzie King beat back external and internal threats to keep the tapestry of national unity from unravelling.

Through *Canada on the Doorstep* you'll discover the births, deaths, storms, international intrigue, and politics that made 1939 so memorable.

DUNDURN
www.dundurn.com

Visit us at
Dundurn.com
Definingcanada.ca
@dundurnpress
Facebook.com/dundurnpress